COMPOSITION IN THE UNIVERSITY

PITTSBURGH SERIES IN COMPOSITION, LITERACY, AND CULTURE

David Bartholomae and Jean Ferguson Carr, Editors

COMPOSITION IN THE UNIVERSITY

↠ Historical and Polemical Essays

SHARON CROWLEY

University of Pittsburgh Press

Published by the University of Pittsburgh Press, Pittsburgh, Pa. 15261

Copyright © 1998, University of Pittsburgh Press

Manufactured in the United States of America

Printed on acid-free paper

10   9   8   7   6   5   4   3   2   1

Library of Congress Cataloging-in-Publication Data

Crowley, Sharon, 1943–

        p.   cm. — (Pittsburgh series in composition, literacy, and culture)

   Includes bibliographical references and index.

   ISBN 0-8229-4056-6 (acid-free paper). — ISBN 0-8229-5660-8 (pbk. : acid-free paper)

   1. English language—Rhetoric—Study and teaching—United States—History. 2. English philology—Study and teaching (Higher)—United States—History. 3. Education, Higher—United States—History.

I. Title.   II. Series.

PE1405.U6C76   1998

808'.042'071173—dc21   97-45367

A CIP catalog record for this book is available from the British Library.

Earlier versions of four of these essays appeared in *Pre/Text* (1991); *Rhetoric, Cultural Studies, and Literacy,* ed. John Frederick Reynolds (Erlbaum 1995), *JAC: A Journal of Composition Theory* 15, no. 2 (Spring 1995); *Composition in the Twenty-First Century: Crisis and Change,* ed. Lynn Bloom, Donald Daiker, and Edward White, copyright © 1996 by the Board of Trustees, Southern Illinois University. Reprinted by permission of the publisher.

FOR MY BRAVE SISTERS

CONTENTS

PREFACE

I have been a teacher of composition for over thirty years. I have been a student of its history for almost that long. And yet I have an uneasy relation with composition. Teaching composition is a rewarding and exciting job. Living with its situation in the university is something else altogether.

This is not an easy book to publish. I fear that its conclusions will be marshaled as evidence by those who want to make universities into the kinds of places they were in the 1960s, before all that antiwar stuff started up, of course, when 95 percent of student bodies were white and when 60 percent of students were men. Freshman English has a role to play in this proposed makeover: the universally required introductory course will once again be used as the gate to the university, as it has been, more often than not, during its not altogether savory history. I do not think this is a good thing, for teachers, for students, or for the future of composition in the university. I risk publishing a critique of the institutional foundation of composition at what is perhaps an inauspicious cultural moment, because, as luck would have it, this is an auspicious professional moment for those who teach composition in the university. We now have an opportunity to decide whether our art and our discipline will remain in thrall to attitudes about and uses of composition that descend from an older, very different kind of university.

Many assertions in the text are supported by large and complex arguments that for continuity's sake I could not rehearse. I indicate that a detailed argument supports something I have said by appending the name or names of its author(s) between parentheses, like this: (O'Neill). This device refers the reader to a source or sources, listed in the Works Cited, in which they can find that argument. If a date or page numbers follow the name in parentheses, that indicates a cite or other specific indebtedness.

Masculine pronouns predominate in this text. In its historical portions I use *men* to mean "human beings," as did the men and women about whom I

ambiguous (and distractingly funny) term *freshperson*. I decided to acquiesce
in an older practice because the alternative was to render the text nearly unreadable by cluttering it with *sics*. Perhaps the insistent use of the male pro-
noun is now unusual enough to call attention to itself, and so the partiality
entailed in its repeated appearance in historical texts—where all teachers or
students are referred to as *he* or *him*—may be apparent to readers.

The necessity of masculine pronouns overlays a gender issue raised by
this study. I analyze a frankly male educational tradition. Sometimes the people
quoted here wrote as though they considered women to be part of humanity,
and sometimes they wrote as if they did not. My decision to write about a
male tradition does not mean that I am not forwarding a feminist agenda.

In this study I use the term *modern* to designate that congeries of cultural
assumptions and ideologies that are also tagged with the term *Enlightenment*.
In other words, *modern* designates dominant fictions that were current during
the eighteenth, nineteenth, and early twentieth centuries of Western history.

ACKNOWLEDGMENTS

My indebtednesses are many. I wish to acknowledge the students who enrolled in my History of Composition classes at Northern Arizona University, the University of Iowa, and Penn State University. You helped me think this stuff through. Thanks. My gratitude to Dick Fulkerson, who read an early draft of chapter 4, literally overnight, and littered the manuscript with helpful comments. Thanks to Andy Alexander for illuminating conversations about the relation of reading to writing in early-twentieth-century composition pedagogy, to Dieter Boxmann for informative conversations about the history of first-year speech instruction, and to Derryn Moten for enjoyable if disheartening conversations about pedagogy and the university. Thanks to Steve Mailloux for very helpful comments on the manuscript and for a great lunch in Phoenix. Thanks also to other reviewers whose names I do not know. David Bartholomae and Jean Ferguson Carr of the University of Pittsburgh Press have been unfailingly courteous and helpful during the preparation of this book. Of course none of these people are responsible for errors that appear in the text.

Many thanks to the people who helped with research for this book. Bonnie Bender, Bill Clark, John C. Gerber, Gene Krupa, Jix Lloyd-Jones, Cleo Martin, Don Ochs, and Dewey Stuitt granted me interviews and lent me stuff. Diane Crosby spent so much time reading in the war years issues of the *Daily Iowan* she found it hard to adjust to peacetime when she emerged from the library. Jan Norton read Norman Foerster's papers and found the good parts. Michelle Morena attended interviews and made clear and useful transcripts of recordings. Debbie Hawhee located obscure publications and helped with the list of works cited. Special collections librarians at the University of Iowa also deserve thanks for their courtesy and resourcefulness. Thanks to Don Bialostosky, who gave me released time to write a first draft. Mostly, I want to thank Colleen O'Neill, Linda Brodkey, Susan Miller, Connie Hale, Susan Wyche, and Tilly Warnock for ethical sustenance.

COMPOSITION IN THE UNIVERSITY

COMPOSITION IN THE UNIVERSITY

> Almost everyone has had occasion to look back upon his school days and
> wonder what has become of the knowledge he was supposed to have
> amassed during his years of schooling, and why it is that the technical skills
> he acquired have to be learned over again in changed form in order to stand
> him in good stead.
> —John Dewey, *Experience and Education*

Ever since the late nineteenth century, instruction in composition
has been required of all students who enter American higher education. The
required, introductory-level course is called "English Composition" or
"Freshman English" at most schools. The delivery of required composition
instruction is a huge enterprise; at many universities the staff of the composition program outnumbers the staff of the Colleges of Engineering and
Business combined. The student body of freshman composition comprises
all but the very few members of each year's entering class who manage to test
out of the requirement as well as the students at the dozen or so elite private
universities that do not impose one. In the academic year 1994–95, there were
12,262,608 undergraduates enrolled in American colleges and universities
("Campuses," 9).[1] If a quarter of these students were freshmen—which is
likely, since freshman classes tend to be larger than more advanced classes—
nationally there were at least four million students enrolled in the freshman
composition course during that year. This means that some one hundred sixty
thousand sections of Freshman Composition were offered, if schools limited
enrollments per section to twenty-five students—as they typically do.

By any measure, required first-year composition uses enormous resources
and takes up large chunks of student and teacher time. Despite this, university faculty do not write or talk much about composition, unless it is to complain about the lack of student literacy. Within English departments, where
composition is usually housed, the center of intellectual interest is not com-

position but literary studies.[2] The typical stance of literary scholars toward composition is figured in two recent histories of literary studies, where its importance is underlined and then dismissed. In his history of the development of the discipline of American literature, David Shumway writes that "English departments owe their relative size and importance and perhaps their very existence to the demand that college students be taught to write" (101). And in his history of English-language literary studies, Gerald Graff acknowledges that without composition "the teaching of literature could never have achieved its central status, and none of the issues I discuss would matter very much" (2). Despite their admissions of the institutional importance of composition, however, neither of these historians is interested in the intellectual and institutional relations of literary studies to the required introductory composition course. Nonetheless it remains true that the required course serves literary studies in many ways, not the least of which is that composition gives literary studies something to define itself against. Hence it is not possible to fully understand the history of literary studies without considering its relation to composition. Something like the reverse is true for people who study and teach composition: it is not easy to imagine the required course outside of the humanist underpinnings given it by its association with English departments.

COMPOSITION STUDIES

An academic field called "composition studies" has emerged during the last twenty-five years. Most of the people who work in this field are currently housed in English departments because scholarship in composition grew directly out of the pedagogical challenges faced by people assigned to teach the required first-year course. Today, scholars in composition conduct challenging and innovative research into the scenes in which contemporary writing is done. They construct theoretical models of composition and they devise pedagogies intended to facilitate composing. Composition scholars are also interested in historical and contemporary theories of language use and in the history and theory of rhetoric. Given the centrality of the required composition course to liberal arts and general education curricula, as well as the huge administrative responsibilities associated with the direction of first-year composition programs, many scholars in composition are also interested in academic and cultural politics.

The recent emergence of this field has made it possible for faculty who are interested in composition to accrue professional rewards and satisfactions that were not readily available to composition teachers before that time. Indeed, such persons are now enjoying a kind of success, at least as success is measured by academic standards. Annual meetings of the professional organization of composition teachers—the Conference on College Composition and Communication—attract thousands of people, and these meetings feature lively debates about theoretical and pedagogical issues. There are more scholarly journals devoted to composition theory and the teaching of writing than have ever existed before, and editors of such journals receive many more submissions than they can publish. A few composition teachers and theorists now hold tenured or tenure-track positions in universities throughout the country. Undergraduate courses in advanced composition and professional writing are thriving. Ph.D. programs in composition are flourishing at dozens of universities, and every year talented students compete to secure spots on their limited admissions rosters. As of this writing, persons who hold Ph.D. degrees in rhetoric and composition are still able to obtain tenure-line positions, although the number of available jobs in the humanities is dwindling. It remains true, however, that such persons are employable primarily because they are needed to supervise massive programs in required first-year composition and not because composition studies is an exciting new field in which new academic priorities are being set.

Academics who profess composition studies go about their professional work somewhat differently than do their colleagues in literary studies. Their interest in pedagogy inverts the traditional academic privileging of theory over practice and research over teaching. Composition scholarship typically focuses on the processes of learning rather than on the acquisition of knowledge, and composition pedagogy focuses on change and development in students rather than on transmission of a heritage. Composition studies encourages collaboration. It emphasizes the historical, political, and social contexts and practices associated with composing rather than concentrating on texts as isolated artifacts. Composition studies also acknowledged women's contributions to teaching and scholarship long before other disciplines began to do so. A list of canonical authors in composition scholarship would include at least the names of Ann Berthoff, Lynn Bloom, Vivian Davis, Janet Emig, Maxine Hairston, Winifred Horner, Janice Lauer, Josephine Miles, Mina Shaughnessy, and Geneva Smitherman, all of whom achieved professional prominence prior to the era of affirmative action in a field of study that readily accepted their contributions.

Given its differences from academic business as usual, it is a shame that composition studies is nearly invisible within the academy. Its unusual professional practices and attitudes admirably fit it to become a theoretical and pedagogical site wherein the sorts of institutional changes currently advocated by materialist, feminist, ethnic, and postmodern theorists could be worked out. The problem is that theorists are largely unaware that composition studies exists. They do know about Freshman English, however.

THE STATUS OF FIRST-YEAR COMPOSITION

The history of composition studies has been written in the fortunes of the required introductory course in composition. Unfortunately, this course enjoys very little status within the university, and so its history and status negatively affect the current status of composition studies.

The required introductory composition course was invented at Harvard in the late nineteenth century. From Harvard it quickly spread to other colleges and universities, and it has been required at most schools ever since. During the nineteenth century the course was taught at Harvard and elsewhere by regular faculty. However, in the early years of the twentieth century, the work of teaching the required course fell onto the shoulders of probationary faculty, primarily because full-time faculty realized that there was no professional future in teaching a course that produced no research (see chapter 6). Graduate students began teaching the course during the 1940s as universities came increasingly to be defined as aggregates of specialized disciplines in which research was the primary pursuit. Their numbers began to be supplemented by part-time teachers during the 1950s and 1960s, when colleges and universities were so overwhelmed by postwar enrollments that they were forced to recruit adjunct faculty to teach the required course. Today, the required first-year composition course is taught primarily by graduate students at research universities that have a sufficiently large pool of people doing graduate study; temporary instructors are employed at universities and colleges where freshman enrollments exceed the available number of graduate instructors. The course is taught by permanent faculty only at two-year colleges and the odd liberal arts college or public university that still retains a primary commitment to undergraduate teaching.

For most of its history, then, the required first-year composition course has been taught by untenured faculty. I hasten to say that this fact is utterly irrelevant to the quality of teaching in the first-year course. Universities and English departments have been given much better teaching in first-year composition than they have any right to expect, given the unprofessional employment practices that are associated with the course. The precarious professional position of its faculty has had much to do with the status and curriculum of the first-year course, however.

Most of the people who teach composition in American colleges and universities are undervalued, overworked, and underpaid. Teachers of first-year composition are routinely employed on a contingent basis, which does not entitle them to the professional perquisites taken for granted by full-time faculty, such as decent salaries and health benefits, and access to secretarial staff, offices, telephones, and duplicating facilities. Composition teachers do not sit on the committees that make decisions affecting their teaching, including committees that choose textbooks and determine teaching schedules or those that write syllabi for the courses. Part-time teachers are sometimes hired the evening before a class begins; they are given a textbook and a syllabus and told to have a good semester (Fontaine and Hunter). Graduate student teachers, some of whom are fresh out of their own undergraduate studies, are typically given an orientation in the week before classes begin. Their subsequent teaching is supervised to the extent that funds are available for such work; such supervision usually requires that at least a few full-time faculty be committed to the composition program.

Composition specialists who have achieved success in the academic terms of promotion and tenure are often reminded—by their colleagues in literary studies—that composition is still not widely regarded as a legitimate field of study. Literary scholars tell their graduate students to take a course or two in composition, not because they are excited by the intellectual work going on in composition studies, but because composition teaching experience is attractive to prospective employers. In many institutions, faculty in literature and creative writing routinely use required introductory composition as a source of financial support for students doing graduate work in these fields. Since faculties in these specialties select students for admission to graduate study on the basis of their scholarly or creative potential, they are ordinarily not interested in graduate students' teaching experience or their suitability as teachers. Hence it becomes quite possible that the people who are selected to teach first-year composition may be uninterested in composition theory or pedagogy; further, they may be temperamentally unsuited to the interactive nature of composition classrooms. Nonetheless, directors of the required introductory course are expected to train such people to teach composition, sometimes in a matter of three or four days.

In colleges and universities that employ part-time teachers of composition, program directors often do not hire the people who teach the courses they are supposed to supervise; in large programs, directors may never even meet all the members of the composition staff. In addition, there is no built-in institutional assurance that people hired to teach composition know anything about it or how to teach it. Many part-time teachers of composition train to teach literature or creative writing and find, when they have finished their degrees, that no work is available in these fields. Hence they become part-time teachers of the required introductory composition course, by default. All in all, directors of composition programs are expected to take moral and legal responsibility for workers they did not hire and who may or may not know enough or care enough about the work they do in order to perform it well. Given these circumstances, it is remarkable, to say the least, that the quality of instruction in required first-year composition is as good as it often is.

The required introductory course in composition is an institution whose rationale did not emanate from some subject matter, discipline, or field of study, as most university courses do. Over the years, then, first-year composition has been remarkably vulnerable to ideologies and practices that originate elsewhere than in its classrooms. An amazing number of rationales has been advanced to justify the universal requirement in composition. I list these in rough historical order: it has been argued that students should be required to study composition in order to develop taste, to improve their grasp of formal and mechanical correctness, to become liberally educated, to prepare for jobs or professions, to develop their personalities, to become able citizens of a democracy, to become skilled communicators, to develop skill in textual analysis, to become critical thinkers, to establish their personal voices, to master the composing process, to master the composition of discourses used within academic disciplines, and to become oppositional critics of their culture. Most of these rationales developed because of composition's institutional proximity to literary studies. Others appeared during interludes in the history of composition in which persons working in other institutional sites succeeded in speaking for composition. The last four goals have recently been elaborated by composition teachers and scholars.

The habit of speaking for first-year composition is well-ingrained in the university. Since the course was not associated with a cadre of professional academics devoted to establishing and maintaining composition as a discipline, in the past no one with the requisite status or institutional power was able to protect its curricula from programs decreed for it by those who harbored educational or cultural agendas that had little to do with the study or practice of composing. Those who spoke for composition were able to dictate to its teachers and students the goals they were expected to pursue as well as the texts they were to study and the curricula and pedagogical strategies they were to employ.

Ostensibly, academics in all disciplines want the required first-year course to teach students how to write. Here *writing* seems to mean that students are supposed to master principles of arrangement and sentence construction; they are also to learn correct grammar and usage. This desire that students master grammar, usage, and formal fluency has remained constant throughout the history of the course. At the turn of the century, for example, Sophie Chantal Hart surveyed professors at a number of eastern colleges (Harvard, Columbia, Cornell, MIT, Brown, Williams, Tufts, Amherst, Vassar, and her own Wellesley) to determine what was wanted from required composition instruction. The replies uniformly complained about student inadequacy: "they can't tell a sentence from an adverbial clause"; "their idea of unity resembles the spokes of a cart-wheel"; "there ought to be more drill in simple English grammar"; "it is of more importance to be able to write intelligently 'It is he' instead of 'It is him,' and give a rational explanation why one is preferable to the other"; "the most difficult thing to overcome is the lack of thought"; "many of our freshmen seem to believe that anything patched up in a grammatical shape will pass for writing" (1902, 372–73). Sixty years later, William D. Templeman had the temerity to ask his colleagues at the University of Southern California what they wanted students to learn in the required Freshman English course. Faculty in Anthropology opined that the most important thing was for students to learn to express their thoughts "in clear and logical language" so that they could write better answers on essay examinations (1962, 35). Astronomy wanted students to "attain some minimum proficiency in spelling," to develop legible handwriting, and to "develop further reasonable facility in expressing ideas clearly," again so that they could write better answers on exams (36). Biochemistry hoped that "a student would learn to write a complete and properly constructed sentence, and a reasonably well organized paragraph" (36). And so on. Thirty years after Templeman completed his survey, the administration of the University of Texas, Austin, canceled an innovative syllabus designed for use in the required composition course there on the grounds that the point of such a course is to teach students the principles of composition *without considering issues or subject matter* (Brodkey 1996, 146–47).

Academics' desire that students master the so-called "basic" principles of composition in Freshman English is understandable, given their own lack of interest in attending to student literacy. Freshman English is supposed to "fix" students' supposed lack of literate mastery once and for all, so that teachers of more advanced courses do not have to bother with such things. The problem is that this desire simply cannot be enacted within a universal requirement that is not intellectually connected to any other feature of the curriculum. Ancient rhetoricians knew that students learned to speak and write most efficiently when their work was motivated by some compelling cultural or professional urgency. Contemporary research confirms that, outside of the freshman classroom, writing always occurs within some motivating context (Petraglia 1995). Research also suggests that the fairly abstract level of instruction that must of necessity occur within a universally required class simply cannot confer the discipline-specific writing skills that will later be demanded of students by their teachers in more advanced courses (Russell 1991; 1988). Anyone who has taught the first-year composition course, or who has even cursorily read its professional literature, knows that its central challenge is to provide students with occasions and contexts for writing that are sufficiently specific and interesting to engage them with the process. But even the most inventive assignments cannot entirely disguise the fact that in the universally required composition class, the primary motivation for composing is to supply teachers with opportunities to measure student performance. In other words, the fact of the requirement provides first-year composition with an institutional motivation rather than a rhetorical one. This makes for a highly artificial writing situation that may explain, at least in part, why such instruction never seems to stick. The writing done in required writing classes is an imitation, or better, a simulacrum, of the motivated writing that gets done elsewhere in the academy and in the culture at large.

Given the difficulty of doing motivated writing within a universally required class, the question arises: why does the requirement remain? I think it serves yet another purpose within the academic imaginary, a purpose that is not often articulated. University and college faculty imagine composition as the institutional site wherein student subjectivity is to be monitored and disciplined. The continuing function of the required composition course has been to insure the academic community that its entering members are taught the discursive behaviors and traits of character that qualify them to join the community. The course is meant to shape students to behave, think, write, and speak as students rather than as the people they are, people who have differing histories and traditions and languages and ideologies.

Now, when I assert that the task of the course has been to impose a universal subjectivity on students, I do not mean to imply that the quality of this subjectivity has remained unchanged over time. When it was invented, the regime used in the required course was meant to produce an educated person, as this was defined within Arnoldian humanism (see chapters 4 and 5). The course was required of all students precisely to insure that only persons who displayed the tastes and habits of educated persons would populate the academy. Humanist goals shape first-year composition curricula even today, although this orientation is currently being challenged by pragmatist approaches. Pragmatist models of education focus teachers' attention on students' activities, trusting that students' repeated engagement in relevant activities will construct the desired subjectivity. Contemporary theorists of composition who adhere to pragmatist curricula argue that the required introductory composition course should engage students in repeated rehearsals of the discursive acts that occur in specific disciplines (Lindemann 1993). In this approach, the required composition course is meant to perform on all students the subjectivizing task that specific disciplines, like medicine or biology or theater arts or anthropology, perform only on students who select them.

And so today there is a paradox at work in the universal requirement that was not so apparent when the required course was expected to create "educated persons," when the curricula of colleges and universities were not determined by specialists in academic disciplines, as they now are. The question whether composition can become a discipline—that is, whether a field of study can be erected around research on composing—is now being raised by teachers and scholars who profess composition studies. The important questions that have not been raised, however, are whether the required introductory course should be part of this emerging discipline, and, if it is, whether the curriculum of that course can retain its traditional function of imparting a universal subjectivity. If the required introductory course is to become a part of the disciplinary practices of composition studies, it must necessarily become part of a sequenced curriculum of courses that introduce students to discipline-specific principles and practices. In other words, the introductory course in composition would serve the same functions for composition studies that Biology 101 and Philosophy 101 serve for those fields. If this happens, the subjectivity inculcated in the course will no longer be universal—that is, the course will no longer produce "the good student" but will aim instead at producing writers or editors or some other more specialized subjectivity. As this analysis implies, the first-year course is a historical holdover from an era in which college curricula were informed by an older sense of discipline, the point of which was to shape students' character and conduct by means of repeated practice and correction. The traditional function of the required first-year course is increasingly hard to reconcile with the professionalization and specialization that now characterize the American academy.

Given the highly disciplined, highly specialized nature of curricula in contemporary colleges and universities, and given too that students from truly diverse backgrounds now enroll in higher education, I have serious doubts about whether a universal student subjectivity is any longer possible or desirable to sustain. And since the required introductory course, considered as an institutional practice, has no content aside from its disciplining function, it is difficult to imagine what sort of content might be appropriate for it apart from that function. Add to this the twin problems that plague the required introductory course—unprofessional employment practices and the intellectual coercion of students and teachers—and it seems that the time has come to reflect seriously on the worth of the universal requirement.

WHO OWNS COMPOSITION?

Since composition is traditionally housed in English departments, the persons who have spoken most frequently for composition have been literary scholars. Unlike composition studies, literary studies is a powerful discipline. It got its start during the last decades of the nineteenth century, when a handful of American scholars and intellectuals realized that English could be subjected to the same sort of philological study that had long been applied to dead languages and created methods to study it in just this fashion (Graff 66). This move permitted them to construct English as a language whose history, grammar, and literature required disciplined study by its native speakers. At the same time, colleges and universities began to institute written entrance examinations in order to test students' mastery of their native tongue.[3] The entrance exams were based on English-language literary texts, and students' performances on them were widely perceived to be miserable. This supposed demonstration of students' inadequate mastery of written English established the grounds for requiring composition instruction of all who entered the university.

Composition and literature have been entwined in an uneasy embrace ever since. I mention above that the study of English is defined within English departments, first and foremost, as the study of literature, and I suggest that this is why historians of literary studies tend to overlook the important role played by composition in the growth of English departments. Graff, for example, attributes the relatively large size of English departments to their adoption of a coverage model for historical periods of literature (7). But an argument can also be made that English departments are large because the required composition course introduces nearly every undergraduate to English studies and thus serves English departments as a powerful recruiting tool. The fact of the requirement also reinforces the impression that everyone needs to study English. Too, the required introductory-level composition course makes it possible for professors of literature to offer small seminars in esoteric literary periods or figures, first, because it supports a large number of graduate students who are thus available to do specialized study, and second, because the practice of hiring teaching assistants or part-timers to teach composition frees full-time professors to engage in highly specialized literary research. Anyone who doubts that composition has contributed to the growth of English departments need only look at the relative size of departments of history or philosophy—where the faculty also employ coverage models—to determine the difference that required first-year composition makes, at least in terms of sheer size.

While historians of literary study have ignored the intimate relationship between literary study and composition, historians of composition have struggled to understand it. Usually, they read the relation in terms of the unequal status accorded to literary study and composition within the academy. For James A. Berlin, composition represents the fallen other against which literary studies measures its own superiority. Following an insight put forward by Tzvetan Todorov, Berlin argues that in the West, rhetoric and poetic have always been entangled in a complicated hierarchical and yet symbiotic relationship wherein "a given rhetoric thus always implies a corresponding poetic and a poetic a corresponding rhetoric" (1987, 25). However, when students of modern poetics began to define the literary text as a "unique and privileged" artifact (as they began to do in the inaugural disciplinary moment of literary studies during the late nineteenth century), it became necessary to devalorize rhetoric, according to Berlin: "in tacitly supporting the impoverished notion of rhetoric found in the freshman writing course, academic literary critics have provided a constant reminder of their own claim to superiority and privilege, setting the range and versatility of their discipline against the barrenness of current-traditional rhetoric, the staple of the freshman course" (28).

Susan Miller also argues that composition is the necessary other half of literary studies, the inferior underside of the discipline to which literary studies can be constructed as superior. Miller reads the literature-composition nexus as a response to America's changing demographics during the troubled last years of the nineteenth century. Immigrants, women, and students whose family status was unclear to the genteel men who ran American colleges—all clamored for entry. And so "the university, ambivalent about its formerly unentitled, newly admitted students, needed to establish an internal boundary, a way to stratify diverse participants in what had been perceived as one dominant American group" (1994, 26). Miller also argues that while literary studies was established as a means of distinguishing a set of preferred texts from those circulating in popular discourse, composition was established in order to distinguish literary writing from all other sorts undertaken inside the university: "in composition, literary authorship could be openly compared to the inadequacies of popular writing and especially to inadequate student authorship. Like early American popular writing, institutionalized writing-as-composition could be implicitly demeaned as unequal to writing from the advanced elect" (1990, 54–55). For Miller, as for Berlin, composition serves literary studies as the despised (because fallen) other against which it can continually measure its own superiority.

About half of the chapters in this book explore the historical relations of literary studies and composition. In chapters 2 through 6 I try to articulate the ideology and practices by means of which literary scholars have managed to keep composition in the place they designed for it—at the bottom of the academic pecking order.

In *Professing Literature* Gerald Graff asserts that the scholars who invented English studies identified with "the Matthew Arnold view of literature and culture" (3).[4] I argue that the scholars who invented the required first-year composition course also identified with Arnoldian humanism. Furthermore, they justified the requirement of Freshman English on humanist grounds, and they designed a curriculum for the course that furthered humanist agendas. Even today some teachers of English wish that the humanist study of literary texts were still an unquestioned mainstay of first-year composition instruction (see chapter 2).

The humanist claim upon composition is typically enacted through the practice of requiring students to read literary texts in the first-year composition course. Literally hundreds of English teachers have asserted that reading literature improves students' writing ability. A few have tried to articulate precisely how the connection between reading and improvement in writing works; generally they argue that students' grasp of style is improved by their unconscious absorption of its finer points as these are demonstrated in the work of great authors. Fewer still have addressed the question of composition pedagogy itself, beyond imagining assignments that ask students to represent their reading or class discussion in writing. Now even if one grants the point that writers can learn something about the way language works through reading, by a sort of osmosis, one need not accept the further claim that literary texts are the best readings to use for this purpose. Historically, though, English teachers have resisted suggestions that nonliterary texts be read in the first-year course. Generally, they justify the necessity of literary reading with humanist arguments: students need to learn values, they need to be acquainted with the best that has been thought and said, and so on (see chapter 5).

A fundamental assumption of this book is that the humanist approach to the first-year course is not the best approach to teaching composition. The problems that confront a humanist agenda for composition instruction are formidable. First of all, modern humanists privilege reading over writing. The point of a humanist education, after all, is to become acquainted with the body of canonical texts that humanists envision as a repository of superior intellectual products of Western culture. My review of the historical arguments put forth to justify the reading of literary texts in the first-year composition course (see chapters 2 and 5) suggests that reading and discussion of literature receive far more attention in humanist curricula than does actual instruction in composition. A second problem posed by humanist composition curricula is that humanism takes a respectful attitude toward already-completed texts, while composition is interested in texts currently in development as well as those that are yet to be written. That is to say, composition is primarily a productive or generative art rather than an analytic or interpretive one.[5] To assert, as I do, that the act of composing differs appreciably from the act of reading is to challenge two fundamental premises of modern humanist pedagogy, namely, that the point of composition is to express one-self and that the point of writing is to represent or reflect upon the quality of one's reading and experience. While teachers of composition do analyze com-pleted texts, they do so in order to gain a better understanding of how texts are composed. People who study and teach composition are also interested in understanding how human events are affected by oral and written texts, and they investigate the ways in which texts put cultural values into circulation among various publics. But they are not necessarily interested, as humanists are, in demonstrating how a given text either questions or upholds a suppos-edly permanent or quasipermanent set of human values. And with the no-table exception of the group of composition teachers and theorists generally called "expressionists," whose ties to humanism are clarified in later chapters of this book, compositionists are not interested in limiting writing pedagogy to instruction in reflexive self-examination (Berlin 1982).

A third problem is posed for humanist composition by the fact that hu-manism has tended to be an exclusive educational tradition, insofar as the humanist impulse is to impart instruction to a select few who are considered able to inhabit a humanist subjectivity.[6] During the late nineteenth century, for example, English teachers reserved literary instruction for those first-year students deemed to be suitably prepared for college by virtue of their educa-tion or family connections, while they associated composition with less able students. Composition instruction, on the other hand, has or can be configured to have a democratic agenda. There is nothing inherent in the notion of teach-ing people to compose that is by definition exclusive. As the example of Plato's response to the Older Sophists suggests, teachers of composing can be scorned by elitists precisely because they are willing to impart their art to all comers *(Gorgias)*. A final problem posed by a melding of humanism and composi-tion is this: humanism—at least in its Arnoldian version—has more in com-mon with metaphysics than it has with rhetoric (Lanham, Spanos, and see chapter 3). Indeed, Arnoldian humanism is hostile to rhetoric, and it is suspi-cious of composition as well (Berlin 1996; Schilb 1996; and see chapter 5).

These differences between humanism and composition are not often ar-ticulated in the discourse of English studies. I take it that this silence has to do with the institutional politics of English departments. If composition's dif-ferences from literary studies were forcefully and repeatedly articulated, it might become much more difficult for English departments to justify contin-ued ownership of the required first-year course.

Certainly, English professors are not the only people who have had designs on first-year composition. Because the course is universally required, it is possible for faculty and administrators to make an argument that composition instruction "belongs" everywhere, or at least somewhere other than English. During the 1970s and 1980s, for example, advocates of a movement known as "Writing-Across-the-Curriculum" (WAC) managed to secure upper-level writing requirements in many universities (Russell 1991, 282ff.). However, proponents of WAC did not succeed in dislodging the universal requirement even though many of them, like David Russell, have repeatedly questioned its usefulness (1995; 1988). Its supposed universality also renders composition susceptible to larger changes in educational philosophy. During the 1940s, for example, advocates of general education argued that the required course ought to be "modern" and "practical"; they insisted that literary study was neither. Their effort to turn the first-year course toward instruction in what they called "communication skills" enjoyed a heady if brief success—the communication skills curriculum did not survive the 1950s in most universities (see chapters 7 and 8). However, its short history demonstrates the tenacity with which humanist assumptions about education cling to first-year pedagogy. It also provides a particularly clear historical example of what happens when an ideology and pedagogy are imposed on first-year composition by people who do not teach the course.

English teachers whose primary intellectual alliance is to humanism have not reacted positively to the occasional association of required composition with nonhumanist rationales. I examine two instances of humanist reaction to interventions in the required curriculum. The earliest of these occurred at the University of Iowa, when Norman Foerster, a prominent humanist literary critic, resisted the implementation of a communication skills curriculum by faculty in the College of Liberal Arts. The second was recently enacted in the pages of *College English* when humanist English teachers responded with alarm to the suggestion, made by a composition specialist, that students enrolled in the first-year composition course could profitably complete their study without reading any literary texts (see chapter 2).

Chapters 7 through 9 trace the influence of another intellectual tradition on the first-year course. That tradition is pragmatic, and it has, on occasion, ostensibly been indebted to the philosophical tradition called "pragmatism." Since first-year composition was initially shaped by Arnoldian humanism, in the history of discussions about the course the terms *pragmatic* or *practical* ordinarily mean "immediately useful." From the point of view of humanist literary study, the first-year composition course certainly looks practical and workaday, and humanists have sometimes distinguished composition from literary study on the very ground of the immediate utility of writing instruction.

The term *pragmatism*, on the other hand, denotes a rich tradition of uniquely American philosophizing, a tradition that is sometimes constructed to include Ralph Waldo Emerson and is nearly always associated with Charles Sanders Peirce, William James, and John Dewey, as well as contemporary thinkers such as Richard Rorty and Stanley Fish. Pragmatism is an action-oriented, forward-looking philosophical orientation that eschews the search for first principles; that is to say, it is more interested in the questions "what shall we do?" and "what are the consequences of our actions?" than it is in metaphysical questions such as "what is true?" or "what is real?". As such it is perhaps better described as cultural criticism than as philosophy (West 5). James Campbell defines the pragmatism developed by Peirce, James, and Dewey as a "philosophical view" that includes an emphasis on "processes and relations; a naturalistic and evolutionary understanding of human existence; an analysis of intellectual activity as problem-oriented and as benefitting from historically developed methods; and an emphasis upon the democratic reconstruction of society through educational and other institutions" (14). Most of the features named have surfaced in composition theory, if not in the pedagogy of the first-year course: a naturalistic understanding of human existence underwrote the communication skills movement, while the turn toward process pedagogy during the 1970s witnessed a marked emphasis on process, experimental method, and problem solving (see chapter 9). However, composition teachers' commitment to social reform through education has been somewhat less marked. During the 1920s and 1930s, for example, English teachers who thought of themselves as progressive educators established student-centered classrooms that had the explicit aim of teaching students "to work together in support of democracy" (Holt 1994, 73). But these efforts to implement pragmatist educational goals in the schools eventually succumbed to pressures exerted by powerful ideological and institutional forces, including a romantic notion of individualist expressionism and the humanist respect for traditional learning (Holt 1993; Russell 1991, 191ff.).

During the 1940s, general education was animated by a specifically Deweyan pragmatism, which held that learning occurs by means of engaging students in activities that induce them to reflect usefully and creatively on their experience (Dewey 1938; Gary Miller). The curriculum of the first-year composition course was altered significantly by the advent of general education. Dewey's work also influenced the development of process pedagogy during the 1960s. Janet Emig, the theorist who is ordinarily credited with the invention of the process approach to teaching writing, asserted in 1980 that Dewey is "everywhere in our work" (1980, 12). Since the pragmatist under-pinnings of process pedagogy gave composition teachers a way of thinking about teaching writing that did not wholly depend on their institutional rela-tion to literary studies, its incorporation into composition lore must be cred-ited, at least in part, with their conceptualization of composition as an art rather than a course. Moreover, the invention of composition studies was intimately connected to the development of process pedagogy because its theorists discovered a way to talk about student writing that authorized teach-ers to think of themselves as researchers.

Pragmatist composition curricula have a distinct advantage over the hu-manist approach to writing instruction insofar as their focus on active learn-ing suggests that people who want to learn to do something should actually practice doing it. However, the appropriations of pragmatism that have made their way into composition studies and first-year pedagogy have limitations. Not the least of these, in my opinion, is that most such appropriations have neglected Dewey's insistence that pragmatist educational efforts ought al-ways to be politically and socially motivated. I argue that with the widespread adoption of process pedagogy, the politics of first-year composition altered from conservative to liberal (see chapter 10). Unfortunately, the instrumen-talist or functionalist character of some strains of pragmatism (and of Ameri-can liberalism itself) have made it possible for teachers of composition to forget Dewey's commitment to education as a primary means of bringing about social change.

COMPOSITION ON ITS OWN

Composition studies may be on the way to establishing itself as a disci-pline. A history of composition studies, considered as a disciplinary entity apart from the required introductory course, has been published (Nystrand et al.). And as of this writing, at least three university composition programs that were formerly associated with English departments have become inde-pendent academic units. Apparently, more separatist moves are in the plan-ning stages.

It looks as though composition specialists, when and if they become in-dependent of English departments, may attempt to maintain the introductory composition course as a universal requirement. I fear that they may have learned only too well the lessons taught them by their colleagues in literary studies—that required composition provides full-time faculty with a firm institutional base from which to operate an academic empire. Given the unethical and intellectually inappropriate practices that motivate the universal requirement, I hope that composition specialists will take a hard look at it before they repeat past practice. In the final chapters, then, I make a series of arguments against retention of the universal requirement.

2

THE TOAD IN THE GARDEN

> . . . imaginary gardens with real toads in them.
> —Marianne Moore, "Poetry"

In the March 1993 issue of *College English,* Erika Lindemann and Gary Tate published a pair of essays in which they discuss the appropriateness of using literary texts in composition classes. Tate and Lindemann are both composition specialists; both have taught and written about composition for many years. In her essay Lindemann argues that writing pedagogy is sufficiently distinct from literary studies so that inclusion of literary texts in writing courses distracts teachers and students from their central task. Her "ideal" writing course

> asks students to read and write a variety of texts found in the humanities, sciences, and social sciences. Such courses should have an immediate connection to the assignments students confront in college. They are not mere skills courses or training for the professions students may enter five years later; they raise questions of audience, purpose, and form that rhetorical training has always prepared students to address. (1993, 312–13)

Tate does not object to the range of texts suggested by Lindemann, nor does he find fault with her emphasis on rhetorical training. He insists, however, that writing teachers be permitted to use literary texts in composition instruction, given their primary interest in helping students to lead rewarding lives. He also rejects "the current focus on academic discourse," not only because such a focus defines composition as a service course, but because he resists what he sees as "the increasing professionalization of undergraduate education in this country" (1993, 319, 320). Tate prefers to think of his students not as "history majors, accounting majors, nursing majors" but as "people whose most important conversations will take place outside the academy, as they struggle to figure out how to live their lives—that is, how to vote and love and survive, how to respond to change and diversity and death and oppression and freedom" (320). He encourages his students to rely on "the resources found in literary works" to aid them in coping with life's struggles (321). Tate acknowledges that his interest in students "as individual human beings who will have private and maybe public lives that transcend . . . disciplines" aligns him with the traditional educational goals of humanism.

Lindemann's and Tate's essays elicited a slew of responses. Four rejoinders were published in the "Comment and Response" section of the October 1993 issue of *College English,* while five more pieces, including new efforts by Lindemann and Tate, were published as a "Symposium" in the March 1995 issue of the same journal. And, it appears, a book is being contemplated, a book that will, presumably, address the issue of whether literary texts should be used in the first-year composition course.

In her second essay in the series, Lindemann expresses puzzlement over the furor raised by her conversation with Tate. She writes: "Colleagues invite us to lecture on their campuses or to appear together at conferences; they include the *College English* essays in their coursepaks for graduate classes; they urge us to make up our differences, unaware that we have been friends for many years and have co-edited a book" (288). She worries that "many readers regarded the Tate-Lindemann debate as a political argument" and that she was cast as "a politically suspect, anti-literature compositionist." She regards the introduction of politics into consideration of this question as reductionist and beside the point as well; the real question, for Lindemann, is not whether literary texts will be used in the required first-year composition course but rather whether English teachers can agree about "what the purpose of a writing course is" (288).

I laud Lindemann's effort to rethink the point of first-year writing instruction and I admire her attempt to find "sufficient common ground for moving the discussion forward." However, I also think that her respondents were correct to perceive this discussion as a political one, and I do not regard the consideration of politics as a reductive move, particularly where the first-year course is concerned. The initial responses to the Lindemann-Tate discussion, all of which defend the use of literature within composition instruction, suggest to me that the content of composition curricula was not at stake in this debate at all, despite Lindemann's attempt to open up that important question. Rather, what was being articulated—however murkily—is resistance to the antihumanist ways of reading literary texts that have been articulated in contemporary literary theory. My analysis implies, of course, that in this dispute the introductory composition course was merely the site on which English teachers staged a disagreement about how literary texts should be read. Now, this may seem like an odd site on which to wage such a battle, especially if it is true that "imaginative literature has not had a secure place in composition classrooms since at least the 1930s," as one respondent avers (Steinberg 271). But, as I try to demonstrate in this book, debate about the use of literary texts in composition instruction is a cover or code for a much larger institutional issue: the status relation between composition and literature within English departments. The curricular practice of using literary texts in composition instruction is implicated with the institutional issue in three ways: first, it affirms that literary study and composition have something in common; second, it affirms the universal importance of literary study; and third, it reinforces the dominance of literary study over composition.

ENGLISH STUDIES AND HUMANISM

Humanism is the common thread that has historically tied literary study to composition. Hence it is no accident that a conversation about the use of literary texts in composition should surface at a moment when humanism has been called into crisis.

Since its inception in American universities, the disciplined study of literature has been justified by a humanist rationale (Graff 1987, 3). The most enduring rationale for required instruction in composition has also been the humanist notion that college graduates should be able to express themselves like educated persons, although there have been vigorous disagreements about what this means and how it might best be achieved. In his history of twentieth-century composition instruction, James A. Berlin argues that proponents of humanist composition "saw colleges as cultivating character by providing aesthetic and ethical experiences through the traditional humanistic studies" (1987, 39). Humanist teachers advocated the reading of literature, along with practice in composing, as the course of study that would create "self-cultivation and self-refinement" in its students.

In the early decades of the twentieth century, English teachers routinely asserted that correct and elegant expression can most readily be achieved through the study of great literature. Some even rejected so-called "direct" instruction in composition on the ground that acquaintance with canonical literary texts sufficed for the cultivation of sensibility. In 1912, for example, William Lyons Phelps argued that "the best way to learn to write is to read, just as one learns good manners by associating with well-bred people" (1912, 127). And in 1915, Charles Osgood wrote in *English Journal* that the object of instruction in the humanities was

> to endeavor by all devices in our power to make each student more sensitive, more accurately and widely observant, more just, more consistent, more spiritual. Just so far as we succeed in this, just that far shall we have carried him toward attaining the gift of utterance. Without something to utter, his utterance is idle. Shall we therefore, in our zeal to make the plant grow gracefully, forget to stir, enrich, and fertilize the soil? (1915, 233–34)

Of course, Osgood's preferred fertilizer was literature, and in consequence he recommended that the study of literature replace "the direct teaching of composition" (233). In 1939 the humanist critic Oscar James Campbell characterized literature and composition not as complements but as enemies. He recommended that English departments abandon the teaching of composition altogether, since composition was not a humanist endeavor. Instead, he wrote, "composition obscures for everyone concerned the extremely important service that English literature, as one of the still living humanities, must render to college students" (1939, 182). While Campbell's venomous attitude toward composition is not typical, it does represent the farthest reaches of a more generally held distaste for composition instruction among teachers of English. Where composition must be offered, humanist English teachers have always preferred to turn the course toward literary study. The association of first-year composition with literary study is so fundamental to the ideology of English studies that conversations about it appear in the professional literature only when the practice is threatened. During the 1950s, for example, there was an enormous surge in the number of essays in the professional literature that defended the use of literature in the required first-year course, because during the 1940s many respected universities had instituted communication skills curricula in the required course. During the 1990s, when English teachers awoke to the fact that an eminent specialist in composition had recommended that the first-year course remain innocent of literary study, they again rose in defense of a time-honored instructional practice.

THE RESPONSES

In his response to the Tate-Lindemann exchange, Leon Knight seconds "with no equivocation at all Professor Tate's position that freshman composition is 'a place for literature'" (676). Knight then rehearses a litany of traditional arguments in support of using literary texts in the first-year course. He posits that literary reading improves reading skills: "learning how to read literature properly is the most direct . . . way of learning to image properly what is read." He suggests as well that reading literature is enjoyable—an argument widely employed during the 1950s to make composition teaching more palatable to reluctant literary scholars. Knight also argues that reading literature develops critical thinking skills because literary texts model the use of evidence and the drawing of conclusions therefrom. This is a variation of an argument that was first put forth during the 1940s, when teachers of literature proposed that literary texts offered a data base from which students could draw arguments for use in their papers. Despite the contemporary terminology in which it is cast, Knight's "critical thinking" argument also retools an argument that was often used during the 1960s, when proponents of the new criticism argued that their preferred textual principles reflected the principles of good writing manifested in the current-traditional essay. And his final argument—that literature encourages awareness of cultural diversity—simply recasts the venerable humanist claim that literary texts are the best or only repository of important cultural or textual values. During the last hundred years, scholars in English have argued that literature constitutes the best or only textual resource in which to find stylistic excellence, philological data, liberal culture, democratic values, universal values, formal perfection, and now, cultural diversity. During that time, English teachers have argued for the inclusion of literary texts in first-year composition instruction on all these grounds (see chapter 5).

It is important to note that, with the exception of the modeling argument, none of Knight's points have to do with the teaching of writing. Rather, all support the pedagogical value of reading literature.

Traditional humanist arguments for the use of literary texts in the first-year composition course also appear in other responses to the Lindemann-Tate exchange. Echoing Tate's concern for the quality of students' lives, Jeannie C. Crain argues for the creation of "literature-based" courses on the ground that "human beings always have more at stake than simply becoming historians, mathematicians, and biologists" (679). She worries that if literary texts were to be excluded from the first-year course, "composition may become only a skills or service course." For Crain, then, discipline-based instruction may abet the reduction of composition instruction to instrumentalism, while the introduction of literary texts can save it from such a fate.

In her response, Elizabeth Latosi-Sawin writes lyrically about the joys associated with the teaching of literature: "To see, as I did recently, a first-semester composition student laugh out loud while he read *The Catcher in the Rye*, or to hear from another 'nonreader' that she 'couldn't put down' *I Know Why the Caged Bird Sings*, is to witness literature being read for life and not for some validation of the entire apparatus of our profession" (676). In her enthusiasm for the life-enhancing properties of literary reading, Latosi-Sawin openly begs Lindemann's question about the appropriate goals of the composition course. She assumes that "the question is no longer whether there is or isn't a place for literature in a composition program, but how literature is to be defined, selected, and used" (675), thus suggesting that the practice of reading literature in first-year composition is uncontested.

I think that Latosi-Sawin is complaining here not about composition pedagogy but about postmodern literary theory, which has indeed caused some confusion about "how literature is to be defined, selected, and used." Tate, Crain, and Latosi-Sawin all oppose "disciplined" ways of reading to "reading literature for life." This interesting dichotomy suggests to me that the arrival of antihumanist theory in English departments has made humanists aware that preferred ways of reading in academic literary studies are highly specialized and hence exclusionary. This awareness was not available to them when humanist ways of reading were the preferred ways of reading within English departments, when reading "for life" did not appear to them to be a "way" of reading at all—it was just reading. To nonhumanists or not-yet-disciplined readers, of course, humanist ways of reading appear to be as disciplined and exclusive as any postmodern approach to literary texts. But for humanist teachers, their preferred ways of reading seem natural rather than shaped by historical and institutional circumstances. To reluctant humanists, deconstructive or neo-Marxist or postmodern feminist ways of reading must look as daunting and exclusive as the new critical way of reading once looked to the bewildered students who made *Cliff's Notes* a successful enterprise in the 1960s.

More to the point of the present context, however, the humanist argument about the connection of literature to life is not a persuasive response to

Lindemann's point that composition instruction "offers guided practice in reading and writing the discourses of the academy and the professions" (1993, 312). Lindemann nowhere indicates her subscription to the larger claims that humanists are wont to make for literary study—that it prepares students to lead rewarding lives, and so on. The point of required composition instruction, to Lindemann's way of thinking, is to offer students practice in the specialized discourses used in every academic discipline. While she might agree that literary studies constitutes one such specialized discourse, I doubt she would be persuaded by Latosi-Sawin's presumption that literature's is a more general and hence more encompassing discourse than those of, say, biology or philosophy or business or engineering.

This insight goes some way toward explaining why Lindemann's position drew so many negative responses. The use of literature in the universally required composition course validates the universality of literary discourse. In earlier times, indeed, its use was recommended there precisely because introductory composition was the only universally required course in the curriculum. As Gerald Thorson put it in 1953, Freshman English offered students their "only opportunity for contact with the poet or novelist" (38). To suggest, as Lindemann does, that literary studies is beside the point of the universally required first-year course is to specify the study of literature, to reduce it from its humanist status as the universal business of educated persons and to define it as simply another disciplinary interest. This is, apparently, a point that some humanists are not yet ready to concede. Further, since every initial respondent to the Tate-Lindemann exchange utterly ignored the question that Lindemann tried to raise—what is the point of the required composition course?—and argued instead in favor of the use of literature in that course, I can only conclude that for these English teachers at least, the point of composition matters somewhat less than the stature of literature.

A SECOND OPINION

In his response to Lindemann's initial essay, Gregory Jay begins with the assumption that "a course in English is not the same as a course in writing" (673). He defines a proper English course as one that "emphasizes the growth of a language, the texts that have contributed to its character, the resources of that language, and the current state of its practice." Whatever this last phrase might mean, Jay effectively equates English studies with literary studies when he writes: "as long as the first-year course is an English course, it ought to accommodate the mission and interest of the department, which includes a substantial attention to the history of imaginative writing and its contribution to the language" (674). He concludes by observing that "if literature does not belong in the first-year writing course, then the first-year writing course does not belong in the English department."

Although he does not rely on humanist arguments, Jay's conclusion is the same as O. J. Campbell's: since composition is not literature, let's get rid of it. Campbell made his attack on composition at a time when literary studies was still consolidating its cultural capital in American universities, and so it was important to him to affirm its importance to the academy, and to distinguish it firmly from composition as well. In 1939, composition presented a certain problem to the discipline of literary studies. While ownership of the universally required course insured a secure institutional base for English departments, the universal requirement, with its erratic hiring policies and perceived lack of intellectual integrity, was an embarrassment to a young discipline trying to establish a definite object of study and a carefully developed set of methodologies for studying it. Campbell's characterization of composition as "an alien intruder, who obscures our values from ourselves and hides them from the rest of the academic world" makes quite clear his feeling that composition threatened the exclusivity and precision that are necessary to the maintenance of an academic discipline (1939, 183).

But times are very different now. English departments are the largest departments in most American universities, and often they are the most powerful departments in the humanities. Literary studies enjoys the protection afforded by a sprawling disciplinary apparatus: a large tenured faculty, clear means of distinguishing tenurable scholars from the untenurable, established journals that operate within a well-defined pecking order, and expansive curricula offered on both undergraduate and graduate levels of study. The arrival of literary theory, which questioned the integrity of "the text" and which was therefore roundly castigated during the 1970s and 1980s as a threat to literary studies, has, in the event, actually catalyzed and renewed the study of literature, which term is now broadened to include noncanonical texts and which practice is now carried on under the head of "cultural studies." And so literary studies certainly does not now need to be protected either from dilution or from institutional invisibility, as it may have done in Campbell's day. Hence Jay may be implying that English departments can now afford to accept Lindemann's position regarding composition's independence from lit-

erature. Since he is not a humanist he has no intellectual or sentimental at-
tachment to the required course, and he apparently thinks that English departments can survive without it.

If composition studies does become an independent discipline,
Lindemann's question about the appropriate course of study in a required
course becomes even more urgent. Of course, she answers her own question
when she suggests that required introductory composition courses prepare
students for the writing assignments that they will undertake while in college.
This suggestion grows out of composition teachers' experience during the
1980s with cross-disciplinary writing programs, in which they discovered that
the traditional institutional definition of writing was far too static and inflexible
to assist writers who work in highly professionalized disciplines. According
to historian David Russell, contemporary academic writing is highly differ-
entiated:

> in the new print-centered, compartmentalized secondary and higher-
> education system, writing was no longer a single, generalizable skill
> learned once and for all at an early age; rather, it was a complex and
> continuously developing response to specialized text-based discourse
> communities, highly embedded in the differentiated practices of those
> communities. Nor was academia any longer a single discourse
> community but a collection of discrete communities, an aggregate of
> competing professional disciplines, each with its own specialized
> written discourse. (1991, 5)

As Russell suggests, prior to the 1980s "writing" had been constructed in the
academy in the monolithic terms of "the academic essay." This model of the
perfect composition, which centers on mechanical correctness and formal
perfection, was invented at the same time as the modern university and the
required introductory course were invented (Crowley 1990). But universities have changed a great deal since the late nineteenth century, and perhaps
the most crucial of these changes is that fields of study have become highly
specialized. Accordingly, their notions of "writing" have become highly dif-
ferentiated.

Thus teachers who learned from their experience with writing-across-
the-curriculum programs during the eighties set about redesigning the function of the required introductory course so that it would assist students in
becoming fluent members of whatever disciplinary community they wished

to join. Hence, they urge, as Lindemann does, that "Freshman English offers guided practice in reading and writing the discourses of the academy and the professions. That is what our colleagues across the campus want it to do; that is what it should do if we are going to drag every first-year student through the requirement" (1993, 312).

To my mind, this proposal is no more satisfactory as a ground for requiring composition than is the humanist notion that everyone needs to learn how to read and write about literature "for life." One glaring limitation of a discipline-centered requirement is that composition teachers simply cannot anticipate every discursive exigency their students will be asked to meet in college or in life. As Tate remarks, "even if I were to focus on the kinds of writing required in the so-called core courses they will all be required to take, those courses exhibit such a wide range of disciplines that the task is hopeless" (1993, 319). If, on the other hand, teachers

> attempt to deal with academic discourse generally, as if there were some features of all such discourse that could be abstracted and taught . . . this abstraction would have to take place at a very high level, a level that would not only be too complex for freshmen but a level that would, in the end, prove impractical if we are seriously trying to help students deal with the day-to-day demands of their academic work. (319–20)

What Tate describes here is precisely what teachers of the required course tried to do during the decades when the pedagogy of the five-paragraph theme dominated composition instruction, when they taught "the academic essay" as though it modeled all possible genres of academic discourse. Many academics still imagine that the academic essay exists, and I would argue that they do so precisely because there is a universal requirement in composition in which, they imagine, this universal discourse is taught. But this superdiscourse does not exist, and belief in it does not solve the paradox presented by a universal requirement in discipline-specific composition. If the required introductory course is to serve specific disciplinary needs, it must either become so specialized that it becomes difficult to see what would hold it together, or it must become so abstract that the work done there would have little reference to actual academic or professional writing.

A second difficulty with the option put forward by Lindemann, to my mind, is that it does not disrupt the historic placement of composition within the university as a service course. That is, Lindemann's proposal simply trades in an old master for a new one, and hence it does nothing to disrupt the un-professional and unethical practices that are currently associated with required composition instruction such as hasty hiring, low pay, low status, denial of academic freedom, and intellectual coercion of students and teachers.

No party to the Lindemann-Tate discussion, it seems to me, faced the very serious questions that are now raised by the universal requirement in introductory composition. Humanism no longer provides an entirely satis-factory rationale for the requirement, if indeed it ever did. And while the disciplinary focus that is being urged by Lindemann and others seems to sup-ply useful elective instruction for students as well as exciting new scholarship in composition studies, it cannot, by its very nature as a discipline-specific endeavor, sustain a universal requirement. I think that composition scholars and teachers, as well as the larger university community, need to question whether or not the arguments that have supported the universal requirement in composition to date can still be responsibly marshaled in its service.

3

THE BOURGEOIS SUBJECT AND THE
DEMISE OF RHETORICAL EDUCATION

> The moral sense is not only itself a taste of a superior order, by which, in
> characters and conduct, we distinguish between the right and the wrong,
> the excellent and the faulty; but it also spreads its influence over all the most
> considerable works of art and genius.
> —Alexander Gerard, *An Essay On Taste*

Opening the second book of *De Inventione*, Cicero recounts the story
of Zeuxis and the five virgins. It seems that the famous sculptor planned a
portrait of Helen, and the citizens of Croton—hoping that one or more of
Zeuxis's works would wind up in their temple—allowed him to search among
their young people for models.

In Cicero's version of the story, Zeuxis, who is anxious to meet pretty
young women, is first taken to see some handsome young men. The Crotoniats
tell him that the bodies of the young men represent strength and athleticism
(the Latin text suggests "dignity" and "manliness"). Cicero makes it clear
that the young men's bodies also represent the city to outsiders such as Zeuxis.
The sculptor is then taken to see the sisters of the young men. As the story
goes, Zeuxis determines which parts of these women are beautiful and which
are defective. He then amalgamates the beautiful parts, and from this amal-
gam he fashions a portrait of Helen.

I am interested in Cicero's story of Zeuxis and the virgins because it can
be read to illustrate a difference in the way rhetoricians and philosophers think
about art. Reading with Cicero, I understand that art is valued for religious
reasons: the Crotoniats want to place a worthy work in Juno's temple. There
is also a touch of civic pride at work, insofar as possession of a sculpture
created by a famous artist gains stature for the city. In other words, art exerts
rhetorical force in a community; it transacts religious or civic business.

Rhetoricians are also interested in the production or composition of art.

In the context of *De Inventione,* the story of Zeuxis and the virgins functions as a metaphor for Cicero's composing process: "In a similar fashion when the inclination arose in my mind to write a text-book of rhetoric, I did not set before myself some one model which I thought necessary to reproduce in all details, of whatever sort they might be, but after collecting all the works on the subject I excerpted what seemed to me to be the most suitable precepts from each, and so culled the flower of many minds" (2.1.4). Even though the notion of surveying the field is an ancient commonplace (Aristotle also used it, as Cicero notes), the importance of discrimination and selection as ancient means of composition should not be overlooked. In fact, Cicero analogized his own powers of discrimination to those of Zeuxis, noting that these powers guided him as he selected excellences from the many treatises on invention available to him. The story of Zeuxis and the virgins allowed Cicero to meditate on authorship, on the issues faced by a composer who wishes to gain control of the available materials.

Now, if I were to read this text as philosopher, reading with Plato, perhaps, I would notice the series of hierarchized representations that animates the story.[1] Zeuxis's gaze first falls upon the specific, sensuous bodies of young men. But these men's bodies are important insofar as they represent the city's values: strength, manliness, valor. The bodies of their sisters, on the other hand, do not so much represent civic virtue directly as they stand in for their brothers' bodies. In other words, their bodies represent civic virtue indirectly, as it is manifested in their families' good breeding. To fashion yet another representation, Zeuxis will select parts of the women's bodies and reassemble them to represent the beauty of Helen, herself represented in story and song as the most beautiful woman who ever lived. Of course, Helen's body moldered away long before Zeuxis thought of travelling to Croton, so that her imagined, perfect, beauty can conveniently be thought to exist aside and apart from actual living, breathing, women's bodies. Reading as a philosopher, then, I notice the relation of the real to the abstract, the material to the ideal. In philosophy, the point of knowing is to abstract the ideal from the real, to move away from the particularities of human bodies and toward the abstraction of ideal traits, such as beauty or justice. In its desire to abstract, philosophical reading differs from rhetoric, which inhabits time and space and which is manifestly interested in people and events—a sculptor's visit to Croton in the fourth-century BCE, a city's desire to foster civic pride—as well as the politics and ethics they provoke and entail.

WESTERN RHETORIC AND AESTHETICS

Throughout most of Western history, aesthetics was studied in the context of rhetorical education. Rhetoricians ordinarily treated aesthetics as Cicero did, as the study of the composition and circulation of art, under which head they included both the plastic and literary arts. During the modern period, however, aesthetics became important, if not central, to philosophical thought. In *The Ideology of the Aesthetic*, Terry Eagleton asserts that

> anyone who inspects the history of European philosophy since the Enlightenment must be struck by the curiously high priority assigned by it to aesthetic questions. For Kant, the aesthetic holds out a promise of reconciliation between Nature and humanity. Hegel grants art a lowly status within his theoretical system, but nevertheless produces an elephantine treatise on it. The aesthetic for Kierkegaard must yield ground to the higher truths of ethics and religious faith, but remains a recurrent preoccupation of his thought. For Schopenhauer and Nietzsche, in sharply contrasting ways, aesthetic experience represents a supreme form of value. Marx's impressively erudite allusions to world literature are matched by Freud's modest confession that the poets had said it all before him. In our own century, Heidegger's esoteric meditations culminate in a kind of aestheticized ontology, while the legacy of western Marxism from Lukacs to Adorno allots to art a theoretical privilege surprising at first glance for a materialist current of thought. (1990, 1)

The burden of Eagleton's argument is to establish that aesthetics became important in modern thought because it is tied to the development of modern bourgeois subjectivity. What Eagleton does not notice is that the new interest in aesthetics stimulated important changes in liberal arts education, which is an important site wherein modern bourgeois subjectivity is developed and disciplined.[2]

At the same time that aesthetics moved to the center of philosophy, modern rhetorical theory, as well as rhetorical education, underwent drastic alteration. Eighteenth-century thinkers, among them Joseph Priestley and Adam Smith, produced new rhetorical theories that drew explicitly on the new science, on philosophical empiricism, and on a notion of taste developed within modern aesthetics. In doing so, they rejected much of the classical rhetorical tradition on which European rhetorical theorists and teachers had relied for over a thousand years.

Until the midpoint of the nineteenth century, American colleges required all students to take four years of instruction in rhetorical theory and to engage in regular supervised practice in oratory and written composition. By the last decades of the century, however, the institutional importance of rhetorical education had been so seriously undermined that instruction in rhetoric disappeared altogether from college and university curricula. Since then, the practice of rhetoric in America has not been connected in any systematic way with education in its principles. This state of affairs was—is—an anomaly in the history of Western education, since rhetoric was taught in virtually every European and American school and university until that time.

I suspect that there is a connection between the importance attached to aesthetics in modern thought and the slackening of interest in rhetoric during the same period. This connection is not a matter of simple replacement or absorption of the one by the other, although it is true that modern aesthetic notions made inroads into the new rhetoric, as is witnessed by the inclusion of the term *belles-lettres* in the title of Hugh Blair's popular *Lectures on Rhetoric and Belles-Lettres* (1783). But the rise of aesthetics and the fall of rhetoric are also linked by their entanglement in larger cultural change.

I take it to be axiomatic that any rhetorical theory that is successful enough to be taught in school will necessarily reflect the dominant subjectivity of its era. The task of rhetorical education in any era, then, will be to discipline and maintain the dominant subjectivity. For example, ancient rhetorical education was constructed to discipline citizens in the practice of civic virtue. In ancient Greece and Rome, citizenship was strictly limited to men whose lineage was very old or who were wealthy enough to render a less respectable lineage acceptable. When Quintilian defined the goal of rhetorical education as the development of the *vir bonus*—the good man speaking well—he was thinking of a relatively small group of people: privileged men who could demonstrate their descent from a preferred *gens*. As long as public business was conducted on a face-to-face basis among persons whose class and cultural affiliations were similar, ancient rhetoric served as an adequate introduction to arts and skills required for verbal negotiation and persuasion. Hence classical rhetorics served as either the foundation or the capstone of liberal arts education in European schools and universities until well past the Renaissance.

During the eighteenth century, however, social and political upheaval wracked Europe and America. There was revolution in France and legislative reform in England. America violently rejected colonial status. After these revolutions and reforms, the aristocratic classes who had deployed ancient rhetoric no longer exerted sole political power in their respective states. With the emergence of capital and a middle class, power was diffused into myriad institutions, as Michel Foucault's studies of the human sciences, medicine, prisons, and schools suggest. Hence discursive power was no longer available only in the direct, person-to-person (actually, man-to-man or man-to-men) fashion that was assumed in ancient rhetorical theory.

During the eighteenth century, rhetoric began to be taught in many more kinds of institutions than previously: in dissenting academies and in new universities established for those who could not get into Paris or Oxford or Cambridge (Tom Miller 1997, 1990). During the early years of the nineteenth century, American rhetoricians such as John Witherspoon and John Quincy Adams taught civic virtue to their students, just as Quintilian had done. By the midpoint of the nineteenth century, however, American rhetoric teachers had developed another pedagogical goal, one that eventually supplanted the older focus on public, civic, discourse. Relying on Blair and on texts redacted from Blair, nineteenth-century rhetoric teachers began the business of developing taste in their students. This shift in the focus of rhetorical education—away from civic virtue and toward the bourgeois project of self-improvement—coincided with the demise of rhetoric as a field of study. That is, when students and teachers became more interested in accruing the cultural and social capital associated with the cultivation of an educated taste than they were in preparing for the pulpit or for politics, the doctrines and principles of rhetoric—classical and modern—began to disappear from the American college curriculum. Late in the century, the study of English-language literature took over the task of disciplining bourgeois subjectivity, a task it still fulfills (Eagleton 1985). Today, outside of speech departments, rhetorical education remains unthought: neither English-language literary study nor English composition have ever included systematic attention to public discourse within their purview.[3]

The bourgeois appropriation of rhetorical education did not amount to simple imitation of the educational and cultural practices of a formerly powerful class. The new rhetoricians thoroughly revised ancient thought about rhetoric: they rejected ancient location of invention within discourse in common use, relocating it in the relation of individual minds to empirical reality and thus yoking rhetoric to the service of science; and despite the countering efforts of elocutionists, modern rhetoricians eventually did away with study of memory and delivery, since the work done by the new class seemed to require literate skills rather more than facility in oral discourse (Halloran 1990). When American rhetoric teachers finished their revision of rhetorical pedagogy in the late nineteenth century, the only bits of classical invention that remained were the topics, put to humble—and literate—service as a means for paragraph development.

Historians of rhetoric have viewed these developments with alarm. According to S. Michael Halloran, "the purpose of education in the rhetorical tradition was to prepare . . . a civic leader who understood all the values of his culture and used artful speech to make those values effective in the arena of public affairs" (1982, 246). Halloran asserts further that "the vitality of the classical rhetorical tradition in the colleges of the 18th and early 19th centuries helped to maintain a standard of public discourse far superior to what we have in politics today" (264). And in a gloomy assessment of the narrowness of modern rhetoric, Vincent Bevilaqua concluded that

> To study rhetoric narrowly as a scientific rather than as an imaginative-poetic concern—to study it in terms of Descartes and Locke rather than in terms of Aesop and Homer—is to see rhetoric as one sees by a lamp at night—the object in focus can be seen with clarity but its background is cut off. One sees only what the narrow lamp of science allows one to see. Little wonder, then, that the modern scientific study of rhetoric has proven both vapid and fruitless; that the modern behavioristic study of rhetoric has in the main delineated the measure of all things while perceiving the meaning and value of nothing. (28)

These historians bemoan the departure of rhetoric from American college curricula because they assume that ethical instruction—instruction in the development of character—disappeared with it. However, this assessment overlooks the fact that such instruction changed its guise and its habitation during the middle years of the nineteenth century. In a new aesthetic guise, ethical instruction was conducted under the pedagogical heading of taste, at first by rhetoric teachers, and later, during the last three decades of the century, by teachers of English-language literature. In other words, American colleges did not abandon ethical instruction when they abandoned rhetorical education; rather, they transferred instruction in the development of character to the study of English-language literary texts.[4] What they did abandon was the ethical subjectivity that was maintained and disciplined within classical rhetorical study: the *vir bonus*. In his place appeared the genteel man of taste.

The pedagogy of taste that developed within early nineteenth-century rhetoric textbooks was explicitly designed to help students discriminate between the tastes of the educated and uneducated classes. Now, ancient rhetorical pedagogy was also classbound; as I have noted, instruction in rhetoric was usually reserved for the sons of nobility and affluence. But classical rhetorical pedagogy did not include explicit instructions to students on how to go about discriminating between themselves and their social inferiors, as did the nineteenth-century pedagogy of taste. This necessity seems to have emerged when rhetorical instruction was taken over by middle-class teachers, whose desire it was to remain in the middle—that is, to remain distinct from both the upper and lower classes. This distinction was to be manifested in the display of an educated taste.

TRADITIONS OF TASTE

Historians have delineated several modern European traditions of taste. British interest in literary taste dates at least from the early eighteenth century. An unauthorized edition of Pope's "Epistle to Burlington," also called "Miscellany on Taste, or Of False Taste," was published in London in 1731. Pope's editors credit this version of the epistle with stirring up interest in taste among learned circles in London, although other scholars argue that its ideas were commonplaces already in general circulation. By the 1750s, in any case, the notion of taste was prominently featured in philosophical discussions of aesthetics: David Hume published "Of a Standard of Taste" in 1757, and Alexander Gerard published his *Essay on Taste* in 1759.

Eagleton traces a rich German tradition of thought about taste (1990). This tradition reached its zenith with the publication of Immanuel Kant's *Critique of Judgement* in 1790. It was Kant who posited the existence of a "pure" taste, a taste that appreciated works of art and natural beauty as things in themselves. By positing this notion, Kant rationalized the familiar distinction now made between "high" and "low" tastes.

A Scottish tradition of thinking about taste seems to have influenced American rhetoricians rather more than either English or German thought. Its theorists defined taste as that capacity, or faculty, which permits persons to discriminate the good from the bad in works of art as well as the virtuous from the vicious in the realm of morality. In this tradition, which probably stems from the work of Frances Hutcheson, the exercise of taste was directly connected to the exercise of public responsibility.[5] The most influential expositor of this tradition of taste in rhetorical theory was Hugh Blair, who devoted the first two chapters of his *Lectures* to taste. In *Rhetoric in North America* (1991), Nan Johnson establishes a firm connection between Blair's philosophy of taste and the cultivation of civic and moral virtue. According to Johnson, "defining rhetoric as a discipline that directs the cultivation of taste, Blair views the study of rhetoric and belles lettres as a process of edification," a means by which the individual can prepare for the discharge of "the higher and more important duties of life" (36; Blair 1965, 12). Thanks to Blair's influential example, nineteenth-century American school rhetoric texts composed in the belles-lettres tradition developed a full-fledged pedagogy of taste.[6]

By the mid–nineteenth century, however, Blair's firm connection of taste to civic virtue had all but disappeared from mainstream school rhetoric texts. In what follows, I examine the accounts of taste given in four rhetoric textbooks that were very popular before and during the Civil War: Samuel Newman's *Practical System of Rhetoric* (1851 [1827]); James Boyd's *Elements of English Composition* (1860); Henry Coppee's *Elements of Rhetoric* (1860); and G. P. Quackenbos's *Advanced Course of Composition and Rhetoric* (1864). These teachers discuss something very different from Blair's ideology of taste as the cultivation of civil commitment.

THE FACULTY OF TASTE

Boyd, Coppee, Newman, and Quackenbos agree that taste is a faculty, which, in the faculty psychology that undergirded the rhetorical theory of the time, elevates it to the same status as the faculties of reason, emotion, or imagination. They uniformly treat taste as the capacity to grasp and evaluate emotional experiences. Coppee defines taste as "the faculty by which we discern and enjoy the beauties of Nature and Art" (61); Boyd names it "that faculty by which we are enabled to perceive and relish the beauties of composition" (43); Quackenbos writes that taste is "that faculty of the mind which enables it to perceive, with the aid of reason to judge of, and with the help of imagination to enjoy, whatever is beautiful or sublime in the works of nature and art" (170); Newman argues that "the decisions of taste are judgments passed on whatever is designed to excite emotions of beauty, of grandeur, or of sublimity" (42).

Boyd posits that anyone who would exercise taste must possess five faculties: first, a lively imagination; second, a *"clear* and *distinct apprehension of things"* (this ability is called "method" by theorists of the period); third, "quick perception" of "those objects that gratify the secondary senses, particularly sublimity, beauty, harmony, and imitation"; fourth, sympathy, the ability to share moral pain and pleasure; and last, *"judgment,* or *good sense,* which is indeed the principal thing, and may . . . be said to comprehend all the rest" (44–45). In other words, the person of taste is equipped with several faculties—imagination, method, perception, sympathy, and judgment—all of which, when working together in harmony, allow him to perceive and evaluate the aesthetic and moral worth of scenes or objects surely and quickly, if not instantaneously. According to Newman, taste aids us in evaluating that which is presented to our emotions. Experience with beautiful or ugly things produces emotions; the capacity to judge or evaluate these experiences, that is, our capacity for taste, is founded on, and grows with, emotional experience. There are three sorts of emotions: moral emotions, emotions of passion, and emotions of beauty. Moral emotions are excited by actions that are vicious or virtuous; passion is generated by objects of desire or aversion; and beauty by experiences of grandeur or sublimity, such as glorious sunsets or moving stories.

These accounts of taste are characteristic of nineteenth-century rhetorical theory in that they use faculty psychology quite uncritically to develop a rather mechanical theory of human response. On this view, people have sensations and experiences; these are stored in memory and simultaneously worked on by a variety of higher faculties, such as reason, emotion, or imagination. People who wished to develop their rational and imaginative capacities were encouraged to have more and better experiences, and to think about them harder and more carefully. Boyd, for example, counseled his readers to improve their faculties of taste by "studying Nature and the best performances in art" (44). He also encouraged them to keep "at a distance from every thing gross and indelicate, in books and conversation, in manners and in language."

TASTE AS DISCRIMINATION AND EXCLUSION

Newman and company advised their students that taste, the ability to discriminate the bad from the good, the beautiful from the ugly, is a sign of excellence that allows discrimination among people, as well. Someone who receives no pleasure from nature or art, according to Boyd, "is said to be a man of no taste" (43). On the other hand, "he who is gratified with that which is faulty in works of art, is a man of bad taste; and he who is pleased or displeased, according to the degree of excellence or faultiness, is a man of good taste." Since taste is natural, all men display it in some degree; Quackenbos points out that "savages . . . by their ornaments, their songs, and the rude eloquence of their harangues, show that along with reason and speech they have received the faculty of appreciating beauty" (171). Obviously, though, this natural capacity does not manifest itself in the same way or to the same degree in all people or peoples. Newman generously reads this difference as a difference in education and class privilege: persons who have leisure and occasion to exercise their emotional responses to beautiful scenes or objects will be able to strengthen that response, whereas the ability to respond emotionally will be stunted in persons who do not enjoy such opportunities. He illustrates with a representative anecdote about a writer who was firmly located in the nineteenth-century rhetorical canon:

> Addison, when he went forth in the evening, and gazed upon the starry heavens and the moon walking in her majesty, felt emotions of sublimity. In accounting for the rise of these emotions, we might say, that he was a man of sensibility—from the original constitution of his mind he was susceptible of emotions of taste to a high degree. His intellectual habits also, and the circumstances of his life, were such as to cherish and strengthen these original tendencies of his mind. Astronomy had taught him something of the size and number and uses of these heavenly bodies; and in this way, or in other ways, many associations were connected with them. On the same evening, perhaps, and in the same neighbourhood, the laborer returning from his daily toil, looked upon the same starry and moon-lit firmament, but felt no emotion of beauty or sublimity. Still this individual might have been originally constituted with as much sensibility as Addison; but such has been his lot in life, that this sensibility has been lost, and he thinks of the moon and stars only as lighting him homewards from his toil. (48–49)

The subtext of this passage cannot have been lost on Newman's young readers: if you wish to be included among the cultural elite, you cannot fail to notice the beauties of nature or art.

Coppee and Quackenbos are unwilling to assign disparities in taste to different kinds of education or circumstance, as Newman does. Coppee associates the capacity of taste not with education or experience but with "the finer powers with which some minds are endued, by which they are permitted to discern beauties and delicacies which are not seen by commoner intellects" (68). And Quackenbos goes so far as to classify people according to the delicacy of their tastes; there are some "endowed with feelings so blunt, and tempers so cold and phlegmatic" that they are nearly insensible to the world around them; others "are capable of appreciating only the coarsest kind of beauties"; while in yet a third class of men "pleasurable emotions are excited by the most delicate graces" (171). It would be disastrous if reason were so thinly dispersed among men, Quackenbos remarks, but since taste has to do only with "the ornamental part of life," Nature has wisely limited its distribution (172).

In these accounts, peoples who exhibit inadequate taste are inevitably non-Anglo or non-European. Coppee asks us to compare "a hut of reeds with a gorgeous palace; an Indian canoe with the floating palaces which cross the Atlantic; an Indian village with one of our great cities—Philadelphia or New York; the barbarous and inadequate dialect of the Hottentot with the copiousness of the English or the graces of the Spanish language" (64–65). Now it would seem that, since taste is natural to some extent, this copious display of natural taste, this diversity of home and boat designs and among languages, should be accepted, if not welcomed. Coppee himself writes: "since we are all gifted with taste by God, each man's taste must be as good as his neighbour's; and therefore there can be no standard" of taste (64). But he abruptly withdraws from this generous insight. In the very next sentence he posits flatly, without explanation or support, that "there is a standard." He announces the existence of "a union, a concurrence of Taste, not only among the refined, but among the barbarous, as far as they can comprehend these things," a unity of taste that "will establish the necessity and existence of a standard of taste" (65). I guess he means that even peoples whose tastes are defined as barbarous by the standard will nonetheless agree that such a standard ought to exist.

Newman defines the standard of taste as "the agreeing voice of such as are susceptible of emotions of beauty, both of those who lived in past ages, and of those now existing" (50). The historical aspect of the standard guarantees its worth for Newman, since works of art that have always been accepted as beautiful can serve as "models of excellence in the fine arts" (51).

Unfortunately, his example of enduring beauty is a statue of George Washington that depicts the American commander bedecked in a Roman toga. Newman reasons that classical drapery "at all times, and to all men, appears graceful and excites emotions of beauty." It follows that this example "both proves, that there is a standard of taste, and illustrates what is meant by it." Newman apparently does not notice that this argument begs the question.

Coppee and Quackenbos, on the other hand, locate the standard in "the concurrence of the right judgment of many well ordered and duly cultivated minds," rather than in a history of expressions of good taste (Coppee 64). In other words, the standard is set by the preferences of those persons whose tastes are widely acknowledged to be accurate and penetrating. Quackenbos explains why only cultivated tastes can set the standard:

> When we speak of the concurrent Tastes of men as the universal standard, it must be understood that we mean men placed in situations favorable to the proper development of this faculty. Such loose notions as may be entertained during ages of ignorance and darkness, or among rude and uncivilized nations, carry with them no authority. In such states of society, Taste is either totally suppressed or appears in its worst form. By the common sentiments of men, therefore, we mean the concurrent opinions of refined men in civilized nations, by whom the arts are cultivated, works of genius are freely discussed, and Taste is improved by science and philosophy. (180)

And so we see that the universal standard is actually set by quite a small group, and a familiar group it is, too: "men" living in "civilized nations" who cultivate the arts and who read science and philosophy. In other words, people just like the people who wrote these textbooks.

Some specious reasoning is at work here. To define taste, as these textbook authors do, in terms of the values or standards held by their group is to create a partial definition. To universalize such a definition is to mistake the part for the whole. To argue that the standard exists because we say it does, and to locate that standard in what we say is good is to engage in vicious circular reasoning as well. Elizabeth Minnich calls such argumentative moves "hierarchical invidious monisms" (the acronym for which, conveniently enough, is "HIM") (53). A HIM is any "system in which one category is taken to be not literally all there is, but the highest, most significant, most valuable, and, critically, the most real category—which sets up all others to be defined and judged solely with reference to that hegemonic category." The hegemonic category soon comes to be seen as controlling the evaluative center, thus relegating other kinds of tastes to the margins, portraying them as coarse, crude, or savage, carefully fenced off, existing altogether beyond the pale.

BOURGEOIS SUBJECTIVITY AND THE PEDAGOGY OF TASTE

Eagleton argues persuasively that the subjectivity of modern aesthetics—the subjectivity manifested as a person of taste—is at least analogous to, if not synonymous with, the bourgeois subject whose emergence marks the modern period. Here is Eagleton:

> From the depths of a benighted late feudal autocracy, a vision could be
> projected of a universal order of free, equal, autonomous human
> subjects, obeying no laws but those which they gave to themselves.
> This bourgeois public sphere breaks decisively with the privilege and
> particularism of the *ancien regime*, installing the middle class, in image
> if not in reality, as a truly universal subject, and compensating with the
> grandeur of this dream for its politically supine status. What is at stake
> here is nothing less than the production of an entirely new kind of
> human subject—one which, like the work of art itself, discovers the
> laws in the depths of its own free identity, rather than in some
> oppressive external power. (1990, 19)

As Eagleton is careful to note, this new form of subjectivity is always already inhabited by contradictions: in the face of its loss of external law, of external sources of authority, the bourgeois subject celebrates its freedom. At the very same moment, however, it internalizes the rule of law, agrees to police itself, to produce from out of itself the rules by which it will govern and restrain itself.

The pedagogy of taste, I would argue, is such a policing mechanism. It is the means through which young men were taught to internalize the marks and limits of bourgeois subjectivity (read "white, straight, male, comfortable, Christian" subjectivity). The ability to discriminate the bad from the good, in concert with his fellows, marks the bourgeois subject for membership in the community. Just as surely, this mark distinguishes him from those others who are not so disciplined, those who are so roughened by toil and hard circumstance that they ignore beauty altogether, like Newman's laborer, or those, like Quackenbos's savages, who revel in the coarse or the bizarre.

Like all ideologies, the ideology of taste works to naturalize that which is culturally instituted. As Eagleton remarks, the bourgeois conflation of taste, morality, and "the natural" entitles its subjects to the claim that "we just know what is right and wrong, as we know that Homer is superb or that someone is standing on our foot" (1990, 64). The ideology of taste assigns socially constructed differences to nature, thus rendering its judgments true, right, and inevitable; at the same time it covers over the real social work it performs, which is to maintain and harden class distinctions. Early nineteenth-century school rhetoric texts teach not so much what, but who, to avoid. The pedagogy of taste helps students to internalize a set of rules that mark their inclusion in bourgeois subjectivity at the same time as it sets them off from members of other classes.

PURE AND IMPURE TASTES

Newman retells the story of Zeuxis and the virgins in the *System of Rhetoric*. Like Cicero, he uses the story to illuminate the process of artistic composition, although he reveals the modernity of his version when he asserts that "taste was evidently the guide of the artist" and shows how facets of the story exemplify Zeuxis's employment of judgment, "founded on the experience of past emotions of beauty" (55–56). The moral Newman draws from the story of Zeuxis is quite different from that drawn by Cicero:

> from this example, we learn, why the most admired productions of the painter are not exact representations of objects and scenes in nature. In natural objects and scenes, that which is suited to excite emotions of beauty, is mingled with objects of indifference and disgust. The artist, under the guidance of taste, collects together these scattered fragments of beauty, and combining them in one view with harmonious effect, presents to us objects and scenes more beautiful than those which can be found in nature. (56)

Here Newman writes as philosopher rather than rhetorician, arguing that the point of art is to abstract absolute beauty from particular instances of earthly beauty. On this reading, nature is not pure enough to stimulate refined sensibilities because it contains impurities to which the cultivated taste will be indifferent; at worst, such impurities may incite disgust.

Newman's remark places his account within the tradition that Pierre

Bourdieu calls "the 'high' aesthetic" or the cult of "pure taste," which is marked by the bourgeois refusal to respond directly to objects or events. In his study of taste Bourdieu writes:

> "pure" taste and the aesthetics which provides its theory are founded on a refusal of "impure" taste and of *aisthesis* (sensation), the simply primitive form of pleasure reduced to a pleasure of the senses, as in what Kant calls "the taste of the tongue, the palate and the throat", a surrender to immediate sensation. . . . "pure" taste . . . is based on the disgust . . . for everything that is "facile". . . . The refusal of what is easy in the sense of simple, and therefore shallow, and "cheap", because it is easily decoded and culturally "undemanding", naturally leads to the refusal of what is facile in the ethical or asthetic sense, of everything which offers pleasures that are too immediately accessible and so discredited as "childish" or "primitive." (1984, 486)

The cultural point of this aesthetic is to establish that art can have no direct political or religious effects upon those whose taste is properly cultivated. Rather, the point of observing art and natural beauty is to manufacture carefully mediated responses to aesthetic experiences. The social point of such learned mediation is to separate those, like Addison, who possess the ability to discuss art or nature as objects of taste from those who treat encounters with them as useful or moving experiences, like the laborer who uses the moon's light to find his way home. For the nineteenth-century rhetoric teachers studied here, taste is a faculty, to be sure, but it is a higher faculty, like reason and the imagination; its possession and cultivation distinguish those who have "natural" responses from those who police themselves, who carefully discipline their responses to the world and to art.

To put this another way: bourgeois aesthetic desire is antidesire. The bourgeois desire is to avoid seduction by art or nature, to avoid noticing the body's immediate responses to experience and particularly to pleasure. When bourgeois liberals defend the circulation of pornography on the basis of the first amendment right to free speech, it is hard not to see the aesthetic of pure taste at work in their claim that pornography does not incite sexual violence. In the terms of bourgeois aesthetics, it is only members of the lower classes who are directly affected by denigrating representations of women, who fail to surround their responses to pornography with the appropriate discursive screens.

In still other words, bourgeois aesthetics simply erases the possibility that middle-class experiences of art and nature may be rhetorical. Cicero and the citizens of Croton believed that nature and art were capable of producing immediate responses in all human beings. The emergence of the pedagogy of taste signaled the end of rhetorical instruction because it also signaled a growing resistance to the very old idea that humans can be persuaded to action by their interactions with nature, art, language, and each other.

4

THE INVENTION OF FRESHMAN ENGLISH

The American collegian is . . . simply a school-boy of larger growth. . . . From the day of his matriculation to the day of his graduation, he is under surveillance more or less intrusive, he pursues a prescribed routine of study, his attendance is noted down, his performances are graded, his conduct is taken into the account, his parents or guardians receive monthly or term reports. In other words, during the entire period of four years the collegian is made to feel that he is looked upon as one incapable of judging and acting for himself.

—James Morgan Hart, *German Universities*

In 1861, like many American men before and after him, James Morgan Hart traveled to Germany to study. He did so partly because it was fashionable for young men to go abroad at that time, but he was also a serious student who wanted to pursue advanced study in law. When he returned to America, Hart published an autobiographical account of his experience, an account that praised German university life at the same time as it condemned the course of study commonly pursued in American colleges. Hart's experience in Germany and that of others like him helped to stimulate profound changes in American higher education.[1] By the end of the nineteenth century the typical American institution of higher learning was no longer a small pastoral college but was well on the way toward becoming a modern elective university.

THE CLASSICAL AMERICAN COLLEGE

Prior to the Civil War, young men went to college in order to become ministers or teachers. Most early American colleges were affiliated with major Protestant religions: Harvard, Yale, and Dartmouth were Congregational; William and Mary and Columbia were Anglican; Princeton and Penn, Presbyterian; Brown, Baptist; and Rutgers, Dutch Reformed. Enrollments were small: during the 1840s, Yale enrolled about 400 students, and in 1856 Harvard enrolled 366 students. The curriculum of the classical colleges was prescribed for all students for all four years—every student took the same courses, in the same order, from the same professors. The course of study generally included Latin, Greek, and sometimes Hebrew; mathematics; rhetoric and logic; philosophy; and perhaps a little history. By 1850, some colleges offered courses in what we now think of as natural and social sciences—geology, mineralogy, geography, and political economy. But colleges more typically adhered to a strictly classical curriculum.

The course of study pursued in the classical colleges was very old even in the nineteenth century. Historian Bruce Kimball traces it to Roman antiquity, where it acquired the name by which it has since been known: liberal arts education (37). Its traditional goal was to train good citizens to lead society. According to Kimball, education in the *artes liberales* was thought "to produce the active citizen who is thoroughly virtuous and universally competent, that is, the perfect orator capable of addressing any topic and assuming any position of leadership in the state" (37). This education was designed for, and limited to, men—specifically those men who qualified by virtue of family background or training to be called "gentlemen" (107ff).[2] In the nineteenth century, the notion of "manliness" was still intimately tied to the ideology of liberal education in general and to the pedagogy of mental discipline in particular. Historian Richard Vesey points out that "educators who believed in mental discipline often linked the word 'manly' to their notion of character. Manliness did not mean softness. . . . Manliness meant power: the kind of power that one gained by a diligent wrestling with Greek grammar" (28–29).

Greek and Latin certainly dominated the arts curriculum of American colleges before the Civil War. At Dartmouth in the early 1850s, "Greek and Latin letters made up at least one-quarter of the curriculum, rhetoric and belles lettres in English another quarter. About one-quarter was devoted to history, moral philosophy, and divinity, and a final quarter to mathematics, physics, astronomy, and anatomy. The pedagogy consisted primarily of recitations, declamations, and disputations" (Kimball 155). The pedagogy of recitation required that students memorize a few pages assigned from a textbook prior to each day's class. During class the instructor called upon them to "recite," that is, to repeat aloud the assigned section of the text. Sometimes students were required to conjugate verbs or to parse constructions found in the texts they read and memorized. Declamation and disputation are classical and medieval rhetorical exercises in which students are assigned a thesis that they must defend or refute in oral or written compositions.

According to Noah Porter, a president of Yale who defended the classical curriculum well into the 1880s, the point of the classical course of studies was to develop men who were prepared "for the most efficient and successful discharge of public duty" (92). But this education was also designed to develop character, and hence the entire course of instruction aimed to inculcate religious and civic moral values in students. The faculty of the colleges were ordained ministers who were charged with passing the religious and cultural values of the educated classes along to the young. Hence they "actively attended to public affairs and schooled their students to attend" (Kuklick 205). But the ministers who taught this curriculum were not men who participated in public affairs. Many did not even have pulpits. Given their relative isolation from the world of affairs, the cultural knowledge they passed on was quite narrow, and it was thoroughly bound up with traditional notions about the proper education for cultured young men. The knowledge passed on by the faculties of classical colleges "mirrored . . . only a narrow, restricted, and genteel life" (Kuklick 205). Such knowledge was infused with Protestant morality, sanctioned by the tradition of gentlemanly education in the liberal arts, and instilled by means of the pedagogy of mental discipline.

According to the Yale Report of 1828, the "object" of a college education was to "*lay the foundation* of a *superior education*"; this was to be done "at a period of life when a substitute must be provided for *parental superintendence*" (Day and Kingsley 278). "Mental discipline" referred to the "sharpening of young men's faculties through enforced contact with Greek and Latin grammar and mathematics" (Vesey 9). By means of repetitive recitation in "hard" subjects that had no discernible use, the classical college "sought to provide a four-year regime conductive to piety and strength of character" (ibid.). In the pedagogy of mental discipline, minds were thought to work like muscles: they were made up of faculties, each of which had to undergo regular exercise so that character would develop evenly and strongly. Thus education would both strengthen the mind and equip young men with what Jeremiah Day, president of Yale, called "intellectual culture" (Day and Kingsley 278). The foundation of intellectual culture was laid in two ways: through disciplining the faculties of the mind and furnishing it with knowledge. Since discipline was the more important of the two foundations, Day recommended that

those branches of study should be prescribed, and those modes of
instruction adopted, which are best calculated to teach the art of fixing
the attention, directing the train of thought, analyzing a subject
proposed for investigation; following, with accurate discrimination,
the course of argument; balancing nicely the evidence presented to
judgment; awakening, elevating, and controlling the imagination;
arranging, with skill, the treasures which memory gathers; rousing
and guiding the powers of genius. (278)

Day argued that a college curriculum had to exercise all of these mental faculties, since the study of any one subject to the detriment of others would
result in a defective character. That is, character was built in young men directly by their studies. In a properly balanced curriculum, study of each subject would be aimed toward developing some necessary facet of character.
Day showed how each classical subject participated in the creation of a properly balanced character: mathematics taught demonstrative reasoning, the
sciences induction and probability; ancient literature was the repository of
"the most finished models of taste," while reading in English taught speaking
and writing; logic and mental philosophy taught "the art of thinking," while
rhetoric and oratory exercised "the art of speaking" (279). Composition especially interested Day: he asserted that "by frequent exercise on written composition" the student "acquires copiousness and accuracy of expression."

RHETORIC AND COMPOSITION
IN THE CLASSICAL COLLEGE

Composition is one of the oldest college courses in America. It was practiced at Harvard (founded in 1636) and William and Mary (founded in 1693)
during the seventeenth century, and at Yale (founded in 1701) during the eighteenth. In 1642, the Harvard Corporation ordered "that all undergraduates
declaiming in their usual courses in the hall: shall after their said declamations ended deliver a copy of each of them fairly written unto the praisident
or senior felow then present unless they have before shewed it to their tutor
for his perusall" (quoted in Perrin, 137). Composition remained an integral
part of the four-year undergraduate curriculum of American colleges until
the last quarter of the nineteenth century (Halloran 1982, 1990). It was taught
chiefly by professors of rhetoric, but since exercises in composing were built
into the entire curriculum the whole faculty took responsibility for seeing to

the improvement of young men's composing skills. According to Washington Gladden, who was enrolled at Williams during the late 1850s,

> no English was required for entrance, and the only English work of
> the first two years was one or two themes each term, with an occasional declamation before the class. There was a speaking exercise
> every Wednesday afternoon at the chapel, which the entire college was
> required to attend, and there were two speakers from each class;
> seniors and juniors presented original orations, sophomores and
> freshmen declaimed. The president and the professor of rhetoric
> presided, and criticized each speaker at the close of his performance.
> (69)

Public performances of compositions were required of students at graduation and other ceremonies as well.

The oral and written discourses composed by students in the classical colleges displayed their grasp of civic and moral issues. At commencements in eighteenth-century Harvard, for example, students disputed the following questions: in 1778, "Is the Voice of the People the Voice of God?"; in 1758, "Is Civil Government absolutely necessary for Men?"; in 1769, "Are the People the sole Judges of their Rights and Liberties?"; and in 1770, "Is a Government despotic in which the People have no check on the Legislative power?" (Morison 1930, 90–91). During the early years of the nineteenth century, Edward Tyrrell Channing, Boylston Professor of Rhetoric from 1819 to 1851, was still assigning topics that we might call "political": for example, he asked his students to discuss their "ideal of a nation's being independent—also of an individual's" and to consider "dependence of the cause of Freedom on the success of our institutions" (Anderson 1949, 78).

Practice in composing was supported by study of rhetorical theory during all four years of undergraduate instruction. During the seventeenth and eighteenth centuries, the model of civic virtue used in rhetorical instruction was compounded from an admixture of classical rhetoric and Christian theology. The close tie between these traditions is nicely reflected in the peroration of John Quincy Adams's *Lectures on Rhetoric and Oratory:* "seek refuge, my unfailing friends, and be assured you will find it, in the friendship of Laelius and Scipio; in the patriotism of Cicero, Demosthenes, and Burke; as well as in the precepts and example of him, whose whole law is love, and who taught us to remember injuries only to forgive them" (1810, 2:397). Adams's students read Cicero and Quintilian in the original Latin; a few were able to read

Demosthenes in Greek. By the mid–nineteenth century, however, classical sources had pretty much disappeared from American rhetoric curricula. They were supplanted by study and recitation from treatises composed by modern British rhetoricians—George Campbell, Hugh Blair, and Richard Whately— or from popular American redactions, such as Samuel Newman's *System of Rhetoric*. Less often, students were also drilled in the finer points of grammar and usage from such popular authorities as Fowler, Lowth, and Trench (Wozniak 33–36; 236–37).

Rhetoric was one of the really masculine studies in eighteenth- and early nineteenth-century American colleges—the ones that strengthened the muscles of the mind. The others were mathematics, theology, and the classical languages. Hebrew, Greek, and Roman literatures were studied for two reasons: to improve students' grasp of the languages in which they were written, and to impart the humanistic heritage. Young gentlemen were expected to read English-language literary texts, to be sure, but they were to do so on their own time, since no one considered such work to be difficult enough to require classroom study. In 1743, the catalog of the Yale library classified the works of Shakespeare, Spenser, and Pope as "Books of diversion" (Broome, 57).

The instruction in English-language literature that did occur in the classical college was conducted by rhetoric professors, who used carefully selected passages of English literary texts to model style—both good and bad. Students never read entire texts written in English for class. Rather, they studied sentences that their teachers selected as examples of elegant composition, or memorized longer passages that demonstrated successful uses of figures. The pages of Alexander Jamieson's *Grammar of Rhetoric* (1818) are littered with quotes from Addison, Akenside, Milton, Shakespeare, and the Bible, among many other exemplary sources; Newman looked to the speeches of Daniel Webster for illustrations of elegant sentence composition; Richard Green Parker's *Aids to English Composition* (1846) cited hundreds of examples for imitation drawn from classical authors as well as English authors such as Scott and Gray.

By the mid–nineteenth century, a number of compendia of English-language literature had been published. The most popular of these were Thomas Budd Shaw's *Outlines of English Literature* (1867 [1852]) and Charles Cleveland's various *Compendia* of British and American literature. Students were apparently expected to read and recite from these huge textbooks, which were popular in part because the collections of many college libraries were small. Despite their bulk, the compendia seldom included actual pieces of literature, and they contained little criticism. Instead, they were massive chronologies of events in the history of English literature, complete with biographies of authors. The range of authors covered in the compendia is enormous: W. F. Collier's *History of English Literature* began with Celtic literature and ended with "the present time" (that is, 1881), and there was an appendix on American literature. Collier included both men and women writers in his collection. His definition of literature was very broad: his textbook discusses the lives and works of poets, dramatists, historians and biographers, essayists, critics, novelists, scientific writers, theologians, scholars, and travel writers. Other compendia took a minimalist approach to commentary, consisting only of schematic outlines of dates, authors, and titles. According to the author of one such text, the point of such schematics or outlines of English literature was to "bring into prominence the chronological relations of the facts they deal with" (Ryland vii).

The authors of the compendia were unabashedly nationalist in their sentiments. Thomas Shaw began his popular textbook like this:

> Within the limited territory comprised by a portion of the British Isles has grown up a language which has become the speech of the most free, the most energetic, and the most powerful portion of the human race; and which seems destined to be, at no distant period, the universal medium of communication throughout the globe. It is a language, the literature of which, inferior to none in variety or extent, is superior to all others in manliness of spirit, and in universality of scope; and it has exerted a great and a continually increasing influence upon the progress of human thought, and the improvement of human happiness. (1867 [1852], 11)

In the introduction to his compendium, Moses Coit Tyler asserted that "the literature of a people tells its life" (1). Tyler urged the study of English literature on openly didactic grounds: "as soon as we can feel that we belong to a free people with a noble past, let us begin to learn through what endeavors and to what end it is free. . . . Let us bring our hearts, then, to the study . . . and seek through it accord with that true soul of our country by which we may be encouraged to maintain in our own day the best work of our forefathers." As Gerald Graff remarks in his history of literary studies, teachers of Tyler's era saw "nothing wrong with treating literature in an instrumental way," and they used it with equal facility to support instruction in grammar and rhetoric or to indoctrinate their students with "civic and religious ideals" (19).

Graff is concerned that the students who used the compendia as recitation manuals may not have actually read any literary texts. He writes that "we can only speculate whether the students who memorized and recited the answers to [questions about Spenser in Cleveland] actually read any of Spenser's verse" (39). But nineteenth-century students were not expected to read vernacular literature in school; it was assumed that any well-bred gentleman who was interested in such literature would read it on his own time. Students studied the history of English-language literature to gain knowledge of their ethnic heritage and to absorb the community wisdom about literary standards that amounted to good taste. Students who memorized the outlines and recited passages from the compendia would be able to talk intelligently about the life and times of admired authors, but they would also understand which authors were of major importance and which were less worthy of attention. Tyler arranged his compendium so that a student could "perceive at a glance the relative importance of certain authors, so that his reading may be either confined to the lives of our great Classics, or extended through the full range of our Literature, without much risk of confusion or mistake as to proportionate greatness" (iv). He justified his massive reorganization of an earlier compendium on the ground that his approach grouped authors together "in such manner as to give most prominence to those who are most important" (viii). Tyler knew who these authors were, and he knew as well which eras of literature were the most important. In other words, he assumed there was broad agreement about the literary canon and the standards of taste. He assumed as well that new works of literature would be evaluated, not solely on their own merits, but on how well they stacked up against works already in the canon. It was tradition, not originality, that counted.

In 1888, Richard Moulton characterized the attitude toward literature that is manifested in the compendia as "judicial criticism" (Graff and Warner 62). Moulton asserted that

> the prevailing notions of criticism are dominated by the idea of
> *assaying,* as if its function were to test the soundness and estimate the
> comparative value of literary work. . . . the bulk of literary criticism,
> whether in popular conversation or in discussions by professed critics,
> occupies itself with the merits of authors and works; founding its
> estimates and arguments on canons of taste, which are either assumed

> as having met with general acceptance, or deduced from speculations
> as to fundamental conceptions of literary beauty. (62)

The job of judicial critics was to assess the worth of each new work in terms of its relation to received standards of taste, and to place it within the received canon according to the degree of prominence it deserved when compared to agreed-upon classics.[3] The writers of compendia of literary history performed a double service in this regard: they imparted widely recognized cultural standards of taste and excellence to students at the same time as they insured that these standards would be disseminated and maintained. The function of English-language literary study in the classical college, then, was to equip students with the cultural capital that would accrue in polite society from their knowledge about America's literary heritage, and to give them widely accepted standards against which they could measure and develop their own good taste.

FROM TRADITION TO RESEARCH

Classical education was challenged after the Civil War, when demographic changes and new cultural pressures threatened to put the old colleges out of business. More people, including women, demanded to study more subjects for other reasons than entering the ministry or teaching.[4] In 1862, the United States Congress passed the Morrill Act, which enticed states to erect colleges that included agricultural and mechanical instruction in their curricula. In addition, wealthy donors were ready to fund vocational and scientific education (Earnest 148). Cornell, unaffiliated with any religion, was founded in 1868; the University of Michigan dedicated itself to graduate research in 1871; and in 1876 Johns Hopkins was established as an institution primarily devoted to graduate studies. But it was emerging American interest in research that brought about profound philosophical changes in the old required curriculum.

The notion of research, imported from German universities by men like Hart, posed a challenge to the American assumption that the point of higher education was to inculcate in students the received civic and religious wisdom of the community. Hart put the challenge in this way: "by *Wissenschaft* the Germans mean knowledge in the most exalted sense of that term, namely, the ardent, methodical, independent search after truth in any and all of its forms, but wholly irrespective of utilitarian application" (1874, 250). This definition of knowledge as a nonutilitarian search for new truths implied a redefinition of the role of teacher. In Germany, Hart wrote, "the professor is not a teacher, in the English sense of the term; he is a specialist. He is not responsible for the success of his hearers. He is responsible only for the quality of his instruction. His duty begins and ends with himself" (264). Hence the German attitude toward knowledge devalued pedagogy. By "quality of instruction" Hart meant quality of research; his narratives about the behavior and attitudes of German professors make clear that these teachers did not feel accountable, and were not made to account, for the quality of their teaching because no one except their students cared whether the knowledge about which they lectured was successfully passed on or not. Furthermore, in the German ideal, teachers were free to determine what they would teach: "*Lehrfreitheit* means that the one who teaches, the professor or *Privatdocent*, is free to teach what he chooses, as he chooses" (250). In German education, teachers were freed from the obligation to instill commonplaces drawn from standard textbooks; they were further freed from the role of moral policeman.

This freedom extended to students as well: Hart translated *Lernfreitheit* as "the freedom of learning," which "denotes the emancipation of the student from *Schulswang*, compulsory drill by recitation" (250). The traditional American pedagogy that insured that students had acquired the *sensus communis* could be abandoned in the new ideal for other activities, such as lecture, discussion, lab demonstration, and independent study. The research ideal also implied that students should be free to learn whatever they liked.

Hart concludes his account of German attitudes toward research and teaching with a sarcastic comparison of German and American pedagogy:

> Were the object of higher education merely to train "useful and honorable members of society," to use the conventional phrase of the panegyrists of the American system, the German universities might possibly change their character. In place of professors free to impart the choicest results of their investigations, they might substitute pedagogues with text-books and class-books, noting down the relative merits and demerits of daily recitation. In place of students free to attend or to stay away, free to agree with the professor or to differ, free to read what they choose and to study after their fashion, they might

create a set of undergraduates reciting glibly from set lessons and
regarding each circumvention of the teacher as so much clear gain.
(260)

In 1874, then, James Morgan Hart was very much aware that the German
ideal of higher education had a different cultural motivation than did traditional American education. The research ideal abandoned fealty to traditional
wisdom; it would instead produce independent thinkers who followed their
intellectual curiosity wherever it led them.

When American universities adopted the research ideal, as they soon did,
profound changes in pedagogy occurred. Lecture, where professors pass on
the results of original research, was preferred to recitation, where students
demonstrate their grasp of traditional wisdom. According to Charles W. Eliot,
president of Harvard, recitation had given way to lectures, "conversational
instruction," and discussion at his university as early as 1879 (Morison 1930,
xliii). Seminars and laboratory instruction were also attempted at universities
with graduate and scientific schools. According to historian Frederick Rudolph
(whose sentiments obviously lie with the new curricular arrangements),

> For professors interested in their subjects and for students interested
> essentially in themselves and their own growth, a whole range of
> devices encouraged the shaping of an environment that honored the
> meaning of the word education in a way that recitations never did.
> Laboratories, field trips, seminars, small group discussions, research
> libraries and related library developments and lectures at their best
> were instruments of liberation. (145)

The research ideal brought about new curricular structures as well. The notion that there are many fields of knowledge worthy of study led to elective
courses of study; the notion that individuals can develop new knowledge led
to academic specialization. Rudolph writes: "An emerging profession of scholars used the elective system to free itself from a tradition of academic book-
keeping, class attendance, and examination by rote and to license the new
professors as investigators, innovators, the advance agents of next year's truth.
The consequence was new: new subjects, new depth, new skills, new truths"
(192). By the end of the nineteenth century, many American institutions of
higher learning had become prototypes of modern elective universities, in
which professors do research and students may major in a variety of courses

of study that are designed to prepare them for entry into a wide number of specialized careers or professions.

But schools are conservative institutions, and late-nineteenth-century university administrators did not abandon the older American tradition altogether. According to Kuklick, the new breed of university president still believed that "an institution engaged in liberal studies would produce public-spirited, service-oriented men. Modern education would foster open minds and broad sympathies, not detached scholarship" (207). Hence many schools retained the traditional arts curriculum alongside the elective curricula developed during the late nineteenth century, offering the two courses of study side by side. Today, students in many colleges and universities may still choose a bachelor of arts degree, which is still thought to provide them with broadly defined civic sentiments—hence the typical requirements in western civilization, history, and philosophy. Some elements of the older arts course of study are still required in many contemporary undergraduate curricula even for people majoring in highly professionalized fields such as engineering or medicine. And there is one classical college course that is still required of everyone nearly everywhere. That course is introductory composition.

In some respects, freshman composition is a remnant of the traditional American college. Its indebtedness to the older model of American education is obvious in the fact that it is still required of all matriculants. But the required course retains more than its traditional institutional position: it still performs the sort of moral surveillance on students that Hart claims was the task of the entire traditional college curriculum. Introductory composition is the only required course in which students are still asked, repeatedly, to express their opinions on a variety of topics not generated by their study of a field or subject matter. Rhetoric teachers in classical colleges felt no compunction about evaluating the quality of the moral or civic sentiments expressed by their students; indeed, they felt that doing so was their duty. And, as we shall see, late-nineteenth-century English professors also felt entitled to comment on students' character and opinions as, they supposed, these were manifested in their compositions. Today, however, universities are more fully (if not absolutely) committed to the research ideal, and composition teachers are the only teachers who are still asked to evaluate students' character rather than their mastery of a subject matter. Contemporary composition teachers are squeamish about this feature of composition instruction, and rightly so, given that this aspect of freshman composition is as outmoded as the curricular philosophy from which it derives. Their reluctance to perform this task may explain why composition teachers have for many years stoutly maintained that they evaluate students' papers on the basis of their mechanical correctness or formal fluency, rather than on the quality or merit of their arguments.

FRESHMAN ENGLISH AND THE ESTABLISHMENT OF ENGLISH STUDIES

After classical colleges were superseded by modern universities, the academic study of rhetoric withered and disappeared. If exercises in written or oral composition were still carried on above the freshman level, they gradually came to be housed in elective courses. Mathematics, classical languages, history, and philosophy became independent departments and developed specialized majors. By 1890, all but the most conservative colleges (Yale for instance) had dropped their freshman requirements in classical languages and mathematics. Linguistics and literary study were coopted by new departments of modern languages—primarily French, German, and English.

English studies grew very rapidly during the final decades of the nineteenth century. Outside of rhetoric teachers' instruction in literary history, there was no systematic study of English language or literature in American colleges before 1870. By 1890, however, the Modern Language Association had been founded, and many universities were offering both undergraduate and advanced course work in English philology and English-language literature.[5] The English Department was the largest unit at the University of Chicago in 1894; twelve faculty members offered forty-eight courses in English to over eight hundred students (Payne 86). At this time, Harvard's English department had only five professors and a staff of fifteen temporary and part-time instructors, but they taught English to almost a thousand students (Payne 44–45). By 1890, graduate-level course work in English was available at many eastern universities (Don Allen 10). In that same year, Harvard president Charles W. Eliot casually referred to the Boylston professorship of rhetoric as "the chair of English" (2). By the end of the century, Eliot found that English was the university's most popular undergraduate major. By then, Freshman English had also become a staple feature of undergraduate education not only at Harvard but throughout the country.

As I suggest above, the Freshman English requirement retained something of the institutional function that composition exercises had fulfilled in the classical colleges: it remained the site wherein students' character could be subjected to the disciplining gaze of the academy, and that is, presumably, why it continued to be required of all matriculants. However, in other respects Freshman English was an entirely new phenomenon, constituting a radical departure from the pedagogy and rationale of the composition exercises practiced in the classical colleges.[6] The confinement of the universal requirement in composition to the freshman level and its location in departments of English were significant departures from classical practice. But the primary departure from tradition was that the intellectual roots of Freshman English were not rhetorical. During the late nineteenth century, the traditional, rhetorical orientation of composition instruction was altered in order to accommodate new, bourgeois attitudes toward composition and literature. These new attitudes made it possible to invent and sustain a new discipline called "English."

In the rest of this chapter, I argue that the invention of Freshman English enabled the creation of English studies. This is of course a partial view because it ignores the efforts of the linguists and literary scholars who inaugurated courses in those fields and who founded professional organizations such as the Modern Language Association. Nonetheless I take this position because it permits me to demonstrate just how central Freshman English was (and is) to the maintenance of English departments. Reading history in this way permits me to argue that the course has always been a service course, and that the initial service it performed was to legitimate English studies as a discipline.

MAKING ENGLISH STRANGE

One of the roadblocks faced by early English professionals was the notion held by other faculty members that since English was supposedly the native tongue of most Americans, neither the language nor its literature required university-level study. In the very first volume of *PMLA*, Theodore Hunt wrote that "the common sentiment, that anyone can teach his vernacular, has been a curse to the English Department. . . . Its philology, it is said, takes us back to the barbarous days of the Anglo-Saxons; its literature ranks among the self-acquired accomplishments of the student rather than among the difficult and 'regular' studies, while its actual expression in composition and literary criticism must be left to natural methods" (1884, 120). Apparently, teachers of classical languages assumed that English grammar was relatively easy to master since English is uninflected. In the same volume of *PMLA*, John McElroy lamented that "there has been no little talk against English grammar in preparation for college. English is called 'the grammarless tongue;' comparatively little time, we are told, 'should suffice, if judiciously used, to teach an intelligent boy the few points of grammar it is most important to know'" (McElroy 200).

Six years later, Le Baron Russell Briggs, who taught composition at Harvard, again addressed the problems posed by the general denigration of English studies. The position of the English teacher, he wrote, "is delicate: he professes to teach nothing but what all the other teachers are presumed to know; and the attitude of these teachers often leads the boys to believe that he is a man who makes a fuss about trifles because he knows nothing bigger to make a fuss about. A teacher of 'Deportment' could hardly be more despised" (Hill et al. 38). (The analogy to deportment is an interesting one.) Nonetheless, Briggs asserted, "English is not easy. Properly studied, it taxes the best powers of both pupil and master" (37). The saving grace for the fledgling discipline of English studies was that phrase—"properly studied." If the new discipline of English were to escape its aura of effeminacy, it would have to overcome the commonplaces that people read English-language literature for "diversion" and that mastery of the English language did not require study. The first step in the process was to define English as a language from which its native speakers were alienated. The second step was to establish an entrance examination in English that was very difficult to pass. The third step, necessitated by the large number of failures on the exam, was to install a course of study that would remediate the lack demonstrated by the examination.

When English-language philologists began to publish massive annotated editions of English-language literature that contained long lists of derivations, sources, and cognate words, they succeeded in "making English seem as hard as Greek."[7] And while this alienating approach to English provided scholars with a field of study, English teachers were busy constructing students as people who did not enjoy sufficient mastery of their native tongue. They accomplished this by limiting acceptable uses of English to a grapholect that Adams Sherman Hill called "pure English."

The notion of verbal purity (*hellenismos* or *latinitas*) is as old as ancient rhetoric. Purity, also translated as "correctness," was one of the four features of style delineated by ancient tradition (the others were clarity, appropriateness, and ornament). According to Cicero, the achievement of correctness came with children's acquisition of their native Latin, providing that young people grew up in the right circles and were given a good education. And so he refused to treat it in detail (*De Oratore* 3.12). With the emergence during the modern period of a middle class, however, the achievement of correctness took on new urgency. In Britain, members of the new middling classes did not have easy access to the circles where the purest English was presumably spoken and written (Tom Miller 1997). In America, where class lines were not so firmly drawn, attitudes toward correctness were conflicted. As Kenneth Cmeil has demonstrated, linguistic correctness was associated on the one hand with cultivation and refinement, thanks in part to humanism's association of refined expression with learning. On the other, democratic access to institutions and the emergence of the popular press served to keep distinctly "unrefined" language in wide circulation. One response to this conflicted situation was the emergence of a cultural practice called "verbal criticism." Interest in verbal criticism reached its zenith after the Civil War, according to Cmeil, when it

> turned into a thriving industry. . . . the language critics . . . thought
> that the mass discipline the war imposed made it possible for the "best
> men" to reassert their dominance in American society; that the post-
> Jacksonian "festival of misrule" would end. . . . Like their "soulmate"
> Matthew Arnold . . . these critics wanted to re-create the cultural and
> social atmosphere of the late eighteenth century, reiterating a vision
> that was humanist at its core. They hoped to maintain the traditional
> civility of refined decorum. Polite language was "reserved," not
> "familiar." The prestige of gentlemen and ladies had to be reasserted.
> The essential morality of style must not be forgotten. The habits of
> thought that drove the late-nineteenth-century critics were, in a very
> real sense, ancient, echoing Cicero's division between the *liberales*
> (gentlemen) and *sordidi* (the vulgar). (123–24)

The verbal critics were anxious about the supposed drifting of words from their moorings in accepted meanings. According to Cmeil, they thought that "Americans spoke too much and without enough care. . . . the fit between signifier and signified was not as tight as it had been. *Calculate* had formerly meant "to ascertain by means of symbols" but it was now vaguely used for "believed," "supposed," or "expected." *Mad*, which meant "crazy," was distended to mean "angry" (125). And so on.

Cmeil locates Adams Sherman Hill squarely in the tradition of verbal criticism (142). Hill attended Harvard as an undergraduate and was a classmate of Charles W. Eliot. When Eliot became president of the university, he made no secret of his desire that English become a strong part of Harvard's offerings (1884, 205). In 1872 he recruited Hill away from his job as a journalist at the *New York Tribune* and appointed him assistant professor of rhetoric (Rollo Brown 50; Kitzhaber 1990, 60). Hill was given the Boylston chair in 1876, and he continued to teach at Harvard for over thirty years, retiring in 1904.

Hill's essays and his textbook, *The Principles of Rhetoric* (1878), display his conflicted thinking about English. On the one hand, he praised the principle that current use was an adequate guide to correct usage; on the other, he actually blamed democratic practices for the "ubiquity of bad English": "Where every man is as good as every other man, every man's English is accounted as good as every other man's" (1890, x). In an essay published in *Scribner's* in 1887, Hill gave two reasons for requiring study in English. He argued that

> of English an educated man should know more than the rudiments, because—if for no other reason—everybody knows, or half-knows, or thinks he knows them; because everybody deems himself capable, not only of criticising the English of others, but also of writing good English himself. Therefore, educated men should know enough to be able to protect pure English against the numerous foes that beset it on every side in these days of free speech and a free press. (1887, 508)

That is to say, the possession of "pure" English distinguishes the educated man from the hoi polloi who think they know the language but who betray by their every utterance that they do not. Furthermore, the possession of "pure" English by a select few would see to its preservation and maintenance. Hill expressed concern that if the standards of pure English were not maintained, the classics of English literature—"Shakspere and Milton, Bacon and Addison . . . Scott and Thackeray, Cardinal Newman and Mr. Ruskin, Hawthorne and Emerson"—would become unintelligible (1890, xv). These utterances align Hill with the Arnoldian tradition of liberal humanism, a tradition distinguished from its classical ancestor by its diminution of the rhetorical impulse and its reverence for the maintenance of the cultural standards exemplified in a textual tradition.

Hill's comments make clear that he located "pure English" in the use of correct grammar, punctuation, and spelling, as well as in students' mastery of the linguistic niceties discriminated by verbal critics. The *Principles* begins with this sentence: "The foundations of rhetoric rest upon grammar; for grammatical purity is a requisite of good writing" (1878, 1). Cicero would have been surprised, I think, to find purity elevated to a first principle of rhetoric. He might have been further surprised to see it given two sections of a textbook written for the use of young men rather than children. Of course, Hill's discussion of grammatical purity was not about grammar at all but about usage. (His remarks on grammar proper appeared in the section on sentence composition). Hill's discussions of usage betrayed his anxiety about the fluidity of class distinctions and his assurance that a proper understanding of pure English would solidify those distinctions. He wrote that "by avoiding pedantry and vulgarity alike" a writer may commend himself "to the best class or readers" but lose "nothing in the estimation of any other class; for those who do not themselves speak or write pure English understand it when spoken or written by others" (7–8). Elsewhere in the text, he claimed that English terms derived from Anglo-Saxon are "the lower classes" of words, so that they cannot perform the "highest" work reserved for terms derived from Latin or Greek (97). In accordance with the tradition of verbal criticism, the *Principles* contains long discussions of the differences between *can* and *may*, *shall* and *will*, *should* and *would*, along with lists of neologisms, archaic terms, slang, and other infelicities to be avoided by the writer of pure English, since "the grosser faults of common speech are avoided by good authors" (48).

Hill was not the only English teacher who was concerned about correctness and what it indicates about one's level of cultivation. As late as 1893 Brainerd Kellogg, who taught at Brooklyn Polytechnic, wrote that

> one's English is already taken as the test and measure of his culture—he is known by the English he keeps. To mistake his words (even to mispronounce them or to speak them indistinctly), to huddle them as a mob into sentences, to trample on plain rules of grammar, to disregard the idioms of the language,—these things, all or severally, disclose the speaker's intellectual standing. One's English betrays his breeding, tells what society he frequents, and determines what doors are to open to him or be closed against him. (97–98)

This is a quite reductive application of the Arnoldian humanist view that the point of acquiring skill in the use of language is to demonstrate the quality of one's cultural and educational attainments, but Kellogg does not hesitate to recommend it to his readers as the only standard worth following.

The influence commanded by Kellogg was small potatoes compared to that wielded by Adams Sherman Hill, who marshaled the considerable prestige of Harvard to orchestrate a national assault on impure English. The device with which he began was an entrance examination.

CORRECT ENGLISH AND THE ENTRANCE EXAMINATION

In the early days of American higher education, students desiring to enter college were examined orally. Examiners were interested in determining the extent of students' previous education, of course, but they also wanted to evaluate their character. Oral examinations were time-consuming, since they required faculty to interview each candidate for admission at some length. Written exams began to be used as early as the 1830s (Smallwood 15). But written examinations did not come into full favor until after the Civil War, when enrollments in higher education nearly doubled.

Before 1800 arithmetic, Latin, and Greek were the only subjects required for admission to American colleges. Faculty who were admitting students to four years of recitation wanted to know the extent of their pupils' preparation in these areas. Hence lists of entrance requirements ordinarily named the texts students were required to know, perhaps from memory: Homer, Xenophon, the Greek testament, Cicero, Caesar, and Virgil. Prior to 1870 entrance examinations seem not to have required knowledge of English literature, English philology, or the more theoretical ranges of rhetoric or linguistics. By that time, however, Yale, Princeton, Columbia, Michigan, and Cornell did require "English grammar" for admission (Broome 53). In addition, Princeton required "a short and simple composition." In 1879 a handbook on admissions summarized the English requirements for admission to most colleges as follows: "A thorough knowledge of English grammar, with such proficiency in the elements of Rhetoric as will enable the student to spell, punctuate, and paragraph correctly" (Nightingale 89).

Mary Trachsel reprints a sample of an entrance examination in English grammar given at Illinois Industrial University (now the University of Illinois at Urbana-Champaign) in 1870:

1. Name the vowells; the labials; the dentals; the palatals.
2. Define Etymology; the name and different classes of words.
3. Give the different modes of expressing gender in English—illustrate each.
4. Give the four rules for the formation of the plural of nouns, and an example under each.
5. Give four rules for the formation of the possessive case of names; and write the possessive plural of *lady, man, wife*.
6. Give the distinction between personal and relative pronouns.
7. What are auxiliary verbs? Name them.
8. Give the third-person singular of the verb *sit* in all the tenses of the indicative mood.
9. He said that that that that that pupil parsed was not that that he should have parsed. Parse the *that's* in this sentence.
10. He that cometh unto me I will in no wise cast out. Between you and I there is much mischief in that plan. I intended last year to have visited you. Correct these sentences, and give four reasons for your corrections (58).

As Trachsel notes, this "exam does not require students to read or compose in English, but simply to describe its rules and its irregularities" (58). In other words, students were expected to have a formal or book-based knowledge of the grammatical rules of English—the same sort of knowledge, in fact, that they were expected to have of Greek and Latin grammars.

The first real departure from classical practice regarding entrance exams occurred at Harvard, which is, not coincidentally, also the birthplace of Freshman English.[8] In the mid-1860s, students desiring admission to Harvard were examined in "reading English aloud" (Hill et al. 55). In 1869, a paragraph was added to the catalog copy suggesting that students should prepare themselves in "Craik's English of Shakespeare (Julius Caesar) or in Milton's Comus." It is unclear whether this meant that students were to read aloud from these texts, or that they took a written examination. It is possible that they were still examined orally, in the traditional fashion, on their knowledge of grammar (prizes were offered). The entry adds the following phrase: "Attention to Derivations and Critical Analysis recommended." Attention to derivations is precisely the sort of commentary that appears in Craik's annotation of *Julius Caesar,* from which students could well have recited in preparatory school.

The earliest mention of written entrance examinations at Harvard appears in 1872–73, when students were warned that "correct spelling, punctuation, and expression, as well as legible hand-writing, are expected of all applicants for admission; and failure in any of these particulars will be taken into account at the examination" (Hill et al. 55). And in 1873 there is the "first demand for a theme," as Byron Hurlbut, one of the early teachers of composition at Harvard, notes in his history of the entrance examination (Hill's account in the same volume dates this demand to 1874) (Hill et al. 46, 8). This first demand for a theme was accompanied by the requirement that students be acquainted with a list of half a dozen literary texts. In 1879, a line was added requiring that "every candidate is expected to be familiar with all the books in this list" (Hill et al. 55). In other words, the entrance examination at that time tested students' knowledge of literature along with their skills in spelling, punctuation, and grammar. It is altogether possible that this exam imitated the long-established pattern for examining students in Latin and Greek, where students were expected to know the canonical literature as well as the grammar of those languages. The readers of the exams were perennially interested in students' command of mechanics, but they disagreed about whether a student could fail the entrance exam because he lacked knowledge of the literary texts from which the exam questions were drawn.

Surely it is no coincidence that the installation of a written examination in composition followed hard upon the appointment of Adams Sherman Hill to Harvard's English staff in 1872. Hill's account of the origin of the written entrance examination in English makes clear his hope that the fact of the examination would improve preparatory instruction in English. He wrote:

> it was hoped that this requirement would effect several desirable objects—that the student, by becoming familiar with a few works holding a high place in English literature, would acquire a taste for good reading, and would insensibly adopt better methods of thought and better forms of expression; that teachers would be led to seek subjects for composition in the books named, subjects far preferable to the vague generalities too often selected, and that they would pay closer attention to errors in elementary matters; that, in short, this recognition by the College of the importance of English would lead both teachers and pupils to give more time to the mother tongue. (Hill et al. 8)

In other words, Hill hoped the exam would improve the taste of both students and teachers. He also hoped it would alter standard pedagogical practices. He wanted to wean teachers away from composition assignments associated with rhetorical instruction—the sort of assignment used by Adams and Channing—which he characterized as themes written on "vague generalities." Clearly, he preferred that teachers use composition assignments drawn from the literary texts canonized in Harvard's catalog announcement. Hill made no secret of his desire to alter the direction of preparatory instruction toward Harvard's definition of "good English." This definition included sufficient acquaintance with literary texts considered canonical by Harvard's English staff.

Anyone who has ever tried to improve the quality of instruction by adopting some sort of ancillary or administrative procedure could have predicted that Hill's ambitious hopes for the entrance exam would be dashed. Harvard's attempt to improve English instruction in the schools by means of its entrance exam was a long uphill battle that engendered bitterness and resentment on the part of many preparatory school teachers, and it upset faculty in other universities as well.[9] Happily, the exam did elevate the status of English among Hill's colleagues at Harvard: "the Faculty frankly accept the requirement in English as standing upon a par with the other requirements" (Hill et al. 9).

Perhaps the exam did not have the pedagogical effects Hill desired because it was a fairly negative experience for all concerned. In 1879, only fourteen of the students who took the entrance exam passed with credit. Half were failed, which raised the issue of what to do about students who could not pass the entrance exam in English but who had to be admitted nonetheless. Here is the prompt used in that year:

> Write a short composition upon one of the subjects given below. Before beginning to write, consider what you have to say on the subject selected, and arrange your thoughts in logical order. Aim at quality rather than quantity of work. Carefully revise your composition, correcting all errors in punctuation, spelling, grammar, division by paragraphs, and expression, and making each sentence as clear and forcible as possible. If time permits, make a clean copy of the revised work.
>
> I. The Character of Sir Richard Steele.
> II. The Duke of Marlborough as portrayed by Thackeray.

III. The Style of "Henry Esmond."

IV. Thackeray's account of the Pretender's visit to England.

V. Duelling in the Age of Queen Anne. (Hill et al. 9)

Perhaps the passage of time illustrates to contemporary readers just how alien Hill's exam must have looked to young men whose preparation did not include practice in the sort of reading and writing skills that would be necessary to pass it. Students would have been required to read the texts named, and they would have to be familiar with literary history as well. Most important, they would have to be acquainted with the definition of "correct" English that circulated at Harvard in order to pass this examination. This definition, in Hill's mind at least, included knowledge of the designated literary texts. He did not hesitate to fail papers whose authors displayed ignorance of the required readings. According to him, 8 to 10 percent of the papers "avowed or displayed utter ignorance of the subject-matter; several, for example, confounded Steele with Sir Roger de Coverley, others the period of Queen Anne with that of Richard Coeur de Lion, others the style of 'Henry Esmond,' the novel, with the manners of Henry Esmond, the hero of the novel" (Hill et al. 9). The rest of the failures were assigned because of mechanical lapses, which Hill excoriated in scathing language: "utter ignorance of punctuation"; unacceptable spellings, perhaps "due to an unconscious effort to represent to the eye a vicious pronunciation"; "grossly ungrammatical or profoundly obscure sentences; absolute illiteracy" (10).

Students never got any better at passing Professor Hill's exam. In 1888, he wrote with a distinct note of despair:

> Between 1873 (when Harvard College for the first time held an examination in English) and 1884, I read several thousand compositions written in the examination-room upon subjects drawn from books which the candidates were required to read before presenting themselves. Of these a hundred, perhaps—to make a generous estimate,—were creditable to writer or teacher or both. . . . In spelling, punctuation, and grammar some of the compositions are a great deal worse than the mass, and some a little better; but in other respects there is a dead level, unvaried by a fresh thought or an individual expression. (1888, 12–13)

Correctness and originality seem to be the criteria by means of which Hill measured student performance throughout his career with the entrance examination, and students seem never to have been able to satisfy him on either of these measures.

In 1892, though, when Hill was no longer in charge, half of the candidates were still failing Harvard's entrance exam (Adams et al. 1892, 151). In 1897, one-quarter of the papers written in English A showed "conclusively that about 25 per cent of the students now admitted to Harvard are unable to write their mother tongue with the ease and freedom absolutely necessary to enable them to proceed advantageously in any college course" (410). The historical record also contains testimony to the fact that preparatory teachers taught to the test, hence frustrating Hill's goal for the requirement, which was to improve instruction in English composition (Hurlbut 49; Payne 51).

Given the immediate and continuing dissatisfaction with students' performance on the entrance examination at Harvard, the question might legitimately be asked: why test for proficiency in English composition at all? Why, in other words, did Hill test the compositional skills of boys who wanted to enter Harvard, and why, when he was so dissatisfied with the results, did he continue the practice? Michel Foucault supplies an answer in his explanation of the machinery that makes power available in modern disciplines such as English studies. Foucault argues that examinations

> opened up two correlative possibilities: firstly, the constitution of the individual as a describable, analysable object . . . in order to maintain him in his individual features, in his particular evolution, in his own aptitudes or abilities, under the gaze of a permanent corpus of knowledge; and, secondly, the constitution of a comparative system that made possible the measurement of overall phenomena, the description of groups, the characterization of collective facts, the calculation of the gaps between individuals, their distribution in a given "population." (1979, 190)

According to Foucault, the power exercised by modern disciplines is invisible. However, that invisible power consists in the ability of discipline's agents to make individuals visible, so that the capacity of each individual may be measured against the (invisible) standards set by the discipline. The examination has the added advantage, from the point of view of agents of the discipline, of putting individual rankings on display, so that the capacity of individuals (or groups, such as those folks labeled by an exam as "basic writers") may be measured against each other or against other groups vis-à-vis their relation to the discipline. As Foucault puts it, the exam provides a discipline with a description of the individual that is "a document for possible use. . . . this turning of real lives into writing . . . functions as a procedure of objectification and subjection" (191–92).

Something like this seems to have happened with the examination papers produced at Harvard. During several years in the 1890s, a committee of Harvard overseers looked at the papers students wrote on the entrance exam as well as papers they wrote for class. Their commentaries in the *Harvard Reports* make clear that the papers could be made to stand in for the people who wrote them, and for their teachers as well. In 1892 the commissioners remarked that "it would certainly seem not unreasonable to insist that young men nineteen years of age who present themselves for a college education should be able . . . to write their mother tongue with ease and correctness" (Adams et al. 1892, 119). Nonetheless, they complained that the papers they reviewed from English A "satisfied the committee that the students were . . . imperfectly prepared," as though the papers were perfect representations not only of the students' skills but of their preparatory education. There is no sense anywhere in the *Harvard Reports* that students might blow off an exam, or that their performance might be affected by anxiety, or that a single performance might not indicate anything at all about overall skill level. In 1895 the commissioners reprinted a number of examination papers in order to demonstrate that "a very large portion of the time of the preparatory school course is consumed in exercises which, in result, so far as good English composition is at issue, seems to obscure at least in the mind of the student the fundamental principles that every sentence consists of a subject and a predicate, and that clearness in the expression of thought is of the essence of good writing" (Adams et al. 1895, 277). They reprinted no papers in the report of 1897, but their commentary on the papers they examined was no less damning than before. In this report, they connected students' papers directly to their level of character development: "the most noticeable feature in these papers [from "Course A"] is their extreme crudeness both of thought and execution" (Adams et al. 1897, 403). The commissioners were shocked that "such a degree of immaturity should exist in a body of young men averaging nineteen years of age, coming from the best preparatory schools in America, and belonging to the most well-to-do and highly educated families."

The unveiling function of exams was not lost on contemporary observers. Writing in the *Harvard Graduates' Magazine* about the "disreputable" state of papers printed in the *Harvard Reports* of 1893, Professor W. W. Goodwin remarked that "a similar test applied to any other department would disclose a state of things in the lower ranks of scholarship which would be proportionally disreputable. . . . It cannot be doubted that a similar depth of ignorance of Geometry, Algebra, Physics, or History might easily be disclosed" (190). But teachers of other subjects did not need to justify their fields of study at the university level, and so they had no need to establish entrance exams that could be failed by the bulk of would-be matriculants. The entrance examination in English repeatedly and continually created appropriate subjects for the study of English—subjects who were visibly, graphically, unable to meet Harvard's standards.

Hill and the Harvard English faculty succeeded in establishing such arcane standards for the use of written English that they virtually insured that many aspirants would fail their exam. In 1888 Briggs defended the exam by arguing that "no candidate ever failed through ignorance of the details of a prescribed book" (Hill et al. 19). Of course this claim contradicted Hill's admitted practice. But if Briggs's description of examiners' practice in 1888 is accurate, this means that mechanical correctness was even more important than it had been under Hill's administration. And yet Briggs confessed that "perfect accuracy" was unknown in the proper use of English (38). In 1882 the examiners began to ask students taking the exam to correct specimens of "bad English." Briggs complained that students did not do well on this part of the exam because they did not take it seriously enough: "The one notion that possesses a boy when he faces the sentences is that something must be changed. His mind saunters up to each sentence, looks at it vacantly, changes the first word that comes half-way to meet him, and moves languidly on" (Hill et al. 31). He condemned teachers in the prep schools, who complained that there was often nothing to correct in the samples of "bad English" used on the exam: "the evils that appear in the [exam] books . . . will remain so long as a single prominent teacher in a single large school suffers slipshod English to be used by his pupils or by himself" (Hill et al. 35, 31). Here are some of the examples of bad English used on the Harvard entrance examination in 1889:

4. So honorable a connection might have been expected to have advanced our author's prospects.
5. Sometimes he would lay awake the whole night, trying but unable to make a single line.
6. Milton was too busy to much miss his wife.

7. Everybody had in their recollection the originals of the passages parodied.
9. He consoles himself with the fancy that he had done a great work.
10. I think we will fall considerably under the mark in computing the poet's income at 600 pounds.

I ask my readers: could you have passed Professor Briggs's entrance exam?

THE EXAM BREEDS A COURSE

During his early years at Harvard, Hill continuously agitated for the removal of the required sophomore course in rhetoric to the freshman level. He was opposed for a time by professors of classics and others whose own freshman requirements were jeopardized by the turn toward elective curricula, but in 1885, thirteen years after his arrival at Harvard, he finally succeeded in getting the requirement moved to the freshman year (Brereton 27–28). His essays do not say explicitly that he advocated this move in connection with his perception that students performed dismally on the entrance exam, but he must have been aware that the exam would not be taken seriously until a serious penalty was attached to failing it. As early as 1879, he was advocating the move to the freshman level as a logical "next best step" after the introduction of the exam (Hill et al. 12). He rationalized the move as yet another way to put pressure on the preparatory schools to expand and improve their instruction in English: "Could the study be taken up at the threshold of college life, the schools would be made to feel that their labors in this direction were going to tell upon a pupil's standing in college as well as upon his admission." In other words, required Freshman English could be used as a club with which to bring instruction in preparatory schools in line with Harvard's definition of good English.

The connection between an entrance examination and a required course is not hard to ferret out. At the founding of Stanford in 1891, according to H. B. Lathrop, the faculty decided to follow the precedent set by the University of California (that is, Berkeley), which was to examine students in English at admission. The humanist connection between literature and composition is apparent in Lathrop's description of the point of Stanford's exam, which was to "test the student's command of the English language," as well as to encourage "the reading of some good books" and suggest "a method of associating practice in composition with the study of literature" (Lathrop

290). It seems that Stanford students had no better luck with the exam than applicants to Harvard had. According to Melville Anderson, chair of the English Department, in 1894 only forty out of 150 students "wrote satisfactory papers" on the entrance examination (Anderson 51). Students' performances were so miserable, according to Lathrop, that Stanford began requiring "at least one year of instruction in English after admission, the object of the course being to bring students to the point of writing with moderate clearness and correctness under all circumstances in which they would be placed" (Lathrop 290). In other words, once Stanford decided to give an examination, the faculty were forced to install course work in order to remedy the deficiencies discovered by the exam. After they had offered the course for two years, however, they found that the professors who taught it "were worn out with the drudgery of correcting Freshman themes" (Anderson 52). Had they not dropped the course, the chair feared, "all the literary courses would have been swept away by the rapidly growing inundation of Freshman themes." So they stopped offering the course and they stopped admitting people to English studies who had not passed the exam. According to Lathrop, students who afterward failed the entrance exam were "conditioned," meaning that they could not graduate until they passed the exam. Such students would be forced to find and pay for private instruction. This feature of the plan worried Lathrop no little, since at that time Stanford's students were not wealthy. Lathrop's uneasiness might well have stemmed from his awareness that the new plan was little short of irresponsible, since the faculty required students to write a composition "on some subject not previously announced," offered no clue as to what was being tested, and expected them to make up a failure on their own time, using their own money (Lathrop 292).

Yale provides a contrary example. In 1892 Henry DeBeers defended his university's refusal to establish an entrance examination in English on the ground that Yale required no course work in that field. DeBeers nicely caught the distinction between the aim of the new research university and that of the classical college when he asked: "What is the theory of an entrance examination? I take it to be this: it is to ascertain whether the candidate is prepared to go on profitably with the studies of the freshman year. It is not its purpose to determine the precise stage of mental development that he has reached" (DeBeers 428). Was DeBeers implying that to test entering students in English was redolent of older ways of doing things, when a boy's "mental discipline" was as important as the extent of his knowledge? He continued: "it is doubtless desirable that a boy should have learned a number of things, of which he will not be challenged to show knowledge at the threshold of the university . . . but so long as knowledge of these does not lead up to and necessarily precede the studies of our freshman year, we do not examine in them, any more than we examine in general information, or in the topics of the day in the newspapers" (428). This is a genteel slap at Harvard. But DeBeers's point is clear: if a university does not require course work in a subject, students needn't be examined in that subject.

So Harvard found itself in the odd position of requiring an entrance examination for a course that was required not of entrants, but of sophomores. This delay did not satisfy Hill, and once again Foucault's work explains why. In his remarks about the disciplinary necessity to punish those who are found deficient by an examination, Foucault points out that within disciplines, exercise is punishment: "exercise—intensified, multiplied forms of training, several times repeated" (1979, 179). If students' performance on an entrance examination reveals that they somehow do not "measure up" to a disciplinary standard, they are to be subjected to repeated exercises in the very deficiency they displayed. The function of the course that followed on the heels of the examination, then, was to establish a site in which students might undergo the repeated and continuous punishment earned by their failure on the exam. This analysis explains the need for the standard assignment used in Freshman English at Harvard and elsewhere for many years: the daily theme. Freshman English was the site wherein students' writing was put on continuous display so that its lacks could be remarked, and so that their papers could be measured against each other and against Harvard's disciplinary standard as well. This reading of the daily theme as punishment-through-exercise explains why no exit exam was demanded at the close of English A, why indeed few Freshman English programs have ever used exit examinations. The point of the required course is not to acquire some level of skill or knowledge that can be measured upon exit; it is instead to subject students to discipline, to force them to recognize the power of the institution to insist on conformity with its standards.

Hill's successors at Harvard learned his lessons well: in their explication of theme correcting at Harvard, Charles Townsend Copeland and H. M. Rideout noted that "the habitual use of correct and intelligent English, is what the instructors try to drill into the Freshmen" (1901, 2). This instruction was highly disciplined. Students enrolled in the courses supervised by Copeland and Rideout were required to purchase Hill's textbook, a composition card that contained Hill's "abbreviated marks of correction," and "the regular theme paper, which has a margin of an inch at the left of the sheet" (3). Instruction began with attention to correctness: "the first effort of the instructors . . . is not to make the daily themes interesting, but to make them correct" (9). The most common failings noted in early themes were "faults in spelling and punctuation, in the use of words, in the construction of sentences, and in the construction of paragraphs" (11). Exams given in the course asked students to rehearse the lessons they were to have learned from Hill's textbook: "Clearness is a relative term. Discuss"; "Explain fully the uses of 'shall' and 'will' in direct and in indirect discourse to express futurity"; "Discuss the principles of narrative writing, and show how these principles are illustrated in 'Adam Bede'" (66, 71, 75). These exams were not intended to test students' ability to use English; rather, they tested their knowledge about stuff taught in an emerging academic discipline called "English."

A few of the specimen themes attached to Copeland and Rideout's monograph were reproduced in facsimile, which allows us to see that readers' commentary consisted of remarks such as these: "use fewer present participles and avoid nominative absolute constructions"; "too many 'ands'"; "too impersonal"; "use fewer words." Terminal commentary was limited to remarks like these: "This is discreditable work. Your spelling is weak, your sentences are a mere slop of 'and' and 'but,' and your paragraphs are bunches of words without any organic relation to the whole composition. The progress of the whole theme is careless and erratic" (93). Freshman English at Harvard was devoted not only to purging students' writing of Harvard-defined infelicities but to reshaping their prose so that it conformed to the very specific stylistic standards set by the course. This aim was not lost on students. In his evaluation of the course, one student wrote: "In an endeavor (and a not very successful one) to conform to certain rules, I have lost all originality,—everything has a sort of labored rehashing, which makes whatever I have to say, dull and uninteresting" (80). Copeland and Rideout were not discouraged by this negative evaluation. They note that it "shows a distinct gain in structure" from the student's earlier work, and remark that "if he has got nothing else from his practice, he has learned to complain more effectively."

CORRECTNESS, CHARACTER, AND THE STUDY OF ENGLISH

The professors who taught Freshman English at Harvard firmly associated correctness with character.[10] The "third hour" of the course, which had been opened up by the move to the freshman level, was regularly taken up with ethical instruction. Copeland and Rideout note: "At the beginning of the year many Freshmen—boys just released from restraint and set to acting for themselves—find their ideas and conduct more or less confused. In affairs both large and small they need sensible advice. And this is what the 'third-hour' talks try to furnish them" (27). When teachers complained about the "bookish" themes and the "translation English" that infected student writing, Barrett Wendell instituted the project of the daily theme, in which students were expected to write about their experiences and their surroundings. The daily theme required no preparation; it was to be a spontaneous recording of the composer's thoughts. According to Copeland and Rideout, the point of the dailies was to get students to "open their eyes, and keep them open, to scenes and events near at hand" (8). What happened, of course, was that reading dailies about students' observations and experiences put the professors in the position of passing judgment on the students' intelligence and character (in this respect, the dailies replicated the function of daily recitation in the classical colleges). The tendency to equate students' writing with their characters could only have been reinforced by Hill's insistence in his textbooks that the primary function of language is to represent thought as clearly and accurately as possible.

Harvard's teachers regularly characterized their responses to student writing in moral language. The most important duty of a composition teacher, Hill thought, was "to prevent the young men and women under his eye from running to extremes" (1888, 91). Hence he urged teachers of writing to impose deadlines and rules on students even if these were a poor substitute for "the self-control which a young man old enough to be in college should exercise in the matter of writing, as in other things" (101). Briggs railed against "pervading inaccuracy," "incontinent oratory," "chronic morality," and "wooden unintelligence" in the themes he read (Hill et al. 30). Copeland and Rideout were concerned about student writers "going astray," and hence their instruction aimed at helping students "steer a middle course" between "the two evils, absurdity and dulness" (55). And the *Harvard Reports* of 1897 described themes written at Radcliffe in just the way we might expect late-nineteenth-century men to characterize women:

> In mechanical execution,—neatness, penmanship, punctuation and orthography,—they show a marked superiority in standard over the papers from the courses of the College proper. . . . In their contents also they reveal unmistakably a greater degree of conscientious,

painstaking effort,—the desire to perform faithfully and well the allotted task. On the other hand, in thought and in form, they are less robust and less self-assertive. A few are sprightly; none of them indicate any especial capacity for observing, or attempt, in pointing out defects and difficulties, anything which might be termed a thoughtful solution of them. (Adams et al., 407)

If the men at Harvard were sloppy, inattentive, and erratic, the women of Radcliffe were self-effacing, unobservant, and thoughtless. A good deal of study in English would be necessary to rectify these character faults.

THE COURSE BREEDS A FIELD

Contemporary sources agreed that Freshman English had much to do with the establishment of English as a university discipline. The connection between Freshman English and the status of English studies was not lost on the authors of the 1897 *Harvard Reports,* who crowed that with the creation of English A, Harvard "manifestly aims at nothing less than elevating the study of English to the same plane of dignity which has for centuries been the peculiar attribute of the classical tongues" (Adams et al. 423). William Morton Payne, editor of a collection of essays about English studies, apparently agreed: he wrote that the furor over students' performance on entrance examinations was "responsible for much of the recent awakening of interest in the subject of English instruction" (12).

So it may well be the case that without Freshman English, English-language literary studies could not have established itself in the university. Certainly the connection between the two endeavors is much more intimate than is usually acknowledged. Both were new fields of study, and they had the same object, even though they carried it out in different ways. Modern composition focused on the bourgeois project of self-improvement, just as English-language literary study did. Their remarks about papers indicate that early teachers of English at Harvard were not so concerned with the quality of students' arguments as they were with students' use of "correct" English, which was now read as a sign that its users inhabited an appropriately developing character. To put this in Foucauldian terms, Freshman English was (and is?) a "political technology of individuals," a pedagogy designed to create docile subjects who would not question the discipline's continued and repeated demonstration of their insufficient command of their native tongue

(Foucault 1988). This project was fully in keeping with the project developed for literary studies, which Terry Eagleton has designated, again in Foucauldian terms, as a "moral" technology that functions to "map, measure, assess, and certify the emotive and experiential aspects of subjectivity" (1985, 97). If Freshman English renders the bourgeois subject docile, the study of literature renders him or her "sensitive, creative, imaginative and so on" (99). Neither of these projects is particularly compatible with a rhetorical orientation to the world, and neither of them, frankly, offers much hope to those who would like to change that world.

5

LITERATURE AND COMPOSITION

NOT SEPARATE BUT CERTAINLY UNEQUAL

> I admit that it is an easier task to inspire young people with a love for great literature—especially if they have it already—and it is still less difficult to reduce literary research to a tedious compilation of insignificant facts. But I am not yet persuaded that the teaching of literature, even at its best, is a nobler endeavor than the teaching of composition.
> —John W. Cunliffe, "College English Composition"

> I delight as much as the next teacher in the opportunity to teach literature. . . . But I still have enough of a professional conscience to recognize that if I am commissioned to teach composition, I should teach composition and not something else. . . . We should resist with all the fortitude at our command the temptation to use writing assignments as a mere subterfuge for teaching what we may be most competent and disposed to teach.
> —Edward P. J. Corbett, "A Composition Course Based Upon Literature"

The meaning of the term *literature* changed radically during the nine-teenth century. Raymond Williams notes that through the seventeenth cen-tury, the term "'literary' appeared in the sense of reading ability and experi-ence" (47). During the eighteenth and early nineteenth centuries, *literature* was still associated with "having letters," that is, with being able to read and write. In another sense, *literature* meant having a liberal education: according to the OED, *literature* meant "acquaintance with 'letters' or books; polite or humane learning" as late as 1880. The sense of *literature* as an expression of national character also began to emerge in the nineteenth century. By the last decades of that century, the term began to take on something like its modern sense of "a special sort of text." According to the OED, the term was then "applied to writing which has claim to consideration on the ground of beauty of form or emotional effect."

Williams argues that the creation of this new meaning was "an extraordinary ideological feat" wherein "the very process that is specific, that of actual composition, has effectively disappeared or has been displaced to an internal and self-proving procedure in which writing of this kind is genuinely believed to be (however many questions are then begged) 'immediate living experience' itself" (46). In other words, the ideological transformation of *literature* involved two steps: the suppression of the role of composition in the production of literature; and the redefinition of the completed literary text as an embodiment of "full, central, immediate human experience." Williams remarks that in its new sense, literature is valued so highly that it can even replace life itself, because "the actual lived experiences of society and history are seen as less particular and immediate than those of literature" (46).[1]

The earliest subjects taught as "English" in American universities were philology and composition. So English studies was established, as Michael Warner points out, "before it began to consider literature its subject" (2). Indeed, literature did not emerge as a professional interest until the late 1880s. Warner argues that the disciplinary need to produce critical work required English teachers to redefine literary texts in such a way that they became appropriate materials for academic study: "In important ways, critical labor— what the critic does, his work and the acceptable forms of his work—did not follow from the literary so much as it reinvented the literary" (2). It is not hard to see how changing definitions of *literature* and *the literary* worked to the advantage of the fledgling profession of English. The notion of literature, defined as a special sort of text that represented immediate experience better than any other sort of text, was soon appropriated into professional discourse. Literature conceived in this way offered teachers of English a body of materials to study at the same time as it justified that study on aesthetic and moral grounds.

Now, even though they may have seized on this new definition of literature to promote their professional advantage, early teachers of English literature rationalized the move by means of Arnoldian arguments about the improvement of taste. David Shumway has pointed out that this move also solidified class interests:

> the literary built class unity not as a special interest . . . but insofar as it defined and was identified with good taste. Such taste was founded on common formal and informal education. . . . by 1890 knowledge of [English literature] remained a significant form of class distinction,

and by teaching it the project of unifying the professional-managerial class with the bourgeoisie could be furthered as the appropriate sense of taste and cultural decorum were inculcated. The point was not to create literati . . . but rather individuals who identified with the culture of the elite. (36)

Shumway's analysis explains why early teachers of English were anxious to move literary studies into the foreground of the new discipline. Speaking at MLA in 1885, James M. Garnett of the University of Virginia argued that while the study of English grammar and philology disciplined the mind, English was also valuable specifically as a *literary* discipline: "the careful analysis of a play of Shakspere, and the study of his delineation of the prominent characters, will furnish an excellent training for the student's taste" (1886 72–73). The notion of literature as a sort of ideal repository of human experience made literary study seem quite different from an older, rhetorical, understanding of literature as a repository of nationalist culture and moral sentiment, as did the modern project of developing individual taste. The phrase *pure literature* appears over and over again in professional literature published between 1885 and 1930. Presumably, the adjective was meant to designate something like literature appreciated for its own sake, unadulterated by historicism or contextualization. Martin Sampson of Indiana eloquently explained the rationale for this approach to literary texts: "the study of literature means the study of literature, not of biography nor of literary history . . . not of grammar, not of etymology, not of anything except the works themselves, viewed as their creators wrote them, viewed as art, as transcripts of humanity,—not as logic, not as psychology, not as ethics" (Payne 96). What this meant in terms of pedagogy was that literature teachers rejected the compendia of literary history that teachers of rhetoric had relied on since the Civil War. The professors who contributed essays to *The Dial*'s series on English departments in 1894 repeatedly noted that they used "whole books" or "real literary texts" in their literary courses. Elsewhere, Brainerd Kellogg complained that a "text-book" like Shaw or Cleveland kept "pupil and author apart" (161). That is to say, commentary came between a reader and direct access to a literary author's representation of experience. After they experienced literature read in the new way, according to Kellogg, the older generation of teachers came to resent a more rhetorical pedagogy: "the wrong that we elders suffered in having thrust upon us a mass of second-hand knowledge concerning authors (Shaw's or someone else's) instead of the authors themselves, rankles in our bosoms yet." In 1896, Theodore Hunt of Princeton wrote as follows about the change in professional attitudes toward literary studies:

> in the study of literature, the main result that is now sought is bringing the student into personal and vital contact with the best English authors, so as to make him thoroughly conversant with their writings, their personality, and their most interior literary spirit. . . . Literature itself, as a visible product, is examined by the student for himself. Authors are studied as far more important than any facts or dates or incidents about authors. The study is thus direct and remunerative; suggestive rather than technical; training the judgement and taste so that the student may choose for himself what is best. (1896, 145)

The object of literary study had become the student himself, or rather, his ability to improve himself.

It wasn't long before professors of English began to think of literary studies as the center of their new discipline. Hunt announced that this new way of reading literary texts required shifts in its relation to other areas of study that might coalesce under the heading of "English." For one thing, philology would no longer be taught on its own merits but would instead perform a service for literary studies, being taught as "the medium of English literature, and mainly as a medium, so as to make the literature all the more emphatic" (Hunt 1896, 149). For another, rhetoric would give way to composition: "as to rhetoric, mere theory is fast giving way to intelligent praxis . . . the writing and use of good English and not the exposition of the views of Quintilian, Whately, Blair, and Campbell, is now the ideal of rhetorical work. Actual product on the part of the student and not the verbal criticism of style is in place, so that English composition shall be a wholesome, vital, mental exercise" (146). Under the aegis of the new discipline of literary studies, composition would usurp the place formerly held by rhetorical theory in English-language instruction. Rhetoric's emphasis on public discourse was not friendly to the new literary aesthetic, while composition, considered as a means of expressing the self, was quite compatible with the aims of the new department of English.

English departments at a few schools—Amherst, Chicago, Harvard—required advanced studies in rhetoric into the early years of the twentieth century, and separate departments of rhetoric were maintained for a while at a few other schools—Michigan, Nebraska, Wisconsin. By and large, though, literary scholars associated rhetoric with "elementary" studies in English. Addressing the very first meeting of the Modern Language Association, James Morgan Hart rang a death knell for rhetoric:

> To my way of thinking, the study of English literature means the study of the great movement of English life and feeling, as it is reflected in the *purest* poetry and the *purest* prose of representative men, those men who have led their people's sympathies. Rhetoric always savors to me of the school-bench. It is, if we look into it scrutinizingly, little more than verbal jugglery. And however clever we may be at it ourselves, however quick we may be at perceiving it in others, we shall be none the wiser in *understanding* an author, the influences that moulded him, his peculiar mission, his hold upon us. The proper object of literary study, in one word, is to train us to *read*, to grasp an author's personality in all its bearings. And the less rhetoric here, the better. (1884–85, 85)

For Hart, then, the study of rhetoric was juvenile and pedantic. Furthermore, rhetoric intruded into the intimate relation that ought to obtain between a literary text and its reader.

But the rejection of rhetoric by those who shaped English studies entailed far more than putting off a clutter of useless rules. Literary scholars' vision now turned inward, toward "experience," rather than outward toward the world. My readers may recall that Matthew Arnold's criterion for modern criticism was *disinterestedness*. However, they may not so readily remember Arnold's argument that criticism was to remain disinterested "by keeping aloof from what is called 'the practical view of things' . . . by steadily refusing to lend itself to any of those ulterior, political, practical considerations about ideas . . . which criticism has really nothing to do with" (588).

Disinterestedness is sometimes voiced within humanism as distaste for popular or mass culture (Huyssen), but it can be read as a rejection of the rhetorical impulse as well. Arnold could hardly have been more clear about the necessity for criticism to rise above public, political discourse:

> It must needs be that men should act in sects and parties, that each of these sects and parties should have its organ, and should make this organ subserve the interests of its action; but it would be well, too, that there should be a criticism, not the minister of these interests, not their enemy but absolutely and entire independent of them. No other

> criticism will ever attain any real authority or make any real ways
> towards its end—the creating a current of true and fresh ideas. (589)

The words *true* and *fresh* indicate Arnold's subscription to what we might call a philosophical romanticism. For Arnold, ideas are produced by isolated individuals who think new thoughts. Ideas produced in this way will be true in the nonworldly sense that they have lasting appeal, and they will be fresh, again in an unworldly way, insofar as they propose new readings of old and timeless issues. Above all, this individual will not be interested; that is, he will have no truck with the local and timely issues that animate the other (lesser?) thinkers who happen to occupy his time and space.

William Spanos argues that modern humanism continually rehearses Arnold's gesture because humanists desire to establish a fixed center, a "metaphysical" space in which there is "no room . . . for the ontological, linguistic, cultural, and sociopolitical questions . . . that would disrupt its still movement" (74). Whether or not we agree that humanism yearns to be a metaphysics, we must accept that Arnoldian humanism manifests a disdain for rhetoric and politics insofar as these endeavors engage ephemeral issues. The rejection of rhetoric that characterizes Arnoldian humanism is nicely if subtly caught in an *Encyclopedia Britannica* entry noting that, even though modern humanists have abandoned "the cumbersome framework of ancient rhetoric," they have retained the ancient notion that the cultivation of humaneness requires wide acquaintance with canonical texts and that "something of the underlying belief survives that effective expression depends on a trained and cultivated intellect and sensibility and is their ultimate sign and seal" (1963, 9:877). Effective expression is important, note, but it no longer has a civic or public use as it did in ancient thought; indeed it is put to no use at all. Rather, the ability to express oneself is the *sign* of the quality of one's reading, a sort of guarantee that one is acquainted with "the best that has been thought and said," to use Arnold's famous phrase. In this formulation the ability to express oneself is not as important as intellectual cultivation; it is the fact of being well-read that counts.

Humanism's loss of rhetorical desire accounts for the peculiar way in which literary texts can be made to stand in for rhetoric in the discourse of English departments. This is apparent in the Tate-Lindemann exchange, where even Tate—a professor of rhetoric—has swallowed the humanist line that literary texts are good places to look for information about how to live one's life, as though reading literature will somehow give students a better grasp of ethics and politics than they can get from studying theology or philosophy or political science, or even from reading the *New York Times* or watching CNN.[2] This expansive attitude about the salient effects of literature on its readers allowed late-nineteenth-century English teachers to fill the pedagogical space vacated by rhetorical instruction with the reading of literary texts.

The devalorization of rhetoric that coincided with the new attitude toward literature and literary study was accompanied by the denigration of composition. Literary scholars lost interest in composition very early in the history of English studies. Historian John Brereton notes that "the major professional organization, the Modern Language Association (MLA), long confined talk of composition to its pedagogical section, and abolished even that from its convention in 1903" (1995, 22). Brereton adds that "*PMLA* hasn't published an article by a composition scholar in eighty years" (24). As early as 1896, William Lyons Phelps of Yale rejected composition as a viable field of study, arguing that no one ever learned to write by working "tread-mill fashion in sentence and paragraph architecture" (Phelps 1896, 794). At a meeting of MLA in 1909, Lane Cooper of Cornell referred to freshman themes as "a mass of writing that has no intrinsic value" (1910, 423). Cooper noticed that Harvard already had begun to reduce the number of composition courses it offered, replacing them with courses in literature: "the tide has begun to drift away from courses in the daily theme and its like at the place from which many other institutions have ultimately borrowed such devices" (422).

To take seriously the notion that composition is a productive art is also to take seriously the suggestion that literary artists achieve their effects by carefully and consciously manipulating the language they use, producing many drafts in the process. Texts that are repositories of "life itself" must be unmediated expressions of experience; the more attention given to craft, the more highly mediated (and hence less intense) the representation of experience. On this model, composition is very much a secondary act; to invoke Shelley's famous phrase, composition is to inspiration as a "fading coal" is to a blazing fire. If literary scholars wanted to keep intact the assumption that literary texts were unlike other texts, it was necessary for them to forget that literature is produced in the same way that all texts are produced: by means of composition. And if they wanted to preserve the supposed universality and timelessness of literature—that is, to preserve its unworldliness—they had to characterize more worldly writing as fallen, alien.

In his last words on the relation of literature to composition, Jim Berlin repeated an argument he had often made: "English studies was founded on a set of hierarchical binary oppositions in which literary texts were given an idealized status approaching the sacred. Against these privileged works, rhetorical texts and their production were portrayed as embodiments of the fallen realms of science and commerce and politics, validating in their corrupt materiality the spiritual beauties of their opposites" (1996, xiv). This analysis explains why, in a humanist intellectual universe, nonliterary composition is defined as a minimalist exercise in the achievement of clarity. Quoting from the 1978 reports that recommended revival of the universal requirement in composition at Harvard, Spanos demonstrates that humanists expect nonliterary writing to feature "the power of 'reasoning and analysis,' of 'discrimination,' of 'judgement' that renders one capable of grasping or comprehending; capable of mastering or appropriating being" (138). In Arnoldian humanism, noncanonical writing is configured as an instrument whose worth is that it articulates or reports on reality or the truth. On this model, reality and truth have always already been discerned by some other means than composition. Deprived of its role as intervention into the circulation of meaning, composing is placed in a servile position as a means of explicating the real, true, or beautiful, all of which are found elsewhere than in composition.

Nineteenth- and early-twentieth-century teachers of English at a few elite universities and colleges eschewed explicit instruction in composition. The reason for this is that the point of humanistic composition is not to create better writers but to display the cultivated character that is the sign of an educated person.[3] In the humanist dispensation, the only way to develop an appropriate character is to spend a lifetime reading the right texts, guided by the example or supervision of appropriate teachers. Arnoldian humanists interpreted explicit instruction in composition as a shortcut, an attempt to inculcate character by circumventing the lifetime of work it takes to become an educated person. And since character was also associated with class affiliation in nineteenth-century humanism, teachers at privileged universities assumed as well that direct instruction in composition was an attempt to climb up the social ladder, made by people who did not own the appropriate family background or the right preparation.

Yet another reason for the general detestation of composition was the drudgery connected with its teaching. In the new approach to composition instruction, teachers insisted that students represent their experiences in their writing, just as authors of literature were supposed to do when they wrote. In Freshman English, though, students' supposedly unmediated access to experience was being produced daily, and few English teachers who got a taste of theme-grading wanted to stick with it for very long. But even though literary scholars rejected rhetoric and composition as scholarly endeavors—just as faculty in other disciplines had rejected the pretensions of English-language scholarship during the 1870s and 1880s—English departments hung on to the required course in introductory composition. And literary scholars saw to it that this course involved students in a good deal of literary study.

The practice of using literary texts in the required composition course carries enormous weight in the politics of English departments. As I argue above, the presence of literature in that course affirms the status of literary studies as the defining activity of English studies.

JUST HOW MUCH LIT IS THERE?

Freshman English has been required at most American universities since about 1900. However, it is difficult to generalize about what was taught when in Freshman English, since massive historical work still remains to be done in university and college archives.[4] As a result, scholars disagree about just how much and how often literature has been used in required composition programs. Of course, the conclusions drawn depend on the point being made and the evidence used. Writing in response to the Lindemann-Tate discussion, Edwin R. Steinberg asserted that "imaginative literature has not had a secure place in composition classrooms since at least the 1930s" (2). Steinberg based this generalization on an odd combination of sources: his reading of selected scholarly texts and recent CCCC convention programs. Tate asserted, on the other hand, that literature was pushed out of composition programs during the 1960s, when "the Rhetoric Police . . . moved in" with an "array of Aristotelian devices" and replaced literature with rhetoric (1993, 318). In his second essay in this discussion, Tate retracted this bit of whimsy, instead citing Richard Larson's recent survey of Freshman English programs that suggests that literature is currently used in about 20 percent of the required composition programs in the country (Tate 1995, 304). Based on his examination of CCCC workshop reports from the 1950s and 1960s, Tate concluded that "although literature certainly did not disappear from the classrooms of many composition teachers, it did disappear from the conversation of our discipline" (he apparently means the discipline of composition studies) (304).

Other historical evidence establishes that literary texts were steadily used in required composition classes from the inception of Freshman English in the 1880s until at least 1970.[5] If Larson's findings are correct, literature is still used in one-fifth of the colleges and universities that require Freshman English (1988). And if the responses to the Tate-Lindemann debate are representative, it seems that many English teachers would like to see the practice revived (if indeed it ever did succumb to the ministrations of "the Rhetoric Police").

The ostensible goals of the required freshman course have remained fairly stable across time as well. I buttress this claim by juxtaposing two studies that appeared sixty years apart. Writing in *English Journal* in 1912, Glenn E. Palmer characterized the available traditions of teaching composition as those of "culture" and "efficiency" (488). The first approach was associated with Yale, the second with Harvard. According to Palmer, the tradition of culture held that "the business of the professor of composition is to produce writers" (that is, people we would now call "creative writers"—authors of fiction, drama, and poetry). Accordingly, advocates of the cultural approach placed "emphasis on the inspiration of literature, recognizing that there can be no literary production without culture." Palmer characterized "the other party" as claiming that "the best we can do for the Freshman student is to cultivate in him good language habits." Thus they laid "stress upon painstaking drill in the writing of short themes, assuming that the average Freshman comes to the university with little knowledge of grammar and less of the organization of the paragraph and the composition."

In 1972, Thomas Wilcox found a similar pair of attitudes toward composition in a large survey of Freshman English programs undertaken during the late sixties. According to Wilcox's study, about half of the English departments in the country "still believe that freshman English should serve the community as a whole by instructing students in techniques of composition they may use whenever they are called upon to write" (1972, 688). The other half asserted "their desire 'to devote [their] interests and utilize [their] specialization in those areas for which [the department] exists, viz., literary art and humanistic thought'" (688–89). Wilcox summarized: "In other words, English departments in the United States are about evenly divided between those which offer freshman *[sic]* utilitarian training and those which offer them something more" (688).

Despite the passage of time, then, English teachers were still able to conceive only two functions for the required introductory course, and these were the same two functions that were discriminated for Freshman English at the turn of the twentieth century: teachers could teach composition as a set of universally useful techniques, in which case the requirement was defined as a service to the university; or they could teach literature in the course, in which case it served higher ends, ostensibly those of humanism and obviously those of literary studies.

DIRECT AND INDIRECT COMPOSITION

The dual model set up by Palmer is a bit of an oversimplification, given that in the early years of the twentieth century, the classical approach to composition was still used at many schools. The classical approach treated literary texts not as repositories of personal human experience but as a resource for models of stylistic excellence, worthy of imitation by all. In this approach, students read literature, to be sure, but the experience of reading literature was not treated as an end in itself; snippets of literary texts were used, rather, to illustrate principles of composition. This approach was a remnant of an older, more rhetorical pedagogy, which was grounded in the notion that clear and elegant expression could be cultivated through principled and explicit study of composing techniques used by admired authors. This approach to instruction had been ideally suited to the classical college, where the aim was to produce gentlemen who were versed in the cultural capital of the nation, whose learning would fit them to become active members of the public sphere. The two approaches that Palmer called "culture" and "efficiency," on the other hand, emerged from modern humanism, where the pedagogical goal was the self-improvement of individuals rather than maintenance of community values. In keeping with the aesthetic bias of Arnoldian humanism, advocates of these new approaches to composition rejected the study of rhetoric. Culture advocates regarded rhetoric as an elementary study of rules, on the order of grammar; efficiency advocates regarded rhetoric as a mummified body of theoretical texts whose study interfered with practice in composing. Indeed, advocates of the "culture" approach eschewed direct instruction in composition altogether, preferring instead to immerse students in reading and discussion of literature. Advocates of "efficiency," on the other hand, engaged students solely in writing practice.

A MIX AT HARVARD

The early history of English A at Harvard shows how easily the classical approach to composition could be conflated with modern humanist attitudes toward literature, which were not at all rhetorical. For example, in one of his essays on composition Adams Sherman Hill recommended the inclusion of literary texts in composition instruction on the classical ground that literary authors provided students of composition with appropriate models for emulation: "knowledge of the principles of the art of composition, as applied by the best writers, ought to help the student to communicate what he has to say in a better form than he should otherwise employ" (1887, 509). However, on the very same page, Hill also resorted to an Arnoldian rationale for the use of literary texts in composition instruction:

> surrendering himself to the influence of genius, [a student] will be carried beyond himself, his mind will work more freely than usual, and his sentences will reproduce his thoughts in more perspicuous and more telling language. A man's mind cannot but be stimulated by contact with greater minds, whether living or dead. Shakspere, Bacon, Burke, George Eliot, feed the powers of thought and the powers of expression at the same time, and thus enable one to think, to talk, and to write to more purpose.

This is a fine statement of the modern humanist position that simple exposure to literary texts improves students' minds and hence their writing, presumably by means of unconscious imitation.

By the time Hill was no longer associated with English A, only hints of its former collusion with rhetorical pedagogy remained. In 1901, the syllabus for English A required reading in works by Shakespeare, Kipling, Thackeray, Macaulay, and Eliot. Charles Copeland and H. M. Rideout, its teachers, justified this practice on the same vague grounds that were used by advocates of the culture approach at Yale: "if a man becomes used to thinking about the work of other writers, he may give more thought to his own" (64). This justification suggests that reading improves writing through some mystified process of imitation. But imitation of excellent models cannot be what was meant, since Copeland and Rideout felt a need to justify their choice of texts, which they admitted were not among "the best in the language." To do this, they resorted to an older argument about the improvement of taste: "young men need training in discrimination; and by reading several unequal and unassorted writers, about whom they must collect something intelligent to say in an examination, they may learn to distinguish the good, the better, and the best" (65). In other words, if students read bad books in school (Kipling?) they would somehow learn to distinguish these from better books, and besides, their teachers needed something to ask them about on examinations. Copeland and Rideout complained that "so few of them have been brought up to read anything at all, or would now start to read of their own accord, that an acquaintance with a few books must be forced upon them. If they are men of the right sort, they will not let the acquaintance drop; at all events, they cannot let it drop until after the examinations" (63). This is a very early instance of the frequent assertion by teachers of English that the point of reading literature in introductory composition is simply that the course is required; if students do not read literature there, the assumption goes, they may read it nowhere in their college careers. Needless to say, this attitude places the required course firmly in the service of literary studies.

CULTURE

The cultural approach to freshman English-language instruction used at Yale and Princeton also served literary studies. On this model, composition was not taught "directly" at all; rather, its teachers trusted that the reading and discussion of literature would suffice to improve students' writing. This attitude also appeared very early in the history of English departments. In 1896, a diatribe against composition instruction was published in *Century* magazine. Its author (probably William Lyons Phelps of Yale) claimed that "a wide reader is usually a correct writer; and he has reached the goal in the most delightful manner, without feeling the penalty of Adam" (794). The "penalty of Adam" was, of course, the direct approach to composition instruction that involved students in "mere grammatical and rhetorical training" or the "practice of theme-writing." In his autobiography, Phelps reiterated his position on the futility of direct instruction in composition: "I am certain . . . that the best way to learn to write is to read, just as one learns good manners by associating with well-bred people. A student who loves good reading, who has a trained critical taste, will almost always write well" (1912, 127).

Thomas Lounsbury, also of Yale, developed this position into a full-scale attack on "compulsory composition" published in *Harper's* in 1911. His scathing denunciation of required composition instruction was the subject of extensive discussion in the professional literature for almost two years after its appearance. Asserting that "the art of writing, like that of painting and sculpture, is an imitative art," Lounsbury argued that "the union of intellectual vigor which comes from hard and intelligent study and of cultivated taste begotten of familiarity with the great masterpieces of our literature" was a product of "slow growth" (876). If imitation of masters was the means by which writing was learned, Lounsbury certainly did not conceive of imitation as the conscious pedagogical procedure it had been in classical rhetoric. For advocates of culture, direct instruction in composition of any kind was a shortcut, an attempt to circumvent the lifetime of reading that brought about true cultivation.

The indirect approach to composition instruction was not without critics. As early as 1896, Joseph V. Denney pointed out that the skills developed by reading—selection, abstraction, imagination—were insufficient for the mastery of composition, which required the student to "organize his own ideas" and to "deal with situations of which he is himself a vital part" (5). Denney could not see how reading facilitated this ability, for which "practice in writing and speaking on subjects within the range of his own observation and experience can alone adequately call into activity." In other words, he thought of composition as independent from reading. Now Denney and his collaborator on several successful current-traditional textbooks, Fred Newton Scott, taught at Ohio State and Michigan, respectively, while advocates of the culture approach worked at elite private universities. As historians have repeatedly pointed out, the culture approach to composition instruction was elitist, based as it was on the culturalists' belief that good taste was firmly associated with good breeding (Berlin 1987, 45; Russell 1988). Phelps himself remarked that "the best way, indeed, to become a good writer is to be born of the right sort of parents" (1896, 794). And Lounsbury's argument assumed that students had access to books, desire to read them, and the time in which to do so. Students admitted to elite universities were presumed to be capable writers already—thanks to their family connections or their supposedly excellent preparation—and so their English-language instruction began with literature rather than composition.

EFFICIENCY

The other modern approach to composition instruction—using neither rhetoric nor literature—was also practiced very early in the history of Freshman English. Here, students wrote daily and fortnightly themes. Their themes were "corrected" by instructors. Specimen themes were read aloud in class, where felicities and infelicities were pointed out and commented upon. Students were then expected to stop making the designated errors.

Some of the respondents to a survey conducted by the secretary of the Pedagogical Section of MLA in 1902 argued that students learned to write most efficiently by writing a great deal. A few pointed out that since composition is an art, like other arts "it can be mastered only by long and faithful practice" (Mead 326). Another suggested that "wide reading has but little or no effect on style."

At least one teacher saw the writing-only approach to composition as a repudiation of rhetoric. Reporting on a survey of composition instruction conducted in 1902, Sophie Chantal Hart of Wellesley firmly rejected the older, rhetorical, model of composition instruction, along with "the incubus of formal rhetoric" from which it derived (365). She recommended that English teachers also reject the traditional sort of assignment in which students write on set themes taken from their reading—"Hamlet's madness or the evils of jealousy as seen in Othello, or Satan as the hero of *Paradise Lost,* or friendship, with pitiful pilfering from Emerson" (367). Rather, she urged that "the true function of English teaching, as I conceive it, is to teach a student to *organize* his experience and knowledge for expression" (365). It followed that students performed best when they were allowed to write about their "daily life and observation" (371).

Hart's reference to "daily life and observation" suggests that she had in mind the pedagogy of the daily theme, which was invented by Barrett Wendell of Harvard. Wendell's reputation as a teacher, along with his popular textbook, *English Composition* (1891), did much to spread the notion among some early teachers of English that the best approach to composition instruction was to elicit bits of personal writing—primarily description and narration—from students. Certainly Hart indicated her subscription to Wendell's principles when she quoted nearly verbatim from the pages of *English Composition:* according to her, teachers could "do something for our students that would count eternally in their development" if only they could "get into the heads of students in our college classes what unity, emphasis, and coherence mean; if we could make them see that these are organizing principles of human thought everywhere, in all the fine arts" (365). Hart did not say why these supposedly integral principles of human thought were inaccessible to first-year college students.

Now, in Wendell's hands the daily-theme approach had impeccably humanist credentials, even though it did not necessarily rely on the reading of literary texts. He felt that daily themes enhanced students' perception of their surroundings and improved their mastery of cultured self-expression. As he told his students in English 12, the point of his course was to "gain from this work training that will make us if not better writers at least better men" (1888). Wendell's pedagogical legacy was twofold, however, since its humanist aspiration toward cultivated self-expression was articulated within an intense concern for correctness. Unfortunately, *English Composition*, like Hill's *Principles*, began by considering the smallest parts of composition—words and sentences. The focus on usage and grammar was necessary because of humanists' interest in policing the development of students' taste and character.

CURRENT-TRADITIONAL RHETORIC AND HUMANISM

Freshman English has its own theory of discourse, which was invented by late-nineteenth-century teachers—Hill and Wendell prominent among them. This theory of discourse has since become known as "current-traditional rhetoric."[6] Current-traditional pedagogy discriminated four genres: exposition, description, narration, and argument (EDNA). It idealized a single format—the five-paragraph theme, which after a brief introduction that stated its author's thesis, presented three highly prescribed paragraphs of support, and concluded. Students were taught current-traditional principles of discourse through teachers' analyses of professional examples, and they were then expected to compose paragraphs and essays that displayed their observance of those principles. By 1900, current-traditional pedagogy had swept the field of competitors for the time devoted to nonliterary matters in the required composition course. By 1910 the standard materials for the course were a collection of readings (either expository essays or literary texts), a handbook, and a rhetoric that expounded the supposedly universal current-traditional principles of unity, coherence, and emphasis.

Historians of composition have attributed the ubiquity of current-traditional rhetoric to its methodical and universalizing approach to the construction of discourse, which presumably rendered it appealing to the scientific and technical interests that invigorated the new American university. James A. Berlin went so far as to associate current-traditionalism with positivism (1984, 74). However, given that both current-traditional rhetoric and Freshman English were invented and maintained by humanists rather than by scientists and engineers, this is an unsatisfactory explanation for its intellectual dominance of the required course. It makes more sense to look for humanist impulses in current-traditional pedagogy, and such impulses are not hard to find.

Despite the name given it by historians, current-traditional rhetoric is not a rhetoric at all. Current-traditional textbooks display no interest in suiting discourses to the occasions for which they are composed. Rather, they collapse every composing occasion into an ideal in which authors, readers, and messages are alike undistinguished. What matters in current-traditional rhetoric is form. Current-traditional pedagogy forces students to repeatedly display their use of institutionally sanctioned forms. Failure to master the sanctioned forms signals some sort of character flaw such as laziness or inattention. All of this is fully in keeping with humanism's rejection of rhetoric, as well as its tendency toward idealism, its reverence for institutional and textual authority, and its pedagogical attention to the policing of character.

Current-traditional textbooks nearly always began with consideration of the smallest units of discourse: words and sentences. This suggests that their authors, and the teachers for whom they wrote, were anxious to correct two features of students' discourse: usage and grammar. Now, principles of grammar and usage are not, strictly speaking, inherent to the mastery of composition. Today teachers of composition pay little attention to these matters (unless, of course, they still subscribe to current-traditional pedagogy). And yet current-traditional textbooks delineated thousands of possible errors in grammar and usage that could be committed by a "careless" or "lazy" writer. In this milieu, an inept choice of words or a comma fault betrayed a student's lack of association with the right people and institutions; worse, it betrayed her failure to care about or to succeed at the bourgeois project of self-improvement. The current-traditional course of study can hardly be called practical in the sense that it prepared students to engage with issues, since it never addressed the quality of a students' argument or its suitability to a given rhetorical situation. However, it was extremely important to teachers who worried about their students' class affiliation. Teachers who subscribed to current-traditionalism obviously thought that observance of its myriad rules might save their students from social stigma, just as they assumed that students' knowledge of selected literary texts might mark them as members of a preferred social class.

Current-traditional pedagogy also solved a paradox created by the proximity of Freshman English to humanist literary studies. After the turn of the century a few universities and colleges that employed selective admissions policies refused to teach composition in their required introductory English courses. Yale, Princeton, and a few other elite schools preferred instead to give freshman students a steady diet of literary texts. This practice implied, at least to those who accepted the exclusivist rhetoric of these colleges, that literary study was suited to students who were deemed to be more capable or better prepared for college-level study. The corollary was that explicit instruction in composition was only necessary for students who were less capable or less well prepared.[7] This meant that the colleges and universities that presumably attracted less capable students had to teach them something other than literature. But what was this to be? Certainly not classical or modern rhetorics. Knowledge of (and respect for) these traditions was at a very low ebb in English departments at the turn of the century, since humanist disdain had driven rhetoric as well as composing theory from the field. What could be taught, and what was obviously needed by less capable students, according to the logic of humanism, was explicit instruction in grammar, usage, punctuation, and spelling. For those less well bred, correct expression could become the sign of an educated character.

Current-traditional rhetoric lent itself beautifully to this need. Indeed, its rules for the composition of correct sentences were soon expanded to account for the composition of larger units of discourse. Wendell's *English Composition* analogized the structure of sentences to that of paragraphs and essays. Wendell inferred from his analogy that universal rules dictated the composition of any kind or part of discourse, and because they were universal, these rules reflected the movement of human thought. When his theory of discourse closed the circuit between correct sentences, formally perfect essays, and straight thinking, it became possible for teachers to infer that any student who could not or would not master the current-traditional principles of discourse was for some reason out of touch with the rules that governed thought itself. Hence current-traditional pedagogy served English studies as an instrument of exclusion. It continued faithfully in this role for many years. Perhaps its institutional high point was reached during the 1950s, when teachers failed as a matter of policy any student theme displaying more than five current-traditionally defined errors, regardless of its quality.

So humanist literary study and current-traditional rhetoric were far from hostile to one another. As we shall see, they happily cohabited in the required first-year course through at least the first half of the twentieth century. This suggests to me that the current-traditional theory of discourse was the perfect vehicle for literary humanists insofar as it allowed them to meet the supposed necessity of installing literate correctness in every student who enrolled in the university at the same time as it exempted them from the responsibility of actually reading students' papers. In current-traditional pedagogy, students' papers are not constructed as messages that might command assent or rejection. Nor do current-traditional teachers constitute an audience in any rhetorical sense of that word, since they read not to learn or be amused or persuaded but to weigh and measure a paper's adherence to formal standards.

Hence the current-traditional theory of discourse is not a rhetoric but a theory of graphic display, and so it perfectly met the humanist requirement that students' expression of character be put under constant surveillance so that they could be "improved" by correction.

LITERATURE IN COMPOSITION, 1900–1930

The use of literary texts in composition instruction was simply taken for granted during the first three decades of the twentieth century. In general, the three approaches to composition that I have already remarked upon were still in use during those years. There were a few courses that harked back to an older, classical, approach, using snippets of literary texts to model principles of composition. There were courses that combined current-traditional instruction with the reading of literature, and courses in which the main business was reading literary texts. This threefold classification is supported by a number of surveys taken between 1900 and 1930. Freshman English has always been a highly surveyed course, and the early years of its history were no exception, as teachers who had adopted the universal requirement anxiously looked about to see what everyone else was doing in the course in which it was realized.

In 1905, Charles Sears Baldwin surveyed forty-four colleges located in "the area north of the Ohio and Arkansas rivers"—that is, in the northeastern United States (385). Baldwin found that literature was used in every program he studied. He divided programs into four categories. The first category, which included programs using the classical approach, was the largest by far, containing twenty-seven schools—over half the schools surveyed. Such programs were "devoted entirely to composition . . . tho there is more or less analysis of masterpieces for the exemplification of rhetorical theory and for models in actual writing" (387). In such programs, "the study of literature as literature is relegated to later courses." Baldwin's remark indicates he was able to distinguish between the classical approach, in which literary texts were put to use as models for composing and the modern approach in which they were read as ends in themselves. Furthermore, his finding is an early manifestation of a theme that recurs across the years: the study of literature is more advanced than composition.

Baldwin's second category, represented at nine schools, included "a larger use of literary models than is directly applicable to the students' writing"; that is, some literature was studied on its own merits. By Baldwin's estimate, such programs devoted about one-third of instructional time to literary study. The third type of Freshman English was "devoted mainly to literature" (388). Such courses maintained "a freer and less perfunctory habit of composition by frequent essays on the books and the literary aspects thus presented." Courses of this type were in place in only five schools in Baldwin's survey: Columbia, City College of New York, Princeton, Rutgers, and Yale. The fourth type, almost as popular as the first, was a two-semester program consisting of one course in composition and one in literature. This last pattern subsisted for many years in schools that required two semesters of Freshman English. The point to be reiterated, however, is that literary texts were used in all the programs that Baldwin surveyed, even though approaches to it differed.

These patterns seem to have remained in place until 1915 or so, when American universities and colleges began to feel the effects of World War I. The war strengthened humanists' determination to preserve the cultural heritage they prized. For example, it facilitated John Erskine's attempts to get his "Great Books" program offered at Columbia; the basic humanities course he taught there grew out of an army directive insisting that the university establish a "War Issues" course (Rubin 166; James Sloan Allen 81). The patriotic (and conservative) bent of this course was apparent in descriptions of it given by its administrators: its point was to silence "the destructive elements in our society" and to prepare students to "meet the arguments of the opponents of decency and sound government" (Gruber 244). In *Professing Literature*, Graff notes that World War I "provoked a general reassessment of educational values" (128). In the case of literary study, this reassessment tended toward affirmation of American nationalism and patriotism.

Two changes of note appeared in professional discussions of the first-year course during this period. The "ideas" approach threatened to turn toward discussion of popular issues, and the efficiency approach increasingly turned toward mechanism. Both tendencies were greeted with alarm by humanist teachers.

Berlin attributed the origin of the "ideas" approach to Harrison Ross Steeves of Columbia. Berlin explained that students enrolled in ideas courses "wrote essays about the traditional issues of rhetoric—legal, political, and social questions of a controversial nature—after reading essays that considered them" (1987, 51). Steeves coauthored a popular textbook (with Frank Ristine) that was the precursor to today's anthologies of essays. *Representative Essays in Modern Thought* (1913) contained essays that presented students with conflicting opinions on important issues—for example, Arnold versus Huxley on the value of science. According to Herbert L. Creek, who was teaching at Illinois at the time, the collection "created a sensation among teachers," although Creek suspected that "the instructors liked Steeves and Ristine very well and the students ignored it as much as they could" (1955, 6). *Representative Essays* had many imitators, and after the war began in earnest, "ideas" collections became increasingly nationalist and patriotic.

Despite his interest in public discourse, though, Steeves was apparently unable to conceive of rhetoric as a body of theory dealing with such discourse. He thought of rhetoric, rather, as the list of rules about sentences and paragraphs to which it had been reduced by Arnoldian humanist thought, which he rightly excoriated as "a needlessly unedifying subject" (1912, 45). Steeves also rejected the daily theme approach to composition, arguing that "if the student is not asked to go outside of his own experience, his rhetorical study is only correcting his ineptitude in matters of form and style, and is not producing nor encouraging intellectual expansion" (47). But he mounted several serious objections to the use of literary texts in required composition, as well. First of all, he wrote, such use "abuses literature by subjecting it to a purpose for which it does not exist" and it possibly "upholds an unpractical and discouraging esthetic ideal in composition" (48). Furthermore, "assigned topics confined to the literary field tax the intelligence and limit the mental freedom of the student." Last, Steeves thought, the combination of literature and composition had the "calamitous" effect of causing students to hate the literary texts they studied in this context. Hence, he suggested that students instead read such authorities as James on ethics, Mill on politics, and Ruskin on economics (51–52). Steeves argued that the only good reason for using literary texts in required composition was the convenience of English departments: "the teaching of the two subjects in a single course effects a saving in time and effort for both teacher and student."

Now, even though these texts are hardly revolutionary, humanist opposition to the ideas approach appeared almost immediately. Frank Aydelotte of Indiana warned of a latent danger—"that of going too far afield in the search for ideas" (1914, 568). He complained that English teachers could not be expected to know anything about "the Panama Canal tolls or the child-labor problem," as though interest in these civic issues was somehow beyond the ken of educated adults (569). Aydelotte also made a virtue of the complaint voiced by Steeves—that literary topics only served the convenience of English departments—by arguing that "the advantage of literary topics for the teacher of English is that he can follow them up and relate them to one another so that they lead in the end to the mastery of a connected body of thought" (569). Current issues were simply too diffuse, too grounded in daily events to suit Aydelotte. Norman Foerster, while ostensibly in sympathy with the ideas approach, cautioned that it "flaunts the banners of ideas and thought and logic (that is to say, of science) and neglects altogether the artistic impulse" (1916, 459). And in 1922, Charles G. Osgood of Princeton pled for the restoration of literary texts to the freshman course—"literature taught humanistically, by devoted humanists—literature employed as the revealer of nature and of life" (164). By "humanism" Osgood meant "the recognition of the human spirit in all its energies and variety" (161). Displaying his ignorance of premodern history, Osgood avowed that rhetoric had nothing to do with humanism; it was a purely technical endeavor that was utterly unconnected with what was truly important in education, that is, the "test and refutation of the true and false values in human life" (162).

During the war years, composition teachers heard—or imagined they heard—a call from citizens to turn the first-year course toward instruction in mechanics. In 1918, Frank W. Scott of Illinois noted that Freshman English had traditionally had two goals: to bestow on students "some degree of facility" in use of the mother tongue and to serve as well as "an essentially cultural influence, the sole, sufficient ornament, the touch of grace and finish in a college curriculum otherwise practical or technical" (512). However, Scott found that "a steady trend toward the practical has left little of the cultural or liberal tincture in the mixture." He attributed this drift toward the practical to "a sincere but mistaken attempt to make Freshman rhetoric meet immediate social and industrial needs" (513). The pressure to offer an extremely practical course of study in Freshman English was also noticed by J. R. Rutland of Alabama Polytechnic, who conducted a survey of the course in 1920–21. Rutland began his report on the study by noting that "recently English teachers have been assailed by the 'socializer,' whose aim of perfecting the language of daily discourse and of business they have accepted" (1). English teachers interpreted the supposed pressure from "socializers" as a desire that students learn to write without reading literature. Rutland noted that

> this age of business and invention is somewhat skeptical of the value of culture. Technical and business leaders who see nothing practical in literary study often prefer readiness of speech to good taste or even correctness. . . . Consequently there is a distinct tendency to eliminate

literature from Freshman English . . . in spite of the fact that most
English teachers still look upon Freshman English as being an
introduction to intellectual culture. (4–5)

Of course, the elimination of literature from the course did not necessarily
mean that instruction had to be reduced to grammar, usage, and mechanics.
But teachers nonetheless read the demands of "technical and business leaders" in precisely this way. Respondents to Rutland's survey reported that sec-
tioning was used because it was "only simple justice" to separate freshmen
"who are keenly interested in literature and who can express themselves with
individuality" from "those who need instruction in spelling, punctuation, sentence and paragraph structure, and logical arrangement of material" (2). The
habitual status distinction made by English teachers of this period—between
better prepared "individuals" who can begin their studies with literature and
the mass of those whose lesser capabilities condemned them to a course in
mechanics—could hardly be more clear. Rutland lamented in his commentary on the survey that "poorly prepared Freshmen, who must spend most of
the year on sentence structure, will miss the joys of artistic self-expression
and the inspiration derived from reading which are emphasized in the advanced sections" (3). Needless to say, his report demonstrates that the habit
of reserving literary study for better prepared and more able students had by
this time penetrated to the heartland.

In 1929, the results of two large surveys of Freshman English were published. Both establish that the use of literary texts in Freshman English was
still widespread. H. Robinson Shipherd of Boston University surveyed sev-
enty-five colleges and universities, attempting to achieve a representative
sample in terms of geography and type of institution. He found that over
half of the schools included in his survey (55 percent) required "a considerable amount—1000 pages or more a semester—of reading in pure literature" (20). He continued: "considerably less than that is required by 25%; and
11% admit not requiring any" literature in the required freshman course.
Another 13 percent put "special stress on literature, such as to turn the course
rather from writing toward reading." This group included "of course, both
Yale and Princeton." I presume that in schools where students were reading
over a thousand pages of literature they were not using these texts as models,
as they would in the classical approach. Interpreted this way, Shipherd's data
suggests that composition courses were still widely used as introductions to
literary study. This assumption is confirmed, I think, by the findings of Warner

Taylor, which established that literary texts were still in wide use in Freshman English instruction by the close of the third decade of the twentieth century.

In 1927–28 Taylor received responses to a questionnaire he sent to over two hundred universities, which he carefully selected to represent "all types" and which were "located in all parts of the country" (3). He established that literature provided the main or adjunct reading in the composition course at older and eastern universities, while it was commonly the subject of the second-semester composition course in the rest of the country (12). According to his findings, 73 percent of middle-western and western schools offered a "straight rhetoric" course to first-semester freshmen, while only 39 percent of eastern and southern schools did so; this means, of course, that some mixture of literature and rhetoric was used in first-semester courses in a quarter of midwestern and western schools and over half of eastern and southern schools. It is also likely that schools requiring a second term of Freshman English used literary texts extensively in that course. Taylor found 9 of 225 schools "giving only literature to Freshmen" (12). This confirms both Baldwin's and Shipherd's findings that the indirect approach to composition was used in only a few universities. A commentator on Taylor's survey suggested that this approach was thought to be viable at "eastern colleges, where there is a higher standard of selection of the student than elsewhere" (Thompson 79). Taylor's survey also indicates that the classical model was still available, as well. He complained of the difficulty of determining the percentages of schools using literary texts because his questionnaire did not permit respondents to specify exactly how literature was taught in their programs: "The trouble lies in the use made of them. If they are studied from a rhetorical standpoint, dissected for unity, emphasis, and coherence,—if, to put it differently, they are employed as models and stimuli for themes, they become a means to an end and lose their significance as pure literature" (12). For Taylor, a pedagogy that analyzes the formal structures of literary texts, in order to facilitate composition, is a contaminant.

In sum: during the first three decades of the century, literary study was a fixture in the required composition course. Even though it was universally required, composition belonged to the English Department, and English teachers everywhere conceived the course as an introduction to the cultured practice of English and the study of its literature. English teachers seemed unable to comprehend that writing instruction might involve anything other than literary study, on the one hand, and drill in grammar, usage, and formal fluency, on the other. They understood required composition instruction to be an exercise in the improvement of character and good taste, which were enhanced, not by practice in composing messages that might actually do work in the world, but by reading good books. In the absence of a viable rhetoric or theory of composition, these teachers simply could not imagine composition as an independent discursive or pedagogical practice.

LITERATURE AS ANTIDOTE

Advocacy for the use of literature in required composition instruction was not a strong theme in professional literature published during the 1930s and 1940s. During the thirties, instruction in the required course settled into a comfortable pattern that combined current-traditional formalism with more or less literary study, depending upon the history and mission of a given college or university and the intellectual bent of faculty who designed the course. During the 1940s and fifties, however, traditional ways of teaching Freshman English were seriously challenged by the advent of interest in communication skills (see chapter 8). Because of the success of this challenge, English teachers' defense of the use of literary texts in the required first-year course resurfaced during the 1950s.

English departments did well during the postwar period. Enrollments in higher education in general boomed after World War II, and many English departments doubled or tripled the number of full-time faculty they employed. The new criticism provided an intellectual rationale for the expansion of literary studies insofar as it encouraged scholars to become critics, which in turn permitted them to develop new and ever more elaborate readings of canonical works (Graff 228). Composition, by contrast, was quite possibly at its lowest institutional ebb ever.

With the notable exception of communication skills, Freshman English underwent almost no theoretical development between 1900 and 1970. In the 1950s and 1960s, introductory composition was still being taught according to the dictates of the current-traditional theory of discourse it inherited from the people who had given the course its original shape in the late nineteenth century.[8] Professional literature about composition instruction testifies to the longevity of current-traditional instruction. In 1955 Herbert L. Creek wrote that when he began teaching composition in 1910, "a pattern of instruction in writing was already established, and in spite of frantic experimentation, there has been no revolution since" (4). Creek read Hill's *Principles* and Wendell's

English Composition as a student; when he became a teacher, he used Edwin Wooley's *Handbook,* which was thoroughly current-traditional (Connors 1983). In 1918, Frank W. Scott, who was Creek's mentor at Illinois, wrote that there had been "a steady diminution in the amount of rhetorical theory offered" in the "stream of textbooks in college rhetoric" (515). "That which has been retained," according to Scott, "has been made more and more elementary, requiring less and less knowledge or study on the part of the student." Henry F. Thoma testified that in 1931 "grammar, usage, and composition were taught from a handbook or a rhetoric. . . . There were certain clear-cut ways to develop a paragraph, and the laws of language were often codified under a hundred rules" (1957, 36). John McCloskey remarked in 1935 that "the teaching of English composition in our colleges has become a conventionalized procedure. . . . A long series of textbooks has established the traditional four forms of discourse and the four laws of rhetoric" (116). By 1950, Kenneth Oliver could refer to adherents of the composition pedagogy based on current-traditional rhetoric as "traditionalists" or "formalists" (3). Such teachers taught "the techniques of structure of the sentence, paragraph, and total theme or essay or report" and were emphatically not interested in the content of their students' work (4). By this time the basic course was so fully routinized that it could be taught in mass settings by a faculty member who lectured once a week while a staff of TAs held smaller twice-weekly discussion sections and graded students' papers.

This was the institutional scene in which English teachers renewed their pleas for the use of literary texts in the required composition course. They were ostensibly motivated by their abhorrence of communication skills, which was at that time the only successful nonhumanist approach to required composition ever undertaken. It is hard to say what feature of communication skills irritated humanist teachers most: its insistence that the basic course should inculcate skills; its emphasis on the practical rather than the cultivated; its interest in public issues rather than personal expression; its use of individualized instruction and its reliance on empirical research; or its focus on mass media. Certainly, when advocates of literature-in-composition weren't belittling the skills movement, they wrote as if it threatened an entire way of life.

In a talk given at the 1955 meeting of the Conference on College Composition and Communication, Harrison Hayford analyzed the intellectual warfare that had been raging over the basic course during the previous decade. He described the required freshman course as having been "under pres-

sure . . . from two sides" (1956, 42). With some justice, Hayford characterized these "sides" in political terms, placing "the 'Communication' wing" on
the left and the "'humanities' or 'general education' wing" on the right (43).
He argued that each side had raised "searching and realistic questions" about
the aim of Freshman English. The questions Hayford posed as emanating
from the right reveal that, in his mind at least, humanists still clung to the
belief that literary texts were more important than any other kind. The first
question suggested that communication skills was "high-school or even grade-
school, instruction in reading and writing" and not, presumably, the demanding sort of course that a study of literature would be. The second argued that
"the humane values derived from literature are so significant, and its instrumental values as model and motivation in composition are so necessary for
mature writing" that the basic composition course should be "*primarily* a literature course, not the simple, contemporary, half-way literature now used,
but great books, by great writers." The third asked: "would not students who
had grappled with great books, who had even glimpsed their scale of human
and literary values, who had written papers in the light of these great models,
be equipped, a fortiori, to read and evaluate all lesser forms both within literature and below it, in the mass media?" Hayford did not indicate whether
his little dialogue was a private fantasy or if he was actually quoting colleagues' hallway conversation. In either case, the questions he imagined for
advocates of literature-in-composition repeat a theme we have seen before in
this history: the superiority of literary texts to all others, and particularly to
popular texts.

Professional literature from the early 1950s amply displays humanist contempt for mass media and popular culture. In 1951, for example, members of
a CCCC workshop agreed that "our age tends to encourage mass feeling and
thinking, and to neglect the culture of individuals" ("Imaginative Writing"
33). Hence they were fearful about the "apparent drift of the freshman English course toward preoccupation with techniques of 'mass communication,'
with probable discard or neglect of techniques intended to develop personal,
humane culture." Kathrine Koller lamented the "visual-minded illiteracy of
a generation of T.V. watchers" (1955, 82). Gerald Thorson complained in 1956
that the typical student "lives in a world of mass media: television, radio,
motion pictures, newspapers, magazines, and comic books" (39). According
to Thorson, communication skills courses only taught what the student already knew, and hence "the cultural uses of language have been excluded.
We have forgotten about books. We have failed to remember that as teachers

of English we are concerned not only with the teaching of skills; we are also interested in the transmission of values" (40).

Humanist worry about mass media was not new in 1950, of course. In 1890 Adams Sherman Hill, who had himself been a journalist, blasted popular media for their negative effects on English usage:

> If newspapers and novels had only a general effect upon a reader's mind, they would still be likely to injure his English; but they have a direct and specific influence upon his use of language,—an influence more wide-spread, more insidious, and more harmful than any other; and this is especially true in the United States, where almost every man has his daily, or, at least, his weekly journal, and almost every woman spends many hours on current fiction. (106–07)

Humanists fear popular texts because they address the current, the common, and the practical. That is, such texts are interested (and interesting, to boot). Humanists also seem to dislike the lack of discipline they perceive in popular culture, where no one seems to be in control of either language or taste.

Certainly, teachers who made humanist arguments in favor of substituting literary texts for mass media in composition instruction during the 1950s did not hesitate to extol the universal and uplifting qualities of literature. Koller offered several justifications for its superiority. First of all, she wrote, literature represents life at least as well as experience itself: "In a great poem, a drama, or a novel, the artist invites us to examine the lives of others; we see human beings like ourselves in action and we know their innermost thoughts" (82). This notion that literature substituted or filled in for life was a commonplace of academic literary theory of the period (see Northrop Frye's *Anatomy of Criticism*, for example). To exemplify this point, Koller used the "delighted student" trope that also appeared in the responses to Lindemann-Tate: "A boy reads 'Michael' and tells me that he had never realized before what emotions his father had, because he had never understood him. . . . No girl I have ever known fails to be delighted by the reflection of herself and her mother, in Chaucer's Pertelote" (82–83). Literature also offered insight into the "richness and complexity of life," according to Koller, thus raising important philosophical questions with which students must grapple—"what is justice?" and "is life tragic—or comic?" (83). Literary texts could also "awaken an appreciation of the beauty of form and begin the development of a taste for the genuine as opposed to the easy and meretricious," and it presented students with democratic ideals, as well. (I have to wonder, parenthetically, whether any literary text achieves this last goal as well as, say, the *Federalist Papers*). After she asserted the capacity of literature to instruct students in philosophy, politics, and ethics, Koller excoriated the comparatively short reach of communication skills in no uncertain terms: "we talk of our responsibility to train the young to communicate; let us not ignore our equally great responsibility to let the great writers communicate with the young. To withhold this privilege is evidence of timidity on our part, of distrust of greatness, and an admission of past failures. . . . not failure but low aim is crime" (84). Koller's assumption that composition without literature is an unwomanly and possibly even un-American undertaking could hardly be more clear.

In 1957 Natalie Calderwood offered a time-honored defense of humanism and the practice of reading literary texts in composition courses. Against the findings of anthropologists and sociologists, she argued that there were "some few certainties, 'permanencies,' which are even yet safe to use as premises from which to think and act" (201). If America found itself in the midst of nuclear anxiety during the fifties, it was not the fault of humanism. Indeed, Calderwood allowed that if a nuclear disaster were to occur, it would not be due to failed "communication" or "mediation"; rather, she opined, such a tragedy would come about because "the mediators are either ignorant or defiant of the universal certainties—the truths in all human experience" (202). There was a certain "presumptuousness" about contemporary cultural attitudes, Calderwood thought, a presumptuousness that was "expressed in our emphasis upon the immediately practical in our composition and communication courses." Her remedy for all of this uncertainty and presumption was, of course, literature. She argued that the student who reads literary texts

> makes an acquaintance with ideas, concepts, feelings, experiences
> which are universal and, as of now, permanent truths. And in the
> acquaintance, through the indirect and subtle moral influence of
> literature which by its very nature is one of its most valuable at-
> tributes, he may even be started on the way to personal moral respon-
> sibility without which language as a tool for mediation or persuasion
> or communication of any sort is, to put it mildly, dangerous. (202)

Once again we see the humanist insistence that reading great literature exposes students to universal values, as well as the argument that reading plays an important role in the formation of character. Given humanists' faith in the moral leverage exerted by literature, I feel entitled to wonder what lessons teachers expected students to glean from the literary texts that were recommended during the 1950s for use in the required composition class. Among these were *Oedipus Rex*, *The House of the Seven Gables*, *Lord Jim*, and *Light in August*.

Obviously the threat to humanism posed by the skills movement drove teachers to find ever more innovative arguments with which to justify the use of literary texts in composition. They found one relatively new ground from which to justify the practice: suddenly, Freshman English needed a "subject matter." Wayne Booth argued in 1956, for example, that "imaginative literature" was "indispensable" in composition "as a stimulus for thinking and writing, as a source of subject matter" (35). The ubiquity of the "subject matter" argument during the 1950s suggests to me that persons interested in communication skills had raised the issue of content in the basic course when they supplied an alternative to the literature–current-traditional nexus. Given humanism's rejection of both rhetoric and composition, and given the absence of disciplines devoted to these fields of study, it never occurred to English teachers that either was a "subject matter." Furthermore, they failed to develop any nonliterary content for the required course precisely so that they could justify their use of literary texts therein. When teachers and administrators who opposed the use of literature in Freshman English made the argument that the course had no content, humanist teachers had little choice but to rearticulate humanist arguments about the superiority of literature as content. And they had to make these arguments to non-English faculty, people for whom this assumption did not go without saying.

The motivation argument for the use of literature in composition was also very popular during the fifties. Teachers who had for years instructed listless or resisting students in the niceties of thesis placement must have welcomed the renewed enthusiasm in the profession for the use of literature in the required course. Gerald Thorson "found the freshman's response much more alert and keen in the study of literature than in the study of editorials or essays. They are more interested in, more eager to express themselves on, 'My Last Duchess', for example, or *Anna Christie* than on 'Radio Doesn't Entertain' or 'Churchill True to Form'" (1953, 38). Some advocates of the motivation rationale even admitted that they had turned to literature as a means of salvaging a theoretically bankrupt freshman course. John A. Hart, Robert C. Slack, and Neal Woodruff pointed to the intellectual disrepair in the course: "experiments have been made in reorganizing Freshman English on a variety of principles, all by teachers bent on giving life to a dying course through new materials and new emphasis" (1958, 236). They then identified "one new development" that "alone shows promise of giving sustained vitality to the course" (237). This "new" development was, of course, the use of literary texts; Hart and his colleagues claimed that students were "thrilled" and "excited" by such works as *The Brothers Karamazov* and *Oedipus Tyrannus*. Further, they claimed, students discussed such works "with eager interest; they respond readily to writing assignments based upon them." Teachers also liked this approach: "teachers seem equally delighted; their accounts of freshman courses in which such books are read are aglow with pleasure over the students' response."

In 1955, Randall Stewart put forward the notion that students could be motivated if the freshman course had a "current of ideas," and hence he preferred that Freshman English be "a course which has to do with the deepest things in man" (17). Of course, Stewart borrowed the notion of a "current of ideas" from the essay in which Matthew Arnold articulated his theory of disinterestedness—"The Function of Criticism at the Present Time." In keeping with the humanist belief that popular reading is a waste of time, Stewart lamented that teachers who used nonliterary materials in the basic course "fritter away our opportunity with miscellaneous, less-than-great reading. . . . The hungry sheep look up and are not fed" (17). To counteract this tendency, he designed a yearlong course in which his students read novels by Hawthorne, Melville, James, Dreiser, and Faulkner. He and the students "built up a substantial subject-matter," he wrote, which "had not been the work of a day or a week, but of months. The subject-matter had become a personal possession, we had lived with it, it had got into the bloodstream" (18–19). Stewart does not say whether this inoculation with the literary virus improved students' writing.

Stewart's essay provoked a number of responses in which literature was characterized as a pedagogical jack-of-all-trades. Harry R. Garvin agreed that "novels can help students (and professors) feel an idea, can animate many of the major issues surrounding the individual and his society in a way that even the best essays cannot" (1959, 176). Kenneth Eble asserted that the restoration of literature to freshman writing was "restoration of an emphasis which should never have been displaced," and he advocated the use of literature in the required course because it stimulated not only students but the teacher of composition, who "needs the daily contact with language in its fullest complexity, power, and beauty, which the pursuit of literature can give him" (476, 477). Other teachers pragmatically adapted their pleas for the use of literature to traditional lore about the freshman course. Helmut Bonheim noted that teachers "would rather teach Dickens than the semi-colon," but he went on to argue that the reading of literature would teach a freshman "how to use commas more effectively than teaching him directly how to use commas" (40, 41). And Kenneth England recommended literature as the "proper" subject matter for the research paper (367).

During the midforties, teachers began to argue that literary texts be used as a data base, a repository of facts, on which students could base arguments. In 1946, for example, Leonard Rubinstein described a new course at Penn State, "the primary intention" of which was to "demonstrate that an assertion is made responsible by particulars, examples, logical structures. Each student must make his own interpretation valid by organizing and citing evidence. Each book in English B must be considered a body of evidence. Each succeeding book enlarges the body of evidence" (275). Students were asked to use evidence from literature to answer very large moral questions in their essays, such as "Does a lack of belief in order and purpose in life lessen one's need for order and purpose in life?" (the data to answer this question were to be gleaned from Hemingway's "A Clean Well-Lighted Place") (274). Rubenstein claimed that teachers and students alike were delighted with this approach; the only drawback was that the teacher of the course "has to rehearse over and over again for himself the peculiar and primitive way literature is used in a composition class. . . . He has to return to the savage need which produces art and which makes art meaningful. He has to regress from the discipline of literature to the origin of literature" (273). Note how composing is opposed to discipline here, how it is redolent of the "primitive" and the "savage" for Rubenstein, who was a creative writer.

Calderwood echoed the literature-as-evidence argument in 1957, asserting that "straight thinking" could be approached "through study of the novelist's or dramatist's discipline 'logic' in presenting the evidence for his characters" (203). Hart, Slack, and Woodruff noted that in a composition course based on literature,

> every student's writing is based on a definite and verifiable ground of reference—a fictional world which is open to examination. The student's perceptions of that world, as expressed in his writing, can be substantiated by the concrete "facts" of that world, "facts" available to every member of the class and to the reader. Misreadings of that world can be quickly detected. (239)

In this approach, literary texts assume the status of current-traditional "facts";

they can be investigated, dissected, and reported on, like frogs in biology class.

The teachers quoted here advocated the use of literary texts in the introductory composition course on the ground that literature represented life's experiences more powerfully and delightfully than anything else could do. They also argued that the presence of literary texts in Freshman English made conduct of the course a more pleasant experience for teachers and students alike—which was undoubtedly true, given the dreariness of the current-traditional alternative. If any of them thought there was a necessary connection between students' reading and the improvement of their writing, though, none articulated a pedagogy that would implement the connection.

LIT-IN-COMP IN THE SIXTIES

Popular composition textbooks suggest that literature was still being used in composition instruction on a wide scale during the 1960s and 1970s. Edgar V. Roberts's *Writing Themes About Literature* first appeared in 1964; new editions have been published regularly ever since, appearing in 1969, 1973, 1977, 1983, 1988, and 1991. Somewhat behind the curve, chapters on "writing about literature" began to appear in comprehensive composition textbooks during the early seventies. Cleanth Brooks and Robert Penn Warren added "Writing a Literary Paper" to the third edition of *Modern Rhetoric* in 1970; in 1972, James McCrimmon incorporated "The Critical Essay: Writing About Literature" into the fifth edition of *Writing With a Purpose;* Robert Gorrell and Charlton Laird wrote "Writing About Literature" into the fifth edition of their *Modern English Handbook* in 1972; and Sheridan Baker added a chapter on the analysis of literature to *The Complete Stylist* in 1976.

Surveys also suggest that literary texts were in wide use in required composition instruction during the 1960s and 1970s. In the early sixties, Albert Kitzhaber read course syllabi from ninety-five four-year colleges and universities. He attempted to construct a representative sample for his survey, including "public and private universities, state colleges, teachers colleges, coeducational liberal arts colleges, liberal arts colleges for men only and for women only, and a few technical institutes primarily devoted to teaching engineering" (1963, 9). He then visited eighteen of the institutions that had sent syllabi to him. Kitzhaber found literature being used in first-semester Freshman English courses in about one-fifth of the colleges and universities he surveyed. He noted that this emphasis occurred at schools "with rigorous

standards for admission—the Ivy League and a number of small, highly selective liberal arts colleges," and noted further that the usual explanation given
publicly for this was that "most students at such schools are better prepared
in English than the average entering freshman" (22). He added that "many of
these colleges have a long tradition of belletristic study in the freshman course
that they are reluctant to depart from." Kitzhaber also found that courses for
advanced students and second-semester composition courses were almost
wholly based on literary texts, a situation that implies that the study of literature was still perceived as more advanced than work in composition.

In 1966–67, Harrison Hoblitzelle conducted a much less ambitious survey
of eight prestigious universities and colleges. His sample included "representative public (in most cases, State) universities with select student bodies"
and three private colleges (596). He found that yearlong courses in required
composition were typical at these schools, and that "the first third is centered
on composition . . . *per se*, with the remaining two thirds devoted to the study
of literature" (597). According to this survey, then, in institutions such as
Berkeley, Michigan, Virginia, NYU, and Stanford students were actually
spending the bulk of their time in the required course studying literature—a
finding that confirms Kitzhaber's hunch about select universities as well as
the findings of surveys taken during the early decades of the century by
Baldwin, Shipherd, Taylor, and Rutland.

In 1967 and 1968, Thomas Wilcox conducted a massive survey of four-
year English programs. He mailed questionnaires to each of the 1,320 such
programs in the United States and received responses from more than 94 percent of them (1973, xi). He seemed surprised to learn that departments of
English "devoted *over 40 percent* of their total teaching effort to this gigantic
educational enterprise" (63). He reported that 11 percent of the schools he
surveyed devoted "the first term of freshman English exclusively to reading
literature and to writing about it; 24.8 percent devote the second term to those
activities; 38 percent combine literature with composition in the first term;
and the same number (but not necessarily the same departments) do so in the
second term" (82). In other words, during the late sixties, at least 40 percent
of entering freshmen encountered literature in their introductory coursework
in English. Interestingly enough, though, anthologies of literature were among
the textbooks most often required for use by departments that mandated that
teachers in all sections use the same text; literary anthologies were required at
55.6 percent of schools reporting, falling behind only handbooks, which were
required in 73.1 percent of the programs surveyed (87). And almost half of

the programs reporting (48.1 percent) required their students to purchase "separate literary works." Needless to say, texts such as these represent the staples of a humanist approach to composition: literary study combined with drill in usage, grammar, and mechanics.

Wilcox also noted some interesting trends in Freshman English. For one thing, teachers now felt that students were coming to college better prepared than in earlier years. He pointed out that this was only a feeling, since "no one, not even those agencies best equipped to do so, has made a historical survey of college students' verbal skills" (1973, 99). Wilcox quoted the senior examiner of the Educational Testing Service, who believed "that whatever improvement is noticed should probably be attributed to changes in the secondary school curriculum, which now permits students to read better works of literature at an earlier age." The senior examiner was probably referring to the supposed effects of Project English, a federally funded program that had supported the rewriting of many high school English curricula during the sixties. Wilcox, however, was not altogether convinced that giving tenth-grade students the opportunity to read *Moby Dick* had done anything more for their writing skills than to make them more "adept at mimicry" (99). Nevertheless, he noted that at many schools the "general preference is for abandoning formal, systematic instruction in composition, for converting the freshman course to a course in literature, or for surrendering that course entirely" (1967, 148). The English teachers he surveyed asserted that it was necessary to offer students "a freshman course which has real substance and which can compete with their courses in the sciences, the social sciences, and other fields to the extent in which it enlarges the mind" in order to hold their attention. Teachers also argued that they were "most competent to teach" literature, and that it was only literature "which is wholly germane to the discipline they profess," thus summarily excluding composition from the province of English studies (149).

Surely there is sufficient evidence in these surveys to convince skeptics that literature was a popular resource in the required freshman course during the 1960s and 1970s. Arguments for its use therein had much more to do with institutional exigency than with pedagogical reality. English teachers knew on some level that required composition was their departmental life-blood even though they despised it mightily. So they turned Freshman English into a literature course, sometimes developing a pretext like student motivation, and sometimes offering no rationale other than that reading literature was a pleasant exercise for all concerned.

A FORMAL PARTNERSHIP

A new and rather bizarre rationale for the use of literature in first-year composition developed between 1940 and 1960: literary texts began to be read as models of current-traditional principles of discourse. In 1965, before he undertook his survey of English departments, Thomas Wilcox published an essay in which he argued that teachers of Freshman English were "committed to demonstrating an analogy—indeed, a continuum—between literature and what is called, by default, 'expository prose'" (71). Taking off a phrase from *Paradise Lost,* Wilcox opined that "most of our textbooks, most of our assignments, and most of our discussions in this course are directed toward instructing students to 'conglobe' their thoughts and experiences into verbal constructs which partake of an order and coherence we assume to be apparent in life itself" (70). Except for the mention of coherence, which is a central principle of current-traditional discourse theory, this account of traditional composition lore could pass as a new critical description of a poem or novel. Wilcox claimed that most English teachers subscribed to a theory of literature based on the principle "that literary works of value exhibit closed patterns, that they include no extraneous matter, that they construe and indeed control experience by containing it in well-designed artifacts" (70–71). Current-traditional rhetoric also valued closed patterns; it also forwarded the principle of unity, which forbade digression; and it prized as well the production of well-designed artifacts in which a student's experience was supposedly represented.

This set of orderly notions also influenced the selection of literary texts for use in composition classes. The choice of literature conventionally taught there, Wilcox thought, was

> determined very largely by our desire to help our students to find
> significant forms, again on the assumption that to discern such forms is
> to learn to fabricate coherently formed non-literary statements. . . . we
> continue to insist that our students produce miniature cosmos every
> time they write. In short, we conceive composition almost exclusively
> as an act of ordering, of fashioning coherent structure, of perceiving
> and replicating harmonious wholes. (1965, 70)

Wilcox was not the only teacher who made an analogy between the formalist textual principles of current-traditionalism and those of the new criticism; however, he was the only contributor to the professional literature who criticized the practice. His criticism was not motivated by the possible harm done to student writing by this theoretical misrepresentation, however; rather, he was concerned that the formalist pattern used in composition instruction misrepresented contemporary literature! "If we were perfectly consistent and honest," he wrote, "we should have to write 'Incoherent (see page 234 of the handbook)' in the margins of nine tenths of the literature offered us today" (72).

This odd state of affairs, where teachers conflated poetic principles with rules for exposition, came about not only because of the institutional proximity of literature and composition, but because of the absolute lack of theoretical innovation in composition. Given this state of affairs, it is not surprising that teachers of the required course—who were, by this time, mainly graduate students in literature—looked to the body of theory they did know in order to derive principles from which to work as they evaluated students' papers. And what they knew was the new criticism. During the 1940s, people interested in literature finally developed a literary theory that could be readily translated into a pedagogy. According to Graff, explication—the favored new critical method of reading—"claimed to be as rigorously 'professional' as any of the methods of philology or history, yet unlike those methods it also claimed to meet the rudimentary needs of students, who could finally be put in touch with literary texts themselves rather than their backgrounds and genetic conditions" (227). In short, the new criticism made literature teachable, even to freshmen. So the graduate students who were practicing new critical readings in their graduate seminars had finally been given a way to tie their graduate study to their teaching of composition.

Thanks to the formalist biases of both the new criticism and current-traditionalism, composition teachers could easily view all texts, not just literary ones, as artifacts having an interior logic whose structural unity testified to their value as repositories of truth. This theory posited that texts accurately represented the completed thought of an author. The structural perfection of a text was proof of its complete representationality. Thus teachers prized formal achievement above all other aspects of composing; they were confident that formal perfection reflected the wholeness of whatever universe of discourse the writer had addressed. When this theory was turned on literary texts, their study was resolved into discussion of their constituent formal elements: situation, character, conflict, theme, structure, symbol, irony, point of view, voice (I borrow this list from the sixth edition of McCrimmon's *Writing With a Purpose* [1976]). When the theory was turned on student themes, their analysis was undertaken in equally formal terms: thesis statements, topic sentences, unity, coherence, emphasis, and point of view. Inevitably, as Wilcox noted, works of literature came to be prized for use in composition instruction if they could be discussed in terms borrowed from current-traditional rhetoric.

Under the mutual influence of current-traditional pedagogy and the new criticism, then, teachers actually found current-traditional compositional principles within literary texts. In 1962, Morris Greenhut of Michigan argued that the *Iliad* "touches on so many basic skills in writing that the instructor could easily devote half a semester to it alone" (138). He paid particular attention to each of the speeches in that poem as "a little essay or narrative having its own proper structure and exhibiting such basic elements of effective composition as movement, coherence, progression leading to a climax, and resolution." Teaching the epic in this way, Greenhut argued, taught students "to read closely and meaningfully." Reading poetry could also help students to distinguish between main and subordinate ideas, to see the relationship of the parts to the whole, and it could make students conscious of stylistic effects. In 1963 Robert L. Eschbacher made the more specifically current-traditional case that "the techniques of definition, classification, and division, comparison and contrast, and process are inherent in a great deal of thinking and writing," and that these can be taught "informally" through reading, and writing about, "a deliberately difficult choice of novel" like *Lord Jim* (22). In 1964, Marvin Bell, a poet in Iowa's Writer's Workshop, posited that the techniques used in the composition of poetry did not differ all that much from those employed in the production of exposition. "Of course," Bell wrote, as if the point needed assertion, "I look upon poetry as a form of composition" (1). The student who studies poetry, according to Bell, "learns that most, if not all, of the same techniques which go into the writing of a good poem are available and/or necessary to the writing of a decent composition." Bell included a list of eleven such techniques, including the necessity for poets to support assertions, attend carefully to arrangement, and to select language that was at once concise and evocative.

The tendency to treat literary texts as models of current-traditional principles also appeared in composition textbooks. Harold C. Martin and Richard Ohmann made the analogical character of the modeling argument explicit in their textbook, *The Logic and Rhetoric of Exposition* (1963), where they posited that "the paragraph is a scene from a play," insofar as it has action, motivation, sequence, and result" (206–07). In his popular handbook on writing themes about literature, Roberts insisted that literary texts, as well as themes written about them, have some central point, mood, or main idea that dictates the organization of the entire piece, and that pieces of literary criticism should look like five-paragraph themes (1973, 9). In 1972, Gorrell and Laird argued that "literature provides ready illustrations of rhetorical principles. A Sonnet shows how form and organization can work; a good poem illustrates precision and economy in diction; a short story or novel may demonstrate the value of direct sentence patterns" (465). And Sheridan Baker told his readers in 1976 that novels had thesis statements: "although working unseen among the details, the thesis also has been there for you to find and state" (291).

Unlike other rationales for importing literature into composition instruction, the formal analogical argument derives its strength from the fact that it assumes some continuity between the study of literary texts and composing. Undoubtedly, there are compositional similarities on some level among novels, plays, and the ideal discourse taught in introductory writing classes, although Martin and Ohmann's application of Kenneth Burke's dramatistic terminology to the structure of traditional paragraphs seems a bit strained. A point to be noticed here, however, is that in all these examples the terms of current-traditional composition theory exerted no little pressure on the interpretation of literary texts. Only in a current-traditional composition class would *Lord Jim* be read as a model for exercises in definition and division. I am tempted to think of this development as the toad's revenge on the garden.

6

TERMS OF EMPLOYMENT

RHETORIC SLAVES AND LESSER MEN

> The pain of being an adjunct is not inflicted in the classroom, but in the
> hallowed halls of academe. My struggle to be seen and heard in this
> discipline is also a struggle to have faith in myself and what I'm doing.
> —Clare Frost, "Looking for a Gate in the Fence"

Today, first-year composition is largely taught by graduate students and temporary or part-time teachers. Full-time permanent faculty regularly teach the required first-year course only in liberal arts colleges, two-year colleges, and the few four-year universities that still privilege teaching over research. According to administrative lore, this arrangement is necessary for economic reasons. No institution, the argument goes, can be expected to staff such a large program as first-year composition with full-time permanent faculty, whose salaries and benefits would simply overwhelm the university's budget.

I like to think of this as "the argument from size," a tactic that does not typically appear in the lists of rhetorical strategies given in composition textbooks. In this case the argument from size is probably true. But it also discloses an arresting contradiction about the status of composition in the university: universities apparently value introductory composition so much that they insist it be universally required, and yet they make inadequate provision for its teaching. (I am not inferring here, or anywhere in this book, that inadequate staffing arrangements translate into inadequate teaching).

Composition was not always staffed the way it is now. Until 1940 or so, composition classes were taught by full-time teachers, although they generally were the newest members of the permanent faculty. This changed when disciplinary specialization began to affect staffing in the undergraduate curriculum.[1] With the narrowing of faculty interests that accompanied adoption of the research ideal, it became increasingly difficult to find full-time faculty who were willing to teach general or introductory courses, and by 1950, American universities with graduate programs had begun to rely on graduate students to staff the required first-year composition course. They had also begun the practice of hiring part-time help to meet staffing demands imposed by the postwar explosion in college enrollments. Richard M. Weaver complained in 1963 that the first-year composition course was then "given to just about anybody who will take it" (1970, 202–03). He continued: "Beginners, part-time teachers, graduate students, faculty wives, and various fringe people, are now the instructional staff of an art which was once supposed to require outstanding gifts and mature experience." Weaver's remark is offensively elitist and sexist; it does not, however, add the insult of disrespecting composition teaching.

The argument from size does not account, all by itself, for the low status of composition and its teachers in contemporary universities. In capitalist cultures, after all, bigger is usually better. Nor does the elementary status of the first-year course fully explain its lowly position in the academy. Teachers of Western Civilization do not necessarily acquire lower academic status by virtue of their interest in or assignment to this course, even though it too is required of entering students at many universities and colleges. I think that the low status of composition teaching in the university accrues, at least in part, from its association with English departments. Throughout most of the twentieth century, faculty in literary studies regarded an assignment in composition as a professional disaster. This attitude emerged long before composition teachers were drawn from the ranks of temporary faculty during the 1970s and 1980s. It antedates as well the full flowering of disciplinary specialization during the 1930s, which ultimately confined the teaching duties of permanent full-time faculty to graduate and upper-division instruction.

The low status of composition instruction means that the situation of teachers of the required introductory composition course is fraught with contradiction. Today, many people become interested in composition because they want to teach, and they enjoy the one-on-one encounters with students that are available in composition instruction (Schell, "Costs"). Many people who choose composition instruction as their life's work also do so in part because they desire to serve the university community by helping students to write better. They find encouragement in the universal requirement in composition, which seems to imply that universities understand and support the importance of writing instruction. Once they are embarked on this career, however, they discover that teachers of the universally required course are underpaid, overworked, and treated with disdain.[2]

For many years and in many parts of the country, I have heard stories about the literal invisibility of composition teachers within English departments. Whether they be part-timers or graduate students, they are excluded from department and committee meetings; hence they are denied a vote in decisions that affect their professional lives. In many schools they are expected to teach from syllabi that they did not design. If they share a mailroom with full-time teachers, their mailboxes are often segregated from those of full-time faculty—the literal separation of the means by which the department communicates with them manifests their imagined distance from departmental affairs. They are not invited to lunch, where, as any full-time faculty member knows, important decisions about curricula and staffing are often made. They are not acknowledged when they pass full-time faculty members in the hallway. I once heard a well-known literary scholar argue at a professional meeting that the literature-composition rift could be mended if only teachers of each subject would sit down and talk about their differences. After he concluded his remarks, a woman seated in the front row near the podium rose to say that she, a part-time teacher of composition, had taught in his department for ten years; this was the first time she had ever heard him speak.

Perhaps the unkindest cuts of all to composition teachers, then, stem from their association with full-time faculty who subscribe to humanism's conflicted attitude toward composition instruction. In the humanist worldview, composition must be maintained in order to maintain the class distinction that is captured in the paired but unequal dichotomy literature-composition. The presence of composition establishes the superiority of literature, just as the presence of the universal requirement establishes a class-affiliated boundary at the gate of the university itself. And yet, from a humanist point of view, there is nothing to teach in composition, because clear and eloquent expression results from the disciplined reading of great literature and the concomitant development of character. That is to say, on a humanist model, composition has no subject and no substance. Perhaps its insubstantial nature explains why its teachers seem to be invisible in the academy.

IN THE BEGINNING

It was not always thus. At Harvard in the late nineteenth century, first-year composition was taught by a group of men who were "unscholarly and idiosyncratic," according to Gerald Graff (66). They included prim, rigorous Adams Sherman Hill; testy, flamboyant Barrett Wendell; gentle LeBaron Russell Briggs, and the irascible Charles Townsend Copeland. Hill, Briggs, and Copeland all held the Boylston Chair of Rhetoric, and all of them had tenure. Wendell and Copeland published a great deal. Indeed, David Shumway argues that Wendell was an important figure in the professionalization of American literature.

Since none of these men possessed Ph.D.s, however, they were never awarded the rank of full professor. By the late nineteenth century, the German research ideal had taken sufficient hold in American universities that the highest professorial ranks were reserved for people who earned a research degree and who continued to do research throughout their careers. And composition teachers, by virtue of their commitment to paper-grading, did not often find time to do research. Men with Ph.D.s did work with the basic course at other universities prior to the twentieth century: this group included John Franklin Genung at Amherst, Fred Newton Scott of Michigan, and G. R. Carpenter at Columbia. But scholars were rare among composition teachers, as Robert J. Connors explains:

> Such figures as John S. Hart, Erastus Haven, Edwin M. Hopkins, A. S. Hill, Barrett Wendell, Le Baron Briggs, G[eorge] P[ierce] Baker, Charles T. Copeland, Henry Frink, Henry S. Canby, and Hiram Corson all were involved deeply in attempting to create a new rhetoric of written communication during the period 1880–1910. Much of their pedagogical work became widely known, and their textbooks sold in the hundreds of thousands. But they had no PhDs, and they could not successfully reproduce themselves through the younger generations of graduate scholars they taught. As this generation died off or became less active during the first two decades of the new century, no one stepped forward to fill their shoes. (1991, 64)

Early teachers of composition, then, more often fit the profile of the model professor in the classical college—the cultural polymath who was perhaps an inspiring teacher (like Corson or Copeland) but master of no special field of study. Their lack of specialization became especially marked after the disappearance of rhetoric as an academic field with which composition teachers could identify.

To put this another way, first-year composition has always been staffed by people identified as teachers rather than scholars—whether this identification is accurate or not, as it was not in Wendell's case, for example. And even in the very early years of professionalization, teaching was not sufficient grounds on which to advance someone to the highest rank. Because of this, by 1900 men with professional ambition had begun to avoid an assignment in composition, if they possibly could. Albert Kitzhaber notes that

> as rhetorical theory settled in its several ruts, and as the composition teacher was reduced almost to a proofreader, the field rapidly lost status . . . . In schools with graduate programs in English, composition teaching was assigned to untrained graduate students. In schools less fortunate, full-time teachers of the lowest academic ranks were given the chore; they looked on it at best as a probationary period which they must undergo before being promoted to literature courses. Composition teaching became, in a very real sense, drudgery of the worst sort, unenlivened by any genuine belief in its value, shackled by an unrealistic theory of writing, and so debased in esteem that men of ability were unwilling to identify themselves with it permanently. (1990, 225–26)

The identification of composition with teaching rather than scholarship, and its abandonment by "men of ability," insured that, increasingly, teachers of composition would be denied access to professional status. It also insured that they would be women, for the most part. I read Kitzhaber's phrase "men of ability" to mean "men able to succeed at research by virtue of their access to powerful men who encouraged them, and by virtue of available time." Women were generally denied academic apprenticeship to men, and if they taught composition, they certainly had no time to do research (Bernard; Hopkins 1912, 1923).

RESEARCH IS TO PROMOTION AS
TEACHING IS TO DRUDGERY

This situation was exacerbated by the practice of requiring English teachers to begin their professional lives by teaching composition. This practice spelled real trouble for aspiring assistant professors because professional advancement was firmly connected to the production of research about literature.

Permanent faculty in English departments were aware, very early on, that a graduate education focused on research did not adequately prepare people to become teachers of composition. In 1916, J. M. Thomas remarked on the odd dissociation of scholarship from teaching English, a dissociation that enabled English departments to award Ph.D.s to persons who were utterly unsuited to the classroom. He asserted that departments must "cease to regard teaching as a safe refuge for those with certain intellectual gifts, but without the personality to make their mark in any other profession" (450). Interestingly enough, Thomas's reservation about scholars' ability to teach lay not with their tendency to specialize; indeed, he granted that "the severe mental discipline which comes from the working out of a dissertation cannot but make a person more rigourous in his own thinking and consequently less tolerant of slovenliness of thought in others" (451). Rather, it was scholars' lack of gentlemanliness that irritated him: "indifference to personal appearance, uncouthness of manners, provincialism in speech, inconsiderateness of the rights and feelings of others . . . certainly ought to prove a bar to recommendation to teach." Unfortunately, graduate faculties persisted in recommending people who possessed these traits as teachers, even though "their very presence in a classroom is a flagrant offense to the good taste of students, which in some of its more important phases it is the function of English to develop."

Thomas's position was a bit old-fashioned in 1916; rail as he might against doctoral training in medieval Latin, Middle High German, Old French, early Norse, and the "not less narrow grubbing at literary relationship"—none of which trained people to teach English, he thought—the professional tide had already turned toward highly specialized research. Thomas dated himself even more thoroughly when he lamented that "too great emphasis has . . . been laid on poetry, drama, and the novel as a prose epic, to the exclusion of the literary qualities of prose itself, to say nothing of that more pedestrian sort of prose which has been so influential in shaping the thoughts and destinies of men"—that is, rhetoric (453). Here Thomas indulged nostalgia for an older model teacher, the intellectual and cultural polymath whose job was to impart knowledge to his young charges and to instill in them the character appropriate to men of affairs. Obviously, this teacher was not being produced by graduate study in philology or literary history, and reproduction of the model became an increasingly remote possibility as the ranks of the professoriate began to be filled by men who had never worked in classical colleges. So two questions arose: Where will novice professors learn about teaching? And who will do the teaching, particularly the onerous variety associated with Freshman English? The answer that English departments gave to the second question was "the newest members of the profession."

In 1916 the MLA commissioned a report on employment in Freshman English, the results of which were presented to the meeting of its Central Division in 1917 and published in the *English Journal* in 1918. The report was written by Frank Scott of Illinois, Frederick Manchester of Wisconsin, and the same Joseph Thomas quoted above, who taught at Minnesota. Their report to the profession indicates that a now-familiar pattern of discriminatory employment was well established in English departments prior to World War I. The pattern was in place even though most English departments were less than thirty years old in 1916.

The committee agreed on one vital point: qualified teachers were indispensable if universities were to offer serious Freshman English courses in which a student was "given a maturer and more largely significant training in thinking and in expression, and in which he is to a considerable extent made acquainted with a correct standard of taste in literature" (592). And yet it was clear to "anyone familiar with the facts" that "distinction of mind, energy of character, humane and thorough education, in addition to literary taste and skill in composition" were not traits that characterized the typical composition teacher, who was too often "inexperienced, unfitted by nature for the work, ill trained, and sometimes, in addition, reluctant and disaffected" (592–93). Scott, Thomas, and Manchester put the blame for this condition not on teachers themselves but squarely on the professional practices that led to their reluctance and disaffection. Teachers who wanted to teach composition, as well as those who were forced to do so against their inclinations,

> may well be disturbed when they observe the actual facts—viz., that in the modern university so much teaching of composition is required; that often teachers of composition are for a long period confined to the one subject with little or no opportunity to share in the teaching of literature; and finally, that in spite of these uninviting conditions these same teachers of composition, whatever their competence, are, with the rarest exceptions, but slightly rewarded in salary and still less in professional rank and dignity. (594)

The committee thus recommended that "the university dignify teaching in Freshman English through prompt promotion of competent instructors and through liberality in salary" as a means of alleviating this situation (595). This recommendation was prompted by their recognition that promotion was not possible "on the basis even of unquestioned excellence in the teaching of Freshman English," since the "ultimate administrators do not, in effect, regard the course as important." This dilemma was compounded by the fact that the amount of work necessary to teach Freshman English prevented its teachers from doing advanced study in literature, which failure, in turn, committed them to careers in Freshman English. The committee thought that promotion and better salaries would at least make this double bind more tolerable, since there appeared to be no way out of it for a substantial number of English teachers.

By this time, apparently, research in philology and literary history was so demanding that commitment to it consumed the available time and energy of aspirants to the Ph.D. degree. Or at least that is how some teachers explained their lack of professional interest in Freshman English. In 1925, a member of the NCTE lamented that "teachers are so wedded to books and the teaching of literature that they are absolutely at a loss to know how to approach the very important subject of composition" (Davis 789). And in 1926, in a spectacular instance of bad faith, Oscar James Campbell defended the Ph.D. in English against an attack upon its irrelevance to teaching by arguing that the highly specialized graduate training given by English departments was not responsible for the dreadful state of affairs in Freshman English. Rather, he wrote, "the course has emanated from the school in which are found the natural enemies of the rigourously acquisitive Ph.D. system. It is the product of those educators who believe above everything else in 'expressing Willie'" (193). In other words, the mindless expressivism that characterized first-year composition instruction was unworthy of the attention of those select few who were fitted to the rigorous study entailed by pursuit of a Ph.D.

Campbell had the chutzpah to assert that the mindlessness of the freshman course had not been fostered within English departments even though he must have been aware that the goal of self-expression was infused into the lore of Freshman English by Barrett Wendell, who had been his teacher at Harvard. Nonetheless, he excused inept teaching in the freshman course on the ground that "young doctors ought not to be deemed failures if they do not accomplish the impossible in this course, which is not of their making and runs counter to much that they believe is pedagogic sense." This is sheer balderdash, of course. Young doctors of English had about the same interest in pedagogy as they had in staying at the bottom of the professional ladder. But Campbell was willing to go even farther in his attempt to separate the required course from the special interests of English departments: he speculated that Freshman English was maintained in universities at the behest of "teachers in other subjects, from history to geology." He was able to write this despite the obvious fact that no other department had as much stake in the required course as did English, where freshman composition was maintained precisely in order to support the advanced work in literature and philology that Campbell defended so vigorously.

By the midtwenties, the pattern outlined in the 1917 MLA report was institutionalized in many universities. Freshman English generally was taught by instructors without dissertations or with new Ph.D.s, while advanced courses in philology or literary history were taught by senior faculty. During the 1930s and 1940s, 60 to 90 percent of composition courses were taught by the newest members of the profession (Hughes 331). Few instructors envisioned the teaching of composition as a lifetime vocation, however. From their point of view, the assignment to composition was a holding tank, or (to switch metaphors) territory that had to be occupied briefly before the real teaching opportunity—in literature—opened up. But this ambition was very likely to be frustrated if a young teacher spent too many years at labor in the fields of composition. In his 1929 survey, Warner Taylor found that teachers who took on the duty of teaching Freshman English faced very serious professional peril: "in some institutions, especially in the larger, there is a rule or tradition—in some cases even a law—that instructors failing to receive promotion at the end of three or four years must resign" (17). Since teachers of the freshman course found it difficult either to pursue advanced research or to be assigned courses in literature, and since promotion depended upon success in literary research and teaching, this rule was a veritable formula for the continuous recycling of new teachers through Freshman English and out of the profession.

Taylor preferred that the freshman course be taught by experienced teachers. His poignant statement of this position is worth quoting at length:

> Mature, efficient, informed, and stabilized service is without question in most institutions needed to a greater extent than at present in Freshman English. And continued devotion to the course, where competence displays the loyalty, should receive recognition. Large universities can absorb, and do willingly, young and untrained teacher-students. But there should always be a solid nucleus of experienced instructors. In some future Eden, perhaps, Freshmen will be taught by the oldest and wisest members of a department—many presidents will tell you that they ought to be so taught;—but while we wait, it might be well to remember that a background in actual teaching is at least as valuable to a department as potential ability to do research work. (17–18)

This plea and others like it did nothing to change the pattern of employment that obtained in English departments throughout the Depression years. In 1940, George Wykoff—a tireless defender of the respectability of composition teaching—noted that "training in English in the graduate schools is primarily training for scholarship, research, and graduate teaching, and secondarily training for teaching literature to undergraduates. . . . Consciously or unconsciously the graduate student quickly learns that literature and research are all-important (he is unaware that composition exists, unless he is a graduate assistant)" (428–29). Contemporary observers agreed that the highly specialized training received by English Ph.D.s rendered them unfit for composition instruction. This fact, when combined with the higher status of literary studies and the senior faculty's resolute inattention to composition theory or pedagogy, was a recipe for disaster for the people who were conscripted to teach the first-year required composition course.

A HISTORY OF ATTITUDES

Anyone who is familiar with colonial studies will recognize the metaphors in which composition teachers have been depicted in the discourse of English studies—as children, serfs, prisoners, and slaves—to be part and parcel of the language of imperialism. Very early in the history of English departments, composition instruction was associated with youthfulness. In 1912, John W. Cunliffe noted that "in certain institutions, under present conditions, the teacher of literature enjoys a position of greater comfort and prestige [than teachers of composition]; that is perhaps the reason why the older teachers of English in almost all our colleges cling to literature with a desperate grip" (592). Taylor testified that in the 1920s there was "often a settled disinclination among older teachers of English, finally entrenched in literature, to do any more of the hard work a writing course entails" (19). He quoted a full professor of his acquaintance who said, in a department meeting, that "no man wants to read themes after he has turned forty."

Composition instruction was also likened to slavery and serfdom. In 1935, Franklin B. Snyder observed that "to the college instructor a section of English A has been, if not an actual symbol of academic serfdom like the iron collars worn by Gurth and Wamba, at least a badge of apprenticeship—something to be accepted as initially inevitable, but from which relief would come with the passing of time" (200). In 1938, Merritt Y. Hughes quoted Henry Sams, chair of the English department at Penn State, who referred to the situation of composition instruction as "the massacre of the innocents in English Departments, which take young doctors of philosophy for instructors of Freshmen and turn them into intellectual proles who have no prospect except discharge and destitution on the one hand or on the other permanent employment in a routine which eats their hearts out" (816). In 1939 O. J. Campbell, who was obviously no friend to composition but who was an astute analyst of the politics of English departments, asserted that

> for the vast majority of those who begin their careers as section hands in Freshman English there is no future in the profession. They cannot hope for even moderate academic promotion. But for all that, crowds of young men and women have been lured into the teaching of English by the great numbers of positions annually open at the bottom of the heap, and there they stick, contaminating one another with their discouragement and rebellion. No wonder they are now organizing, as other proletariats the world over are organizing, to assert and foster their class interests. . . . Their work, they realize, has no relation whatever to the subject to which, in hopeful youth, they resolved to dedicate their lives. . . . I know of large departments of English in which no one has been promoted from an instructorship to an assistant professorship for over ten years. Instead, men from other institutions have been brought in over the heads of the wretched section hands. This process is natural—yes, inevitable—because the work of a Freshman English instructor does not fit him for the teaching of literature. (181–82)

Composition teachers were also depicted as poverty stricken, a description that was all too accurate in many cases. In 1941, Theodore Gates argued that the willingness of senior faculty to turn over "the job of teaching composition to . . . the generally ill-clothed, ill fed, and ill-housed" had deprived the freshman course of attention from the profession's most respected thinkers. Gates asked, rhetorically: "where will you find a full professor concentrating his best thought and energy, or even a fair portion of it, on the problem of teaching adequate control of thought and the clear expression of it?" (69).

In 1949, Wykoff noted that teachers of literature disparaged "the life, the work, and the achievements of teachers of composition. Some seem to take a fiendish delight in ridiculing and discouraging those about to enter or already in the field," he wrote (321). By this time, the double bind in which English department practices entangled young instructors had apparently become invisible to senior faculty, who attributed its doleful outcome to the incompetence of the young instructors who were being recycled through required composition. Wykoff quoted a professor of literature as saying that "any man who will submit to a composition assignment for more than two years is worthy of nothing but contempt" (321–22).

Fifteen years later, the situations described by Campbell and Wykoff still obtained in English departments. In 1954, Andrew Schiller reported that any instructor of English "can talk for fourteen straight hours about Milton's heterodoxy in the concept of free will, has read every learned article on 'his subject' and can cite the hardcover books; moreover the latest learned article, which makes reference to every one which has gone before, he wrote and mailed only last week to P.M.L.A." (110). And yet, Schiller continued, this instructor's teaching load consisted of "three sections of composition and one of literature." Once a week he graded three sets of student themes "chockfull of comma-splices, dangling modifiers, misspellings, sentence fragments, incoherences, and inanities." Schiller concluded: "the good gray professor who guided his dissertation never told him it would be like this."

Workshop groups meeting at the Conference on College Composition and Communication during its early years continued the litany. From a 1952 report: "the teaching of composition is often regarded as an apprenticeship leading to 'good courses,' and the teacher is likely to get a feeling of diminished returns after a few years, compared to his experience in teaching literature" (Rorabacher 10). Workshop participants noted further that composition teachers were held in "low esteem" and that a "stigma attached to their work." Also in 1952, Adolphus J. Bryan observed that "most teachers who enter the field of English look upon composition as a necessary evil to overcome on their way to the goal of literature teaching" (6). Nor was Bryan misled about the institutional arrangement that supported the department's more esoteric studies in literature: he noted that Freshman English paid "the bill for expensive advanced courses" (7). In 1955, Edward Stone remarked the "schizophrenic" character of employment patterns in English:

> Trailing clouds of the glory of the graduate school . . . the young
> Ph.D. finds himself not only with the shades of his first prison term
> falling on him, but its manacles securely locked on his guiltless and
> unaccustomed wrists. Fuming and fretting like Tennyson's jilted
> young lover, he finds the doors to all the literature courses . . . barred,
> each ceaselessly guarded against trespass by its balding senile porter

> insolently clanking the keys of his office (or rustling his offprints). . . .
> Not only is he not permitted to teach an elective—not to mention a
> graduate—course for which he is qualified: he knows absolutely
> nothing about the subject of rhetoric, which he will spend the greater
> part of the next three or thirteen years teaching! (92)

In 1959, Philip R. Wikelund echoed terminology used earlier to characterize
teaching assistants in composition as "helots" and "slaves" (227). Again in
1959, a report on the teaching of English stated that "the teaching of composition is regarded as drudgery, is paid badly, and offers little opportunity for
advancement in rank. Typically it is thought to be only a steppingstone to the
teaching of literature" ("Basic Issues," Item 32). Indeed, the composition
assignment could be used as a punishment. Graff reports that Yvor Winters's
department chair at Stanford "kept him teaching freshman composition for
many years" because he disapproved of Winters' interests in poetry and criticism (153).

In 1971, Ray Kytle recounted his history as a teacher of composition. At
the large university where he did his graduate work, he noted, "composition
was taught almost exclusive by 'slaves,'" that is, by graduate students (339).
At another university, where he was then employed, Kytle noted that "composition is taught primarily by serfs—untenured and, by present criteria,
untenurable instructors. These people, most of whom would prefer to be
teaching literature, can expect to remain on the faculty for no more than 3 to
5 years." By the 1970s, English departments had begun the practice of admitting more people to doctoral-level graduate study than could possibly find
employment as full-time teachers of literature. While this practice provided
plenty of students for graduate seminars in literature, it had the unhappy
effect, Kytle thought, of lowering the status of composition instruction:

> To my mind, almost everything that is wrong with college composi-
> tion can be traced to the predominance of these two "solutions." For
> neither slaves nor serfs can be credited with important and significant
> insights and, perhaps most significantly, the occupation of slaves and
> serfs, in this case the teaching of composition, is inevitably reduced to
> the status of those people who are engaged in it. The profession does
> not respect college composition because it does not respect the people
> who teach it. (339)

Perhaps I should point out that Kytle is not remarking on the quality of instruction in required first-year composition. He is, rather, complaining about an institutional attitude, an attitude that is directly tied to hiring practices.

Certainly there is sufficient evidence here to suggest that English departments have colonized composition. An assignment to teach composition was used as a means of exclusion and as a way to punish teachers who were unfortunate enough to arouse the ire of some powerful figure. Thankfully, the image of slavery is no longer used to characterize people who teach composition. Nonetheless, a postdoctoral assignment to composition is still read by full-time English faculty as a professional deficiency. Even today, people who labor overlong at teaching composition find themselves shut out of tenurable positions in English departments.

7

"YOU CAN'T WRITE WRITING"

NORMAN FOERSTER AND THE BATTLE
OVER BASIC SKILLS AT IOWA

It is our present education which is highly specialized, one-sided, and narrow. It is an education dominated almost entirely by the mediaeval conception of learning. It is something which appeals for the most part simply to the intellectual aspects of our natures, our desire to learn, to accumulate information and to get control of the symbols of learning; not to our impulses and tendencies to make, to do, to create, to produce, whether in the form of utility or of art.

—John Dewey, *The School and Society*

On April 5, 1944, the faculty of the College of Liberal Arts at the State University of Iowa approved a new undergraduate program in general education. This program required all students enrolled in the college to take a foreign language and physical education, plus core courses in natural science, social science, literature, and history. The new program also required students to take a series of courses called "basic skills" if they could not demonstrate sufficient levels of competence in speaking, writing, and reading.

Iowa's new undergraduate requirements did not differ much from those adopted by many American universities during the forties under the headings of liberal or general education. At Iowa, however, adoption of the program was accomplished only after intense struggle among faculty and the administration. At least two prominent faculty members resigned because of their dismay over the program, and the unpleasantness surrounding its adoption may have played a role in the decision of the dean of liberal arts to take a presidency elsewhere, as he did in the year following the program's implementation. One of the faculty members who resigned was the eminent scholar and critic, Norman Foerster. In his letter of resignation, Foerster claimed to

be upset about a faculty promotion that had been made without his knowledge (he was director of the School of Letters at the time). However, other
documents and books, articles, memos, and letters written by Foerster himself suggest that his discomfort went far beyond chagrin at the supposed circumvention of his administrative authority.

Foerster joined the faculty at Iowa in 1930 as professor of English and
director of the School of Letters. Immediately after his arrival, he managed
to implement a two-year, twelve–credit hour course in literature that was
required of every student who matriculated in the College of Liberal Arts.
This hefty requirement was in keeping with Foerster's humanist sympathies,
which mandated that the development of taste and moral sensitivity was a
lengthy process. The course, at first called "Literature and the Art of Writing" and then simply "Reading and Writing," expected students to confront
"some of the central questions of human life as they have been represented in
literature" (1936, 15). Students read classical and Christian literature, including works by "Homer, the Greek tragedies, Plato, the Bible," and "works of
Chaucer, Shakespeare, and later English and American authors to suggest the
continuity of the tradition" (1946, vii). According to Foerster, the course
was not a "historical survey or a study of literary art; it was a study of human
values." Instruction in composition in the course supposedly took place in
connection with students' reading.

This ambitious course was not without problems. It was taught chiefly
by graduate students, since professors were not especially inclined to take on
a teaching responsibility that might interfere with their advancement (undated unsigned memo, Foerster papers).[1] The English Department worried
that the graduate students were inexperienced, overworked, and underpaid.
Certainly they were overworked: the typical teaching load was two sections,
and since each section could enroll as many as fifty or sixty students it must
have been difficult for the TAs to give much attention to students' writing.

Faculty in other departments complained about transgression of intellectual turf. The philosophy department expressed concern about the inclusion of Plato in the required course, and faculty in religious studies objected
to its use of the *King James Bible*. Apparently there were also complaints that
teachers of the course "indoctrinated" students (Foerster to Newburn, 15 May
1943). A professor of chemistry argued that if students were to be educated
in citizenship, twelve hours of political science would be preferable to the
same amount of literary study: "while every student should have a basic command of English, it seems to me as ridiculous to attempt to make all students

literary geniuses by cramming ancient literature down their throats as to make all students chemists or painters" (Glockler to Newburn, 23 August 1943). But Iowa's faculty had a more fundamental problem with the course, according to John C. Gerber: "there was a great deal of dissatisfaction in the faculty about that literature program. They admitted that the literature staff did a very good job teaching literature, but they thought it did a terrible job with writing. And they wanted more attention given to writing" (1993).

The two-year literature course came under concerted attack when planning for the new undergraduate program got under way. Late in 1943, the steering committee for the new curriculum proposed that composition be taught apart from literature. By that time Foerster was no longer attending meetings of the steering committee, although he had been a member since its inception in 1942. It is unclear whether he chose to absent himself from crucial meetings of the committee during December 1943 and January 1944 or whether he was asked to do so. At any rate, at those meetings the committee approved a plan that included a substantial component in the "basic skills" of reading, writing, and speaking. An individualized testing and advising program would be put in place in order to determine each student's abilities in these areas. Students who were deemed deficient in any of these skills would be required to take coursework until they could demonstrate competency. Literature, on the other hand, would be one of four "core" areas of studies in which students were expected to take eight hours of coursework.

Foerster responded to these decisions with an angry letter to the dean in which he argued vigorously against the proposed plan. He was particularly upset about the basic skills proposal which, according to him, separated reading and writing even though these arts are organically connected (Foerster to Newburn, 14 January 1944). He also asserted that the proposed plan abolished writing at the college level (apparently on the assumption that basic skills was not a college-level course); further, the new plan destroyed the twelve-hour literature course. This letter represented one of several attempts by Foerster to change the committee's decision. He resigned in protest from the steering committee. He enlisted the help of colleagues in the English Department in his cause; one historian of these events thinks that "other members of the English Department undoubtedly saw [the argument] in part as a battle to preserve departmental integrity" (Flanagan 206). In February, he presented the president of the university, Virgil Hancher, with the results of an informal survey he had undertaken in which he asked English teachers at other schools their opinion of the best way to teach freshman to write.

According to Foerster's reading of the data, none supported a plan like that proposed by Iowa's steering committee. In late March, Foerster presented an alternative core plan to the faculty at large, apparently attempting to circumvent the university curriculum committee's impending adoption of the proposed undergraduate program. He also requested Hancher's permission to appear at the meeting of the State Board of Education where the new program would be presented; his request was denied.

The debate became public in the spring of 1944. The citizens of Iowa were kept informed of its progress by local and regional newspapers that often relied on Foerster as their source. According to the *Des Moines Register*, for example, "officials of the school of letters charged that the committee had moved to separate writing from reading courses, and revamped literature courses, without consulting the head of the school of letters, the English department, the subcommittee on basic skills and the sub-committee on literature" ("Await"). In March, Foerster wrote a letter to the student newspaper, *The Daily Iowan*, in which he pointed out that he had resigned from the steering committee before its report was made public. Therefore, he claimed, the *DI* had misrepresented him by listing his name as a member of the committee and hence implying that he supported the proposal. He included his letter of resignation from the committee in this communiqué and asked the paper to reprint it, which it did.

Despite Foerster's efforts to derail it, the proposed program was brought to a vote of the college faculty and was approved, after heated discussion, by a vote of 105 to 80 (Crary 150–51). Foerster took the defeat very hard. In July he resigned his posts at the university and sent copies of his letter of resignation to Iowa newspapers. He claimed in this letter that it was not the new program that stimulated his resignation but the fact that he had lost his "freedom to administrate" ("Foerster Resigns"). Moreover, he feared that a "hard time" was in store for those who would not "collaborate with the new order." Despite his protestation, the *Cedar Rapids Gazette* leapt to the conclusion that Foerster had resigned because the vote had not gone his way: "the issue which led to Foerster's resignation was debated for months and it was decided against him by the liberal arts faculty itself" ("Foerster Resigns"). The *Gazette* also reported that he was "said to have believed the curriculum was becoming too vocational." Foerster's personal correspondence suggests that the newspaper's surmise was correct: he considered tendering his resignation four months earlier, before the plan had even gone to the faculty for a vote (Foerster to Boyd, 27 March 1944).

This outline of the events at Iowa demonstrates that a great deal was at stake in the argument over basic skills, intellectually and ethically, for Norman Foerster. In order to understand why the proposed undergraduate program was so repellent to him, it is necessary to know something about his educational values. Foerster was sufficiently interested in pedagogy and educational policy that he wrote extensively about both. A fuller explication of his program for humanistic education will explain why he felt that he could no longer continue working at a university that required independent courses in composition where writing was defined as a "basic skill."

FOERSTER'S HUMANISM

Norman Foerster's humanist credentials were impeccable. He studied at Harvard with the neohumanist Irving Babbitt, and many of his humanist beliefs were in deep sympathy with Babbitt's (Hoeveler). Even though he published a good deal of critical and historical work and edited a very successful anthology of American literature, Foerster is not now characterized as a great critic or a formidable scholar. Historians do agree, however, that he was extremely important to the disciplinary development of literary studies and creative writing. Graff (214) and Shumway (136) each credit him with the legitimation of American literature as a field of academic study. Shumway argues that Foerster's work was influential in diminishing the hold of historical scholarship on literary studies, thus opening up a space for criticism. He asserts as well that Foerster's readings of American literature played an important role in shaping its current canon. Graff notes Foerster's important role in legitimizing creative writing as a field within English studies (138). This work began at Iowa, where, in his capacity as director of the School of Letters, Foerster convinced the graduate college to accept so-called "creative" scholarship in lieu of a critical or scholarly dissertation, which provision opened the way for the development of the Writer's Workshop (Wilbers 44).[2] The present incarnation of the workshop would not please Foerster, who had no use for creative writing as an end in itself. Rather, he intended that provision for a creative thesis would strengthen literary study, on the assumption that graduate students' attempts to produce imaginative literature would enhance their understanding of it and hence improve their critical skills. He told the *Daily Iowan* that "the success of this departure in graduate study cannot be judged by the production of masterpieces of imaginative and critical literature"; rather, its object was "to give all types of literary students a rigorous and appropriate discipline" ("Iowa's School"). Foerster also altered the complexion of the English Department during his tenure at Iowa; in 1939 he hired Austin Warren and Rene Wellek, which in effect moved the department away from scholarship and toward criticism. In 1941, Foerster, Welleck, and Warren, along with linguist John McGalliard and writer Wilbur Schramm, published *Literary Scholarship, Its Aims and Methods,* a manifesto that argued against scholarly specialization.

Foerster undertook all of these efforts as means of realizing his humanist ideals. Much of his scholarly work, including his innovative readings of American literary texts, was also undertaken in this attempt. Between 1928 and 1946 he published half a dozen books and essays that outlined his humanist program for American education.

In *Toward Standards* (1928), Foerster defined humanism as "a general idea, an attitude toward life or way of life. It represents man's effort to define or realize his humanity as distinguished from his animality, on the one hand, and his divinity on the other" (6). Foerster articulated his humanism in response to what he took to be the current intellectual and moral climate of the country; he called this climate "naturalism." Against naturalist skepticism, he insisted that belief is inevitable:

> we live by belief, by faith, by that which we provisionally know: that which appears to us most nearly to correspond with reality, or rather with experience, or rather still with those portions of experience that we choose to value. Shrinking from the spectre of sterility—that everlasting No—we make our affirmations, today no less than in the past, identifying our belief with the truth. (158)

This confident association of humanist belief with truth was the main source of contemporary complaints about its doctrinaire stance. To admit the provisionality (and multiplicity) of belief and yet assert that one's own belief is the truth seems at best contradictory and at worst arrogant. Yet Foerster persisted in this creed, since to him the perceived alternative was worse. That alternative, which he characterized as a "deterministic monism," was the naturalistic assumption that reason and empirical investigation could explain the behavior of all creatures, including human beings, since all creatures were motivated by their biological natures (159).

Foerster argued to the contrary that science was helpless to assist in "the main concern of man" since the essential experience of human life lies within the realm of values (160). His attitude toward science was subtle: he acknowledged that the natural sciences had "done valuable service in acquainting man intimately with the bond that exists between him and external nature" (153). However, he rejected explanations of human motivation that were grounded in nature or natural explanations. Moral habits, he wrote, could not be "explained by the process of evolution." This was so because of the saving remnant of human nature—its spiritual capacity. According to Foerster, human beings have a dual nature, which distinguishes them from other creatures: while subject to their biological natures to some extent, humans can also exert free will. His warrants for this argument were "the Greek and the Christian" textual traditions, both of which certified that "men are still conscious of an inner conflict, insusceptible of reconciliation, between the expression of a natural desire and the will to conform to a standard of values." Since humans had free will, they were free, within the constraints of tradition, to choose their paths in life. This meant, in turn, that they were responsible for their actions (165). This provision secured humanism from what Foerster took to be the disastrous determinism of naturalism, which explained human behavior in terms of biology, psychology, or physiology. He was concerned that biological and psychological determinisms released human beings from their obligation to behave ethically. He was further disturbed by the naturalist assumptions that man was a "unitary rather than a dual being" and that "the creative expression of the self must not be hindered from without by convention nor from within by inhibition" (151). He doubted whether the creed of the self could give "full play to the individual" and at the same time offer "the needful amount of protection to society."

Foerster's commitment to humanism deepened during the late 1930s and into the 1940s. Like many Americans, he interpreted the Second World War as a conflict over values, and he did not hesitate to associate the humanities with the right values. In the preface to *The Humanities After the War* (1944), he positioned humanist values as the entire point of the war effort:

> what the humanities seek to preserve and promote constituted the very aim of our fighting in a world in danger of being overwhelmed by the inhumanities. Against an expert barbarism misusing science we proposed to defend the values of civilization—justice, decency, tolerance, freedom, including academic freedom to pursue knowledge. These values we had foolishly taken for granted. After the war, if we are not to repeat that tragic error, they must be cherished and extended. (v)

In this volume Foerster argued passionately for the resurrection of the "true" humanities—history, literature and the arts, philosophy and religion—as a means of bringing about an intellectual and spiritual reorientation. He argued with equal passion against those who, he implied, were in some way responsible for the war since they "place political and economic planning in the foreground" and find "the internal excellence of man" in "externals, in things, in a certain minimum of possessions, from which they go on to argue that lasting peace depends upon a constantly rising standard of living throughout the world" (29). While Foerster at times showed respect for the so-called "common man" he was not above excoriating "the people": "the public lives in the present, not in history; looks to literature and the arts for entertainment and the adornment of life; leaves philosophy to the harmless specialist; and has been all but weaned away from its religious loyalties" (30). However, he unhesitatingly placed blame for this situation on purveyors of the "false humanities," historians who preferred facts to interpretation or "some kind of economic interpretation of the past"; literary artists and scholars who were more concerned with developing technique or amassing facts than they were with inculcating values; materialist and naturalist philosophers; and religious leaders who grew "more and more secular" (30). All in all, university intellectuals seemed to Foerster to have adopted the methods of social science and to have abandoned all that was worthwhile in tradition: ethics, creativity, idealism, faith.

Foerster's humanism was unrelentingly conservative. He took the conservative's dim view of human nature, in which human beings—who are suspended between their animal desires and their spiritual aspirations—need discipline. Foerster thought that the appropriate discipline would be instilled by an education that taught time-honored values. His humanism was also conservative in its reverence for a patriarchal past. However, Foerster assumed that all people were teachable, and so he counted his views as superior, not necessarily to those of the untutored masses, but to the views of educated persons who bought into what he took to be a wrongheaded and potentially evil ideology. He thought that social scientists and professors of education, in particular, ought to be counted among this group.

Foerster's animus toward naturalism was repeatedly directed at those who attempted to adapt the values as well as the methods of science to the study of human nature. He condemned "scientism," which he defined as the "disposition to believe in general progress and to attach one's hopes, not to any tradition or folkways carried over from a dying past, but to the contributions of science in the vital present and the unborn future" (1937, 120). He particularly resented the scientistic pretense to ideological neutrality, when, after all, scientism preached materialism, relativism, and evolutionism. He averred that naturalistic scholars possessed the sort of "literal mind" that caused little harm in the natural sciences, where it was checked by the rigor of scientific method, but which "works havoc in subjects like sociology and education, where it is free to run wild in disregard of complexities and intangibilities" (128). Such a mind was utterly undisciplined, Foerster thought, spending "much of its time in thinking what it wishes."

From a humanist point of view, this is not an unfounded rant. Humanists believed, correctly, that adoption of the ideal of scientific research had led universities to reject prescribed curricula and to embrace the elective system. For thinkers like Babbitt and Foerster, it followed that electivity had led to the decay of standards, since in the context of naturalism the elective system prompted educators to build curricula around individual needs rather than received tradition. Babbitt thought that the elective system was the institutional expression of naturalists' tendency to "identify the ideal needs of the individual with his temperamental leaning" and to "exalt instinct and idiosyncrasy" (1908, 121). He noted sarcastically that naturalists "in their endeavor to satisfy the variety of temperaments, would push the principle of election almost down to the nursery, and devise, if possible, a separate system of education for every individual." Foerster, too, bemoaned the new emphasis on individual needs: "we find enthroned in the modernist school, not Latin, history, and mathematics, but Tom, Dick, and Harry. . . . Each individual, having found his hobby, is to ride it to the limit" (1938, 42). The principle of electivity implied that any human interest could become an academic field of study, and the absence of prescription further implied that all courses of study were equally valuable. Foerster was aghast at the implication that fields like psychology and sociology were on an ethical par with literature, history, and philosophy. Sifting through college catalogs, he found plenty to excite his ire: courses in celestial mechanics, hygiene and plays of childhood, the League of Nations, first aid, applied shorthand theory, upholstery and weaving, philosophy of business, business English, and urban sociology (1937, 86). The diversity and lack of center betrayed by this bewildering array of studies were anathema to him.

HUMANISM AND EDUCATION

Foerster realized that his was a minority voice. In 1938, he predicted a bleak future for the traditional liberal arts, since educational philosophy seemed to be turning more and more in the pragmatist direction espoused by John Dewey (Foerster 1937, 4). Foerster characterized Dewey as a contemporary sophist who had rejected "all permanent values and all tradition" (1946, 19). He did not hesitate to speak of Dewey and Marx in the same sentence, arguing that their rejection of traditional values permitted them to suppose that they were free to remake human nature so that "we shall all delight in serving everybody else; we shall all be happy cogs in the world machine, the world beehive, and nobody will want to sting anybody else, because everybody will be secure and appreciated" (1938, 4). Foerster was not convinced that human happiness could be achieved through social engineering of any kind, including education; in his opinion the result of such engineering was more likely to be a "slave state." He sincerely doubted that human beings could be induced to behave themselves through having all their physical wants satisfied, and so he feared the social impact of any educational philosophy that attempted to develop individuals who were free to pursue their interests wherever they led. He detested the lack of discipline that he associated with Dewey's approach to education:

> Humanism is not content to let Nature take her course. Education does not consist in throwing down the reins. As Aristotle suggested, we become human largely by resisting our own natural tendencies, pulling ourselves back toward the mean just as people straighten pieces of wood that are warped. The child, the youth, must be preserved from his imperious natural temperament and from the tyranny of his special aptitude by the imposition of human culture. (1937, 254)

This characterization is unfair to Dewey, who never advocated nonintervention in students' lives (Holt 1994, and see chapter 8). But it does point up the fact that irreconcilable differences existed between Foerster and advocates of progressive education. Where progressives began with students, he would begin with subjects and texts; where progressives idealized individual potential, he valorized a common cultural heritage.

Now if the point of education is indeed to transmit the cultural wisdom contained in canonical texts, it makes perfect sense to establish a common curriculum in which most or all of the coursework is required. Foerster would have been quite happy to restore the sort of education that took place in the classical American college, although he knew that such a proposal would not find many adherents in the late 1930s. So he did the next best thing: in *The American State University* (1937) he devised an ideal liberal arts curriculum that could be required of all students. The point of such a program would be "the requirement of direct contact with some of the first minds of the ages, as the primary means of learning how to think" (259). Imposition of this requirement would eventually cleanse the entire university curriculum of the excrescences it had recently developed: "it would soon begin to force a pruning of the curriculum, for there are many fields of study in the present state universities in which great minds have never interested themselves." Subjects dear to naturalistic educators, such as "hygiene, psychology, logic, and English," would give way to a curriculum featuring only those subjects in which great minds were interested: mathematics and natural science, history, literature, and philosophy and religion (259–60).

Foerster's rejection of "English" underscores his scorn for modern disciplinary boundaries. He disdained what he took to be the scholarly pedantry associated with philological research, and he was contemptuous of composition instruction conducted apart from literary study. His categorical rejection of English also highlights his belief that literature was not just the property of a single department; rather, it was a central concern of the humanities. His notion of literature was very broad, in keeping with his humanist conviction that all students should become acquainted with the best that has been thought and said. As we have seen, Foerster's common curriculum in literature encompassed study of the Bible and of ancient Greek literature, as well as masterpieces of English literature. But he would also include what he called "American state papers"—the Constitution, the Declaration of Independence, Jefferson's work, the Federalist Papers, the "Gettysburg Address." He also recommended the study of "foreign" languages on literary grounds. In his ideal curriculum, students would be required to take two of six "principal languages"—Greek, Latin, Italian, French, Spanish, and German—in order to gain access to "the great literature of the Occident" (1937, 261). His chauvinism clearly emerged when he remarked that even though Greek was a dead language, it is "far more alive, more vital to us, than many 'living' languages, such as Portuguese—not to mention the African dialects—which do not unlock comparable treasures" (262).

Composition also had a place in Foerster's ideal curriculum, but the kind of composition that was to be studied in English departments would be different from that expected elsewhere. While it was "plainly the responsibility of the department of English to afford training in well-organized communication of facts and ideas," he thought, training in composition could "produce a regular habit rather than a casual capacity" only if faculty in every department saw to it that students' writing possessed "a decent correctness and clearness" (263). When Foerster wrote about composition, he always distinguished its "remedial" aspects—spelling, punctuation, sentence construction—from the higher-order functions that were presumably best taught in connection with literary study. He subscribed fully to the modern humanist assumption that an informed acquaintance with great texts was adequate preparation for those who wished to express themselves in writing.

THE STRUGGLE OVER THE CORE

Foerster must have realized in 1942 that talk at Iowa about a new undergraduate program represented an opportunity for him to implement the ideal course of study he had depicted in *The American State University*. Surely he would not have agreed to serve on the steering committee had he not had some such goal in mind.

The undergraduate curriculum was the brainchild of the newly appointed dean of the College of Liberal Arts, Harry K. Newburn. It is not clear whether Foerster knew that Newburn was a progressive educator. In a lecture given in 1943 Newburn argued that education should be conceived "in terms of changes in individual behavior rather than in terms of subjects to be studied or courses to be completed" (104). To his way of thinking, students were not to be made to measure up to predetermined standards; rather, during their stay at the university they were to be given whatever was necessary "to further their intellectual and emotional growth" (105). Foerster would certainly have been alarmed by the new dean's rejection of prescribed subjects and his focus on students' needs, if he were made aware of them. And so he may have wangled an invitation to serve on the steering committee precisely in order to head off this sort of talk. Whatever his reason for agreeing to serve, a clash became inevitable when the formidable humanist began to discuss curriculum with Newburn and the group of scientists and social scientists who constituted the steering committee. As is often the case in university settings, the participants in this drama tried to work out their vast epistemological differences by maneuvering in committee.

The struggle between Foerster and the steering committee focused on the size and content of the core courses. At a meeting of the committee in January 1943, Foerster moved the adoption of a thirty-two-hour core, of which the largest section was a twelve-hour literature requirement (ten hours were allotted to natural sciences and ten to history and social science). This motion was unanimously approved. It is unclear whether Foerster actually supported this relatively small core or whether he simply made the motion in order to get discussion started. In any case, he later proposed larger core course plans ranging from forty-two to sixty hours. Now, Foerster had two reasons for supporting a larger core: first, he truly was interested in requiring students to get an education in the liberal arts as he defined them; second, as discussion progressed, committee members and other faculty who supported a smaller core inevitably suggested that the literature requirement be reduced. An undated unsigned document in Foerster's papers justifies the scope of the literature course, thus suggesting that the size of the requirement had indeed come under fire:

> This two-year course is conceived as an organic whole, and can neither be telescoped into one year nor cut off at the end of one year. If only 6 hours are required, the course will have to be abandoned, and something put in its place. What? Shall we have to take the reactionary step, at a time when world literature is fast growing in importance, of returning to the pre-1930 setup of a year of "Constructive Rhetoric" followed by a year of "English Literature"— indeed, not even that, but requiring only one of these courses? It might well be wiser to make English a wholly elective subject. (Foerster Papers, University of Iowa archives, Iowa City)

Foerster's handwritten notes on this document suggest that he considered dispersing the literature requirement into other departments—history, art, philosophy, political science, and religion. So it is clear that he was not merely defending turf when he defended the size of the literature course; indeed, he was even willing at this point to remove English studies from the core.

By April 1943, proposed curriculum changes had been discussed in a meeting of the liberal arts faculty as a whole, subcommittee reports had been circulated, and presumably the workings of the various committees were the subject of hallway conversations. By that time at least three core plans were in circulation among members of the steering committee, all of which reduced the literature requirement to eight or ten hours. In May of that year, Foerster tried one more time to enlarge the core. He proposed a cleverly designed forty-hour plan to the steering committee. This plan divided required coursework into six areas: physics, biology, history, social science, the "quest for human values (literature, philosophy, religion)," and two years of writing instruction ("For the Steering Committee," 1 May 1943). He then noted that the smaller program suggested by the dean involved the "sacrifice" of "two-thirds of the above common or socialized education"; either one of the sciences, history or social studies, or writing, had to go if the dean's plan were adopted. Of course there was no question for Foerster of dropping the values portion of the plan, and he would have considered the retention of history at the expense of social science to be a positive gain. He was also ready to jettison writing instruction, if it came to that.

In notes made for a joint meeting of the steering committee and the literature subcommittee two days later, he again appealed for adoption of a forty-hour core, allotting twelve hours each to literature, social studies, and science, plus four elective hours. He could see "no reason," he wrote, "to destroy the common core and set up flimsy courses—when these sacrifices can be avoided by a plan calling for 40 hours instead of 36" (unsigned, 3 May 1943). In this meeting, Foerster's objections to the smaller core revolved around the possible elimination of history and the reduction of the literature requirement to eight hours, which would, in his opinion, require the "omission of American literature and contemporary literature," as well as "neglect of the aesthetic approach," which was serious in his view because there was no common core requirement in the fine arts. Furthermore, it was "a large order" for an eight-hour course in literature to attend to the "spiritual, emotional, and aesthetic development" of students.

But Foerster's views in this matter did not prevail. At its meetings on December 27 and 30, when Foerster was "out of the city," the steering committee approved a thirty-two-hour core that included an eight-hour literature requirement. In March 1944, well after the steering committee had approved its plan, Foerster scheduled a conference with Newburn. At that meeting he tried one last time to enlarge the common core, arguing this time for a sixty-hour plan, with fourteen hours allotted to science, twelve to history, eighteen to foreign language, and the rest, presumably, to literature, religion, and philosophy. According to Foerster's notes, Newburn insisted on limiting the core to thirty or forty hours, in which eight hours each would be devoted to science and social science and none to history and language. After this meeting, Foerster began to characterize Newburn as an "educationist," a term that was, for him, a specific variant of "naturalist."

THE ENGLISH DEPARTMENT AND BASIC SKILLS

Early on in planning for the new curriculum, Newburn apparently realized that the issue of "basic skills" ought to be considered apart from the question of core courses. During the summer of 1942, then, he appointed a subcommittee to study this issue. This committee was chaired by a member of the English department, Bartholow V. Crawford. Two assistant professors of English, Carrie Stanley and Joseph Baker, sat on the committee. Baker was an outspoken Foerster partisan; "Miss Stanley," as she is everywhere referred to, ran a writing laboratory in which she oversaw individualized instruction for students who had demonstrated a need for it. She ran this lab because her rhetoric course had been displaced in 1930 by Foerster's twelve-hour literature course.

Aside from its considerable presence on the Basic Skills Committee, members of the English Department showed little interest in this part of the developing curriculum. They were much more interested in the literature subcommittee, which had been charged with the responsibility of returning a plan for a literature core to the steering committee. Foerster attended the first meeting of this subcommittee, and the minutes of that meeting record his remark that the study of literature was not to be confused with the acquisition of skills (Minutes of the Subcommittee on Literature, 25 May 1942). The minutes also note that "Professor Foerster spoke at some length on the place of the humanities in the curriculum."

After reinforcing his views at the initial meeting of the subcommittee on literature, Foerster did not regularly attend meetings of the group. Nonetheless, his influence cannot be missed in its discussions or in the report it eventually approved and sent to the steering committee. On May 17, 1943, for example, the literature subcommittee responded negatively to the sample curricular plans being circulated by the steering committee, on the ground that the proposed eight- or ten-hour requirements in literature would seriously reduce the time available for class discussion. Such a reduction, in fact, would "mean the virtual omission of classroom instruction in writing at the college level." In other words, if the size of the literature requirement were to be reduced, composition would have to go. In its final report, the subcommittee asserted its belief that "the study of literature is fundamental" to liberal education; consequently, they "were opposed to any attempt to reduce the amount of literature which has hitherto been studied in the required course in English, and are convinced that, instead, the present program should be strengthened" ("Report: Subcommittee on Basic Skills," 1). The authors of the report resorted to solidly humanist grounds to support the position that composition instruction should be carried on in connection with literary study: "effective self-expression is, in fact, characteristic of the cultivated man; his speech, including conversational style, shows the influence of his reading, and his writing shows it" (2). Members of the subcommittee could tolerate the establishment of "a separate course in the basic skills of composition (grammar, punctuation, spelling, sentence structure, diction, and paragraphing)," but, they noted, since such a course was "remedial" in nature, "it will hardly point toward that positive and effective use of language which is best taught with the constant challenge of the masters of the art of writing" (6). That is to say, composition taught in connection with literature is a college-level study. The subcommittee on literature simply could not imagine an intellectually serious composition course independent of literary study.

On January 29, 1944, Seymour Pitcher, who directed the twelve-hour literature course at that time, paid a visit to Dean Newburn. This visit occurred on the day before the steering committee adopted the basic skills plan. Pitcher wrote a memorandum of the meeting, a copy of which made its way into Foerster's papers. During their conversation, the dean apparently mentioned concern on the part of scientists on the faculty that "composition should not be taught 'narrowly' to serve the purposes of literary study" (Pitcher, Memorandum, 1). When Pitcher asked if the aim of the proposed basic skills course was to teach students how to write scientific articles, the dean countered that its point was to teach students to think, "but not necessarily in connection with problems advanced in literature" (1). Composition ought to get about the same amount of attention in literature as it does in sociology, the dean thought, thus indicating his assumption that literature was a discipline like any other. Newburn also assured Pitcher that the basic skills course was indeed college-level work. What was new about it was that the teaching of composition would be "fitted to the individual student's needs."

A note in Foerster's handwriting appears at the bottom of this memo. It says: "wash our hands of B. S."

FOERSTER ON COMPOSITION

Norman Foerster did not teach the twelve-hour literature course that he tried so hard to protect. In fact, he did not teach composition after he advanced to senior rank in 1914. Despite his lack of teaching experience in basic courses, Foerster nonetheless fancied himself something of an expert on their design. In his January letter to Dean Newburn, he recounted what he took to be his credentials in this area:

> I was invited to North Carolina as chairman of the course, and over a period of eight or ten years sponsored three different plans. I became the author or editor of seven textbooks for freshman and sophomore English, two of which have been used more widely than any others in the field (but I have never recommended any of them for adoption at Iowa). At Iowa I found what seemed to me an unsound and outmoded plan, and proposed the course we have developed experimentally through the years. . . . As President of the College English Association, I urged my ideas and found widespread approval of them. In regard to freshman students deficient in writing, I believe I have known intimately all the ways of dealing with the problem of basic skill. . . . I have read much in the professional journals in English, and better than that, have secured inside reports from other institutions and the "lowdown" of confidential oral comment. (14 January 1944)

All of this, Foerster thought, made him an authority on composition. Most assuredly, he was not defending a "vested interest" when he proposed to substitute a literature course for the proposed basic skills program; he merely advocated what he knew to be sound practice.

Foerster did not mention in this letter that many of his textbooks were anthologies. Aside from the early *Outlines and Summaries* (1915), he wrote only two composition textbooks, both in collaboration with J. M. Steadman of Emory University (Brereton 1988, 47). *Sentences and Thinking* (1919) and *Writing and Thinking* (1931) are fairly ordinary redactions of current-traditional lore about the composition of various units of discourse—sentences, paragraphs, essays. Their single departure from tradition is the somewhat surprising attribution of their theory of invention to Samuel Taylor Coleridge. Both books begin by asserting that writing and thinking are "organically" related. The authors tell their readers, in fact, that thoughts grow into mature compositions just as seeds grow into trees, and they illustrate the principles of sentence composition with diagrams that represent branching trees. According to Foerster and Steadman, great literary artists did not "plan their compositions with rule and compass and cleverly arrange fine words —did not work mechanically—but, having a given idea to express, they allowed it to grow from within, nourishing it with a mental and spiritual attention, till it was ready to issue as a work of art" (*Writing and Thinking* 4).

This theoretical stance committed Foerster and Steadman to a strong version of the current-traditional canard that writing represents thinking: since literary artists work organically, the form in which their work is found is "the only possible form for the particular thought they had" (*Writing and Thinking* 4). In fact, sentences themselves are exact representations of thought; the perfect sentence "must express a thought, one thought, not part of a thought, nor more than a thought" (5–6). Hence paraphrase and translation are impossible, since to alter even a word is to alter the thought.

A more thorough contempt for composition would be hard to find, unless it is Shelley's assertion that "when composition begins, inspiration is already on the decline, and the most glorious poetry that has even been communicated to the world is probably a feeble shadow of the original conceptions of the poet" (511). Shelley admitted that his theory of composing required poets to be in touch with the divine. Whatever Foerster and Steadman thought about poets' access to divine inspiration, their adoption of this organic theory of composing put them in something of a pedagogical bind. If it is true that each of us exactly expresses our thoughts in language (when we are in organic harmony with our natures at least) there is really no point in discussing the art of composing—each of us simply records our thoughts onto paper and has done with it. It follows that the quality of our productions is exactly representative of the quality of our thoughts—the better we think, the better we write. Of course the obverse is also true: if the writing is "vague and feeble, we may safely assume that the writer's thought was vague and feeble" (*Writing and Thinking* 6). No amount of attention to composition can make up for lacks in the writer's thinking.

Given the very small role played by composition in this theory of invention, Foerster and Steadman should have been hard put to justify the more than four hundred pages of rules that followed their enunciation of this bit of romantic nonsense. They justified the imposition of rules by simply exempting students from the scope of their theory: "it would be fatal for the student of composition to assume . . . that all the rules of syntax and rhetoric are superfluous, that he need merely contemplate his thoughts and depend upon them for the sentences that will convey them to other men" (7). Students were not to use the organic theory of composing in their own work, since

> after all, the sentence organism has certain definite laws that may be
> learned and applied. While it is true that the thought determines the

expression, that my thought requires my expression, it is also true, happily, that in the main all men think alike. We are all individuals, but individuals of the same species. Broadly speaking, our thoughts are those of all other men; if they were not, other men could not understand us. (7)

Of course this contradicts the theoretical position they had just taken about the utter congruity of an individual's language with her thought process. In the absence of a theory of composition that posed language or ideology as a source of commonality among humans, Foerster and Steadman were forced to attribute the fact of communication to species-specific similarities among "men," a position that should have alarmed Foerster the ardent antinaturalist.

The problem was that on the Romantic model there is no way to explain the perceived superiority of some literary texts without the notion of individual genius, unless critics are willing to fall back on a more rhetorical critical theory that maintains that standards of taste are constructed by the communities that produce and consume art. Romantic critics are ordinarily averse to doing this. So when their professed organicism led them to a theory of radical individualism, as it inevitably must, Foerster and Steadman immediately drew back into the humanist refuge of universals—all "men" think alike. They did so, perhaps, because of the humanist desire for a firm and universal center; to accept radical individualism is to accept the principle of difference, and Foerster's tirades against progressivism demonstrate that he was not willing to accept such a principle. But this fallback involved them in contradiction once again, because of the scarcely hidden contempt in which humanists hold composing, particularly when it is being done by students. Foerster and Steadman simply could not bring themselves to apply to students a theory of composing that requires a notion of genius. A humanist theory of composition requires some notion of a superior individual, just as romanticism does. The difference is that humanists allow for the effects of education; the ability to express oneself is the product of superior breeding, but it may also be cultivated by reading the right books, going to the right schools, and hanging about with the right people. Students, by definition, are still undergoing this process of education, and hence they cannot be thought of as contenders for the status of genius.

Perhaps it is unfair to indict Foerster in this way on the basis of a brief passage that appears in coauthored textbooks. Quite possibly, the contradiction resulted from the collaboration. However, the passage cited above appears in all editions of both textbooks, unaltered over a period of better than twenty years' time and through many editions. What is even more strange is that the romantic theory of composition on which Foerster and Steadman relied in these textbooks is part and parcel of the naturalism that Foerster rejected so vigorously in the scholarship I have already reviewed.[3] I can only conclude that he either did not notice or did not care about the contradiction that marred the textbooks on the basis of which he claimed expertise in composition.

AFTER IOWA

In the summer of 1944 John C. Gerber, who had been teaching in Mortimer Adler's "Great Books" program at the University of Chicago, was chosen by the heads of the departments of Speech and English at Iowa to head up the new program in basic skills. At the time of his appointment, Gerber was unaware of the conflict that resulted in Foerster's resignation from the university. He recounts that in August, as he was unpacking his books, Foerster appeared briefly in the doorway to his office and said: "I want you to know that I don't blame you for what has taken place" (Gerber 1993).

Apparently, Foerster was not able to forget what happened at Iowa even after he left Iowa City. In 1949, he contributed an essay to a collection of articles dealing with communication and general education, edited by Earl J. McGrath. McGrath had been appointed dean of liberal arts at Iowa upon Newburn's departure, but he had subsequently become secretary of the federal Department of Education. A prominent essay in McGrath's collection, written by one John C. Gerber, described Iowa's flourishing program in communication skills. Other contributors wrote glowing accounts of the successes achieved in communication skills programs. It is difficult to guess why Foerster agreed to participate in this project, since most of the essays describe freshman programs that he would have detested. Perhaps he felt that his contribution, called "Teaching the College Student to Write," represented a necessary corrective to other work in the collection written by linguists, general semanticists, clinicians, and teachers of speech.

In his essay Foerster quoted with approval from an article written by a former colleague at Iowa, Wendell Johnson. This is a bit odd, since Foerster and Johnson were not at all intellectually compatible. Johnson was a psychologist who ran a speech and hearing clinic at the university, and he was a fellow traveler with the general semantics movement. He, too, had been vocal during the curriculum revision, but he had argued that Iowa should adopt a curriculum with "a consistently scientific orientation" (A Core Curriculum, 17 September 1943). He proposed that core courses consist of a three-hour course called "Basic Mechanisms of Language Behavior," plus three hours each of psychology, social science, and fine arts, and six hours each of mathematics, science, and literature. Nor was the essay from which Foerster quoted compatible with humanist attitudes toward composition. Entitled "You Can't Write Writing" and published in *ETC: A Journal of General Semantics,* Johnson's piece castigated English teachers who had supposedly concentrated their teaching on grammatical correctness with such intensity that they had failed to teach his graduate students to write "with significance and validity" (102). He blamed this failure on English teachers' focus on writing as writing, rather than on writing about something. Johnson made an analogy to reading classes, in which he saw a similar failure:

> one cannot read reading. One can only read history or geometry or biology, etc. If the child reads such material in the reading class, then it is difficult to see how the reading class differs appreciably from the classes in history, geometry, and other subjects. If the child does not read such material in the reading class, then the reading class must differ from these others, but in a puzzling way, for it may be that the reading teacher is actually making the amazing effort to get the child to read reading. (102)

Of course this is a specious argument that turns on a subtle shift in the use of the term *reading*. Classes using the same readings may approach those materials in a variety of ways, and, as we now know, there are as many ways of reading as there are of complaining about English teachers' failure to teach their students to write. Nor does the analogy of "reading reading" to "writing writing" quite hold; Johnson asserted that "what one writes about writing will have little, if any, significance, except insofar as one writes about writing about something else" (103). This remark of course overlooks the whole of literary criticism as well as an enormous body of commentary on composing written by poets, writing teachers, and psychologists.

Johnson also explicitly rejected the sort of writing instruction advocated by Foerster. He argued that trying to learn to write by reading literary texts was "like trying to learn to bake a cake by eating one" (108). And with an embarrassing echo of the theory of composition adumbrated in Foerster's textbooks, Johnson argued that a central problem with English teachers' teaching of writing was that they believed that since writing is an art, it "cannot be taught at all. Only God can make a tree; the teacher of English can only water the tree with verbal dew in the hope of keeping it green" (109). Needless to say, Johnson thought that this was so much romantic hogwash.

Nonetheless Foerster used Johnson's argument to authorize his own position that writing could not be taught apart from some subject matter, and of course the subject matter he preferred was literature. He argued yet again that "what is needed is a two-year course in literature and in writing about it," given that literature was the subject "in which the English department is most competent and most interested" (1949, 210). By this time Foerster was able to see that "writing about something" and "writing for someone" were rhetorical principles. But he was utterly unable to comprehend that rhetoric itself might be an appropriate "subject matter" for composition; indeed, he seemed unaware that rhetoric had any content at all. That may be why he was so intent on using literature as a source of rhetorical inspiration.

In 1946 Foerster published a slim volume entitled *The Humanities and the Common Man: The Democratic Role of The State Universities.* While this essay once again rehearsed the educational policies he advocated throughout his career, it is hard not to read it as a scarcely veiled attack on the faculty and administration at Iowa. The book begins with a litany of the intellectual sins committed by faculty at universities in the "Middle West"; adherents of these "half-truths and errors" believed in naturalism, materialism, scientific neutrality, relativism, contempt for the past, elevation of research over teaching and skills over knowledge, job-centered education, student-centered education, vocational education, and individualization of instruction (10ff). Foerster railed against core courses; he railed against the use of faculty advisers because it entrusted "the cause of liberal education" to "the specialist" (17). He took yet another shot at "educationists," those professors of education who followed in the footsteps of Rousseau, Darwin, Spencer, and Dewey, who thought that experimental studies would teach them how to teach, who substituted individualized attention to students for the possession of real knowledge. In the section of the text devoted to "the great faculty," he opined that excellent professors must be hired by humanistic department heads "because the dean, as likely as not, will not know the difference between the right sort and the wrong sort" (49). In his peroration, he reminded those who would plan the universities of the future that "an educational leadership of faith and courage may be defeated in the end, but it is better to be defeated in the end than at the beginning" (60). Perhaps Foerster felt that he had been defeated by events at Iowa, but his career was hardly over. He secured other positions and continued to write long after his retirement from teaching.

Moreover, the humanism that Foerster defended so fiercely has not died. It has in fact been powerfully resurrected by the likes of Lynn Cheney and William Bennett, both of whom have used their national prominence as a bully pulpit from which to argue for a return to the traditional values honored within humanist education. In an eerie echo of Foerster, E. D. Hirsch, author of *Cultural Literacy* (1987), recently took issue with "educational naturalism," which he associates with progressivism (Kelly). He advocates, rather, that American schools return to a "'knowledge-based curriculum,' heavy on content so that students become conversant with the cultural underpinnings of their world." And Stephen Balch and Rita Zuercher of the National Association of Scholars recently bemoaned the demise of required courses ("Less Costs More"). At the same time, they noted with alarm "a dramatic increase in the number of schools offering what best can be described as 'remedial' composition courses (though the word is avoided), frequently for credit." Presumably the NAS approves of a universally required freshman course as long as it upholds "standards" and does not pander to students' needs.

One thing remains intact that would not please Foerster, however. The "basic skills" course at the University of Iowa is still required of all entering students who cannot demonstrate a sufficient level of competency in speaking and writing. The use of literary texts in the class is still discouraged. I do not know what Foerster might make of the fact that the course is now called "Rhetoric."

8

FRESHMAN ENGLISH AND WAR

Since World War II, teachers of composition have had to endure an extraordinary amount of dogma and nonsense that has been sprayed over the composition course by the theologicians of communication. Teachers have been afflicted by the fancies of semanticists, communications skillists, and linguisticians, singly and en masse. They have been pragmatized, scientificated, and sometimes nearly obliterated. . . . Like street cars, a new delusion came along every hour.
—A. M. Tibbetts, "A Short History of Dogma and Nonsense in
   the Composition Course"

When it does not please us, we call it propaganda; when it does please us, we call it education.
—Norman Foerster, *The Future of the Liberal College*

Universal requirements prosper in wartime. Wars cause university teachers and administrators to circle the curricular wagons, to multiply requirements, and to clamp down on electivity. Historian Robert J. Connors remarks that "wars seem to create a desire for tradition and stasis where they can be achieved on the home front" (1996, 2). Certainly the advent of World War II firmly cemented in place the universal requirement in introductory composition, even though it brought about enormous changes in the curriculum of Freshman English itself. These changes occurred directly, through the armed forces' intervention into the curriculum of the basic required course, and indirectly through the war rhetoric that accompanied and followed the actual conflict.

The required course was also influenced during the war years by its centrality to general education and its teachers' interest in communication skills. The communication skills episode affected the history of Freshman English in a number of important ways. For one thing, the development of this new approach to the basic course instigated the establishment of a professional association for its teachers: the Conference on College Composition and Communication. The definition of writing as communication rather than expression moved teachers to consider rhetoric as a possible theoretical resource for composition instruction for the first time since the course was invented. The advent of communication skills upon the scene of Freshman English also marks the first time that English departments' ownership of the basic course was challenged by authorities who had sufficient clout to divert it from its humanist moorings in literature and current-traditional pedagogy. These authorities included teachers of speech, college deans, and the United States armed forces.

THE MILITARY GOES TO COLLEGE

In 1943, the U.S. Army, Navy, and Army Air Force implemented training programs at a number of American universities. These programs were instigated at the behest of leaders of academic organizations who were anxious not to repeat the experience of the first World War, when, in the absence of academic planning, the military had virtually taken control of college campuses (Cardozier 4). This time around, academics planned to be ready when the military needed its services and facilities. Even before America officially entered the war, then, officials of the American Council on Education urged President Roosevelt to take advantage of colleges and universities as training centers for military personnel. Roosevelt agreed, and training programs were hastily planned by academics and members of the military, some of whom had been professors in civilian life. Once implemented, these programs did not last long, since soldiers were badly needed in the war effort: the Army Specialized Training Program (ASTP), for example, was initiated in the spring of 1942 and phased out in the spring of 1944. The navy's V-12 program lasted somewhat longer, terminating in the fall of 1945. Despite their brief lives, the military programs altered the way things are done on American campuses. (They suggested to administrators, for example, that summer school was a profitable endeavor).

One of the biggest changes the military programs wrought was in the curriculum of Freshman English. In addition to coursework in engineering, medicine, and veterinary science, the programs called for a set of "basic" studies, in which English was included. But the aim of basic English looked very different to the military than it did to English teachers. The objectives of the ASTP English course were outlined as follows:

> The end-product of the Army Specialized Training Program is an officer candidate who will, after further specialized training, function effectively in a position of command. He must, therefore:
>
> 1. Be a clear thinker.
> 2. Possess the skill of orderly, concise, and appropriate communication, both oral and written, including the ability to observe and report accurately.
> 3. Possess the ability to listen and to read understandingly.
> 4. Know the basic forms of military communication.
>
> In view of the limited time available for instruction in English, it is particularly important that this instruction be reinforced by requiring trainees in all classes to write and speak with deliberation, clearness and correct language. (Tressidder 388)

Specific goals were then listed for instruction in reading, writing, and speaking. As far as the army was concerned, the aim of all basic instruction was to promote clarity and efficiency of communication. The navy program did not differ in this regard:

> The aim of this course is to teach the student to say and write what he means concisely and with a purpose, and to read and listen with precise understanding and discrimination. Problems in oral and written communication; practice in the kinds of expression which students will be called on most often to use—reports of events, summaries of reading and lectures, explanations of problems or situations, Navy letter and report forms, short informal talks, class recitations and discussion. . . . Readings from periodicals and books, especially of contemporary American writings, to gain information, to extend the student's experience, and to show modern practices in varied types of expression, technical and popular. (Tressider 388–89)

There is much in these descriptions to alarm teachers of the traditional Freshman English course: the emphasis on oral communication; the reading of popular media and technical manuals; the absence of attention to self-expression; and, perhaps worst of all from a humanist point of view, no literature.

It is interesting to imagine English teachers' responses to this program of study, particularly within the institutional context brought about by war. Most colleges and universities had sought contracts for the military training programs in order to keep their faculties employed. While many faculty members, primarily those in scientific and technical fields, were absent from campus because they were engaged in the war effort, the war also decimated student populations, particularly in all-male colleges and state universities. And so the military training programs offered employment for the faculty who remained on campus, especially those in the humanities who might otherwise have lost their jobs. In a sense, then, faculty were conscripted into teaching in these programs. What did professors of literature, history, and philosophy think of this new teaching duty, which entailed fifteen-hour loads and six-day weeks, and which cycled through twelve-week sessions all year long with no summer vacation? Apparently most accepted this onerous schedule with grace; it was "all part of the war effort" (Cardozier 190). What teachers of English did not accept so graciously, apparently, were the alterations made to Freshman English by the military objectives for basic study.

In December 1944, Argus J. Tressidder, a lieutenant in the Naval Reserves on leave from the University of Louisville, reported the results of an "informal" survey of English department heads in some forty schools where both army and navy training programs had been established. According to Tressidder, the survey showed that the programs had failed to produce "really satisfactory results" (389). A host of institutional reasons can be imagined to account for this failure: the programs were hastily designed and implemented; too much was attempted in too little time; servicemen were not used to the rhythms and requirements of academic study; and faculty and facilities were inadequate on many campuses (Wykoff 1945). Too, military and academic mindsets were not at all compatible—the army, for example, thought that academic study was conducted at far too leisurely a pace.

But the responses to Tressidder's study also reveal a disciplinary conflict. While the army and navy had of course not intended to shake up academic disciplinary boundaries, their inclusion of oral communication in the ASTP and V-12 curricula weakened English departments' claim to ownership of the required course by challenging the assumption that literate discourse was its obvious and proprietary subject. The military curricula also established that studying oral and written discourse together could reinforce students' grasp of both mediums. Even though the military programs were usually administered out of English departments because English had the institutional resources to mount large instructional efforts, English departments employed teachers of speech in the programs on campuses where they were available, either on a part- or full-time basis, to provide the necessary expertise in oral instruction (Bagwell). The speech teachers taught public speaking to the soldiers every other day or for a few hours a week, alternating days or hours with teachers of writing. In a few cases, specialists in speech correction worked with soldiers who needed their help. The close association with professional teachers of speech necessitated by the military programs made some English teachers aware that there was more to teaching oral communication than simply asking students to stand up and talk. At other schools, where teachers of speech were not available or were not encouraged to participate, English teachers gave whatever attention they could to oral communication. I suspect that more than a few counted class discussion as fulfillment of their obligation to teach speaking.

A few of the department heads who responded to Tressidder's survey liked the blending of speech and writing in the basic course. One reported that "the small amount of extempore speaking that we have been able to include in the navy course has proved to be useful and may be continued in the regular composition course"; another wrote that "we like the oral approach, even when the main interest is in written composition. We like the analytical approach, also" (Tressider 391). But most complained that there was too much ground to cover in the military course, "especially in speech" (390). Another head agreed that "too much time is given to speech," and yet another considered the navy program more successful than the army's because "it put less emphasis on oral work." One respondent was opposed to the emphasis on oral communication because it forced "cancellation of attention once paid to instruction in reading verse and more difficult varieties of prose." Another remarked that "a freer course in literature, involving some writing and speech (instead of a formal discipline) would better serve the ends of the Navy in preparing officers" (391).

The omission of literature from the basic course had been the army's idea, and so Tressidder was not sanguine about English teachers' willingness to refrain from using literature in the basic course after the military departed from campus. He quoted an article in *Harper's* that suggested that the army had dropped ASTP because English departments had reverted to teaching English and American literature in the course, and he concluded his own summary with these remarks:

> Only a very few English teachers admit that the old freshman compo-
> sition courses should be scrapped and a new one built and that in the
> freshman year there is little place for the study of literature. A similar
> survey among teachers of speech (a fairly impracticable attempt in a
> course dominated by English departments) would certainly reveal less
> conservative opinions and more revolutionary suggestions. (392)

Obviously, Tressidder preferred that the basic course include oral composition, and his article further makes clear his distress that neither English departments nor the armed forces were sufficiently aware that speech was itself
a discipline with a distinctive body of knowledge and practices to impart.
Taking his bias toward speech into account, it is nonetheless telling that
Tressidder depicted English departments as conservative enclaves holding
back the wave of the future. He noted that before the war some colleges had
been experimenting with courses in which "oral and written composition are
blended," and he noted as well that such programs "have made a sincere attempt to restore the classical concept of rhetoric, which admitted no artificial
divorce of the principles of speaking and the principles of writing."[1] Such
courses in communication, he thought, had anticipated the planners of the
military programs.

Certainly the military's inclusion of oral instruction in their basic programs opened up the question of disciplinary ownership of the required basic course. If the required course aims at the improvement of students' use of
language, there is no reason why oral communication should be excluded
from its purview. To put this in institutional terms, the programs designed by
the armed forces made it more difficult for English teachers to argue that
materials and skills taught in the basic course were specific to their discipline.
The military course presented English departments with a part-whole problem that they have been unable to resolve since, as the Lindemann-Tate discussion demonstrates. Either the basic course "belongs" to English departments, in which case English teachers are perfectly justified in insisting that
its content reflect the instructional mission that they take to be primary, that
is, literary study; or the course "belongs" to the college or the entire university, since all students, regardless of disciplinary affiliation, are required to
take it. From this supradisciplinary point of view it can be argued that basic
course curricula should reflect the interests of all students and teachers, and
on this view, literary study is as relevant to the course as physics.

Furthermore, the military emphasis on technical and analytic composition simply displaced the claims of literary study on the course, thus lending support to those who had argued over the years that the composition practiced in the freshman course ought to be utterly practical and hence dissociated from literary study.[2] The military's approach would perhaps have been no more influential on the curriculum of Freshman English than had other arguments to this effect, were it not for its conjunction with general education, which was gaining influence in American universities during the early 1940s, once again thanks to the war.

EDUCATION FOR DEMOCRACY: GENERAL OR LIBERAL?

The simplest way to account for the rise of interest in general education is to suppose that it was a response to the elective system put in place near the end of the nineteenth century. Once the notion of elective study was adopted by American universities, no theoretical limits could be imposed on the proliferation of courses. In addition, once their adoption of the research ideal released faculty members from the duty of teaching a received common curriculum, they quickly realized the professional advantages inherent in specialization (Bledstein). Specialization in its turn enabled unwieldy fields like the social sciences to split into subdisciplines, each of which then quickly developed the professional apparatus that permitted their adherents to think of themselves as subscribing to distinct disciplines. This happened within English studies after 1910, when teachers of oral composition formed separate departments of speech in which to teach elocution, public address, and dramatic interpretation (Cohen).

Specialization and proliferation flourished virtually unchecked (though not without criticism) during the first three decades of the twentieth century. In 1944, when Harvard published its report on general education, over four hundred courses, taught by three hundred faculty, were offered in arts and sciences on that campus (*General Education*, 183). The only universally required course at Harvard at that time, as at many other universities, was Freshman English. People who were appalled by this state of affairs often argued that students could "get through" a college education without having studied mathematics, science, literature, or whatever—critics usually named the lack that caused them the most professional or personal distress.

General education was in part, then, an attempt to bring some order into the chaos of courses and specialties that university curricula had become. Most general education programs had three components: one or more basic courses (usually in English, physical education, and perhaps mathematics), required of everyone who could not test out of them; core area requirements or courses in three large categories of knowledge—science, social science, and the humanities; and a major field of study. Advocates of this threefold division argued that it gave individual attention to students who needed academic work in basic skills and required them to come in contact with fields whose study was considered fundamental to a Western education at the same time as it allowed for the specialization that was becoming increasingly important to undergraduates, who, by this time, had begun to view college as preparation for a career.

But general education was also motivated by quite different concerns that were foregrounded by the advent of a second world war. Once America entered the war, educators lost no time in arguing that the point of education was the preservation of democracy, and those who touted general education advertised it as the means by which the education of citizens in a democracy should be pursued. In other words, the war and its attendant rhetoric fomented desire for a return to the older, more centralized and unified approach to higher education that had formerly been designated "liberal" (Gary Miller). But it is important to remember that general education was not the same as liberal education, although contemporary sources often assumed affinity between the two. For example, Tremaine McDowell, a professor of English at Minnesota, asserted in 1946 that the term "general education" was "a tacit admission that 'liberal education' has not fully adjusted itself to the present century" (353).

In order to clarify the distinction between general and liberal education, it is necessary for me to make an all too brief detour into the educational philosophy of John Dewey, which influenced the general education movement.[3] Unlike advocates of liberal education such as Norman Foerster, who proposed a prescribed curriculum of master subjects, Dewey focused his philosophy of education on the experiences of learners. For Dewey, "experience" was a name for an individual's ongoing interaction with her environment. This interaction is mutual: as the environment shapes individuals, so do an individual's actions alter her surroundings.

> When we experience something we act upon it, we do something with
> it; then we suffer or undergo the consequences. We do something to
> the thing and then it does something to us in return: such is the
> peculiar combination. The connection of these two phases of experi-

ence measures the fruitfulness or value of the experience. Mere
activity does not constitute experience. It is dispersive, centrifugal,
dissipating. Experience as trying involves change, but change is
meaningless transition unless it is consciously connected with the
return wave of consequences which flow from it. When an activity is
continued *into* the undergoing of consequence, when the change made
by action is reflected back into a change made in us, the mere flux is
loaded with significance. We learn something. (1985 [1916], 146)

Any experience in which learning takes place, then, requires engaged activity
rather than passive reception. The only action that accrued meaning was
reflective experience, in which an individual tried to determine the outcome
of an action upon the environment. In a sense, then, for Dewey education *is*
this sort of experience, insofar as interactions with newer and more complex
environments stimulate people to change and grow. The point of formal
schooling is to provide challenging and provocative experiences for learners:
"the next step is the progressive development of what is already experienced
into a fuller and richer and also more organized form, a form that gradually
approximates that in which subject-matter is presented to the skilled, mature
person" (1938, 73–74). Hence the name applied to Deweyan pedagogy: "progressive education." This progression means that teachers must intervene
and control the pace, sequencing, and variety of experiences that children
undergo in school.

Humanist critics often accused Dewey of dismissing traditional learning, since he rejected their notion that education was "a process of preparation or getting ready" for some imagined future adult life (1985 [1916], 59;
1938, 47ff). Such critics missed Dewey's point, however. He sanctioned the
consumption of traditional subject matter as a means of learning more about
one's cultural environment so that meaningful interactions with it could take
place. What he objected to was the one-sidedness of traditional education, where
teachers dispensed received knowledge while learners passively ingested it.
In fact, he sanctioned humanism, if that term were redefined to mean "being
imbued with an intelligent sense of human interests. The social interest, iden-
tical in its deepest meaning with moral interest, is necessarily supreme with
man" (1985 [1916], 297).[4] He was contemptuous, however, of arid scholarship:

knowledge *about* man, information as to his past, familiarity with his
documented records of literature, may be as technical a possession as
the accumulation of physical details. Men may keep busy in a variety

of ways, making money, acquiring facility in laboratory manipulation, or in amassing a store of facts about linguistic matters, or the chronology of literary productions. Unless such activity reacts to enlarge the imaginative vision of life, it is on a level with the busy work of children. (1985 [1916], 297)

Dewey insisted that the point of education was not the accumulation of knowledge but instillation of the desire to grow and become wise (James Campbell, 216–17).

Dewey insisted as well that education has a social end. The education he envisioned could only take place in a democratic polity:

A society which makes provision for participation in its good of all its members on equal terms and which secures flexible readjustment of its institutions through interaction of the different forms of associated life is in so far democratic. Such a society must have a type of education that gives individuals a personal interest in social relationships and control, and the habits of mind which secure social changes without introducing disorder. (1985 [1916], 105)

In other words, Dewey's educational philosophy was far from disinterested: the point of formal education is to give individuals a stake in the outcome, not only of their own lives, but of the affairs of the entire polity. Education is meant to equip individuals to become active members of the group, influencing it and being influenced by it. Gary Miller puts it like this: "Dewey saw inquiry as an instrument of personal and, ultimately, social transformation. His concern was less with the fixing of belief than with the transformation of situations to achieve a more satisfactory environment" (62). Dewey did not disparage belief in any way; he thought that individuals could not live or learn without it. But he was not sympathetic to those who discouraged people from changing their beliefs in accordance with reflective experience.

Dewey's adherents, called "progressive educators," achieved some remarkable successes during the early decades of the twentieth century (Cremin, Zilversmit). As is apparently the case with any subtle body of thought, however, principles deduced from Dewey's theory of education were absorbed into educational practice in fairly reductive ways, abetted by scientism and an absorption with method (Holt 1993, 1994; Gary Miller 68ff). The influence of progressivism on Freshman English was first felt on a wide scale during the 1940s, by which time some of its principles had made their way into talk about general education. Its advocates agreed that a primary point of general education was to develop the relationship of the individual to the culture in which she lives (Gary Miller 106). In other words, general education would immerse students in a critical examination of their present circumstances and their relation to those circumstances.

This focus on present needs was, of course, anathema to humanists. Norman Foerster scorned the notion that "the people" knew what they needed, and hence he scorned the educationists' belief that

> a state university is a people's university, of the people, for the people, and, in the end, by the people. It must offer them what they spontaneously want, or what they are supposed to want, not what they need and might be taught to want. Of course it is hard to say what they need, or even what they want, but as a working hypothesis we will assume that they want what is useful and practical, not in a remote and indirect way but immediately, something tangibly marketable. (1946, 14)

For Foerster, general education was little better than pandering. If people were allowed to choose what they wished to study, they would always opt for something other than what was best for them, he thought. This passage can also be read as a poke at the tendency of general educationists to take for granted that the individualized and pragmatic education they espoused is what all individuals want. Foerster also responded negatively to the notion of individualized instruction. He noted sarcastically that "the half-truth that men are created equal has been supplanted by the new declaration, which affirms the half-truth that they are created unique" (1946, 16).

Unfortunately, in their efforts to tailor an educational program to fit each individual's needs, progressive educators sometimes asserted a will to test and measure. And, as we shall see, many of the communication skills courses associated with general education programs used a battery of tests that determined how long each student would remain in basic studies. The interest in individualization also led to the use of advisors, who were expected to help each student plan an individualized curriculum that suited her needs and interests. Foerster did not fail to note the contradiction implicit in the notion that students needed guidance in order to find out what they wanted to do: "it is the business of the personnel service and the faculty to prod [students] into finding themselves, that is, into learning what occupational groove they could be made to fit, what sort of tool they were created to be" (1946, 15–16). Foerster's conservatism found little to like in the frank individualism espoused by adherents of general education. He jibed at their beliefs that students were "happily self-motivated" and that they "knew at the start what they want to prepare for" (15).

Dewey's texts do not exactly authorize the focus on individualized instruction that characterized early programs in general education. To be sure, one of his complaints about traditional education was that it overlooked students, emphasizing instead the interaction between teachers and texts or subject matters (1938, 41). Furthermore, he argued vigorously that "every individual shall have opportunities to employ his own powers in activities that have meaning" (1985 [1916], 179). But this remark occurs in the context of a critique of original genius, the notion that some people are endowed by nature with more or better intellectual and creative capacity than others. Dewey insisted, on the other hand, that all thinking was original and creative, and that all people could do it (1985 [1916], 166). And so his interest in individuals was an interest in furthering the principles of democracy. Indeed, he emphatically rejected any rights-based individualism that would privilege the desire of a given individual over the needs of the social group (1935, 29–31).

Dewey's emphasis on the social authorized some progressive educators to espouse socialism during the early years of the twentieth century. Dewey himself resisted Marxist socialisms, primarily on the ground that they advocated violent revolution (1935, 54). He preferred a politics he called "radical liberalism," by which he meant the "perception of the necessity of thoroughgoing changes in the set-up of institutions and corresponding activity to bring the changes to pass" (45). But such nice distinctions within leftist politics were lost on most Americans, and because of its perceived lean to the left, progressivism fell on hard times during World War II and after. Cold-war rhetoric simply conflated progressivism with socialism, the ideology whose agenda for the world reputedly involved the eradication of democracy. But these years also saw a subtle shift in popular attitudes toward democracy itself, a shift that had a profound effect on the meaning of general education. According to Miller,

> in the postwar and Cold War years, people began to define democracy differently. Democracy was no longer seen as a *process* that encouraged change; it was a political ideal that was to be *preserved* in the face of the communist threat. The focus was not on the individual's right to change society but on the individual's responsibility as a citizen to protect democracy, which was now identified with the status quo. (Gary Miller 117)

If Dewey had hoped that education would be reconceived as a process of continual change, he must have been disappointed by the rhetoric of general education during the war. During the early 1940s, defenders of democracy reassigned the point of general education to the development of democratic values within individuals in order to insure that every citizen would be prepared to defend America against actual or ideological aggression from without or within. As Miller notes, this new emphasis on the preservation of values made general education difficult to distinguish from liberal education (119).

Indeed, some plans for general education, such as that forwarded by a committee of Harvard professors in *General Education in a Free Society* (1945), were a blend of liberal and general education. According to the terms of this report, known familiarly as the "Redbook," students at Harvard would be required to take a course each in science, social sciences, and humanities, which was a typical division of studies in general education. However, the point of these core courses was to furnish "the body of learning and of ideas which would be a common experience of all Harvard students, as well as introductions to the study of the traditions of Western culture"—a sentiment that would not have displeased Irving Babbitt (196). But when they came to consider the required course in composition—the venerable English A—the Harvard eminences took a radical position. On the ground that "what is desired is not primarily skill in writing literary English or about English literature," the committee recommended that English A be abolished (199). In its place, composition would be "given . . . in connection with the courses in general education then being taken by the students" (200). Composition actually was taught in connection with GE courses at Harvard during the 1950s, although this innovation didn't last long (Russell 1991, 254).

It is worthy of note that Freshman English was the only course that remained as a universal requirement throughout the fifty years (1880–1940) during which the American professoriate created a large number of specialized disciplines and expanded their curricula accordingly. This lone requirement, although taught by a single department, was widely accepted as so necessary for students' advancement that it remained inviolate throughout the years of growth, diversity, and specialization. Norman Foerster was astute enough to notice that its presence in the curriculum actually compromised the principles of electivity and equivalence on which the new university throve. With typical acerbity, he remarked that the "new men" in "education, sociology, educational sociology, and many other subjects" forgot that "once the essentiality of a single subject is admitted" the way is opened to require "other essentials" (1937, 89–90). That is to say, Freshman English was an ubiquitous contradiction of the curricular philosophy entailed in the elective system. But nobody except Foerster seemed to notice, or care, about this anomaly. Much less did anyone question the salience, worth, or appropriateness of the universal requirement. And when general education began to be touted as a remedy for past curricular sins, its advocates simply swept the requirement into their plans.

COMMUNICATION AND DEMOCRACY

The "basic skills" course instituted at the University of Iowa in 1944 was much more securely grounded in the philosophy of general education than was the Harvard plan. In his introduction to the new program, President Virgil Hancher outlined the principles on which it was based:

> students are not alike, and some need different things from the University than do others. The liberal arts curriculum, then, should be revised not backward toward tradition, but forward toward needs. It should be designed so that every student will have a chance to acquire both the basic skills and the fundamental understandings he needs to live in the modern world and to meet the social and ethical responsibilities which he must face as a good citizen in a democratic nation. These, we felt, he would acquire more readily from a dynamic and active process of learning than from passive receptivity to teaching. (*The New Program*, 1945)

The basic skills portion of this program was as thoroughly individualized as the institutional situation permitted. Students who were able to demonstrate competence in speaking, writing, and reading upon entrance would be excused from further work in those areas. Those who could not would register for a four-hour course called "Communication Skills," wherein they would be "instructed according to their needs as revealed by their performance on objective examinations, in speaking and in theme writing." Students would stay in this course until they could demonstrate that they had reached "the desired level of competency" (n.p.). This could occur in one semester, or four, or never: students who did not achieve the desired level would be denied graduation. Even more specialized instruction was available in reading, writing, and speaking clinics for those who needed additional help.

It is not entirely clear how the "basic skills" program at Iowa came to be known as "Communication Skills." Gerber attributes the term to Harry Newburn. This may be correct, given that the dean used the term *communication* early in 1943, when he enumerated a list of skills he took to be fundamental to a college education (Gerber 1993; Newburn 7).[5] As we have seen, in 1944 Tressidder used the term *communication* to describe basic courses that, prior to the war, had combined speaking and listening. Very few such courses were in existence prior to 1943. Perhaps he was thinking of an experimental program at Stephens College, which had begun in the 1930s (Wiksell). A general education program was put in place at the University of Florida as early as 1935, but its basic skills course was called "Reading, Speaking, and Writing" (Wise 1949, 157). The University of Illinois set up a Division of General Studies in 1940; its basic course was called "Verbal Expression," since the term *communication* was not in use at that time (Hultzen 113). Suddenly, though, in 1943–44 a half-dozen courses or programs called "Communication Skills" were put in place in American universities, usually within the context of general education programs or separate colleges called "Basic Studies" or "General Studies." In that academic year, programs or courses that combined instruction in speech and writing appeared at Drake, Florida State, Iowa, Minnesota, and Michigan State. The timing suggests that wartime had something to do with this flurry of curricular innovation, since planning for such programs had begun in most of these universities in 1941–42. In 1945–46, Colgate, Denver, and Southern California also established communication skills programs. According to James A. Berlin, by 1948 over two hundred colleges and universities had established communication courses (1987, 96).

While all of this activity was no doubt stimulated by professional interest in general education, the emphasis on communication itself was a direct result of the rhetoric of war. Educators attributed the onset of the Second World War to a lack of communication—among Americans and between nations. They were convinced that attention to communication would prevent another such horror, because they assumed that if people could just make themselves clear to one another, they would cease to fight and disagree. In an address before the War Problems Conference in 1943, for example, Lennox Grey urged American educators to adopt a spirit of unity:

> Now, if ever, teachers need to come together—elementary school, high school and college teachers—liberal arts teachers, and professional educators. The sniping that goes on between the liberal arts colleges and the professional schools of education is as shameful as the

sniping between the Mihailovich and Tito factions in Yugoslavia, or as the factionalism that brought about the fall of France. It can have serious consequences for education, at a time when democratic education is more seriously threatened than most of us realize. (132)

Grey used these dramatic analogies to urge teachers to unify their instructional efforts around the "growing realization" that "communication is the basis of all human community—the basic factor in all education, in all human relations, in all national union, in world federation" (133). He pointed out that "Hitler and his Nazis" had used "new instruments of communication" such as radio and television to spread their message of hate, and so he urged his audience to investigate the uses of these instruments as well, in order to "see to it" that they were used "to further human understanding, not to exploit human ignorance." Grey explicitly rejected the disinterestedness of contemporary literary study, urging its teachers to pursue their work in connection with concern about world events: "we may be skilled in discussing the playing of Hamlet or the technique of a novel of Dickens'. We have thought all too little about the crucial bearing of all this on the future of nations and races."

John J. DeBoer echoed this sentiment in 1945: "the most promising development in the teaching of English is the gradual emergence of clear-cut social purposes" (292). He too used the threat posed by the enemies of the hour as goads to action: "The Nazis have developed the arts of psychological warfare to a high level, chiefly by skillful use of the means of communication. The Germans under Hitler and the Japanese are not only highly literate, but thoroughly efficient in the use of all the vehicles for the transmission of thought." Both writers implied that American teachers' failure to become familiar with new communications technology, as well as their disinterest in world affairs, had put their country at a disadvantage during its time of need.

Two themes that informed the communication skills movement appear in this war rhetoric: the faith that contradiction and hostility can be erased by communication, and the realization that modern communications technology enhances distribution of powerful rhetorics. Today a theorist might remark the naivete of the assumption that differences among people can be resolved by means of efficient communication. But during wartime, clear communication seemed to be a weapon that could be deployed against powerful antidemocratic ideologies. And when new theories of communication were translated into pedagogy and implemented as goals of the universally required course, they had the potential to bring about enormous changes in its curriculum. Perhaps the most important of these potentials was the emphasis on communication rather than expression. To make communication central to a pedagogy suddenly makes audiences, messages, and situations important. In such a milieu the humanist focus on self-improvement fades from view, and teachers' attention is wrenched away from texts outward, toward the world and its problems.

COMMUNICATION SKILLS PROGRAM

In 1945, a symposium on communication skills was held at Northwestern University. It is perhaps worth noting that no literary scholars spoke at this meeting. Talks were given by Lennox Grey, James O'Neill, Robert Seashore, Porter Perrin, Paul Witty, James McBurney, Major Irving Lee, Lieutenant Argus Tressider, Robert Pooley, and Franklin Knower. Two members of this group—Grey and Tressider—have already appeared in this narrative. Lee, O'Neill, and McBurney were professors of speech, as was Knower, who had been active in the design of the new undergraduate program at Iowa. Seashore was a psychologist, Witty a professor of education. Grey and Pooley were the only English teachers among this group, and both were primarily interested in English Education. Pooley and Perrin brought new grammars to the attention of English teachers during the 1940s and 1950s. Perrin was a professor of rhetoric and the author of a very popular rhetoric handbook for use in the first-year course, the *Index to English* (1942), which took a nontraditional approach to grammar and usage. Perrin wrote his dissertation on the history of American rhetorical education, something that was quite rare at the time (1936).

In his response to the papers presented at this meeting, Glen Mills pointed up many of the contradictions and difficulties that would accompany the implementation and orchestration of communication skills programs during the next ten years or so. Mills was rather cynical about what he took to be administrative efforts to reduce costs by combining instruction in speech and English, and he doubted whether the two fields were so easily compatible as the sudden proliferation of communication skills programs seemed to imply. A speech, after all, was "not merely 'an essay standing on its hind legs'" (41). There were obvious differences between speech and writing, such as the fact that "debate, several kinds of group discussion, and parliamentary procedure" had no written counterpart (41). Furthermore, there were differences

in the invention, arrangement, delivery, and style of oral and written discourse. Speakers were under immediate constraints imposed by the social
nature of oral discourse—in particular the actual physical presence of an
audience, whose response might force a speaker to adjust not only her ethos,
but her arguments, vocal register, and gestures to the occasion as well. Such
social constraints did not face writers, who worked in "psychological isolation." Mills further pointed out that many English teachers were unaware of
the pedagogical sophistication that was necessary to teach speech well. He
listed the principles taught in his own speech program as follows:

> the importance of communication rather than exhibitionism, the idea
> that winning the desired response is the end, the role of techniques of
> bringing attention to a peak on the response, the disarming simplicity
> and spontaneity of effective speech, the desirability of being an able
> person in good emotional state and with a proper attitude toward
> himself and his audience, unconscious control of subliminal cues, and
> the communicative functions of free, properly-motivated bodily
> action. We seek to develop in addition to these attitudes and adjust-
> ments, specific skills and abilities. . . . these include self-confidence in a
> speech situation, directness, meaningful action, expressive voice,
> general preparation, specific preparation, analysis of subjects'
> arrangement, means of support, constructive use of suggestion, and
> oral style. (43)

I suspect that analysis of arrangement and style were the only principles listed
that were readily adaptable to the typical Freshman English course. Indeed,
humanist English teachers might have regarded Mills's attention to students'
bodies, voices, and emotional development as childish, if not shocking.

Nonetheless, hardy teachers in many colleges and universities attempted
to develop courses in communication skills that combined instruction in speaking and writing. A wide range of philosophies and theories of discourse governed such programs. Depending on the degree to which speech teachers
were involved in their design, they incorporated more or less general semantics, communication theory, group dynamics, and social psychology. Depending on the degree to which English teachers on a given campus were interested in semantics or linguistics, the courses bore marks of those interests.
One truly radical communication skills program, based on Freudian psychology, General Semantics, and life-adjustment educational theory, was implemented at the University of Denver.[6] At some schools, communication skills

programs were put in place alongside a traditional Freshman English course, and students were either placed into one or the other program or were allowed to choose between them.

Some schools were forced to make do with the six hours that had traditionally been reserved for the Freshman English requirement, while others were fortunate enough to be able to fold in a three-hour block formerly used for a basic speech course, thus making available a nine-hour requirement in communication skills. Some universities turned this block of time into a four- or five-hour course lasting two semesters. In an attempt to get around the uniform timetable imposed by the semester system, many programs tried to individualize instruction by combining large lecture sections with discussion sections and periods of work in a writing laboratory. Students could remain in these smaller sessions until their work was deemed good enough for them to advance. Usually, but not always, communication skills courses were offered in conjunction with a general education program. Sometimes they were housed in a separate College of Basic Studies or General Studies. In this case, the staff for the course—particularly in labs and clinics—was more likely to be drawn from both English and Speech departments, and from psychology or other social sciences as well.

Programs at many schools were given the administrative support necessary to develop an array of machinery and approaches aimed at individualizing instruction. In schools that could afford it, clinics and laboratories were supplied with a good deal of equipment: microphones, tape recorders, phonographs, ditto machines, opaque projectors, and film projectors. Many programs also attempted to find venues outside of class in which to publicize students' communicative performances. Iowa, for example, published a magazine of student work and produced students' radio shows.

An impressive battery of tests was in use at some schools. Stephens, for example, subjected students to the Cooperative English Test, the Fowler Vocabulary Precision Test, the Chicago Test of Clerical Promise, the Stephens College Knowledge Locator Test, the Stephens College Test of Survey Reading, the Stephens College Article and Text Comprehension Test, and the Wiksell-Filkin Library Instructional Test (Wiksell 144). In addition, students were observed by teachers and clinicians while they underwent several "performance activities" during the first weeks of the semester: presenting an informal report, participating in group discussion, speaking and reading aloud, writing a social letter, presenting a talk, listening, writing a critical review, and participating in conversation (144–45). As was true at most schools with communication skills programs, Stephens students who performed well on a given test were exempted from further work in that area. Students who were thought to need more intense individualized instruction in a given area were sent to clinics in reading, writing, listening, or speaking, where they worked with tutors or teachers in small groups.

Some programs incorporated standardized testing into the classroom scene as well. Ironically, this was done in the name of individualization. At Michigan State, for example, all grades earned in course activities were "interpreted only as an index of the quality of a student's work at a given period of time" (Bagwell 85). Students who earned an "F" at the end of the first or any term were nonetheless allowed to pass the requirement if they passed a comprehensive examination given by the College Board. Students could take this test whenever they (and a counselor and the dean of the Basic Skills College) felt that it was "advisable." Students who passed the exam, no matter when they took it, were "given full credit for the course and excused from taking further work."

But these arrangements obtained only in a few universities where the communication skills program enjoyed widespread administrative and faculty support. In most schools, a typical curriculum used in communication skills simply supplemented the traditional curricula of Freshman English. The sort of communication skills programs put together by English departments were generally distinguished from traditional Freshman English in only a few ways: their syllabi announced an allegiance to communication that was couched in the rhetoric of democracy or the social; they included attention to speaking and sometimes listening; and they used textbooks that contained information about communication, linguistics, or semantics. James McCrimmon's venerable *Writing With a Purpose* (1950) is a fine example of the sort of textbook produced for use in such programs, written by an English teacher, informed with new attitudes toward linguistics and grammar, and yet thoroughly committed to current-traditional rhetoric (Connors 1981). In such programs the course or courses were administered and taught by English departments and teachers. Some programs hired directors, while others did not. Sometimes teachers of the course were given preliminary or regular training in communication skills materials and sometimes they were left to their own devices.

The introductory program at the University of Florida was typical of the sort of institutional compromise that English departments achieved with communication skills. It was based on the following assumptions:

(1) Every use of language involves, broadly speaking, a social situation; (2) ideas are of prime importance, and teaching the communication arts is fruitless when attempted apart from ideas meaningful to the student; (3) language arts, like other arts, may be mastered only by regular practice; (4) the communication arts are so closely interrelated that progress in one makes progress in each of the others surer and easier—in fact, that they operate in a complementary manner; (5) the most effective approach in the development of the communication arts is through reading. (Wise 131)

Many of the "general aims" of the Florida course sound familiar enough to a student of Freshman English: to read with speed, comprehension, and enjoyment; to listen and take notes accurately; to communicate ideas effectively (132). Evidence of students' mastery of these aims was their ability to "analyze another's writing, discovering the writer's central purpose and his pattern of thinking"; "to use in their exact meaning a wide range of words;" to write abstracts, summaries, and precis; to read literature with enjoyment; "to exhibit an increased interest in the voluntary reading of books which have been accepted as desirable"; "to speak with clearness, accuracy, and sincerity, exhibiting poise and confidence"; "to gather thought material, arrange it in an appropriate form, and finally present it in effectively written discourse." This course was offered for five hours' credit; one hour per week was given in a large lecture section while two more hours met in discussion section and two hours per week were spent in writing. Lectures centered on "ethical, political, or social problems which are subject to debate." This hour supposedly fulfilled the obligation to teach listening and note-taking. During the first semester of the course, students read expository essays, which were discussed in the small sections; during the second semester they read literature. The point of discussion sections was to enhance reading ability. Teachers pointed out "key words, topic sentences, and central themes." Students also gave speeches in the discussion sections; those who performed well were allowed to speak before the entire assembly during a lecture session. A student's work in the writing laboratories was kept track of by means of a worksheet that showed results of tests in mechanics, as well as "his weekly essay with the number of pages, total pages written to date, the instructor's score and the instructor's approval of the student's correction of the paper" (133). On the reverse side of the worksheet, a student recorded "a profile chart of his errors week by week. Very soon each student knows—and his instructor knows—just what type of error is the student's greatest fault." All in all, one gets the feeling that the Florida program had not been severely impacted by the philosophy of communication skills.

In 1956, near the end of its heyday, Jean Malmstrom proposed a fourfold classification of the kinds of communication skills programs that were then in place in American colleges and universities. Her first category covered programs like Florida's, which took the expedient way of simply combining exercises in writing and speaking. Courses in such programs focused on students' achievement of correctness, just as traditional composition courses had. Malmstrom explained that oral and written work in such courses was often "discrete," by which she meant that teachers used two textbooks instead of one, so that it was difficult for them to discover that instruction in oral and written communication might be mutually reinforcing. In other words, such courses were an administratively convenient way to meet the demand for communication skills. They also allowed teachers to forego development of a theory of discourse that might include both media.

A second category of courses had appropriated "a specific body of subject matter" around which to organize their basic courses (Malmstrom 22). Here teachers used "class periods for the study of certain areas such as linguistics, semantics, ethics, social psychology, group dynamics. Communication is thought of as a body of knowledge to be understood like the material in a course in chemistry or history." This approach was clearly superior to the first type, although it did pose some dangers, Malmstrom thought. While there were many "fresh, intriguing texts" that could be used, and while its teachers had "a fine and uncommon feeling of having something solid to teach," they were also tempted to lecture "like other subject-matter professors, since they 'know' and the students don't." Too, subjects like social psychology and group dynamics were really more at home in the social sciences than in English. Last of all, teachers who took this approach were "confronted by the difficulty of translating the language of linguists and semanticists so that freshmen can understand it"; such teachers were faced as well with the task of proving that linguistics or semantics really did fall under the head of "communication."

Communication skills programs that fell into Malmstrom's third category organized themselves around "self-understanding" (23). This is no doubt a reference to the short-lived program at the University of Denver, which depended upon a frightening battery of psychological tests and measures to help students "adjust" to life. Malmstrom disapproved of this approach on the ground that "a little psychiatry is a dangerous thing. Freudian analysis is alluring, but a layman may tamper inanely, or worse, disastrously with the students' already complicated personalities."

Malmstrom's preferred sort of course constituted her fourth category. Here she located communication skills courses that met

> the first stipulation of the original mandate from the armed services: that language be studied as an instrument for communicating ideas in a social system. Skillfully taught, it may also well meet the armed services' second demand: that language be conceived of as an instrument of mediation among individuals, groups, and nations. We Americans like to have both practical and idealistic motives for our truly important actions. Students motivated by the obviously practical job-getting value of decent speaking, writing, reading, and listening, plus the idealistic concept of keeping democracy dominant in the world, will learn communication. Actually we need only to guide them, and get out of their way while they learn. (23)

In this passage Malmstrom names all the innovations brought to the required first-year course by persons who were truly informed and interested in communication skills: its emphasis on the social, its insistence that the point of language use is communication rather than expression; its melding of the practical with a patriotic ideal; its trust of students' willingness and ability to learn on their own.

COMMUNICATION THEORY AND PEDAGOGY

The sort of course idealized by Malmstrom was quite rare because its success depended to a certain extent upon teachers' acquaintance with contemporary research in language use. According to Thomas F. Dunn, the new subject of communication drew upon an array of research in fields as disparate as philology, linguistics, semantics, psychology of language and learning, philosophy of mind and language, anthropology, electronics, neurology, and acoustics (31–32). This situation made heavy demands on teachers of communication courses. Since communication was a subject matter supported by a body of theory and research, its teachers had to be receptive to change because new data and new techniques were constantly appearing. Dunn also noted that recent findings made in information theory had caused teachers to rethink their understanding of language. Since "communications engineers have found that they must distinguish between the code and the message," teachers of communication had "adopted the principle of studying the code more directly and thoroughly rather than taking the code for granted" (32). As Dunn suggested, information theorists regarded language itself as capable of influencing meaning. While this insight was ordinarily understood negatively to mean that language could not be trusted, when this attitude toward language was put into play in communication skills courses it complicated teachers' attitudes about language use. To think of language as a code was to open the possibility that miscoding could occur in the transmission itself. Hence the difficulty or subtlety of language, rather than students' ineptitude, could account for miscommunication. If language is able to frustrate a composer's intention, in other words, the onus of miscommunication does not lie entirely with the composer. Indeed, the pitfalls of language must be catalogued and studied in order that miscommunication be avoided.[7] This pedagogical goal carried a certain force, because the onset of the recent war was widely attributed to lack of communication.

The third development that teachers of communication had to take into account, according to Dunn, was recent psychological research into the learning process, which established that "learning is by imitation. That is, a child learns to speak by copying the actions of those around him who can already speak, and our students come to college with the speech habits of their community and the writing habits of the reading they have done most extensively" (36).[8] This insight legitimated the teaching of all four communication skills: students observed models of language in use while listening and reading; they imitated those models while speaking and writing. This approach also rendered instruction compatible with social scientific methods of investigation that, according to Dunn, relied on observation and imitation. In courses centered on communication theory, instruction focused on students' language habits and on language in production, rather than on already completed texts. Communications courses asked students to read a lot, but their instructional emphasis was on the activity of reading itself, rather than on the quality of the texts selected. In fact, popular oral and written texts selected from radio shows, films, magazines, and newspapers were preferred in such courses, since they presumably modeled language as it was currently used in students' communities.

The communication skills program put in place at the University of Minnesota in 1945 represented an attempt to incorporate as many of the theoretical and pedagogical insights gleaned from new theories of communication as was possible within the time and space limitations imposed by university calendars. Entering students at Minnesota were given a brochure that described the program as follows:

> The year's work will include elementary consideration of the principles by which meaning is conveyed verbally, of the principles of sound linguistic usage, of the principles of organizing materials for communication, and of the principles of persuasion. Study will be made of the press and of the radio, and, briefly, of the motion picture, as agencies by which information is transmitted and modified and by means of which opinions and attitudes are formed. (Harold Allen 1949, 59–60)

This program rested on several assumptions, some of which read as though they were generated in direct opposition to the assumptions that governed Freshman English. The designers of the Minnesota program assumed that communication is a socially necessary activity and that the primary function of language is to convey meaning; they did not number the development of taste or the achievement of cultured self-expression among the goals of the program (60). The designers also assumed that it was more important to get meaning from listening and reading, and to put meaning into speaking and writing, than it was to observe conventions of usage. In other words, the circulation of meaning was more important than the observance of correctness. As Allen put it, "acceptable language standards depend upon appropriateness to the user, to the subject, and to the situation rather than upon arbitrary rules" (60). Appropriateness is, of course, a rhetorical concept.

But the truly remarkable feature of the Minnesota program was its focus on popular media as vehicles for the transmission of important social meanings. Allen's rationale for this emphasis is worth quoting at length:

> in a democratic society some meanings which are conveyed through public and semipublic agencies and organizations to great masses of people are of social importance. The imperative corollary is that citizens in such a society, where public opinion is significant in government, obtain some understanding of the special characteristics of these agencies insofar as they produce or affect the meanings which they convey. Only with such understanding can the adult citizen exercise critical discrimination in receiving mass communication calculated to influence his opinion and attitudes. Only with such

> understanding, furthermore, can he intelligently provide active, direct, and constructive criticism of the mass communication agency. (60–61)

No doubt these sentiments were motivated in part by cold-war hysteria about "undesirable private, group, and governmental influence upon press and radio" (Harold Allen 1949, 61). Whatever their motivation, the emphasis on the content of messages, the importance of public opinion, and the attention to citizenship in the Minnesota program mark a radical departure from business as usual in Freshman English. During three quarters of coursework, students were introduced to scientific linguistics, logic and theories of persuasion, and mass communication. Writing and speaking projects involved students in rhetorical and logical analysis of political speeches and other ideologically charged uses of language. They listened to radio programs, contrasting the styles of news commentators. They read daily newspapers and pamphlets published by "special interest groups" and did contrastive studies of these media "in order to determine factors affecting editorial policy, content, and style; that is, such factors as ownership, advertising, location, circulation, and readers" (64). If instruction in this program actually lived up to its billing, in 1945 students at the University of Minnesota were being given a first-rate course in linguistics and rhetoric.

FRESHMAN ENGLISH VERSUS COMMUNICATION SKILLS

In 1947, at the annual meeting of NCTE, Harold E. Briggs, a teacher of English, and Clyde W. Dow, a teacher of speech, read a pair of papers about the comparative advantages of communication skills. Briggs opined that "the traditional freshman English program is pretty much satisfied with things as they are or as they used to be. The traditional mind is always a closed mind" (327). The teacher of communication skills, on the other hand, was forced by the very innovativeness and philosophy of the field, "to have an open and receptive mind." It particularly irritated Briggs that traditional Freshman English teachers refused to incorporate "new techniques and bodies of knowledge" into their courses: "the day is not far past when English looked with disdain upon such raw new disciplines as psychology and speech. But, like it or not, the new knowledge presses upon us, and being honest men, we cannot deny its validity and usefulness. The traditional English teacher grants this but wants speech and psychology to stay where they belong" (330). Dow, on the other hand, noted that the emergence of communication skills programs had integrated instruction in writing and speaking, which he took to be "a great advantage to the student" (332). Teaching staffs had improved, as well, thanks to the establishment of in-service programs. He also liked the increased profile of speech. But the single most significant development in communication courses, Dow thought, was "the separation of written expression from literary appreciation" (334). He hoped that the exclusion of literary texts from the required freshman course would gradually wean students away from their "erroneous belief that writing is an impractical, useless, and an academic barrier to be surmounted with the least possible effort." In other words, in the opinion of this teacher of speech, the literature-cum-grammar content of the traditional Freshman English course was to blame for students' lack of interest in writing.

Whether these assessments are fair or not, they do establish that contemporary teachers saw traditional composition instruction as very different from communication skills. And they were correct. The goal of Freshman English was to create humanist subjectivities. Its pedagogy centered on the examination of humanist texts. Its instructional tools—literature, current-traditional discourse theory, and traditional grammar—were treated as exemplars or standards to which students were expected to measure up. Communication skills courses, on the other hand, were grounded in theories of discourse borrowed from the social sciences. Their indebtedness to social science was apparent in their use of empirical testing, in their emphasis on the social uses of language, and their interest in public rather than private uses of discourse. Such courses supposedly fitted instruction to students' abilities rather than the other way around. Communication skills courses utilized popular texts and popular media: radio, television, even comic books. Where traditional Freshman English courses had given very little if any attention to the actual *practice* of composition, communication skills courses demystified the communicative arts by articulating and teaching tactics that students could use to improve and perhaps master their use. Furthermore, the emphasis on communication opened the course outward toward the world rather than inward toward students' expression of their experiences and insights.

It is no accident that the founding of the Conference on College Composition and Communication followed hard upon the advent of communication skills programs. The graduate students and new instructors who were typically conscripted by English departments to teach the required introductory course were not prepared to teach communication skills, since their graduate training fitted them to teach literature. And once the basic course was attended to by departments other than English, the limits of its staff's qualifications for teaching communication (and for teaching writing, for that matter) became apparent to other faculty and to deans. Moreover, with the advent of communication skills programs, full-time tenured academics were in charge of designing and administering the required first-year course for the first time since the late nineteenth century. The need for regular staff meetings became immediately apparent, given the innovation and complexity of the typical communication skills syllabus and the fact that teachers of the course hailed from two or even several disciplines (Gerber 1947; Harold Allen 1952). Staff meetings encouraged talk about the course among its teachers, and they awoke a desire in program directors to invent and stabilize teacher training programs. This desire stimulated in its turn a need to talk to other directors who were in the same boat. Hence, a professional organization was created (Gerber 1950, 1952; Wilson; Berlin 1987, 104ff).

John C. Gerber, who was active in the organization of CCCC, remembers its founding moment as follows:

> It all started [in 1947] at a meeting of the National Council in Chicago
> . . . on freshman programs. And 80 or 100 people turned out, which
> was unusual. I was chairman of the meeting, and they wouldn't close
> it. They wanted to talk. And finally I said, "Suppose we have a
> meeting just on this subject, the freshman program, next spring. How
> many of you would come?" and all the hands went up. So we had one
> the next spring and 500 people were there, which indicated that we had
> a bear by the tail. (1993)

NCTE had called the 1947 meeting in order to provide a forum for administrators and teachers to discuss the combined teaching of reading, writing, and speaking in communication courses. Gerber was chosen to chair it because he directed one of the premiere communication skills programs in the country, at Iowa. He remarked in his published account of the 1948 meeting that it "suggested to many the need and potential usefulness" of a professional organization for persons engaged in this new sort of freshman program (1952, 17).

And so it was communication skills, and not traditional composition, that inspired teachers of the required introductory course to move toward professionalization (Hackett). In an interview, Gerber explained that in the late 1940s there were two distinct kinds of freshman programs: "some kept the old composition programs, but others had moved over to communications. So in the early programs of the CCCC we always had to set up meetings for the two different kinds of programs. Since the communications programs were new and exciting, those of us heading communication programs tended to dominate. So we insisted that Communication be added to Composition" (1993). Later on in his career, Gerber would insist that it was communication skills that returned interest in rhetoric to English departments:

> the revival of interest in rhetoric began, really, in our composition
> classes in the late 1940s with the great emphasis at the time on commu-
> nication skills. Designed primarily for returning veterans and largely
> pragmatic in purpose, most of the communication skills courses did
> not last long, at least at the college level, but in their short life they
> broke up the notion of the successful composition as a static discourse
> needing only unity, coherence, and emphasis for its success. (1967, 353)

Gerber realized that current-traditionalism was not a rhetoric. Communication skills, on the other hand, was sympathetic to the notion that language use was only meaningful in social contexts.

THE INEVITABLE DEMISE

Most communication skills programs had been phased out by 1960, although some of the apparatus they initiated, such as placement testing, remains as part of current composition programs. Given the intellectual demands that communication skills placed upon teachers, and given the administrative support necessary to fund labs, clinics, support staff, and equipment, it does not surprise that communication skills programs did not last long. But resistance to communication skills on the part of traditional English teachers cannot be discounted as a factor in its demise.

Traditional teachers began to express their skepticism about the new approach early on in its history. In 1947, for example, Samuel Middlebrook caricatured the basic communications course at Denver as the "fruit of a marriage of the English and speech departments, plus some sound advice on when to shut up" (140). He recommended "a second thought about the adjustment to the life of Poe, of Wordsworth (before he got 'adjusted' and fell into prose), of Shelley and Shakespeare" as an alternative to the life-adjustment philosophy that drove the Denver program (143). In 1950, Kenneth Oliver took issue with communicationists' rejection of the "cultural uses" of language—that is, literature—which he described as "perhaps the most effective use to which language has ever been put" (5). Oliver cleverly used cold-war rhetoric to turn the communicationists' political argument against them. To refuse instruction in literature was "as dangerous to democracy as is the traditionalists' failure to teach competently evaluative response to slanted reports and the persuasive propaganda of special-interest writers and speakers." This was so because American individualism, which was reinforced in composition instruction by literary reading and written exercises in self-expression, was the only available weapon against "what sways the crowd, or collectivism."

In 1960, near the end of its heyday, Aerol Arnold found little evidence in "the best thinkers of our time" to support "the easy optimism of those teachers of communication who believe that once we teach more people to avoid two-valued judgements and 'achieve singleness of meanings through precision of expression' we will have achieved the 'miracle of shared living'" (12). As Middlebrook had done, Arnold positioned literature as the body of authoritative texts that established the sham perpetrated by communication skills. He doubted whether "the sense of loneliness in the world" which "pervades much of contemporary literature" could be combated by the puny array of instructional devices favored by partisans of the movement. But the locus classicus of complaint about communication skills was written by A. M. Tibbetts, who opined in 1965 that it was "one of the silliest doctrines ever to exist in American education" (91). Communication skills was "the best of times" for the "experimentally minded," Tibbetts wrote. "A student could get his lisp removed at the speech clinic in the morning, and in the afternoon he might learn to read the *Reader's Digest* faster and faster." Tibbetts was cheered by the reintroduction of rhetoric into composition instruction, but he suspected, perhaps rightly, that rhetoric was "crowded out" of the course by its teachers' inadequate level of preparedness and the general level of confusion that emanated from communication skills programs (92). From the point of view of the relatively fat 1960s, the serious wartime exigencies that gave birth to the communication skills movement must have seemed remote indeed.

FRESHMAN ENGLISH AND WAR

I began this chapter with the observation that the onset of war stimulates university faculty to prescribe curricula. The Vietnam War may seem at first glance to constitute an exception to this generalization, but it does not. Curricular reaction to that war was only delayed until the late 1970s, by which time student protestors had departed from the universities they had earlier tried to shut down. Under pressure from students, many universities dropped the universal requirement in composition during the early seventies (Smith; Hoover; Connors 1996). However, it was firmly back in place by the late 1970s, thanks no doubt to the media's fabrication of a literacy crisis and the supposed impact of open admissions on "standards." These events should probably be held together with a stronger connective than "and." John Heyda has made a forceful case that *Newsweek*'s "Why Johnny Can't Write" hysteria was an attempt to heap scorn on efforts by a few composition teachers (like Mina Shaugnessy at City College) to help new students acclimate to the university. And the *Newsweek* furor was followed by the publication of yet another sour report from gray eminences at Harvard, who recommended yet another curricular circling of wagons.

William Spanos argues that calls for more "unified" curricula, such as the general education movement, are responses to humanist realizations—brought on by the internationalist perspective that wartime inevitably imposes—that people living in other parts of the world do not necessarily accept the ideological positions reified within American culture. In the face of ideological threats to humanist concepts such as "freedom" or "man," general education (like liberal education before it) was an attempt to reaffirm the singularity and superiority of American culture. Here is Spanos, commenting on Harvard's "Redbook":

> by surveying, not history as such, but the monuments of western history, students would recover standards of judgment that would give certainty and direction to their intellectual pursuits and their sociopolitical practice, standards an "ominously" antidemocratic social philosophy in the "East" and "radicalism" at home were threatening to undermine. The vicious circularity of the logic of this pedagogic project should not be overlooked. Education in this view from above is not a process of generating critical consciousness but of gaining confirmation, of reaffirming at the end the (Western/American) standards of judgement that determine the pedagogical process from the beginning. (127)

While I am not inclined to accept uncritically Spanos's assumption that general education was a reaction to the perceived threat of socialism, I do agree that its educational effect was to blot out large sections of world history and ideology, to make certain events and points of view unreadable, as it were.

The irony is that such an education is put forward as education for freedom. For all its rhetoric of liberation, general education is constraining, particularly when it is couched in the more reactionary rhetoric of humanism, as it was during World War II. The "darker agenda" of humanism, Spanos avers, is "the production of 'subjected subjects,'—of individuals who are not only subordinated to the identity of the state, but who also work actively to enhance its hegemony" (126).[9] Spanos is correct to expose the hoax of liberation that attends institutional rhetoric about curricular requirements. Both liberal education and general education were couched in the language of democracy and freedom, and yet, in the most obvious ways, they reduced students' freedom to study whatever they like, to determine how many hours were required to get a degree, and to select their teachers. General education also subjected students to a battery of standardized tests, which, in the name of individualization, simply placed them on one or another predefined rung of the educational ladder. Most seriously, from the point of view of this study, general education offered the university a new rationale to support the universal requirement in introductory composition. It takes considerable rhetorical chutzpah to tout a universal requirement as a liberatory practice, but American universities got away with doing precisely that during World War II. With the single exception of brief and spotty interruptions brought about by student protests during the early 1970s, also motivated in part by the onset of war, universities have successfully imposed the requirement on students ever since.

9

AROUND 1971

THE EMERGENCE OF PROCESS PEDAGOGY

> The process approach was always there waiting for us. It was what we
> should have been doing all along and would have had we not confused the
> basic human act of discoursing with the kind of knowledge you can store in
> vaults, just because they were both being taught in the same buildings.
> —James Moffett, "Coming Out Right"

"Teach the process, not the product." This slogan enjoyed wide
currency among writing teachers during the 1970s, and it now serves professional writing teachers as a popular thumbnail history of writing instruction.
Around 1971, the story goes, composition teachers stopped relying on the
correction of finished essays as their primary means of instruction—the product—and instead began to offer assistance to students while they actually
composed, thus intervening in the process.[1]

THE PROBLEM AND TWO SOLUTIONS

A large body of textual evidence attests that a pedagogical turn of this
sort was widely recommended in professional literature published during the
late 1960s and throughout the 1970s. Advocates of process generally made
one of two sorts of recommendations: that teachers pay attention to students'
composing before they had actually begun to write, and that teachers adopt a
set of so-called "student-centered" classroom practices. In an early example
of the first sort of recommendation, David V. Harrington pointed out in 1968
that "the common emphasis in rhetorics, handbooks, guides to composition, is
upon organizing, correcting, and polishing the theme which has already been
thought of or discovered" (7). He recommended, on the contrary, that "the
time has come . . . to begin to concentrate primarily on what goes into the

discovery and development of ideas, which he characterized as an "earlier stage of the writing process" (7). Later writers would label this stage of the composing process "invention," after the practice followed by ancient rhetoricians.

In 1972, Donald Murray published an example of the second sort of recommendation in an essay entitled "Teach Writing as a Process, Not Product." Murray claimed that "teaching process" had the following implications for the composition curriculum:

(1) the text of the writing course is student writing;

(2) students find their own subjects and use their own language;

(3) students write as many drafts as are necessary to discover what there is to say;

(4) students write in any form that is appropriate, since "the process which produces creative and functional writing is the same";

(5) "mechanics come last";

(6) students writers must have enough time for the process to occur;

(7) individual papers are not graded;

(8) since student writers, as individuals, differ from one another, their writing processes may differ, too; and so "there are no rules, no absolutes, just alternatives." (91–92)

By means of this list, Murray implied that teachers who used traditional pedagogy focused on texts other than those composed by students, ignored the discovery process, insisted that students compose only one draft of each assignment, confined student writing to certain forms or genres of discourse, gave prominent attention to mechanics, did not allow sufficient time for composing to occur, graded every paper, and forced every student to follow the same absolute rules. What he described by omission, then, was the pedagogy of current-traditional rhetoric.

Teachers who recommended adoption of process pedagogy suggested that current-traditional instruction was the cause of bad student writing of the sort caricatured by Walter S. Minot in a 1974 issue of CCCC:

> Statement of Intent: My purpose in this theme is to define very specifically the real meaning of true friendship.
>
> In today's modern world, true friendship is very rare and hard to accomplish. Webster defines friendship as the state or fact of being friends. Thus it can be easily seen that in order of friendship to have a

state of existence there must be friends, because without friends there would be no friendship.

True friendship denotes more than just being friendly with someone. We are amicable with many people who are not really true friends. This is not true friendship. Truly real friendship happens only when two people are really true friends. In order to have a friend, you must be a friend first, or you won't have any friends. Everyone needs a friend, or his or her life will be very alienated.

A friend is a person who helps you up when you are down. You may have many acquaintances, but you can have only a few true friends. A friend is someone who will continue being your friend even if you do something bad to him. He will adhere to you through thick and thin, through rain or shine. If you took your best friend's girl away from him, he would still be your friend.

On mutual respect is based true friendship. A good example of this is the friendship between Allen Whitehall and Robert Epstein. If Al needed a dime to buy flowers for his widowed mother who has arthritis and Bob had a dime, he would give it to him no matter what the cost of the personal sacrifice.

As I have shown, true friendship is the greatest thing anyone can have. Without friends, no man can stand alone. I can only finalize my definition with these words: True friendship is eternal and it should last a lifetime. (154)

Murray argued that such writing was itself a response to product-centered teaching: "we teach writing as a product, focusing our critical attention on what our students have done," and yet our "conscientious, doggedly responsible, repetitive autopsying doesn't give birth to live writing" (89). In 1973, Jean Pumphrey also claimed that the bad writing typically produced in traditional composition classes was in fact taught to students by those very classes. "Few of us," she wrote, "would like to think that this is what we're teaching, but when we stand outside the process, pushing the student too quickly into communicative language, leaping past the expressive function of language, I believe we are, unwittingly, teaching the style we then sit back and criticize" (41). And in 1977, Linda Flower and John Hays lamented that "we still undertake to teach people to write primarily by dissecting and describing a completed piece of writing," while outside of school "writing is a highly goal-oriented, intellectual performance" (269). Flower and Hayes concluded that "this gap between the textbook and the experience is a problem composition must face." Even though these teachers complained about different features of traditional instruction—its critical focus on completed student writing, its focus on exposition, its focus on text rather than on performance—all were concerned with its inadequacy.

HISTORIES OF PROCESS PEDAGOGY

The thumbnail history encapsulated in "teach the process not the product" still animates composition lore. Recently, Lad Tobin "caricatured" the story composition teachers tell themselves and their graduate students about the advent of process pedagogy into first-year composition instruction:

> Writing teachers, realizing, finally, that less is often more, began throwing things overboard—grammar lessons, lectures on usage, old chestnut assignments, the modes of discourse sequence, prose models, grades, rules, prescriptions. And they began experimenting with exciting new techniques—freewriting, mapping, peer editing groups, one-to-one conferences, writing workshops, portfolios. Students began to write essays that other humans might actually want to read. And, not coincidentally, teachers began to think that composition wasn't just a service course, a burden, a dues-paying debt on the way to real teaching, but actually a real field in its own right and, for some, even a calling. (4)

Tobin has nicely caught the heady atmosphere of the time, it seems to me, particularly with reference to composition teachers' reconceptualization of their roles. With the advent of process pedagogy the classroom truly was a more interesting place to be, because the burden of filling three class hours a week was now shared by students who were doing peer reading and group brainstorming. The classroom was also much more interesting to think about than it had been prior to the advent of process, because composition teachers now gave themselves permission to think of their students as writers and themselves as people who had something to teach. Composition teachers, in short, began to think of themselves as professors of a field of study.

Many histories have been written about this period in first-year composition, in part because it truly was an exciting time, coinciding as it did with "the sixties" (which actually happened between 1965 and 1975, at least in my memory). I suppose it could be said that another such history is superfluous, and perhaps that is so. I have written this one, however, because it seems to me that a few features of composition teachers' turn to process have not received the emphasis they deserve. Process pedagogy brought about three rather remarkable changes to composition in the university. Most important, it professionalized the teaching of first-year composition. This was accomplished by means of the theoretical discovery of something on which to do research: students' composing processes. Another way to characterize this contribution is to say that the discovery of the composing process was at the same time the discovery that composition could be theorized. Second, if it ushered in a reconceptualization of composition teachers as disciplined professionals, process pedagogy also stimulated a reconceptualization of students as people who write rather than as people whose grammar and usage needs to be policed. Last, but certainly not least, the advent of process pedagogy made composition a lot more fun to teach.

On the other hand, one improvement often claimed for process pedagogy simply did not occur. Its partisans pictured process as an antidote to current-traditional pedagogy. However, the two pedagogies are not antithetical but complementary, and it will be part of the burden of this essay to show how this is so, and to demonstrate as well that current-traditional pedagogy remains alive and well in composition in the university.

PROCESS AS A FIX FOR CROWDED CLASSROOMS

It is a central assumption of this chapter that process pedagogy was welcomed by composition teachers in part because process-oriented teaching strategies were useful as means of alleviating difficulties imposed by the fact of the universal requirement. Indeed, the earliest advocates for process pedagogy wanted to exploit its potential for relieving the teaching situation brought about by the universal requirement. Barriss Mills began his 1953 essay entitled "Writing as Process" by pointing out that "everyone complains of our young people's inability to write clearly and effectively" (19). He pointed to a number of rationalizations that could explain this state of affairs: "the lack of time for instruction in writing, the overcrowding of our schools, the democratization of education, bringing students with poor backgrounds in English into the schools and colleges, the widening gulf between the written and the spoken languages, and even the movies, the comics, and television." Now, complaints about students' lack of preparation for introductory composition are part of the lore of Freshman English, and they date back to the invention of the composition requirement itself. Mills's complaints about television and comics are of course humanist complaints about popular entertainments of the 1950s. Overcrowded universities were in part a result of the GI Bill, which brought thousands of returning veterans back to school and had put severe strains on college and university faculties and facilities all over the country (Olson). But those students were probably not the ones Mills was thinking of when he worried about "democratization" and "poor backgrounds"—the veterans who returned to school after World War II were the most serious and successful group of students who had ever entered American higher education.

Mills argued that teachers' "unwillingness or incapacity to think of writing in terms of process" resulted in failed teaching. He criticized the outlines, drills, workbooks, and the "police-force" notion of usage associated with current-traditional pedagogy, as well as the standardized theme assignment typical of mass instruction in writing, because "learning to communicate effectively is very much an individual affair; mass methods simply will not work" (25). Even though Mills attributed his insight about the virtue of treating writing as a process to an intellectual climate that included semantics, linguistics, propaganda analysis, and psychologically informed literary criticism, one gets the impression that Mills's crowded classrooms were the real instigation of his recommendation (20). Confronted with so many students whose levels of writing ability differed, Mills preferred "individualized instruction." He wrote that a "style of expression is a matter of individual outlook and personality," and hence "some sort of laboratory approach seems to be the best method" to teach writing. Writing laboratories "make possible a more or less continuous co-operation between student and teacher during all steps in the writing process." He far preferred this individualized, process-oriented approach to "the old method of making a theme assignment, letting the student flounder alone through the process of writing it, and then triumphantly pointing out its many weaknesses." Mills was twenty years ahead of his time when he argued that "even mechanics can best be solved in the midst of the process of actual writing; the student learns more about grammar and punctuation by solving usage problems as they arrive" (25–26).

But Mills was not alone in recommending process-oriented tactics as means of stretching institutional resources. The "Oregon plan," developed by Charlton Laird and John C. Sherwood and partially funded by a grant from the Ford Foundation, was intended to alleviate the workload imposed on teachers of Freshman English by "the run-off from the post-depression and World War II baby deluge" (Laird 131). Laird devised his scheme of peer workshops and small-group conferencing in order to meet quite pragmatic exigencies: "we assumed that if I could teach the class in seven or eight hours without worse results than I should have expected from eleven hours, we could theoretically increase an instructor's load twenty-five to thirty percent without either him or his class suffering appreciably" (132). The gist of the plan was this: composition teachers met with a class once a week only; during the other two class sessions, students met in small groups in order to criticize one another's work. In the meantime, instructors held conferences with individual students. Laird crowed about the advantages of this system: students did much of the "routine correction" of papers; student attitude improved, as did "both the mechanics and the rhetoric" of their papers; the number of late papers decreased, as did plagiarism; and "tension between teacher and student lessened" as well, since "the student now felt he knew the teacher as a human being, and the teacher was no longer his severest critic" (134). Laird attributed these improvements to the fact that "the student receives less instruction in *writing*" and "more help in *learning to write*" (134). Furthermore, under this system students took personal responsibility for their work and for that of their colleagues (135). So while these early proponents of process pedagogy turned to it as a means of alleviating the difficulties associated with mass instruction, they soon found, to their satisfaction, that students' writing, and their attitudes about it, improved as well.

Since composition is universally required of entering students, its teachers feel the burden of enrollment increases as soon as they occur—sometimes long before administrators become aware of their impact on university resources. Composition's vulnerability to increased enrollment is compounded by the fact that composition teachers grade student papers. University faculty and administrators who have not taught composition often seem oblivious to the difference that this pedagogical necessity makes. An unforeseen (or unannounced) increase in freshman enrollment may impact, say, the biology or psychology or history departments, but such an increase can often be absorbed simply by finding a larger lecture hall. This is not true in composition, where each additional student means additional papers to grade. As a consequence, composition teachers are hyperconscious of the need to carefully husband the time available for grading and conferences. The strategies recommended by Mills and Laird made more time available by reducing the number of hours that teachers spent preparing and delivering lectures on current-traditional lore. Presumably, peer criticism also saved teacher time, since students' fellow writers could take care of any errors in grammar and usage that appeared in early drafts.

Early advocates of process tactics, then, turned to them as means of relieving the pressure put on teachers by the institutional situation of composition. They discovered the happier effects of process pedagogy only after they implemented it in order to save teachers' time and sanity.

THE DEVELOPMENT OF COMPOSITION THEORY

In 1982, only ten years after Murray's essay appeared, Maxine Hairston wrote that "the admonition to 'teach process, not product' is now conventional wisdom" (78).[2] Hairston noted that process pedagogy had been adopted only by the "vanguard of the profession," however; she doubted that "the overwhelming majority of college writing teachers in the United States" had yet had access to the literature on process pedagogy. Nonetheless, she claimed that "the move to a process-centered theory of teaching writing indicates that our profession is probably in the first stages of a paradigm shift" (77). Hairston borrowed the notion of the paradigm shift from Thomas Kuhn's *Structure of Scientific Revolutions* (1961, 117–18).[3] Paraphrasing Kuhn, she defined a paradigm as "a common body of beliefs and assumptions" or a "conceptual model" that "governs activity" in a given profession (Hairston 76). The regnant paradigm determines what are "the problems that need to be solved, the rules that govern research," and "the standards by which performance is to be measured."

Hairston's essay does not clarify whether she takes the supposed "paradigm shift" in composition to have fundamentally altered the profession's ways of knowing—that is, she does not say whether she takes this shift to have occurred on the level of epistemology. She reviews intellectual developments that may have contributed to teachers' uneasiness about product-centered instruction—"intellectual inquiry and speculation about language and language learning that was going on in . . . linguistics, anthropology, and clinical and cognitive psychology" (80). She also notes demographic changes brought about in student populations by open admissions and by the dropping of the universal requirement at a few schools. But for Hairston the key indicator of a paradigm shift within composition was the fact that "for the first time in the history of teaching writing we have specialists who are doing controlled and directed research on writers' composing processes" (81).

If paradigm shifts can be said to mark changes in the ways in which a professional community views itself and its practices, then Hairston was quite right to proclaim the advent of process pedagogy as a paradigm shift. She put her finger precisely on the real achievement of advocates for process pedagogy: they supplied composition teachers with something to study, something on which a field could be erected and a discipline could subsequently be based.[4] Even though the pressure to professionalize has been constant in American universities since the late nineteenth century, composition resisted this pressure until relatively late in its history. College teachers of composition did not have a professional organization that represented their specific interests until 1949, when they formed the Conference on College Composition and Communication in order to monitor and improve instruction in the required introductory course (Wilson 128). That is, prior to the 1970s, composition teachers had focused their professional attention on the maintenance of a course rather than on a body of research. This focus changed around 1971, because composition teachers discovered a subject upon which they could do research: the composing process as practiced by students.

During the 1960s, post-Sputnik anxiety made federal money available for research in the humanities. Among the English teachers to take advantage of this windfall were D. Gordon Rohman and Albert O. Wlecke, whose 1964 Project English study introduced a new term into composition teachers' lexicon—"Pre-writing." As far as I can tell, their study represents the first attempt since the late nineteenth century to theorize composition in the university.

In choosing sources for the design of their study, Rohman and Wlecke were typical of other early process theorists such as Janet Emig and James Britton's research group, whose interest in creativity stemmed primarily from two sources: accounts given by artists and scientists of their creative processes, on the one hand, and work being done in developmental psychology, on the other. Rohman, for example, cited accounts of composing by the poet John Ciardi and the novelist Dorothy Sayers alongside his citations of the work of Jerome Bruner, a developmental psychologist. Certainly, interest in creativity was in the air during the middle years of the twentieth century. Brewster Ghiselin's collection of essays about creativity, published in 1952, was often cited or alluded to by theorists of process during the sixties. The collection featured an account by French mathematician Henri Poincare about his partially unconscious creative process, an account on which both Emig and James Britton's group obviously drew (Emig 1964; Britton et al. 22–32). *The Paris Interviews: Writers at Work* began to be published in 1958. Creative writing programs experienced phenomenal growth during the middle decades of the century, and so creative writing teachers' talk about the writing process and workshop pedagogy circulated in the discourse of English departments during that time as well (Myers, Wilbers).

Three of Bruner's works seem to have been especially stimulating to process theorists: his account of a conference of "scientists, scholars and educators" who gathered in 1959 to discuss improvements in scientific pedagogy, entitled *The Process of Education* (1963, vii); his collection of essays on nonrational thought, entitled *On Knowing: Essays for the Left Hand* (1962); and *Toward A Theory of Instruction* (1966).⁵ Bruner's speculations on pedagogy included the repeated observations that traditional education emphasized rational knowing at the expense of other means of learning, and that teachers too often concentrated on teaching specific skills rather than on imparting more general levels of understanding. The complaint that knowing rather than doing takes center stage in traditional education is of course reminiscent of Dewey's educational philosophy, as is the distinction between lower- and higher-order experiences (Dewey 1938a, 44; 1989, 15–16). Interestingly, Bruner's critique of traditional education could be aimed directly at current-traditional composition instruction, which imparted knowledge of the humanist canon at the same time as it drilled students in the mechanics of written discourse; neither practice aimed at providing students with a "general understanding" of composing.

Chief among Bruner's candidates for alternative means of learning were what composition teachers now call "heuristics"—disciplined yet open-ended techniques of discovery or inquiry. Bruner defined discovery as "a matter of rearranging or transforming evidence in such a way that one is enabled to go beyond the evidence so reassembled to new insights" (1962, 82–83). He hypothesized that continuing practice in inquiry would teach children how to apply their learning to new areas; in other words, "it is only through the exercise of problem solving and the effort of discovery that one learns the working heuristics of discovery; the more one has practice, the more likely one is to generalize what one has learned into a style of problem solving or inquiry that serves for any kind of task encountered—or almost any kind of task" (94). He pointed out that he had "never seen anybody improve in the art and technique of inquiry by any means other than engaging in inquiry."⁶ Bruner argued further that real understanding of any subject came about only when a learner achieved a grasp of its "conceptual structure" (120). It is important in this context to note that Bruner's notion of "general understanding" was not to be achieved by the passive study of specifics such as the canonical texts recommended by humanists. While such study might acquaint students with the trivia of history, it had no power to equip them with organizing concepts that would enhance their further learning. Bruner defined culture as "the development of great organizing ideas"; the power of such ideas is that "they permit us to understand and sometimes to predict or change the world in which we live" (120). Like Dewey, then, Bruner was not opposed to the study of history or literature, but he wanted instruction to focus not on texts but on learners' activation of what they found there.

Rohman's account of his and Wlecke's experimental study clearly indicates that they preferred that writing instruction operate in what Bruner called the "hypothetical mode," wherein "the student is not a bench-bound listener, but is taking a part in the formulation [of the material] and at times may play the principal role in it" (Bruner 1962, 83). This approach, Bruner argued, offered a distinct gain over traditional teaching insofar as it increased a learner's "intellectual potency." That is to say, when learners approached tasks as opportunities for discovery, they were far more likely to become self-motivated—to continue to learn because they were rewarded by the joy of discovering things for themselves (Bruner 1962, 88). Rohman interpreted this directive to mean that composition instruction could no longer "'program' students to produce 'Letters and Reports for All Occasions'" (1965, 108). Rather, the point of composition instruction was to "enlighten" students "concerning the powers of creative discovery within them." To do so would render composition instruction both liberal and responsible.

In other words, Bruner authorized Rohman and Wlecke to switch the focus of instruction away from texts and onto students. At the same time, they constructed a new subject of composition—the self-directed student, the person who, according to Rohman, "stands at the center of his own thoughts and feelings with the sense that they begin in him. He is concerned to make things happen and not simply to allow things to happen to him; he seeks to dominate his circumstances with words or actions" (Rohman 108). The construct of the self-directed student allowed Rohman to theorize the scene of composing in very different terms than those given by the humanist pedagogical tradition. The subject of Brunerian pedagogy would no longer be a passive receiver or transmitter of texts. The student would become, rather, a person who actively reflected upon experience, someone who could, in

Brunerian terms, assimilate the conceptual structure of a subject and alter it to fit conceptual structures already in place in his or her mind; the student would, in other words, learn (Bruner 1963, 11).

Discovery was central to Rohman and Wlecke's theoretical innovation. They isolated a stage of composing called "Pre-writing" and defined it as "the stage of discovery in the writing process when a person assimilates his 'subject' to himself" (106). They hoped that with their invention of Pre-writing that they isolated "the characteristic combinatorial principle . . . that underlies all writing" (106–07). Now, in *On Knowing*, Bruner defined "combinatorial activity" as "a placing of things in new perspectives" in such a way that new knowledge comes about (20). If Pre-writing is such a principle, it must name the means by which writers discover new ways of combining materials, ways that lead them to new discoveries. However, as a principle it is not specific to the discovery process used in a given composing situation, for which Rohman reserved the theoretical term "pattern" (106). Nor does it have anything to do with the arrangement or organization a writer will eventually impose on a completed discourse. Pre-writing is a much more general term; indeed, Rohman virtually equated it with thinking, which he defined as

> that activity of mind which *brings forth* and develops ideas, plans, designs, not merely the entrance of an idea into one's mind; an active, not a passive enlistment in the "cause" of an idea; conceiving, which includes consecutive logical thinking but much more besides; essentially the imposition of pattern upon experience. (106)

Thinking, or Pre-writing, was active reflection on experience that imposes order or pattern upon it. When writers do not employ Pre-writing, according to Rohman, they can achieve only a "remote" or "abstract" understanding of whatever it is they wish to write about: "it is not enough to know *about* goodness; we must know it from experience" (107). This emphasis on experience provided Rohman with sufficient grounds for rejecting current-traditional or any other inherited lore about composing. He defined "bad writing" as the "sort of book" in which writing problems are "identified and solved in advance of any person's encountering them"; "good writing" on the other hand, was "the discovery by a responsible person of his uniqueness with his subject" (107–08).

In Rohman and Wlecke's work, Pre-writing seems to represent both kinds of learning discriminated by Bruner: specific and nonspecific transfer. A basic principle of learning, for Bruner, was that "grasping the structure of a subject is understanding it in a way that permits many other things to be related to it meaningfully. To learn structure, in short, is to learn how things are related" (Bruner 1960, 7). Commenting on this passage, Rohman noted that "in writing, this fundamental structure is not one of content but of method" (1965, 107). He thought that if researchers could "isolate the principle that underlies all writing," students could then "practice that principle in whatever 'subjects'" they might choose. For Bruner, learning occurred through two sorts of transfer: through "specific applicability to tasks that are highly similar to those we originally learned to perform" and through "learning initially not a skill but a general idea, which can then be used as a basis for recognizing subsequent problems as special cases of the idea originally mastered" (1960, 17). Learning to hammer nails, for example, helps one learn how to hammer tacks or to chip wood. These are cases of specific transfer. Bruner gave no examples of nonspecific transfer, but I think we can assume that in regard to composing, for example, he would underwrite the notion that a general understanding of how composing works in writing would enable a student to grasp how composing occurs in, say, music.

On the analogy of hammering and chipping, it seems to follow that learning to write an essay would facilitate specific transfer to, say, the writing of poetry. However, Rohman and Wlecke treated Pre-writing as the sort of general principle that facilitates nonspecific transfer of learning: "we sought to isolate the structuring principle of all Pre-writing activity and then to devise exercises to allow students to imitate that principle in their own 'Pre-writing'" (112). Much of the student writing that was produced during their research was of the kind "which immediately follows the discovery of fresh insight"; as such, it was not suitable to all possible occasions for discourse. Nonetheless, they argued that "writing grounded in the principle of personal transformation ought to be the *basic* writing experience for all students at all levels, the propaedeutic to all subsequent and more specialized forms of writing." Here, in other words, is an argument for the primacy of expressive discourse as a fundamental kind of writing, an argument that, as far as I can see, is not authorized by Brunerian educational psychology. In this passage Rohman and Wlecke substituted the nonspecific sense of Pre-writing—the composing process in general—for one of its specific manifestations: writing to discover. The privileging of personal or expressive writing would become a central theme in process pedagogy. It is hard to say whether this preference stems from its early theorists' interest in the composing accounts of literary writers or whether it reflects the humanist assumption that the point of composing is the expression of one's cultivation. Perhaps the preference has to do with the ideology of liberal individualism that undergirds process pedagogy (see chapter 10). Or maybe process theorists preferred expressionist discourse simply because, to their way of thinking, it was not current-traditional.

Rohman and Wlecke did not follow up another opening offered them by Bruner's work: the opportunity to define what might constitute the "structure" of composing, defined as a field of study. They did not do this, I think, because they were less interested in theorizing composition than they were in dissociating Pre-writing from current-traditional composition instruction, which they referred to as the "knowledge of standards" and "the rhetoric of the finished word" (106). To be sure, in 1965 almost no one thought of composition in the university as a potential site for theory; virtually the only incentive to theorize about what went on in Freshman English was teachers' discontent with the actual scene of teaching. And so it makes perfect sense that Rohman and Wlecke devised their theoretical innovation in reaction to the instructional status quo. Despite this, their notion of Pre-writing remained frustratingly consistent with current-traditionalism, since they insisted that heuristic work is done entirely in the mind and that such work precedes writing or drafting. Rohman's discussion of Pre-writing makes explicit his continuing subscription to the current-traditional convictions that "thinking must be distinguished from writing" and that "in terms of cause and effect, thinking precedes writing." In other words, the inventors of the term *Pre-writing* did not acknowledge the points that would be made later by Bruner and other process theorists: that the use of language can stimulate invention and that invention can occur while a composer writes (Bruner 1966, 111).

Historians of composition associate teachers' widespread adoption of process pedagogy not with Rohman and Wlecke, but with the work of Janet Emig, particularly her 1971 monograph entitled *The Composing Processes of Twelfth Graders*. James A. Berlin claims that "the effect of Emig's study was widespread and significant" and that "her effort resulted in more teachers calling upon the process model of composing" (Berlin 1987, 160–61).[7] But Emig began to make important theoretical contributions to composition even before she published her famous monograph.

Emig's disgust with current-traditional rhetoric cannot be discounted as a motivating force in her turn to process pedagogy. An essay published in 1964, entitled "The Uses of the Unconscious in Composing," features a decidedly unrestrained attack on contemporary composition instruction, which then depended on in-class essays and the "theme-a-week assignment" (6).

Here is Emig on contemporary textbooks:

> It must be acknowledged that the writers of these texts do not promise
> more than mere competency of product: if method is surface,
> expectation is appropriately low. There is no wisp or scent anywhere
> that composing is anything but a conscious and antiseptically efficient
> act. Nowhere in such an account is there acknowledgment that writing
> involves commerce with the unconscious self and that because it does,
> it is often a sloppy and inefficient procedure for even the most
> disciplined and longwriting of professional authors. Nowhere are
> there hints about preverbal anguishing and the hell of getting under-
> way; of the compulsions and fetishes governing the placement of the
> first word or phrase on the page—the "getting black on white" of
> deMaupassant; of subsequent verbal anguishing; of desert places; of
> the necessary resorting to the id as organizer and energizer. It could be
> said that I am asking—primal sin—for such books to be something
> other than they are meant to be; and perhaps they are used chiefly for
> their prescriptive annexes on usage. But nonetheless, one longs for
> them to make at least a small obeisance in the direction of the untidy,
> of the convoluted, of the not-wholly-known, of a more intricate self
> and process. (7)

Emig's scorn for traditional pedagogy was no less marked in the 1971 monograph, where she characterized the five-paragraph theme as a mode "so in-
digenously American that it might be called the Fifty-Star Theme. In fact,
the reader might imagine behind this and the next three paragraphs Kate Smith
singing 'God Bless America' or the piccolo obligato from 'The Stars and
Stripes Forever'" (97).

"The Uses of the Unconscious in Composing" appeared in an issue of
CCC sandwiched between pieces by poets Marvin Bell and William Stafford.
But Emig's essay was no paean to the mysteries of inspiration. She established that professional writers consciously relied on settings and devices that
stimulated them to composition—music, incantation, habit, and ritual. Most
of the citations in this essay were to the work of novelists and poets—Stein,
Cather, Poe, Kipling, Spender, Lowell, Hemingway—although Emig did
mention Bruner in passing. In *The Web of Meaning* (1983), a retrospective
collection of her early work, Emig mentioned that when she wrote the 1964
essay she was particularly taken by Stephen Spender's differentiation of composers into "Mozartians" and "Beethovians," since for her, writing was "such

an agony" (44). That is to say, Spender's recognition that some writers, like Beethoven, took a slow, evolutionary, painful, and sometimes aimless approach to composing justified to Emig the difficulty that she experienced in her own writing.

Emig's most important contribution to composition theory may have been this habit of treating her own composing process—as well as those articulated by professional writers—as exemplary sources of insight into composing in general. Her innovation was to assume that all human beings face the same problems and issues when they compose; students were no different from professional writers in this regard. While this does not seem like an earth-shaking discovery on the face of it, in the context of current-traditional instruction Emig's insight was revolutionary. In that milieu, students' composing processes were thoroughly prescribed. Moreover, students' writing was sharply distinguished in kind from that produced by the poets and novelists they read in class, which was presented to them as though it had been created in an instant by the inspired insight of "great" minds. In the new dispensation ushered in by Emig's work, poets, novelists, teachers, and students alike struggled while composing. Furthermore, composing processes were as varied and as idiosyncratic as the people who deployed them and the occasions on which they were used. With the benefit of this insight, composition teachers could focus on tactics or strategies for instigating and maintaining each student's process as it developed on each composing occasion, and hence students themselves, rather than the texts they produced, became the locus of instruction.

In an essay entitled "On Teaching Composition: Some Hypotheses as Definitions" (1967), Emig applied what she had learned about human intellectual processes to teaching itself. She defined teaching not as analysis and evaluation of completed texts, but as "the intervention, usually by an older person, into a process, usually of a younger person, to improve that process or the product of that process" (128). She suggested that interventions have two modes: proffering freedoms and establishing constraints. The freedoms she listed are very like those that Murray would mention five years later:

> the provision of stimuli; the extension of options, including the acceptance of divergent writing behavior . . . allowing the student to choose his own subject and style of approach; permitting him, tacitly or explicitly, to break off in process and not complete a given piece of writing; withholding any form of evaluation . . . and giving sanction for the student in some instances not to write at all. (1967, 129)

It is worthy of note that Emig characterized these process-oriented teaching strategies as "freedoms," while she treated as "constraints" tactics that are obviously associated with current-traditional instruction: the rationing or removal of stimuli, the establishment of parameters, the insistence that writing be completed and evaluated (130). She posited, further, that there might be other processes of composing that did not follow the monolithic, linear approach implied by current-traditional attitudes toward invention: "instead of a process or processes inexorably made up of three 'stages,' there may be more or fewer components. Writing may be recursive, a loop rather than a linear affair—one can write, then plan; or one can revise, then write" (131). This possible multiplicity of processes supported, once again, the wisdom of proffering students freedom to compose however and whatever they chose.

In this essay Emig wrote as though she believed that process pedagogy most often produced expressivist discourse, while the traditional approach most often produced expository discourse. Furthermore, expressive discourse was produced with the least teacher intervention; its pedagogy focused on "nonintervention or upon intervention enacted chiefly as the proffering of freedoms"; the production of expository or communicative discourse, on the other hand, required teachers to help students "to acknowledge growing or changing sets of constraints" (134). Composition teachers relied far too much on constraints, Emig thought, which created a view of teaching that is "dangerously truncated, irresponsible, and anti-humanistic" (129). She connected this habit to American pragmatism: "This exclusiveness can be formulated as follows, 'The imagination is no damn good unless it propels events in the 'real' world, such as the hanging of witches, or the dropping of napalm'" (132–33).

In Emig's early work, then, a theory of composing was generated from an odd conflation of sources. Expressionism—as articulated over and over by the subjects of the *Paris Review* interviews—combined fruitfully with her reading in philosophy and psychology. Emig was correct to associate expressivist writing with humanism; as D. G. Myers argues in his history of creative writing instruction in America, its original impulse was intimately tied to humanist literary education, and expressive writing is of course the premiere genre of creative writing pedagogy (4). Emig's association of exposition with pragmatism was mistaken, however, since exposition also has a humanist heritage, via current-traditional pedagogy (see chapter 5). Exposition can only be called "pragmatic" from inside a humanist point of view, where it does indeed look workaday because it is paired off against "creative" or "expressive" writing. Expository prose as it is configured within current-traditional pedagogy is not particularly pragmatic, since it usually functions as a medium of graphic display. Nor should Emig's unflattering depiction of an unimaginative and amoral pragmatism as "what gets the job done" obscure the extent to which her own work is indebted to philosophical pragmatism, insofar as the developmental psychology from which she drew her later work is very much at home in a pragmatist tradition of educational philosophy (France).

There is almost no documentation in the 1967 essay, although Emig did suggest that teachers and students read *Writers at Work* (25). She later remarked that she read "a great many pieces on processes of writing" during a seminar she took in 1961 with Priscilla Tyler, to whom she gave credit for bringing the notion of process to her attention (1983, 44, 61–62). During the late sixties, she apparently began to read extensively in developmental psychology. The documentation in the 1971 monograph is about equally divided between poets and novelists, on the one hand, and cognitive/developmental psychologists and philosophers of mind, on the other. Early in the 1970s Emig also discovered the work of James Britton and his colleagues, to whom she referred as "the London group" (1983, 97–98).

Britton's group published the results of their massive study of the development of children's writing abilities in 1975. Britton and company concerned themselves with writing as a process because they were interested in writers' development (1975, 20). They assumed that "as writing becomes more complex and its varying functions become distinguished and developed, so too do the processes by which the writing is achieved." It is obvious from their discussion of these matters that they thought they were entering relatively uncharted waters, and that a better understanding of the development of writing processes would immeasurably improve writing instruction (19, 21). However, this study, too, was apparently provoked in part by the perceived inappropriateness of current-traditional rhetoric. Britton and his colleagues wished to provide teachers with a "model" that would "characterize all mature written utterances and then go on to trace the developmental steps that led to them" (6). Since their examination of the writing of mature adults demonstrated that there were many more genres of writing than the four forms allowed by current-traditional rhetoric (exposition, description, narration, and argument), they rejected this scheme and developed one of their own based on their examination of actual student writing. Working inductively, they produced a threefold "functional" scheme in which student writing was categorized as "expressive," "transactional," or "poetic." Unfortunately, this generic scheme influenced composition teachers more than did their detailed discussion of the writing process, primarily because Britton's categories recognized expressive discourse as a distinct mode of composition (Gradin 51–52). This, as well as the humanist strain in traditional composition instruction, authorized teachers to concentrate instruction on expressivist discourse (France 87ff).

PROCESS AND STUDENT UNREST

During the late 1960s, students began to express their dissatisfaction with business as usual in the freshman writing class. Sometimes this dissatisfaction was expressed quite compellingly: at the University of Iowa, for example, the rhetoric building was burned down. Responding to student pressure, perhaps, many universities reduced the number of hours in the requirement or lowered the standard for exemption (Smith). Teachers rationalized these moves by convincing themselves that students were better prepared for college work than they had been in the past (Wilcox 1973). A few universities abandoned the composition requirement altogether, and those that did so found to their surprise that enrollments in the elective composition course remained high (Hoover).

Process pedagogy offered teachers a much less radical way to respond to students' insistence on "relevance" in their courses. In a recent interview, Gary Tate remarked that in 1971 "there were . . . experimental courses going on around the country as teachers, under the influence of changing social, political, and educational attitudes, began trying to make the classroom more student-centered, more responsive to the rapidly changing world outside the classroom" (McDonald 37). Tate's observation is born out by the professional literature from the period. In 1970, for instance, Harvey Stuart Irlen pointed out that traditional composition instruction was no longer suited to its students, since "the operating word is 'now.' Traditional freshman-English courses are not now; and, increasingly, freshman are" (35). Irlen urged the adoption of small-group instruction in writing and reading in the name of three key terms: freedom, relevance, and responsibility. Each of these values was impossible to achieve in traditional instruction, Irlen thought, because "we have set an arcane body of knowledge between ourselves and the students" (36).

Hip teachers demanded that Freshman English be turned into a "happening." In 1967, Charles Deemer urged teachers to remove their authority and to engage "students' active participation"; the goal was "a class of students actively aware and participant, a class that does not swallow the 'teacher's' remarks but considers them" (123). Deemer recommended that teachers use surprise and shock to upset students' expectations about traditional authority relations in the classroom; he recommended, among other things, that teachers "speak, not from behind a podium, but from the rear of the room or through the side window" and that they "discuss theology to Ray Charles records" (124). In 1971, William Lutz explicitly connected the happening to process, arguing that happenings focused teachers and students' attention on the fact that "writing is creative" (35). He defined a happening as "structure in unstructure; a random series of ordered events; order in chaos; the logical illogicality of dreams."

To give them their due, Deemer and Lutz realized that current-traditional instruction was tightly implicated with the hierarchical and authoritarian structure of the university, and, in line with that realization, they recommended restructurings of classrooms and realignments of institutional authority along with more sweeping innovations. Lutz, writing with tongue firmly in cheek, put it this way: "we need to look anew at the student, the role of the teacher, the classroom experience, the process of writing, human nature, original sin, and the structure of the universe" (35). If nothing else, then, student unrest caused composition teachers to ponder ways in which they might redistribute authority in their classrooms. One way to do this was to reject current-traditional rhetoric, which channeled authority from institution through teacher to student.

As we have seen, teachers characterized this rejection as a transfer of attention from "a body of arcane knowledge" to the lives and experiences of their students. This distinction between texts and people was not lost on contemporary observers. Robert Gorrell observed in 1972 that "this concern for what the student is rather than what he does . . . provides at least some basis for a distinction between new and old or traditional" (265). Made uncomfortable by the pedagogy of happenings wherein "making scrapbooks or collages or films" sometimes replaced instruction in writing, Gorrell argued for a more balanced perspective: "the development of the student seems to me infinitely more important than the sanctity of the topic sentence or rules for using a semicolon. But I do not believe concern for the student's growth precludes trying to give him some help, even some information" (266). Gorrell worried that, in their rush to eject current-traditional rhetoric from the introductory course, teachers were in danger of rejecting substance altogether.

Another way to redistribute authority in the classroom was to disperse it among students. The turn to process, with its emphasis on students' activities, was admirably suited to the adoption of teaching tactics that supposedly dispersed composing authority among all members of a classroom. Accordingly, during the early 1970s, composition teachers began to experiment with workshops and peer review. These tactics were aimed at giving student writers a greater voice in the development, revision, and editing of their work in progress. But composition teachers also wanted to displace some of the responsibility for classroom activity away from themselves and onto students.

Workshops have a long history in the American academy. Historians variously attribute their origin to progressive education or to nineteenth-century literary societies (Gere, Myers). However, workshops came into their own as a pedagogical tool during the middle of the twentieth century with the establishment of programs in creative writing. The first such program in the country, at the University of Iowa, was (and still is) actually called "The Writer's Workshop." At Iowa, workshops "involved small groups of students meeting weekly with an instructor, discussing the work submitted, and offering suggestions to each other on how to improve it" (Wilbers 97).

Nor were peer review and workshops new to composition instruction in the 1970s. Many early teachers of composition, including George Pierce Baker and Gertrude Buck, offered regularly scheduled writing courses that were called "workshops" and that presumably relied on peer criticism. And, as we have seen, Charlton Laird and his associates had utilized both tactics during the 1950s in order to maximize efficiency of instruction. But during the 1970s, workshops enjoyed an enormous surge in popularity among composition teachers. Ann Gere has established that there was three times more professional talk about "writing groups" during that time than had appeared during either of the previous two decades (1987, 29). Gere attributes the renewed popularity of workshops to teachers' acquaintance with developmental psychology and new theories of language learning. But I think that historians should not discount student unrest, as well as teachers' weariness with the teacher-centered pedagogy of current-traditional rhetoric, as important stimuli to the adoption of workshop pedagogy.

PROCESS PEDAGOGY AND INVENTION

During the 1970s, writing teachers assumed a close relation between process pedagogy and the rhetorical canon of invention. In his 1976 survey of invention, Richard Young remarked that

> it is no accident that the gradual shift in attention among rhetoricians
> from composed product to the composing process is occurring at the
> same time as the reemergence of invention as a rhetorical discipline.
> Invention requires a process view of rhetoric; and if the composing
> process is to be taught, rather than left to the student to be learned,
> arts associated with various stages of the process are necessary. (33)

Young was correct to associate the renewed interest in invention with the
emergence of process pedagogy. Even though current-traditional rhetoric
had a truncated theory of invention, current-traditional teachers did not pay
explicit attention to invention when they made writing assignments. In current-traditional classrooms, students wrote outside of class, except when they
were asked to compose an impromptu theme in the space of a class hour.
(This exercise was intended to insure teachers that at least some student writing was not plagiarized). Students' work was read and evaluated with an eye
toward their mastery of formal correctness rather than the quality or extent
of the material discussed. Hence the notion that teachers or peers might intervene in students' composing was something of a novelty, as was the notion
that students might complete more than one draft of an assignment. Also
new was the suggestion that teachers might evaluate the quality of students'
thoughts—something that was certainly implied by the use of some heuristics, such as the ancient topics, which enjoyed a brief vogue during the 1960s.

Invention, as understood by ancient rhetoricians, is any systematic search
for, and generation or compilation of, material that can be used to compose a
discourse suitable for some specific rhetorical situation. Invention may go on
throughout the composing process; as delinquent students know, invention
often begins anew during editing. Since invention can rely solely upon a
composer's linguistic and memorial resources, it can occur at any time—when
the composer is doing other things than composing. Invention may or may
not include writing or speaking; for example, medieval composers invented
in memory, using writing or speaking only if they wished to publish their
compositions (Carruthers). Invention was configured as a wholly mental activity in current-traditional lore, and so the theoretical transfer of invention
from mind to pen might be said to be a hallmark gesture of the shift to process pedagogy. The contribution of literate heuristics by a number of composition scholars during the 1970s consolidated teachers' dawning awareness
that invention might take place in writing itself.

A few truly challenging inventional systems—the topics of ancient rhetoric, for example, and the tagmemic model developed by Richard Young, Alton Becker, and Kenneth Pike—were touted in innovative textbooks as well as the professional literature of composition, but neither was widely appropriated by teachers of the required first-year composition course. Free writing, which was brought to the attention of composition teachers by Ken Macrorie and Peter Elbow, fared somewhat better, as did a collection of heuristic strategies borrowed from heterogeneous sources—brainstorming, cubing, dual-entry notebooks, journal-keeping, and the like.[8] These free-floating, all-purpose heuristic strategies survive in current best-selling composition textbooks, while inventional systems that depend on students' and teachers' acquaintance with a complex theory of discourse, like ancient rhetorics or tagmemic linguistics, have fallen by the pedagogical wayside. It might be worth considering why this happened.

During the 1960s a distinguished group of composition theorists recommended that the inventional schemes adumbrated with ancient rhetorics be appropriated in the teaching of composition. This group included Dudley Bailey, Edward P. J. Corbett, Frank D'Angelo, Gorrell, Richard Weaver, and W. Ross Winterowd, among others. Despite the professional authority commanded by its advocates, the use of ancient rhetorics never caught on among teachers of introductory composition. Their limited appeal is not surprising. The extant texts of ancient rhetorics are expensive and hard to obtain; they are also difficult to use without a fairly thorough grounding in ancient history and culture. Although Corbett's elegant *Classical Rhetoric for Modern Students* (1965) remains in print, it has largely been used in graduate rhetoric classes or in teacher training, uses which testify to the perceived difficulty of its subject.

The sheer foreignness of the ancient notion of *copia* poses a more serious difficulty to modern teachers who wish to adapt ancient rhetoric to composition instruction. Ancient teachers insisted that their students develop an abundance of topics on which to elaborate. Such copiousness, hoarded and filed in a well-trained memory, went with a rhetor wherever she traveled; a copiously supplied rhetor had no need to retreat to one of the few sparsely stocked libraries that existed in ancient times. Ancient invention also drew on communal epistemologies that privilege the commonplace; that is, they began with tradition, precept, generally accepted wisdom, what everybody knew. The communal bias of ancient invention is evident, for example, in its deployment of values (justice, honor, expediency, and the like) which its teachers assumed to be shared, at least rhetorically, by all members of a community. These emphases on copiousness and communal knowledge are foreign to modern thought and hence to current-traditional rhetoric, which reveres economy and privileges the individual author who can originate and own new ideas.

Teachers who advocated the use of ancient rhetorics in the required composition course during the 1960s tried either to overlook or to erase the epistemological incompatibility of ancient rhetorics with current-traditionalism, but, as Susan Miller has argued, they did not succeed (1989). I suspect that ancient schemes of invention feel "added on" in a current-traditional milieu; that is, teachers who define writing in current-traditional terms recognize on some level that ancient rhetorics are theories of composing in their own right, theories that are not epistemologically consistent with current-traditional pedagogy. So, while it is possible that the so-called "revival" of ancient rhetorics during the sixties did provide historical authority for a renewed interest in invention as a viable part of composing, ancient inventional systems were never widely adopted by teachers of the required first-year composition course (Connors, Ede, and Lunsford).

A similar fate befell another well-formed theory of invention: the particle-wave-field heuristic adumbrated in Richard Young, Alton Becker, and Kenneth Pike's *Rhetoric: Discovery and Change* (1970). This book enjoyed modest success during the early seventies in introductory composition courses. Since then, however, it has accrued the curricular status of Corbett's text— often cited, often plundered for classroom use, occasionally serving as part of graduate students' introduction to rhetoric. The particle-wave-field heuristic is perhaps the most complex heuristic ever developed for use in composition instruction. It required students to "view" the "unit" they were studying across six different perspectives: particle-wave-field and contrast-variation-distribution (127). That is, they were to analyze changes that occurred when they shifted their perspective on the unit from the vantage points of time and space, and when they considered it as part of a larger context, or "system." The complexity of the tagmemic heuristic undoubtedly mitigated against its wide adoption. Serious engagement with it interrupts the linear progress of composing advocated within current-traditionalism. Students who were used to the quick production time typical of current-traditional pedagogy must have been frustrated by a heuristic that forced them to concentrate on invention so intensely and thoroughly. Teachers who were not used to evaluating the content of students' papers may have felt constrained by the tagmemic heuristic's focus on the invention of material.

This is not to say that nobody appreciated the scholarship on which the tagmemic heuristic was based. In a lecture delivered in 1970, justifying teachers' interest in the composing process, James McCrimmon asserted that "the writing process is a process of making choices"; he cited as support an essay on style by Young and Becker, along with Pike's early work with tagmemics. This reference to Young, Becker, and Pike's scholarship was in keeping with McCrimmon's habitual intellectual eclecticism. Three years earlier, he had incorporated the term "pre-writing" (from Rohman and Wlecke?) into the fourth edition of his successful current-traditional textbook, *Writing With a Purpose* (1967, 4). And in a 1969 essay he allowed that "Prewriting, of course, is nothing new. It goes back at least to Aristotle's search for the available means of persuasion and in one form or another it has always been encouraged in the schools, usually by the injunction 'Think before you write'" (125–26). Now, while Aristotle invented many Western notions, he can hardly be saddled with responsibility for this current-traditional canard about invention. But McCrimmon was not finished making connections. He linked Prewriting to I. A. Richards's notion of "feed-forward," implicated Kenneth Burke's theory of motives with his own notion of purpose, and tied Burke's concept of identification to the work of Anatol Rapaport, who probably got it from Burke, or maybe Carl Rogers (127). McCrimmon's flattening eclecticism demonstrates just how accommodating current-traditionalism can be. It is so accommodating, in fact, that it has happily appropriated the process pedagogy that many teachers thought would finally displace it from the first-year composition course.

THE CONTINUITY OF CURRENT-TRADITIONALISM

Process-oriented composing strategies, while indeed new to the introductory composition course around 1971, were easily adapted to current-traditional instruction. Indeed, such adaptation occurred almost as soon as process talk appeared in the professional literature. As early as 1967, McCrimmon included heuristic exercises in *Purpose*. In 1970, Ray Kytle advocated the use of "pre-writing" to help students produce current-traditional texts. For Kytle, pre-writing was a three-stage process during which students examined their chosen subjects from a variety of points of view, limited the subject, and developed a thesis. Narrowing a subject and finding a thesis are, of course, hallmarks of current-traditional invention.[9]

The continuing prominence of current-traditionalism belies that any significant epistemological shift has occurred in teachers' thinking about composition instruction. Signs of current-traditionality appear in descriptions of composition programs at colleges and universities all over the country, where the first course is labeled "exposition" and the second "argument," or where students are expected to write a long research paper, or where formal fluency and correct usage determine teachers' evaluations of student writing. Too, current-traditionalism still informs the best-selling composition textbooks.[10] Their authors typically incorporate process-oriented composing strategies into a current-traditional scheme by suggesting that students use heuristics to compose current-traditional essays. Take, for example, *The Bedford Guide for College Writers*, third edition dated 1993, written by X. J. Kennedy, Dorothy M. Kennedy, and Sylvia A. Holladay. The rhetoric portion of this huge tome, which also includes a reader and a handbook, is divided into four parts: "a writer's resources," "thinking critically," "special writing situations," and "a writer's strategies." The first three sections feature process-oriented exercises divided into stages called "generating ideas," "planning, drafting, and developing," and "revising and editing." The fourth part, on composing strategies, begins with a section on generating ideas that includes instruction in brainstorming, free writing, keeping a journal, asking a reporter's questions, and seeking motives. This eclectic collection of heuristics is followed by a process-oriented discussion of drafting that easily accommodates current-traditional formalism: "planning" includes advice about stating a thesis and outlining; "drafting" includes advice about topic sentences and coherence; "strategies for developing" include examples, classification, analysis, definition, comparison and contrast, cause and effect. These are, of course, the current-traditional modes of development. Under the heading of "revising and editing," the authors give students a short course in the detection of logical fallacies, another inheritance from the current-traditional theory of discourse. Like current-traditionalism, process is an accommodating pedagogy; it absorbed the expressionism that undergirds free writing as easily as the Burkean dramatism from which Kennedy et al. claim to have derived the tactic they call "seeking motives."

The easy accommodation of process-oriented strategies to current-traditionalism suggests that process and product have more in common than is generally acknowledged in professional literature about composition, where the habit of contrasting them conceals the fact of their epistemological consistency. A truly paradigmatic alternative to current-traditionalism would question the modernism in which it is immersed and the institutional structure by means of which it is administered. Process pedagogy does neither. It retains the modernist composing subject of current-traditionalism—the subject who is sufficiently discrete from the composing context to stand apart from it, observing it from above and commenting upon it. Furthermore, this subject is able to inspect the contents of the mind and report them to a reader without distortion, using language that fully represents a well-formed composing intention. Nor did process pedagogy change the institutional situation of composition: the introductory courses are still required, and composition teachers are still overworked and underpaid, just as they were prior to 1971. (Indeed, the adoption of process pedagogy may actually have increased teachers' workload, given its emphasis on revision). The failure of process pedagogy to dislodge the universal requirement is particularly pointed, since its early advocates argued that process-oriented instruction was especially adapted to the composing needs of individuals or small groups of students working in laboratory settings. Its more widespread advocacy during the 1960s and 1970s, then, presented teachers with an opportunity to rethink what Barriss Mills called "mass methods" of instruction (25). Unfortunately, this did not happen.

CONTEMPORARY POSTSCRIPT

In 1992 the University of New Hampshire hosted a conference entitled "The Writing Process: Retrospect and Prospect" (Tobin and Newkirk, ix). In his introduction to the collected papers from the conference, Lad Tobin recounts the success of process pedagogy during the 1970s and 1980s. He is careful to note that process was a product of its time, and that times have indeed changed:

> Like rock music, free love, political protests, and other trends that
> flourished in the late 60s, the writing process movement has begun to
> get squeezed by the past and the future, by the right and the left. The
> critique from traditionalists, including many administrators, teachers,
> and parents, was expected: the writing process was just another fad, a
> product of its time—interesting and maybe even understandable in its
> way, but, in the end, excessive, soft-headed, and irresponsible. Now,
> traditional opponents of process pedagogy argue, is the time to get
> back to the basics; that is, back to grammar, usage, logic, argumenta-
> tion, belles lettres, great literature. Back to standards and models. (5)

As Tobin perceptively notes, process pedagogy has become the doctrine of the very establishment it once critiqued; Elbow, Emig, Murray, and Macrorie are now names to conjure with in composition studies. And so process has recently come under attack from the Left as well. Oddly, the Left, as Tobin depicts it, sounds suspiciously like the Right, with its supposed "attack on student freedom" and its insistence on "content" (6).

A truly radical suggestion about writing pedagogy does appear in this volume. In an essay entitled "Coming Out Right," James Moffett, author of *Teaching the Universe of Discourse* (1978), recounts his struggle since the 1960s to alter the way in which writing is taught in American schools. According to Moffett, activist supporters of process pedagogy have not yet succeeded in redefining writing in the schools as anything other than a means of record keeping and examination. "The problem is not likely to go away," he avers, "until schooling is placed on another footing than compulsion and testing" (23). With reference to composition in the university, Moffett has it exactly right.

10 ⤙

THE POLITICS OF COMPOSITION

> I celebrate teaching that enables transgressions—a movement against and beyond boundaries. It is that movement which makes education the practice of freedom.
> —bell hooks, *Teaching to Transgress*

There's a canard about teaching that goes like this: "Just when you design the right syllabus, the wrong students walk in the door." Unlike academics who construct their pedagogical task as passing on knowledge (that is, unlike teachers in almost every other academic discipline), composition teachers profess the development of students' abilities. Hence the canard applies to their work with particular force.

Preparing a syllabus involves making predictions about how a semester's work will be orchestrated. The obvious predictions made by a syllabus are about timing and pacing. But a teacher preparing a syllabus also makes predictions about who students are and what they want from her class, and she predicts as well how what she knows will be integrated into the class. An experienced teacher of writing knows that what she knows will be modified by the experience of teaching a composition class, and she must admit as well that the conduct of any class is affected by her desires as well as her health and her well-being. All of these things can change on a daily or even an hourly basis. When she is preparing a syllabus, she has to guess about how all of this will affect her plans as the group grows or shrinks, as students work together for fifteen weeks, and as their desires, health, and well-being affect classroom interaction. No wonder that syllabi are difficult to write.

The teacher who prepares a syllabus is asked to make generalized predictions about a time-bound and localized activity. The activities that go on in writing classes may be much more localized and temporal than they are in a class where the aim is to impart knowledge rather than to improve abilities. And in other fields where it is important to impart skills to students, such as medicine or engineering, there is a body of knowledge and procedures that precede each student's immersion in the discipline. These protect each student, to some degree, from making innovations or errors that might result from eccentric or uninformed responses to the discipline. On the other hand, in writing instruction (according to the ideology of process pedagogy, at least), the entire point of instruction is to help students to produce eccentric or individualized responses.

To put this point in theoretical terms, I am suggesting that disciplines like medicine and engineering create what Foucault called "relations of governmentality," wherein a technology of power creates and controls a technology of the self—the engineer, the doctor (Foucault 1991). This relation of governmentality regulates teaching in these disciplines in such a way that the predisciplinary subjectivities of students and teachers are less important to their practice than they are in composition instruction. That is to say, the subjectivity we call "doctor" or "engineer" is expected to replace, to some extent, the predisciplinary subjectivities with which students embark upon the study of medicine or engineering. However, in first-year composition instruction, students' predisciplinary subjectivities are the very materials with which they and their teachers are expected to work.

I am not suggesting that first-year composition has no discipline. Indeed, its disciplinarity is to be found in the discursive mass of hints and plans and procedures that Stephen North calls its "lore," as well as in the host of institutional practices that configure the universal requirement—textbooks, standardized syllabi and assignments, grading scales, and the like (23ff). Curiously, though, throughout its long history, the technology of disciplinary power that is the universally required composition course has not been considered to produce a postdisciplinary subjectivity that might be called "the writer," in the sense in which this term is usually understood outside of composition classrooms. Nineteenth-century teachers like Adams Sherman Hill, Barrett Wendell, and Charles Townsend Copeland knew very well which subjectivity they wished to develop in their students by means of writing instruction: the gendered, classbound subjectivity that marked them as Harvard men. Hill and Wendell did the non-Harvard world the dubious favor of packaging and marketing that subjectivity as current-traditional rhetoric, which continued to discipline composition teachers and their students for much of the twentieth century. And even though current-traditional rhetoric is said to have disappeared from the scene of composition instruction, the institution of the universal requirement continues to do its policing work. The universal requirement is, in Foucauldian terms, an ethical technology of subjectivity that creates in students a healthy respect for the authority of the academy. The requirement makes clear to students that they are not to write in their own voices, despite what their textbooks tell them. To the contrary: they must produce discourse that will satisfy their teachers in Freshman English and beyond. In other words, the subjectivity produced by the requirement can be characterized as something like "docile student." The ethical technology that is the requirement, I submit, supersedes anything that specific composition teachers operating in local spaces may want to do for their students in the way of helping them to become writers; it gets in between teachers and their students, in between students' writing and their teachers' reading.

What I have just written explicates a view of first-year composition instruction that is not widely shared among composition professionals in the university. Since the 1970s, dedicated composition teachers and specialists in composition studies have tried to intervene or to circumvent the subjectivizing function of the requirement. They have generally done this by reconfiguring the pedagogy used in first-year composition. Process pedagogy is a good example of this sort of attempted intervention, since its adherents directly addressed the matter of students' subjectivities. Theorists of process constructed a self-directed student who would take control of his or her own writing process; this projected student subjectivity was to replace the docile, rule-bound, grammar-anxious student subjectivity produced by current-traditional instruction. The institutional paradox, of course, is that students are *forced* to take the class in which they are to be constructed as self-directed writers.

This talk about the creation and maintenance of subjectivities suggests that composition pedagogies are not innocent of politics. Even though teachers who espouse current-traditional rhetoric, or process, or some other approach to teaching composition may assume that their practice is governed purely by personal preference, or expediency, or tradition, or lore, it remains true that pedagogies and practices are implicated in the politics of the institutions in which they work and with ideologies that are in wider circulation as well (Althusser, Bizzell 1992, Fish). In this chapter I make a case for the political implications of the major pedagogies that teachers of composition have espoused during the history of the required first-year course—current-traditionalism and process. An explicit argument in support of the political implication of pedagogy is necessary, I think, because many teachers of composition, as well as some leaders in the field of composition studies, maintain that it is possible to offer instruction that is politically neutral (for example, Hairston 1992). I argue further that the switch to process pedagogy can usefully be described as an ideological alteration of the politics of first-year composition instruction from conservatism to liberalism. I will also try to establish that the liberal politics of process pedagogy is an insufficient and inappropriate response to the contemporary situation of composition in the university.

THE POLITICS OF COMPOSITION PEDAGOGIES

Current-traditional pedagogy is conservative in the ordinary sense of that term insofar as it resists changes in its rules and preserves established verbal traditions and institutional lines of authority. Current-traditionalism preserves traditional social and academic hierarchies insofar as students are taught to observe without question rules of discourse that were constructed long before they entered the academy and to submit their native grapholects to grammar and usage rules devised by a would-be elitist class. Current-traditional pedagogy is teacher-centered: the teacher dispenses information about the rules of discourse and evaluates the students' efforts in accordance with those rules. Students themselves are constructed in current-traditional rhetoric as potentially unruly novices whose work needs to be continually examined and disciplined.

As this analysis implies, current-traditional pedagogy is also conservative in an explicitly political sense. Political conservatism is marked by a "quest for a realistic concept of order which acknowledges the ineliminable tension at the heart of the human condition" (O'Sullivan 52). Norman Foerster's insistence on the dual nature of the human being, poised between its animal and spiritual natures, is a fine example of a conservative's typically low estimate of human potential. Conservatives view human beings as creatures caught between reason and desire, and, unlike liberals, conservatives generally have a healthy respect for the power of human desire to overcome reason. Given conservative pessimism about the perfectibility of human nature, the institutional practices of surveillance and examination—associated with current-traditional instruction from its beginnings at Harvard—make perfect sense. Current-traditionalism and the institutional practices associated with it represent an attempt by those in authority to impose order on student discourse. This explains why a teacher who opposed some universities' decision to lift the universal requirement in the early 1970s could write that this trend was "but a small part of a national trend of leniency" that was occurring "in a sociopolitical milieu which . . . at its worst is a cover for irresponsibility and laziness" (Patrick Shaw 155).

The adoption of process pedagogy marked a sea change in the politics of composition instruction, since process pedagogy is undeniably indebted to liberalism. Teachers who have adopted process pedagogy encourage novice writers to write as though they are free and sovereign individuals who have unimpeded access to their (supposedly unique) "selves." Each such individual is encouraged, as the textbooks say, to find her own voice. The free and sovereign individual is, of course, a central assumption of liberal thought (Arblaster). The liberal individual is imagined to possess the capacity to reason, which capacity insures his autonomy and sovereignty.[1] Liberals assume that this individual has clear and unmediated access to whatever desires motivate behavior; that is, with sufficient reflection, the sovereign individual can become aware of the reasons that support his decisions and actions. This reflection is assumed to occur in a perfectly private arena of individual thought, which is, ideally, uncontaminated by either communal memory or public discourse. That is to say, the private reflecting individual of liberalism is thought to be able to make rational decisions about behavior as though these decisions were not affected by the ideologies that circulate in culture, his history, or his desires and those of others.[2]

Conservatism and liberalism differ significantly in their assessment of the worth of human nature. While conservatives retain a healthy respect for the inherent human proclivity to go wrong, liberals assume that individuals are either inherently good or are subject to shaping toward it by supportive environments. Hence liberal educational theory is motivated by the metaphors of emancipation and empowerment (Bowers). Unlike conservatives, who assume that the point of education is to acquaint new generations with respected traditions, liberals assume that the point of education is to help individuals get better at whatever they want to do. Education accomplishes this by enhancing individuals' capacity to reason and to think through problems on their own. As a corollary of their faith in education, liberals assume that education allows individuals to overcome the impact of circumstances on their development. Indeed, liberals are fond of referring to such circumstances as class, race, and gender as "accidents" whose cultural liabilities can be overcome if individuals will only work hard enough and acquire sufficient education.[3] Since liberalism rejects the authority of tradition and common sense—since, in short, it rejects ideology—liberal teachers must insist that the effects on people of class prejudice, sexism, or racism can be overcome with sufficient individual effort.

Process theory constructs students as unique individuals who should be encouraged to develop their personal voices. Hence its premiere genre is the expressive or exploratory essay, which is assumed to represent authentic access to students' experience. Process-oriented teachers view students as naturally capable writers whose abilities have for some reason lain dormant prior to their encounter with the process-oriented classroom. Liberals place great faith in progress, and this faith is everywhere apparent in the professional literature about process: process-oriented teachers believe in their students' abilities to improve their writing with the help of process-oriented instruction, and they believe that composition theory itself progressed with the discovery of process pedagogy. Since all individuals are constructed as equals in this pedagogy, until very recently process theorists did not acknowledge that class, gender, or racial differences can affect the dynamics of workshop groups and peer review. Much less did process-oriented teachers consider that as power is unequally distributed in culture, this unequal distribution would be repeated in student-centered classrooms.

Of course, practices are never politically pure. Institutional practices in composition typically represent the general history of the course as well as the history of influential teachers and administrators on a given campus. Current-traditional rhetoric lingers on in composition textbooks, not because it is of much use to writers, but because the academy is comfortable with it. Literary texts linger on in the second-semester course because literary study has always been constructed as more advanced than the direct instruction in composition given in the first semester. Many composition programs are marked by a mix of liberal attitudes toward students and conservative, humanist, attitudes toward texts. Sometimes concepts borrowed from current-traditionalism and process pedagogy are used to rationalize the same set of institutional practices. For example, many composition programs distinguish the two semesters of introductory composition from one another in current-traditional terms, characterizing the first semester's work as a course in exposition and the second as a course in argument. Other programs adopt the terminology associated with process pedagogy, characterizing the first course as a series of exercises in personal writing and the second as devoted to public writing assignments. The current-traditional distinction between exposition and argument is generic, while the distinction between public and private is ideological, having been borrowed from liberal thought. And while many programs say that they move students into the composition of argumentative or persuasive writing in the second course they actually focus on composition of a research paper, which is a current-traditional exercise in exposition rather than in argumentation. Others confine students in the second course to the practice of writing about literature, a special form of argumentation that cannot be called "rhetorical" or "persuasive" in the ancient sense of that term, since its highly specialized audience resides mainly within English departments and always already knows much more about literature than do the students who write the papers.

LOCATING STUDENTS IDEOLOGICALLY

Even though liberal composition lore suggests that writing instruction is a highly individualized activity, composition teachers continue to think of students in generic and idealized terms. As Richard Ohmann noted over twenty years ago, composition textbooks depict the student as "newborn, unformed, without social origin and without needs that would spring from his origins. He has no history" (1976, 148). Ohmann was referring, of course, to the class blindness manifested in best-selling composition textbooks of the day. The same charge can still be brought against textbooks, and it can still be made with some assurance about contemporary composition lore and research. In other words, composition teachers have still not begun to account satisfactorily for our own and our students' location in physical and ideological space. And if I am right that students' subjectivities are the material of contemporary writing instruction, their (and our) location in these spaces utterly compromises the liberal depiction of students as free and self-sovereign individuals.

In composition research and lore, composition teachers speak of "the classroom" as though this space is similarly constructed at Yale and at San Jose Community College. And yet teachers know, even if they have never set foot on either campus, that the students who attend Yale are subjected to very different relations of governmentality than are the students who attend San Jose Community College. Contemporary colleges and universities are credentializing institutions, but they credentialize in different ways. A student may attend a local community college in order to attain information and skills that she needs to get a job; she goes to Yale, on the other hand, to attain a social credential or to solidify one she already has by virtue of family connections. Stanley Aronowitz and Henry Giroux argue that a student who obtains an MBA at Harvard Business School has received no better education than she would have obtained in the School of Business at most other universities in the country (1985). What the Harvard degree offers, that most others do not, is access to extremely powerful social and business connections as well as the social status that this association brings.

Research on the demographics of universities and colleges suggests that students' placement in a particular kind of institution results primarily from their class affiliation and secondarily from geographical location. In other words, the primary factor determining admission to a given university is class; the second is place of residence. The politics of class and location are complicated by two well-established hierarchies that operate among and within institutions: a ranking hierarchy distinguishes worse from better kinds of institutions, and a status hierarchy distinguishes privileged teachers and students from those who are less so. The ranking hierarchy (as if it needs repeating) privileges older, private, eastern universities. Large public universities called "research institutions" come next, while "teaching" universities and two-year colleges come last. The status hierarchy that operates among disciplines places the sciences at the top; composition is at the bottom. This complex intertwining of privilege, rank, and status explains why composition is not required or taught at older, private, eastern universities; their students (by virtue of native intelligence? class affiliation? family connections?) are assumed not to need it.

And yet composition scholarship and lore often proceed as if the politics of class, status, and location were not operative in our classrooms. We tend to think of "students" in terms of the (liberal) subjectivity we have constructed for them in our professional imaginations, rather than as middle-, upper-, or working-class persons who hail from Los Angeles or Philadelphia or Milltown or Mayberry. It is perhaps less difficult for composition teachers to remember our place within the university. Those of us who are senior can remember a time when we were treated as nuisances by our colleagues (Crowley 1988). Composition teachers who are new to the profession are reminded daily—by the fact that they are expected to teach someone else's syllabus—that they work at the very bottom of the academic pecking order.

I am painfully reminded of the politics of location when I get letters like this one from a former graduate student. I quote, omitting details that identify him or his institution:

> Dear Dr. Crowley: Thanks for your response to my note. I am sorry to be such a bother. The fact that I dislike [State] is compounded by the fact that parts of it don't like me. My Division Chair seems to not

want to make my life here any easier. If you recall, he didn't want me
to be hired, he preferred a local. I have come to the conclusion that it
was foolish for me to try to swim upstream against the political tide. . . .
Many of the people who live here do not trust anyone from the
outside. All of us who came from the outside feel the same kind of
isolation. The best we can do is hang together. . . . It just seems better
for us to leave than fight.

This person teaches four sections of composition every semester. During his
first semester at this institution, someone put sugar in the gas tank of his vehicle. Now, a liberal might wonder what is wrong with him—what could he
have done in class to deserve such treatment? I suggest, rather, that he has put
his finger precisely on the difficulty: he is an outsider working in an insular
community. Nothing he could have done, or can do, will change his status
vis-à-vis that community, at least in the short run. Such are the politics of
location.

Communities can be ideologically located, as well. Before I tell some
stories that illustrate this point, I want to note that what I am about to say
goes against the grain of the prevailing etiquette in composition studies, which
mandates that teachers never criticize or blame students, at least in public.[4]
This etiquette is in place for a good reason: it repudiates a historical practice
in current-traditional composition, where for many years students were imagined as stupid and irresponsible louts who couldn't learn to spell or punctuate
properly no matter how hard institutions tried to teach these skills to them.
Composition teachers seem to have learned that students' inability to master
these arcane arts has as much to do with institutional settings and practices as
it has to do with students' willingness to learn or their level of preparedness.
However, we have overreacted to this past, I think, to the extent that we no
longer see students as they are, as people whose discourse is immersed in the
master discourses of our culture. When I examine students' immersion in
these discourses, I am not student-bashing, or at least I'm not doing it for fun.
What I am trying to do is to locate students in ideological space.

When I teach the required first-year course, I ask my students to read the
student newspaper or a daily newspaper on a regular basis. During one session of such a course, the class discussed news reports and editorials concerning our university's decision to disallow the use on campus of sports
mascots that offend any group of persons. Students in my class professed to
be nonplused by this decision. They simply could not see, they said, in what

ways the mascots of the Florida State Seminoles or the Kansas City Chiefs could be offensive to anyone. Much less could they see how such a symbol could be perceived to be racist. I believe my students when they say that they believe such things, but I cannot allow them to leave class without knowing that such beliefs are contested—indeed are vigorously contested—by others, including their teacher. This requires that I explain to them how racist beliefs circulate in culture; where this particular set of racist beliefs came from and how it is maintained; and why, finally, such beliefs are unethical. I also need a theory of discourse that accounts for the circulation of sets of beliefs such as racism and for the commonplaces that sustain them—commonplaces such as the assumption that "Chiefs" and "Seminoles" are harmless titles, disassociated from any racist history or practices. Nothing in either conservative or liberal composition lore prepares me to do such teaching.

Another story: a student in my required first-year class itched from the very first day to make a homophobic speech. The word *homophobic* is mine, not hers; she was astonished to learn that there is a word for her attitude toward nonheterosexuality. I thought I had convinced her in a series of conferences that her position was so unsavory to me that she would, like a savvy rhetorician, use one of the other topics she and her classmates had generated in workshop. Imagine my chagrin when she stood up, late in the semester, to proclaim that she would leave the university were she assigned a gay roommate. As she continued to speak, repeating most of the homophobic commonplaces that circulate in public discourse, I wondered what on earth I could say in response to her talk. I ended the stunned silence that followed her conclusion by saying: "You know, Muffy, if the statistics are correct, there is at least one gay person in this class." From a corner of the room a loud voice responded: "You bet your ass there is." Another student had chosen this moment to out herself to the class, thereby creating what is known in our trade as "a teachable moment." Thanks to her intervention, the class began to contest Muffy's position, and some ideological work was done that day. Unfortunately, teachers cannot always count on students to perform such work. Nor should we.

Sometimes the politics of location utterly confound the premises and standardized practices that typically organize the mass instructional setting of the first-year required course. For example: two students in my class made a series of speeches about the regulation of drugs. One student was from a suburb of a small city; his position was that drugs should be entirely deregulated. He had been a debater in high school, and he was anxious to make the university's debate squad. His topic was thoroughly researched, and he occasionally argued his position with brilliance. The second student hailed from downtown in a large urban area. His position was that drug trafficking should simply be stopped by whatever means were available, including the use of force. His arguments were drawn from his experiences on the street, and he spoke with power, often with eloquence. How, I asked myself, am I supposed to grade these guys? The grading scale used by my department listed specific criteria that I was to use in evaluation. The rules also required me to award so many A's, B's, C's, D's, and F's, and so, implicitly, it required me to rank these performances against one another. Taken together, the arguments advanced by each speaker were convincing even though they held opposing positions on the issue; but their persuasive power was achieved by entirely different means. Neither was clearly right or clearly wrong. Class response was no help: many students in the class accepted the argument that drug traffic ought to be thoroughly regulated or even stopped, but they did so for entirely different reasons (some of them racist) than those advanced by the student who argued that case.

I recently received the worst teaching evaluations of my career from a class of students who took their required first-year composition course with me. One of the students in the class was forthright enough to explain what had gone wrong. She pointed out that several members of the class, all white men, had felt silenced by me. Her revelation made me angry on several counts. First of all, I was angered that she felt she had to speak up for the men, who, despite her remark, were perfectly capable of speaking for themselves. Women continue to feel, apparently, that they must clean up after men. I was angry as well that this matter was not brought to my attention while class was in progress. In fairness, I must say that I probably would not have encouraged the men in question to speak more, had I known about their resistance, since I remember the class as a struggle by women students to speak and be heard. But I would have liked the opportunity to discuss their feeling of being silenced, with the men themselves and with the class as a whole. So in a sense, their commentary after the fact elided discussion of the entire issue of gender relations and teacherly authority. To put this another way, their hostile silence about these issues silenced the rest of us.

In this case, students resisted what they took to be my feminism. A liberal might say that I should just shut up in class about my "personal" ideological convictions because I am unjustly imposing them on students. Whether or not it is possible to hide one's convictions from students in this way is an arguable point, as is the ethical question it entails. But I also think that the students in question resisted my teacherly authority because I am an old woman—a figure who is typically constructed in American culture as relatively powerless (Walker). These young men did not like being in a class where an old woman had opinions, expressed them with force, and was, to boot, their professor. There is absolutely nothing I can do about this particular ideological construction—except to challenge it.

And yet I am not unaware that I speak and teach from a position of relative privilege: I teach at a relatively privileged institution and I hold rank and tenure within that institution. Bad evaluations no longer scare me because they do not endanger my job. Of course none of this is true for most teachers of writing. If the teacher of the first-year course is unranked, untenured, and utterly without academic status, she does not have the luxury of responding angrily to bad evaluations. And bad evaluations happen to untenured teachers of the required first-year course for the same reason that they happened to me in this instance: students resist a teacher's ideological location. For example: a teaching assistant is asked by students in her class just how much Native American blood she has. The question comes from a group who had read and discussed essays written about precisely this manifestation of white racism. Another TA is harassed in her classroom by a male student who persists in remarking upon her appearance. A white student asks an African-American teacher whether he has sufficient credentials to teach the class. Another TA is told repeatedly by his students that they do not wish to study multicultural issues because multiculturalism has nothing to do with them.

And so Maxine Hairston is just wrong when she claims that "we can create a culturally inclusive curriculum in our writing classes by focusing on the experiences of our students" (1992, 190). Hairston's sunny liberalism overlooks the fact that students' experiences are saturated with their disparate access to cultural power. The "accidents" of gender, race, sexual orientation, ability, age, and class do make real differences in classroom interaction: whites own more cultural power than people of color; males own more power than women. These disparities hold even when the person of color or the woman in question is the teacher of the class, and they may be deployed with powerful effect if he or she has no professional status. Most teachers of composition have no professional status whatever. I have my doubts whether ideological and cultural differences can always be negotiated into the warm "community" that Hairston depicts as her classroom ideal: "real diversity emerges from the students themselves and flourishes in a collaborative classroom in which they work together to develop their ideas and test them out on each other. They can discuss and examine their experiences, their assumptions, their values, and their questions. They can tell their stories to teach other in a nurturant writing community" (1992, 191).

No matter how nurturant the teacher, the so-called community of the classroom is rife with the ideological differences that students and teachers bring with them to class. These differences will inevitably be put on the table, as they might not be in a history or biology class, because liberal composition pedagogy insists that students' identities *are* the subject of composition. Within the context of the universal requirement, which forces people to take and teach the class, this seems to me to be a recipe for pain.

11

A PERSONAL ESSAY
ON FRESHMAN ENGLISH

English A will go on until doomsday.
—Bernard DeVoto, "English A"

Freshman English is a sentimental favorite in America, like big bands and Colin Powell. If you don't believe me, talk to your colleagues and neighbors about the introductory English course they took as undergraduates. Some will depict it as an endless drill in grammar and mechanics but will assure you nonetheless that knowledge of those arcane arts contributed to their survival in college. Others will recall their course as a comfortable seminar taught by a tweedy professor who introduced them to the Great Texts of Western culture. In either case people will remember their experience positively, if not fondly. Freshman English is a lot like "hell night" in fraternity initiations: people do it because it was done to them, everybody sentimentalizes it by forgetting its more painful aspects, and nobody notices its potentially deleterious effects until somebody complains or gets hurt. When this happens, administrations may put a stop to it for awhile. But it inevitably creeps back into place and is soon thriving once again.

As we have seen, the Freshman English requirement has a continuous history within the modern American university—except for a brief period during the 1970s when a few English departments made the course elective, in response to students' declaration of its irrelevance to their intellectual lives (Smith). Today, at least one semester or quarter of the course is universally required in most American colleges and universities. Many universities require their students to complete two semesters or quarters of the course. Surely such unanimity about the institutional status of Freshman English should imply unanimity about its efficacy as a college course. Not so. Serious complaints have been made about its intellectually thin curriculum and its haphazard pedagogy ever since the course began.[1] Complaint can be made about contemporary coursework in Freshman English as well. According to a Ford Foundation study, about half of the Freshman English programs in the country do not teach writing at all; rather, they instruct their students in current-traditional rhetoric (Larson 1988, 1992). Half of these (or 25 percent of the total) do not concentrate instruction on the current-traditional essay, but instead teach traditional grammar, orthography, and punctuation. In many so-called basic writing classrooms this instruction is accomplished by means of memorization and drill or through the use of commercially prepared worksheets.

The repetitive and repressive curriculum of Freshman English is directly linked to its institutional status as a required introductory-level course. Freshman English is attached to a huge administrative enterprise on almost every college campus in the country. Its very size subjects its administrators, teachers, and students to unprofessional and unethical working practices on a scale that is replicated nowhere else in the academy.

In this chapter I review the cultural and academic-ideological forces that keep Freshman English in place as the only universally required course in the American academy. I also reflect on my work with the Wyoming Resolution—an effort to alter the working conditions of postsecondary writing teachers—and on what this work taught me about the importance of hierarchy in the academy. These reflections suggest to me that the reasons for the stability of Freshman English are deeply seated within cultural and academic expectations about who should have access to higher education.[2] Given the ideological work that Freshman English does, alterations to its curriculum or pedagogy seem almost beside the point. Near the end of this chapter I suggest an institutional alteration to Freshman English that, if carefully implemented, could disrupt some of the ideological work now being done by the course.

FRESHMAN ENGLISH AS CULTURAL CAPITAL

At the University of Texas at Austin, the required composition course isn't "Freshman" English, strictly speaking. It is E306, but it is, nevertheless, a required undergraduate writing course. In 1990, the committee charged with overseeing this course designed a new syllabus for it. Called "Writing About Difference," the syllabus asked students to read a set of court cases in which plaintiffs had run afoul of some practice that elided their difference(s) from other members of groups with whom they worked or associated (Brodkey

1996, 211ff). The cases were selected for two reasons: first, there were associated documents in each case that took a variety of positions with regard to its merit—majority and minority opinions from several courts along with law review articles; second, each case raised the issue of what it means to be defined as different from mainstream American culture. Using Stephen Toulmin's data/warrant/claim model of argumentation, students were to discuss and write about some of the cases, both in large and small groups. The syllabus also contained some quite traditional writing assignments, such as summaries, precis, and the like.

A very public uproar followed the English Department's adoption of this proposed syllabus. The uproar eventuated in the apparently permanent postponement of its implementation at Texas, although other schools agreed to pilot the syllabus. On the face of it, the uproar was politically motivated. Conservative critics of the proposed course, who included the Texas branch of the National Association of Scholars and commentator George Will, interpreted the focus on "difference" as a politically correct indoctrination in racism and sexism.[3] But what I find equally interesting about the furor is the fact that faculty outside of English departments as well as members of the press felt quite comfortable in defining what sort of course required English ought to be. People who literally had no professional or financial stake in the design of the course, and who had only the faintest academic interest in it, felt entitled to criticize a syllabus developed by the teachers and scholars put in charge of it by the university, teachers and scholars who are professionally identified with composition studies. It is as though the curriculum of Freshman English is owned by the community at large.

I suppose this is not an unreasonable position, given that taxpayers fund a certain portion of the budgets of state universities like Texas. But Freshman English is almost an anomaly in this regard. I cannot imagine the press or community creating such a fuss over a new syllabus in Chem 101 or even in introductory sociology or religious studies. In fact, only one other college course has been imagined to be the intellectual property of persons not directly associated with its development or administration: that course is Western Civilization. Messing around with the syllabus for Western Civ can generate the same sort of political uproar that occurred at Texas, as was attested by the well-publicized debate over the freshman curriculum at Stanford (Pratt). Western Civ and Freshman English share another interesting institutional similarity. Even though both are often required of students at the introductory level, neither are ordinarily considered to be introductions to university-level study of history or English. Both courses, then, seem to serve extradisciplinary or even extrainstitutional constituencies, which fact gives them a unique curricular status. The curricula for such courses are conceived as cultural capital—as the mutual property of all persons who conceive of education as a site for transmission of a received dominant culture. Where this is the case, it is easy to understand why discussions about curricula can become heated.

My readers may not be immediately convinced that the standard fare of Freshman English plays any cultural role. But it always has, and it still does. Freshman English originated as punishment for failure to master a highly idealized version of the written dialect of a dominant class. The required first-year course still serves American universities as a border checkpoint, the institutional site wherein students either provide proper identification or retreat to wherever they came from. In America's cultural imagination, mastery of "correct" English still signifies that its users are suitable for admission to the class of educated persons. This criterion is generally wielded negatively; that is, "correct" English is used as a handy standard of exclusion by those who practice racial or class discrimination. Because of this, I would be morally remiss to deny the social force exerted by the ideology of "correct" English on people who suffer because they think they don't have it but ought to, or those who suffer because their mastery is questioned by others.

Whatever ways may be found to alter this unfair and misguided feature of American ideology, it will not be changed by giving every American university student a dose of Freshman English. Most Americans do not attend universities or colleges. Setting this aside, it remains true that class and race discrimination can easily find other sites of purchase, even if dedicated composition teachers succeed in eradicating "incorrect" written English from the face of the earth. For the sake of argument, I will concede that, in theory, somewhere in America, some students who sit through a one- or two-semester required course in Freshman English master "correct" English, especially if these hypothetical students harbor a burning desire to succeed at the project. But I seriously doubt that this success is widespread, or repeatable, or predictable, since it depends on something that is manifestly not within English teachers' control: students' desire to conform to the academic and class standards represented in "correct" English.

Ironically, "correct" English might not exist without support from the institution of Freshman English. Certainly it would be much harder to define. No one, including its teachers, has ever agreed exactly what mastery of "correct" English amounts to: the ability to spell correctly? to avoid grammatical error? to punctuate conventionally? to paragraph logically? to string sentences together intelligibly, if not effectively? to write like an English teacher? a poet? a scientist? a corporate executive? All of these standards have been held up at one time or another as literacy ideals for Freshman English. Given this plethora of implicit or explicit standards, the universal Standard of Written English pursued by students, teachers, course designers, test makers, and textbook authors should have long ago been recognized as the chimera it is. This has not happened in part because Freshman English performs the important ideological work of sustaining belief in "correct" English; it is the institutional site wherein the rules of "correct" English are given clear definitions.

Research into teachers' commentary on student papers, conducted by Robert J. Connors and Andrea A. Lunsford, yielded the finding that definitions of "error" are historically and culturally bound: teachers' ideas about error definition and classification are products of their times and cultures. What seem to us the most common and permanent of terms and definitions are likely to be newer and far more transient than we know. Errors like "stringy sentences" and "use of would for simple past tense forms" seemed obvious and serious to teachers in 1925 or 1917 but are obscure to us today (399). However, Freshman English textbooks cover over this transience. Connors and Lunsford note that the list of the ten most common errors included in recent editions of John Hodges's enormously successful *Harbrace Handbook* is exactly the same list that appeared in the first edition, issued over fifty years ago (1941). Hodges derived that list from a study of twenty thousand student papers supplied to him by teachers working mostly at the University of Tennessee-Knoxville during the late 1930s. This timely and local list of errors has transmogrified over the ten editions of the *Harbrace* into a set of rules that define "correct" English. While the errors made by students change, and while teachers' definitions of error change, the institutional paraphernalia that name those errors do not. The point is not only that textbooks are not representative of student and teacher practice. The point is that, without Freshman English and its attendant paraphernalia, the content of "correct" English would be much harder to define and stabilize.

FRESHMAN ENGLISH AS TURF

Academics share the proprietary attitude toward Freshman English that is irregularly manifested in the culture at large. Some admit to a quite proletarian aim for the Freshman English program: it is to "remediate" students' writing ability, bringing their skills up to snuff in order to meet the demands made on them by the more specialized, discipline-specific writing they will supposedly do in advanced university coursework. Others, feeling equally proprietary, insist that the course teach students the conventions of "the academic essay."

However, people who work with writing-across-the-curriculum programs can easily demonstrate that there is no such thing as "the academic essay," since each discipline defines its preferred genres in its own terms. Writing successfully within a discipline involves learning when to use quite subtle linguistic nuances such as an authoritative tone or a specialized vocabulary or syntax. Because of this, immersion in the language of a discipline and instruction in its conventions and genres constitute the most appropriate tactics for learning the rhetorical features peculiar to discipline-specific prose. Freshman English seems to be left with the task of instructing students in the composition of a mythical genre.

The idealist notion of "the academic essay" (a euphemism for the five-paragraph theme) assumes that rhetorical situations are similar or the same across a certain range of possible settings, that instructors can forecast the parameters of such settings, and that students can adequately meet the terms of any given discursive situation by applying a handy set of discursive formulae. Over forty years ago, Wallace Stegner pointed out the absurdity of these assumptions when he reminded readers of *College English* that "anyone writing honestly creates and solves new problems every time he sits down at his desk. Nobody can solve them for him in advance, and no teacher had better try" (1950, 431). The myth of the academic essay continues to nurture massive Freshman English programs for reasons other than its salience to writing instruction: it fosters and supports the persistent American belief that universal standards of literacy exist, and it legitimizes and covers over the social and institutional functions of Freshman English.

Recent professional essays about composition instruction suggest that teachers abandon the myth of the academic essay as an instructional goal and substitute an altogether more lofty purpose in its stead: they should aim to empower their students by giving them access to the literacy used in academic and other bureaucratic discourse communities. In this context, "empowerment" seems to entail energizing or transferring some sort of control to students—control of their own language or someone else's. Presumably, students may then employ that mastery to achieve yet other personal or professional ends when they leave the composition classroom. These aims are laudable. Remarkably, they center on students. This makes them rare, if not unique, within the American academy, which has been becoming steadily more discipline-centered ever since the late nineteenth century. Nevertheless, the most sympathetic critic of composition instruction must admit, I think, that the aim of empowering students, however worthy, is so encompassing that it can never be reached, and so vague that to articulate any usable meaning for it is nearly impossible. Talk of "mastery" and "control" involves composition teachers in academic projects whose ethics and politics are insufficiently considered (Malinowitz; Stuckey). In addition, the argument for literacy as empowerment begs a number of important questions: can we impart literacy in a quarter or a semester or a year? what is literacy, anyhow? and whose literacy do we teach? can literacy in fact empower anyone who has achieved it? how does this work? what sort of empowerment are we talking about— political? ethical? intellectual? financial? and if in fact literacy does empower people, for whose purposes does it do so?

I am not denying that reading and writing empower some people in some places at some times. I do not readily doubt Donna Haraway when she observes, for example, that "writing has a special significance for all colonized groups" for whom "releasing the power of writing" is "about access to the power to signify" (175). I do doubt whether universal literacy is an unmixed blessing, however. When mass literacy became available in England during the Industrial Revolution, after all, people used it to read their bibles and newspapers; but they also went to school, where they learned to submit to authority.

I fear that English teachers' love affair with the powers of literacy says more about us and our class affiliation than it does about the realities of American cultural and economic life. Literacy empowered us; we hope it will do the same for our students. But our clinging to this hope may cover over the different realities that hold for us—mostly bourgeois as we are—and those of our students. Along with Pat Bizzell, I worry that "in the present morally vexed times" the term "literacy" "may be exactly what's called for to screen out the social and political considerations that we do not feel prepared to deal with" (1991b, 318–19). Along with J. Elspeth Stuckey, I think that it is absurd and cruel to conflate economic inequality and racial discrimination with a literacy problem.

Of course, composition teachers do not all speak the same language. Conservative teachers want their students to be able to fit in with currently established cultural rites and institutions. That's why they teach the formalist rituals of traditional grammar and the five-paragraph theme. Liberal-humanist teachers want their students to become empowered, so they use student-centered pedagogies and teach students to compose on their own. Leftist composition teachers desire that their students be alerted to the oppressive and debilitating means by which their culture defines them and their relations; they desire as well that students be empowered by their awareness of oppression to change the means by which it is maintained (Berlin and Vivion; Bizzell 1992; Sullivan/Qually). The role of literacy in achieving these desires is only fuzzily mapped out in each of the three camps.

I share the goals adumbrated within the camp of leftist composition teachers. Because of this affiliation, I must enter a serious caveat about any project that would use Freshman English as a venue for a radical instructional politics. Leftist composition teachers must remember that we inherit an oppressive institutional history and a repressive intellectual tradition. We inherit an institutional structure that was created in order to serve as a social and intellectual gatekeeper. Its operational status was and still is grounded in nineteenth-century hopes for literacy, assumptions about who was, and who could become, "an educated person" and about the most efficient ways of fitting people to compete aggressively, if obediently, in a capitalist society. Freshman English has always been a gesture toward general fears of illiteracy among the bourgeoisie, fears generated by America's very real class hierarchy. Hence I question the wisdom, as well as the possibility, of turning Freshman English to radical purposes.

In fact, I wager that Freshman English will continue to exist in its traditional form for a long time to come, despite the efforts of leftist composition teachers to alter its focus toward social change. I have several reasons for suspecting this. First, the traditional required course reassures taxpayers that their children are getting one final guaranteed dose of "correct" English. Second, Freshman English is a cheap way for university faculty to salve their guilt about their own teaching, which is discipline-centered and which forces students to accommodate to the discipline's ways of knowing or to fail. Third, the emergence of composition studies has enabled a few writing teachers to do research, to publish professional discourse, to get grants, rank, and tenure, and thus to assume power in English department and university politics. Freshman English is our daily bread. Newly enfranchised professionals will want to think twice before tampering with a sure thing. In short, I doubt whether it is possible to radicalize instruction in a course that is so thoroughly implicated in the maintenance of cultural and academic hierarchy.

CONTRADICTION AND COMPROMISE

I learned about the staying power of Freshman English the hard way—
by trying to tamper with it. In 1987, I was among those who began working
to implement the Wyoming Resolution. This resolution, which is named for
the conference at which it was generated, deplores the conditions under which
most teachers of introductory-level writing courses are hired and fired and
under which they must work.[4] Jim Slevin put the case for the urgency of their
situation in eloquent and compelling terms:

> We should no longer hide from ourselves or from others that our
> profession, as it is now practiced in this country, rests on, is based on, a
> foundation of despicable inequality. . . . I do not think we can consider
> this, any longer, simply an unfortunate consequence of bad times. . . .
> I want to insist that this is a central feature—not an incidental
> feature—of the profession now. . . . We know, for example, that half
> the teachers at two-year colleges are part-time. We know that over
> one-quarter of the faculty at four-year colleges—one in four—is part-
> time, and that of those three full-time faculty it is almost certain that
> one will have only a temporary, non-tenure-track appointment. . . .
> While undergraduate catalogs regularly speak with rapture of writing
> instruction's central contribution in preparing America's citizens and
> future leaders, such centrality is not apparent in the status of those
> who teach these courses. (1991, 2)

I do not speak for Slevin here, nor for the other dedicated people who have
tried and who still are trying to better the working conditions of postsecondary
writing teachers. I do agree that the situation Slevin describes is permanent,
not transitory, and that it is morally suspect as well.

Given the contradictory status of Freshman English as cultural capital
and initiation rite on the one hand, and its lowly intellectual position at the
bottom of the academic pecking order, on the other, I should not have been
surprised at the complexity entailed in trying to alert the profession of English studies and the larger academy to the unethical character of its typical
employment practices. But I was surprised, and I learned some powerful lessons from the experience. Looking back on this work (with which I am no
longer associated in an official capacity) I am amazed by the theoretical and
political naivete with which I undertook it. Working with the Wyoming Resolution brought home to me the force of the Marxist canard that contradic-

tions necessarily arise within class struggle. It forced me to acknowledge the insidious workings of class privilege within the academy. I had to be hit over the head with this last realization, because I am among the academically privileged. Let me try to demonstrate how my privilege blinded me to certain political realities.

The first draft of a statement written by the Committee on Professional Standards was vigorously opposed by the very persons the Wyoming Resolution was drafted to help: part-time teachers. At a large CCCC session where the statement was discussed, a few contingent faculty objected to the portion of the statement that condemned the use of permanent part-time positions to staff Freshman English. In response, members of the committee redrafted their original version of the statement to make its terms more palatable to people who wanted to retain the possibility of some kinds of permanent part-time employment that are not ordinarily thought of in connection with the teaching of Freshman English, such as a professional writer's holding a part-time short-term appointment, or two people sharing a single position so that each may write and teach, or people teaching Freshman English in a (mythical?) university that recognizes and rewards their contributions to teaching and curriculum design with equable salaries, tenure or security of employment, and promotion. But beyond making these exceptions, the committee hung on to the concept of tenure, which we thought was the best available ground from which to assail the increasing use of temporary part-time teachers in postsecondary writing instruction. Granted, tenure is crucial to the maintenance of the hierarchical thought that is the lifeblood of the American academy. Granted also that tenure is awarded primarily for achievement in highly specialized kinds of research, and granted too that writing teachers ought to try to redefine prevailing standards for security of employment and promotion so that good teaching can be suitably rewarded. On the other hand, the term *tenure* carries a significance that was crucially important to the committee's argument that all college writing teachers who present the appropriate qualifications and who are hired under appropriate circumstances are entitled to the same academic benefits enjoyed by any other college teacher, including and especially academic freedom.

Academic freedom is, historically, the notion that entitled university faculty to relative security of employment. That achievement was a long, hard battle, and it isn't over yet, not by a long shot (Hofstadter and Smith). Obviously, the increasing use of temporary faculty in American colleges and universities is a direct assault on tenure and on the concept of academic freedom itself. The centrality of this issue to the maintenance of academic hierarchy was made clear during the debate over E306 at Texas. People who opposed implementation of the new syllabus raised a hue and cry about the possible abridgement of the academic freedom of those who would be forced to teach a mandated syllabus designed by somebody else. This is noteworthy since such an outcry has never been raised before, not ever in the hundred-year-plus history of Freshman English. Through all the dreary years that the prescriptive formalist visions of Adams Sherman Hill dominated prescribed instruction in the introductory writing course, there was no outcry about violations of its teachers' academic freedom. No outcry in 1950, when Freshman English was overwhelmed by the numbers of postwar students coming to colleges and universities and people were literally yanked off the streets to teach the course. No outcry through most of the 1960s, when current-traditional rhetoric was nearly universally prescribed for writing assignments in Freshman English, no matter who taught it. Though I obviously can't document this claim, I will cheerfully wager that during all those years, most institutions of higher learning in America mandated a textbook, a syllabus, perhaps even assignments and a grading scale for use by teachers of Freshman English.

Let's face it: if you hire teachers under circumstances that preclude use of the elaborate screening procedures involved in hiring tenure-line or tenured faculty, you have absolutely no assurance that such teachers will teach what you want them to. They may decide to teach cooking, or nothing at all, for all you know. Of course if they do that it's easier to get rid of them than tenured or tenure-line faculty who do that: you can just fire them on the spot. Historically, however, most institutions have solved the problem of hasty hiring in Freshman English by mandating a syllabus that, as the textbook publishers say, "teacher-proofs" the course. That is, the syllabus and its imposing textbooks are designed to keep Freshman English teachers from teaching what they'd prefer to teach if they had the chance.

If I've got this right so far, what it means is that the right to academic freedom has never applied, and does not now apply, to the huge corps of teachers who, year in and year out, teach Freshman English. The truth is that academic freedom is tied to security of employment; if you don't have the one, you don't have the other. Hence the bulk of Freshman English teachers, the bulk of English faculty, not only never did have tenure; they never will, as long as the universal requirement imposes a prescribed curriculum on them and their students, no matter what their abilities or affinities.

For conservative academics to raise an outcry at this late date about Freshman English teachers' putative right to academic freedom, then, is an instance of very bad faith indeed. Of course conservative teachers' real complaint about the E306 syllabus was that its politics was not their politics. The traditional literature-cum-grammar curriculum of Freshman English is conservative, has always been conservative. This politics was maintained in the course for many years precisely because its teachers do not enjoy academic freedom. This state of affairs will not change if liberal or radical academics merely redesign the course syllabus and continue to impose it on its conscripted teachers. Tenured academics have always dictated the terms of Freshman English teaching to its staff, and it is tenured academics who fight over its curriculum.

It was also tenured academics who dictated the standards of professional instruction and who put limits on the implementation of the Wyoming Resolution. Which brings me to the first lesson I learned from working with it: do not presume to speak for others who do not enjoy your privileges. In my anxiety to preserve whatever academic privilege is enjoyed by the very few teachers of composition who are tenured or are on tenure track, I wanted to upgrade the status of our profession by altering the fact that disrespect for it is reflected in the professional status of most of its teachers. Furthermore, in presuming to speak for temporary teachers and teaching assistants, I simply erased the reality that many English teachers must teach on a temporary basis if they wish to work at all.

My work with the Wyoming Resolution forced me to talk with temporary and part-time teachers and teaching assistants all over the country. Thanks to this experience, I am no longer impressed by the argument made by Richard Ohmann, that college writing teachers possess "the cultural capital and class resiliency to make lives for themselves somewhere other than the ghetto, prison, or homeless shelter" (1991, xiii). Ohmann is correct to assume that part-time teachers can sometimes find other means of employment; many do "leave the academy," as they say. Within the current economic situation, however, more and more well-educated persons who have dependents to feed and clothe are without full-time work. Many temporary part-time teachers have invested in at least five or six years' worth of higher education; many have Ph.D.s. Nonetheless, they cannot get full-time, permanent work in the profession for which they spent so much time and money preparing. So they must teach by the piece, offering one or two classes at two or more different institutions. Some universities and colleges pay as little as $1,200 per section of Freshman English. At that rate, even if they worked every available hour of the week, part-time teachers would not be able to support themselves, let alone a family, by teaching. Their class and ethnic privileges do not obviate the fact that their children need to be fed, clothed, and sheltered.

Second lesson learned: organizations like CCCC and MLA can do only symbolic work (not that this isn't important). The third provision of the Wyoming Resolution called upon CCCC to censure institutions that failed to comply with the employment guidelines developed by the committee on professional standards. CCCC hasn't yet censured any institutions of higher learning, even though something like 90 percent of American colleges and universities are currently in violation of the organization's standards for professional quality in postsecondary writing instruction. The organization hasn't censured those institutions because professional academic groups don't know how to make institutions pay attention to censures. Furthermore, CCCC simply doesn't have the financial or professional resources necessary to enforce sanctions. And it will continue to have none until its members and their leaders are willing that the organization establish a political action arm (which means, among other things, hiring lobbyists and attorneys to represent their professional interests to legislatures and university administrations).

The Wyoming Resolution addresses a class issue that is repeated in the hierarchal distribution of specialties in English, but which is not entirely attributable to it. Most teachers of literature have permanent full-time appointments; most teachers of composition have temporary, part-time appointments (Schell 1997). The resolution also raises a gender issue, since most part-time and graduate teachers of writing are women, while most full-time, permanent, ranking faculty are men. And it raises the issue of racial discrimination as well. I'll give just one example of how this works. In many two-year colleges (where, nationally, over 60 percent of the faculty are employed part-time) the permanent faculty is firmly tenured in, and has been so since well before the effects of affirmative hiring were felt. So the only way that such institutions can put teachers of color into writing classrooms is by hiring them on a temporary, part-time basis. If CCCC were to try to abolish part-time positions altogether, institutions in this position would lose their teachers of color.

Which brings me to the third lesson I learned: if you work in a corrupt system, you have to face the fact that making things better for people working in one part of the system may make things worse for people who work in another part of it. We have to think hard about the wisdom of developing universal solutions for a set of problems that have been generated by the imposition of a universal requirement upon very different kinds of institutions.

A MODEST PROPOSAL

Bearing this caveat in mind, and ever mindful of the difficulties entailed in altering institutions that perform powerful ideological work, I nevertheless entertain hope that the cultural and institutional roles played by Freshman English might be interfered with. We ("we" meaning college and university English teachers) won't do this solely by tampering with its curriculum. However, we might be able to alter the functions of Freshman English by altering its institutional status. In this spirit, I offer a modest proposal. Let's abolish the universal requirement. Let's just stop insisting that every student who enrolls in a two-year college or four-year university must take a required composition course. Please note that I am *not* proposing the abolition of introductory-level writing courses. I suggest, rather, that universities simply stop insisting that every student who matriculates must somehow deal with an introductory-level composition requirement, either by taking a course or testing out.

Perhaps it is well at this point that I bring together and summarize my objections to the requirement, some of which have been suggested by the historical investigations undertaken in this book. Here they are:

The universal requirement exploits teachers of writing, particularly part-time teachers and graduate students. The working conditions of teachers of universally required introductory composition courses are ordinarily less rich than those of other university faculty: such teachers usually are paid less, have no access to benefits or job security, have little or no advance warning about what and when they will teach, and have inadequate office and communications facilities. While my complaints about teachers' working conditions apply primarily to temporary and part-time teachers, my reservations about the compromise of academic freedom in a universally required course apply to graduate students as well. Their lack of academic freedom is directly tied to the absence of job security in such positions, since the notion of tenure was established precisely in order to protect academic freedom.

The universal requirement exploits students. Freshman composition is the only course that is required of every student who enrolls in a college or university, no matter what her desires, her experience, her age, or her major. Students invest time, money, and energy in the required introductory courses, which often create a good deal of stress for them since the classes are small and performance-oriented. It seems reasonable that their investment should be backed with some assurance that the required effort is indeed necessary or even useful. I have never seen convincing evidence that the required intro-ductory composition course has any effect at all on the students who take it. Please note that I am not claiming that the course has no effects; I am only pointing to the curious silence within our profession about measurable ef-fects of the universally required course.

The requirement has negative curricular effects. I think that the required nature of the introductory course affects the quality of its curriculum. It is difficult to design a course or courses for a large and amorphous audience when, moreover, the course fits into no discernible disciplinary or scholarly sequence. In curricular terms, the introductory composition requirement comes from nowhere and goes nowhere. And while it is true that innovative and exciting curricula have been written for the required course, they are difficult to implement and sustain because of the size and impermanence of composition faculties. I also think that innovative and exciting curricula for the required introductory course will be resisted wherever they are imple-mented, as they were at the University of Texas, because of the academic and cultural beliefs that the role of the requirement is to induce students to em-ploy correct grammar and usage.

In large universities and colleges, sections of the course are offered nearly around the clock and are scattered across the campus, so that writing pro-gram administrators or their administrative staff stand little chance of visit-ing sections even once. Part-time teachers hurry from one campus to the next, pick up their mail once a week (if they have a mailbox), and are not invited or are unable to attend curriculum planning sessions. And while graduate stu-dents have shown themselves to be capable designers of curricula for the re-quired introductory course, they do have other work to do while they are teaching and administering the required program. Those who succeed at that other work soon leave the programs whose curricula they helped design to become composition professionals elsewhere; those who do not succeed hang around a little longer, but inevitably they, too, either become part-timers or take up other careers altogether.

The requirement negatively affects classroom climate. The required status of the introductory composition courses causes resentment on the part of some of its students. The required course feels like high school, and so stu-dents employ high-school resistance tactics on its teachers. While their use of this strategy may not present serious problems to experienced professors, it can be devastating for young, inexperienced teachers. The small size and the performance orientation of the introductory composition course bring teachers and students into closer contact than is the case in other college courses, and so it is impossible for teachers to ignore students who act out their resentment over their temporary incarceration in terms given them by the society in which they live, particularly if their teachers are women or are marked by them as members of minority groups.

The requirement has negative disciplinary and institutional effects. The required introductory course in composition maintains and promulgates a definition and ideology of writing instruction that is quite narrow. University faculty, including English faculty in literary studies, view writing and writing instruction in the terms traditionally used in the required introductory course. Since faculty who are not professionally associated with composition instruction still assume that the required introductory course teaches grammar, spelling, punctuation, and organization, they view composition faculty as literacy gatekeepers rather than as intellectuals and teachers. Despite its radical and ground-breaking discoveries about pedagogy, composition studies nevertheless remains almost invisible within academic hierarchies, primarily because of its association with the traditional required course. I suspect that the effort required to maintain the required course has kept those of us who profess composition studies from thinking of our discipline in more expansive curricular terms.

The requirement has negative professional effects. Composition studies is far too invested in the universal requirement. We composition professionals have used the requirement to establish a firm institutional base, and hence we are implicated in all of the unsavory institutional practices it entails. We are so invested in maintaining the requirement, I suggest, that we have hesitated to claim the disciplinary legitimacy of what we know and do. Some days I think that we have so little faith in our field of study that we fear the university will get rid of writing instruction (and of us) if we unhook our discipline from the requirement. However, without the administrative burden imposed by the requirement, composition specialists could begin to work toward installing writing instruction throughout the curriculum vertically as well as horizontally, toward establishing departments of writing in institutions where that is appropriate, toward strengthening writing centers, and toward offering writing courses outside of the academy.

HOW IT MIGHT WORK

To deny that all students need to jump over the hurdle of Freshman English is to begin chipping away at the course's historical function as a repressive instrument of student and teacher legitimation. I give just one example of how this might work. Abolishing the universal requirement rids us of one of the more appalling surveillance functions of Freshman English—the placement exam. Many universities use students' ACT scores to "place" them in one or another tracks of Freshman English—the lowest track is usually called "remedial" or "basic" writing and the highest is called "honors" or something equally laudatory. Composition directors who work in universities that exempt high-scoring students from the requirement can (and do) in effect abolish the requirement for high-scoring students by placing them in shorter courses of study or by exempting them altogether. They can also control enrollments by lowering the exemption score until the size of the group deemed to need instruction is small enough to fit the size of the available teaching staff. Faculty at other universities determine placement by means of objective tests that quite frankly measure students' grasp of grammar and usage rather than their writing ability. Others ask students actually to write essays. In some schools teachers administer an essay exam to the students enrolled in their classes; in other schools essay examinations are administered en masse in large halls where proctors prowl among the students to insure that no one cheats. The students' papers are then read in holistic reading sessions. Piles of papers are placed on tables; rows of readers are "normed" to improve their uniformity of response and are then set to reading. I find it inconceivable that people who design and administer these discursive gangbangs think that writing produced outside of any rhetorical context can actually be read. The institution provides motivational context for the placement exam, of course, since students have to pass the exam in order to get into, or out of, Freshman English. But one can refer to the activities associated with mass examinations as "writing" or "reading" only if one is willing to define these acts as obtaining under circumstances where authors' names are expunged from their texts, where all who write respond to the same prescribed prompt, and where all who read do so not to find out what an author has to say but in order to determine who goes and who stays. If Freshman English is not required, we can stop participating in this expensive and embarrassing hoop-jumping ritual.

In addition, the modest proposal offers the attractive administrative advantage of returning control over enrollments in the introductory English course to the people who support, administer, and teach its sections. As things currently stand, staffing in Freshman English is driven by enrollments. The uncertainty entailed in tying numbers of sections to enrollments implicates English departments in low-rent hiring practices, makes us complicit in the direct assault on tenure that is a feature of the increasing use of temporary part-time teachers in untenurable budget lines, interferes with quality training and supervision of teachers, and makes planning for controlled enrollment growth or shrinkage nearly impossible.

Departments adopting the modest proposal will be in control of course enrollments, offering only the number of sections that can be responsibly staffed and supported. And, since such departments will know how many sections of the introductory course they plan to staff, far in advance of any given semester or quarter, they can redesign their hiring practices to meet professional standards as well as the needs of teachers of writing who reside nearby. They will be able to staff sections of the elective course with trained and enthusiastic teachers; they can pay teachers in accordance with their skill and experience; they can hire them well in advance of their scheduled teaching assignments. I hope it is not utopian to imagine that in some schools, these practices might lead to others: promoting teachers of writing based on the work that they do, and offering them security of employment in accordance with the standards that are used for all faculty at that institution.

Adoption of the proposal will allow an English department of any size to determine the number of graduate assistantships it can responsibly award and support. Departments that need fewer TAs can pay each of them more, if its administrators are skilled enough rhetors to convince their superiors that current levels of funding will be more efficiently deployed under the terms of the proposal. Maintenance of a good writing center, along with a series of good elective writing courses, would allow graduate students some flexibility in their teaching assignments. Freed from the enrollment demands placed on them by the required course, departments that wished to do so could more easily assign graduate assistants to help faculty in pursuing research projects or in teaching other courses, within and outside of the department. In addition, graduate assistants would have more flexibility in planning and scheduling their teaching assignments from term to term, so they can better balance the demands of graduate study with their teaching responsibilities, and so that their resumes reflect a larger variety of teaching experiences.

BETTER CASES

Good and bad arguments can be raised against my proposal. The only really good argument against it that I can think of goes like this: if the requirement is lifted, some composition teachers may lose their jobs. I think that demand for elective writing courses will remain high without the requirement, especially if they feature high-caliber instruction. Nonetheless, I grant that the universal requirement protects employment for the very people I want to help.[5] Nor am I unaware that faculty and administration at some universities will read the modest proposal as an invitation to eliminate or reduce the number of part-time and graduate student teaching positions at their schools, rather than engaging in the hard work and planning that are necessary to upgrade teaching positions, institute meaningful professional development, and write curricula for new elective composition courses. I leave it to my readers to decide whether the risk entailed in adopting the modest proposal ought to be undertaken at their schools.

Here is another, less good, argument against the modest proposal: if we don't require the course, students who need it might not take it. I am skeptical about students' "need" for Freshman English as the course has traditionally been configured (see chapter 12). On the other hand, I am quite willing to admit that a very good introductory course in writing can help students make their way through the university and perhaps even enhance their lives after college. It should be apparent by now, though, that I don't think it likely that very good writing courses can be invented or maintained within a universal requirement. My first response to this argument, then, is this: let's trust students to determine whether or not they "need" an introductory course in writing. In documented cases where the requirement has been lifted, high numbers of students have continued to enroll in an elective introductory course (Brannon; Hoover). My second response is that universities that still feel paternal toward their students can retain some sort of testing device in order to insure that students who are deemed to "need" an introductory writing course do in fact get one. I offer this possibility in the interest of honoring the politics of difference and location, but I must say that it makes me very uneasy because I suspect that much placement testing evaluates class affiliation and linguistic background rather than writing ability (whatever that is, outside of some legitimating rhetorical context).

WORSE CASES

Bad arguments against the modest proposal are legion. A second version of the needs argument is a bad argument. Here it is: minority students particularly need a course that introduces them to the literate skills that enable them to succeed in college and in life. I have heard this patronizing and racist claim made by writing teachers on more than one occasion; I suspect it is the version that some teachers have in mind when they put forward the needs claim in support of the universal requirement. I will pass by its appalling racism and simply observe that to acquire the literate skills prized in the academy is actually to become a member of a valued but nonetheless minority culture. Persons who desire to enter academic culture must pay a price. To the extent that they adopt the language of the academy their entitlement to their native languages and cultures is compromised or diminished. The modest proposal does not entail that students who wish to do so be denied the opportunity to learn the language of a privileged minority. It does question the assumption that all students should be forced to learn it by means of a universally required course in academic literacy that, moreover, ineluctably confronts them as a requirement upon their very entry into the academy. The universal requirement of Freshman English comes at the very beginning of students' careers in higher education. There are no firmly institutionalized practices that insure that beginning students are alert to the political, ethical, and cultural effects of their being forced to take a course that advocates their adoption of the values entailed in acquiring standard written English, or liberal culture, or a leftist politics. No matter what its ethics and politics, students (and many teachers) don't know (or won't admit) that Freshman English has an ethics or a politics. This deception is especially hypocritical when Freshman English is advertised or conceived as a "skills" course.

Requirements in first-year composition raise a set of very large questions for me. Here they are: isn't it administrative overkill to require the course of everyone since it may be needed by some? And how do we know who needs the course? Do we really find this out by testing students in massive holistic grading sessions? Who says that the tests we use actually measure the skills students need to pass the required course (especially since most of them only measure first drafts), much less that they measure the skills students need to succeed in college or in life? Wouldn't it be saner to allow students to self-select the course, or to be recommended into it after undertaking some college work? Do we know that a one- or two-semester residency in a Freshman English course actually teaches students the literate skills they need to succeed in college or in life? How do we know this? If we were to impose a universal exit test on the course, would its results tell us that students can write well enough to succeed in college or in life? If we were sure that students did achieve this level of mastery, could we be equally sure that they maintain it without further, constant, practice? And do we want to equip students to succeed in a culture that is devastating its natural environment, that fails to care for children, elderly, and poor people, that subjects people to verbal or physical abuse on the basis of gender, ethnicity, or sexual behavior, and that wages war on other peoples for self-serving reasons? Do we want to force students to take a course whose traditional practices aim at making them oblivious to all of this? If we do want these things, we should be candid about our desires. But we should then think hard about the gap that exists between our desires and our ability to implement them by means of three or six hours of required composition instruction. In short, we should stop hoping or wishing or assuming that Freshman English accomplishes the mighty goals we set for it in our professional imaginations.

Another bad argument is generated by the desire of English departments to maintain their institutional hegemony by maintaining their sheer size. It goes like this: abolishing the universal requirement will diminish the availability of financial support for graduate students, and hence will diminish the number of students available to take graduate courses in English. Granted. Perhaps it is time for English departments to admit that the size of graduate programs in English has been inflated by the ready availability of support for graduate teaching assistantships. Our desire for graduate students has made English departments complicit in an exploitive staffing policy that nets the institution a very great deal of skilled teaching for almost nothing. Too many departments award too many doctorates in English without asking whether their graduates can find employment, or whether they will, after teaching under exploitive conditions for four to eight years in graduate school, be willing to teach for many more years under the same or worse conditions as part-timers and freeway fliers.

Another bad argument: if English departments don't offer the universally required course, somebody else will. It is easy enough to envision some other department or some new institutional entity springing into the breach left open by an English department's abandonment of its historical commitment to instruction in formal fluency. This is still a bad argument, though, for all the reasons discussed above. English departments that consider abolishing the universal requirement will have to discuss how to head off such a development, should it develop, before they make public their decision to quit underwriting the cultural and academic myths that have kept Freshman English on a minimal-support system all these years.

CODA

I wrote the first version of this essay in 1990. It now seems to me that the people who tried to implement the Wyoming Resolution seriously underestimated developments during the late 1980s and early 1990s that would further entrench the universal requirement and worsen the unprofessional and unethical working conditions associated with it. During that time, universities adopted a post-Fordist pattern of employment, retiring senior faculty and replacing them with temporary, part-time workers (Robin Murray, Lauter 1995). Standards for tenure have become ever more stringent, insuring that fewer and fewer people actually gain tenured positions in the academy. At the same time, neoconservatives are attacking the notion of tenure because they want to rid universities of teachers whose politics are not their own. The neoconservative movement to restore traditional humanist values to higher education would, it seems to me, cheerfully retain Freshman English in its exclusionary role as gatekeeper to the university.

12

COMPOSITION'S ETHIC OF SERVICE, THE UNIVERSAL REQUIREMENT, AND THE DISCOURSE OF STUDENT NEED

> We tend to ask, "Do they write well enough to get by?" and if we think they do we usually exempt them from part or all of the Freshman course. A more proper question, I think, would be, "How much better can they be taught to write?" for writing is a skill with no top limit.
> —Albert Kitzhaber, "Death—Or Transfiguration?"

> There's gotta be a couple of ways we can do this.
> —Tommy Lee Jones as Quint in *Black Moon Rising*

Since its beginnings in the late nineteenth century, university-level composition instruction has maintained an ethic of service. Its teachers and supporters have argued that composition instruction served the needs of the academic community, as well as those of students and the community at large, by teaching students to write error-free expository prose. Since the late nineteenth century, this instrumental ethic has provided most American colleges and universities with a rationale for requiring introductory composition courses of all students.

The instrumental ethic of the introductory course has been supplemented from time to time with other, more general, aims. During the 1920s and 1930s, for example, the introductory writing course was conceived as a site wherein students could be exposed to liberal culture (Berlin 1987). During the 1940s, in the aftermath of world war, the required course was reconceived as a venue for the inculcation of citizenship and the distillation of democratic values. Recently, radical composition theorists have urged that college teachers of writing use their classrooms to make students aware of social inequities (Berlin 1991; Bizzell 1992; Clifford; Cooper and Holzman). Despite attempts to update or expand the definition of its service ethic, however, the required introductory composition course has always been justified, at bottom, in instrumental terms: this is the site wherein those who are new to the academy learn to write its prose.

In an essay entitled "After Progressivism," Michael Murphy argues that the service ethic of composition studies is so pervasive that it affects the thinking of even the most careful, and most radical, theorists of composition. Murphy claims, for example, that complicity with the service ethic mars the earlier work of James Berlin:

> All that is potentially radical about Berlin's deployment of "social-epistemic rhetoric" . . . seems to me . . . quickly coopted by its implicit association with composition's progressivist baggage. The progressivist discourse of educational democracy—along with its allied senses of duty ("our responsibilities as teachers and citizens" [493]) and social welfare ("the greater good of all" [490])—is so fundamental a part of the language of composition scholarship that it can effectively underwrite the work of even as guarded an anti-foundationalist as Berlin. (355; quoting Berlin 1988)

The problem with compositionists' subscription to agendas set out for them by the academy, according to Murphy, is that in the absence of sustained critique of those agendas "the compositionist is enlisted in the service of a transcendent good embodied in the proper function of the institution, and the composition student is left, once again like the discipline itself, inadvertently but undeniably disabled" (356). In this analysis Murphy implies that composition cannot serve its own ends, or those of its students, as long as it serves the ends of the institution. And composition cannot cease to serve institutional ends as long as compositionists cannot critique their history of complicity with institutional values such as "faith in social progress" (345).

Murphy connects the service ethic of composition to its failure to achieve disciplinarity. However, Burton Bledstein's study of the rise of professionalism in America establishes that the inauguration and maintenance of disciplines are ordinarily justified by a service ethic (36–38). And so it might be said (although it is not, often) that most academic disciplines bear a service mission. The natural and social sciences can be construed to exist for reasons other than facilitating the disinterested pursuit of knowledge or the professional advancement of their practitioners; and it can fairly be said that the research produced by natural and social scientists has, on occasion, contributed to human health and happiness. Too, the examples of medicine and law suggest that a powerful discipline can be developed around an explicit service ethic. In other words, a service ethic is not necessarily incompatible with disciplinary status.

What is distinctive about the service ethic associated with composition studies is its low status. Within the academy, the work done by composition teachers is not imagined to be as worthy as that of scientists, social scientists, musicians, artists, historians, literary scholars, or philosophers, all of whose professional work is imagined to perform some valuable service either for the academy or for the culture at large. Periodic attempts to alter the image of composition—by associating it with loftier goals like liberal culture or democratic values—have been unsuccessful in dislodging its connection to the laying of academic groundwork.

THE UNIVERSAL REQUIREMENT AND
THE STATUS OF COMPOSITION

Susan Miller argues that the service ethic of composition is held in low repute for social reasons. She situates her critique of the invention of composition within the historical evolution of American universities, after the Civil War, toward admission of people who would formerly have been barred from university educations because they lacked the appropriate family connections. She argues that the pairing of composition instruction with literary studies, under the rubric "English," offered growing universities with newly elective curricula a way to insure that traditional class boundaries were maintained:

> The university, ambivalent about its formerly unentitled, newly admitted students, needed to establish an internal boundary, a way to stratify diverse participants in what had been perceived as one dominant American group. As the symbolic domain of a national vernacular literature was suddenly produced to control an actual public realm, an equally new but easily identifiable, low, and now alien "writing" could simultaneously represent a murky, improper realm of language. That is, nonliterary writing by the unentitled became an organized discourse on composition, the unentitled domain that would perfectly complete the formation of a newly conceived, privileged, and discrete literary canon. (1994, 27)

Writing done by the unentitled would be put under continued surveillance in required composition courses. Students would remain in such courses, their writing subject to such scrutiny, until it displayed the requisite conformity or until they left the academy.

This is the instrumental service ethic of the required composition course: to make student writing available for surveillance until it can be certified to conform to whatever standards are deemed to mark it, and its authors, as suitable for admission to the discourses of the academy. When the Harvard overseers instituted English A, the target language was that spoken by the genteel white male upper class. Today, the target language is called "academic discourse," which term testifies to the current importance of disciplinarity within the academy. But this change in focus has not altered the social point of the requirement: exclusive practices need someone to exclude. The marginalization of the entire freshman class (except, of course, for those few elect—usually English majors—who are exempted) serves to underscore and reinforce the exclusivity of academic discourse, both with regard to the academy's newest members (students and teachers alike) and with regard to the culture at large.

Even though the cultural roles played by universities and by literary studies itself have changed enormously since the instauration of English studies, the lowly functions envisioned for composition instruction by the Harvard overseers still remain in place in American colleges and universities, fulfilled then and ever since by the universal requirement in introductory composition. Disciplines younger than composition, such as English-language literary studies and the social sciences, are now firmly established in the academy. However, composition teachers and theorists did not make serious moves toward achieving disciplinarity until the 1970s—eighty to ninety years later than most fields of study in American universities.

I think that the universal requirement in introductory composition, which is the institutional manifestation of composition's service ethic, has kept the traditional goals of disciplinarity—the pursuit of knowledge and the professional advancement of practitioners—beyond the reach of composition studies until very recently. The difference made by the universal requirement is manifested in the history of the professional organization of composition studies—the Conference on College Composition and Communication—which was founded, not to advance knowledge, as were MLA or SCA, say, but in order to help its teachers manage the universally required course and to protect them from exploitation (Gerber 1952). Accordingly, until 1970 or so, composition research concentrated on teacher practice and its effects on students' writing, and this research was usually undertaken, not in the disinterested pursuit of knowledge, but in order to improve teaching practices. By 1990, though, composition studies had developed a body of research and theory that differed from its more traditional work, and CCCC has become a forum for the publication of scholarship undertaken primarily to advance knowledge about writing. In this regard, composition studies can now be considered to have met the first requirement for disciplinary status.

What remains is for composition studies to improve the status and working conditions of its practitioners. Composition's recent bid for disciplinarity has been hampered not only by its history of unfair employment practices but by the emergence of post-Fordist hiring practices in the academy at large (Faigley 1992, 10–13; Robin Murray). Post-Fordist institutions rely on part-time or other disposable faculty, such as graduate students, to do the teaching. The advantages to management of part-time faculty are economy (lower salaries, fewer benefits) and flexibility (layoffs in hard times are relatively simple). Whatever might be said about the evils of disciplinarity, until recently its institutional practices impeded the full-scale implementation of part-time instruction in the academy. Recently, however, tenured faculties have become complicit in their own demise; as tenured faculties continue to raise the standards for tenure—as they have over the last ten years—they accelerate the creation and maintenance of post-Fordist employment patterns in the academy.

It remains to be seen whether post-Fordist employment practices will reduce or negate the power of disciplinarity in American universities. In any case, composition's bid for disciplinarity could not have been made at a worse time. Moreover, the imagined construction of composition as "low" work exerts so much ideological force within the academy that even if composition were to achieve a disciplinary status that is recognized beyond its own borders, its image might not alter appreciably within the academy. Those few composition teachers who have achieved rank, commensurate salaries, office space, and lower teaching loads are aware that their colleagues in other disciplines still regard their work as not truly academic. And such perks do not now and probably will never accrue to the thousands of teachers who teach four, five, or even six sections of the required introductory course every semester, precisely because their work is perceived to be instrumental, even remedial.

SERVICE AND THE REQUIRED INTRODUCTORY COURSE

In the minds of most of its teachers and everybody else who thinks about it, composition instruction is firmly associated with the curriculum of the required introductory course or courses in composition. This is unfortunate, since the traditional pedagogy of this course maintains and promulgates a definition and ideology of writing instruction that is quite narrow, configuring it as a series of exercises in formal fluency plus instruction in usage, grammar, spelling, and punctuation. The fact of the requirement itself ought to be a tipoff that the work of the course is widely considered to be distasteful: modern universities require courses only when they think that students will not elect them.

When composition directors or teachers attempt to design syllabi for the required course that are not distasteful to students, they inevitably jettison or downplay the pedagogy of formal correctness. However, a case can be made that such attempts will fail to the extent that faculty outside composition, or the public at large, become aware of them. Linda Brodkey, who collaborated on the design of the aborted syllabus for E306 at Texas, writes that opposition to it emanated from the "common sense" that obtains about the required introductory course:

> Common sense prevailed at Texas. Alan Gribben [a vocal opponent of Writing About Difference] was later reported in the *Chronicle of Higher Education* as declaring simply: "'If you really care about women and minorities making it in society, it doesn't make sense to divert their attention to oppression when they should be learning basic writing skills.'" . . . Another professor of American literature circulated his own countersyllabus, based on principles of copyediting. . . . A professor who writes handbooks . . . published an editorial in the student newspaper identifying rhetoric as "the subject matter to be taught and learned," and defining an introduction to rhetoric as focusing "on the logic and validity of arguments, the development and enrichment of ideas, the appropriate arrangements of subject matter, and the power and correctness of language." (1995, 232–33)

Persons who protested the redesigned syllabus at Texas may have done so for political reasons, but they covered over their uneasiness with the syllabus by insisting that the required introductory course be firmly associated with the pedagogy of formal correctness, which is, incidently, perceived to be politically neutral.

Lest anyone think that such common sense obtains only in Texas, I quote a recent essay wherein David Bleich meditates on the ways in which faculty at the University of Rochester view the required composition program:

> It remains the case that most faculty, perhaps even most English department faculty, would like to continue their own work without changing the role that writing as a subject has had in the curriculum for perhaps more than a century. . . . I imagine that those reading this essay understand "this role" to mean: writing programs are a subordinate and lower status part of the English department. The teaching of writing is not considered to be a subject with a scholarly literature and a body of knowledge, but a service and training area, a staging area, perhaps, for the "real" work in science and technology. (136)

Despite its pedagogical innovations and its ambitions toward curricular expansion, then, because of the universally required course and its unique function within the academic imaginary, composition studies is still associated with composition's earliest and most familiar pedagogy: the pedagogy of grammar, spelling, punctuation, and formal fluency. Because of this association, composition is regarded as instrumental or remedial work.

Unfortunately, as Murphy points out, composition theorists and teachers themselves maintain faith in the universal requirement, thus participating in the continued maintenance of their profession's low academic status. When I and others have suggested at professional gatherings that composition theorists and teachers rethink the continued usefulness of the universal requirement, the suggestion has been met with vigorous resistance. This resistance does not seem to stem primarily from fears that jobs may be lost if the requirement is lifted. Rather, the major argument used against lifting the requirement is ideological, and it invokes composition's traditional service ethic. It goes like this: "Our students need what we teach."

Sometimes this claim is buttressed by a second one: "at-risk students particularly need what we teach." Apparently, studies do exist indicating that at-risk students' chances of staying in college are increased when their initial coursework includes a small class with a supportive environment where they get a good deal of individual attention (White). This is welcome news; however, it is not an argument for imposing a universal requirement in introductory composition. If such supportive environments are more typical of composition classrooms and writing centers than of other disciplinary sites, that is a largely unsung tribute to people who teach writing and who profess composition studies. But this evidence does not support the claim that at-risk students are specifically served by instruction in composition.

And when evidence about the retention of at-risk students is used to support the claim that minority students profit from required instruction in writing, at-risk status is equated with minority status—an equation that I resist. Indeed, it is my desire to resist equations like these that in part drives my resistance to the universal requirement, which tends toward standardization and away from the recognition of students' diverse abilities and desires. If I am right that the required introductory course remains in place in order to socialize students into the discourse of the academy, to the extent that it succeeds in this it supplements or even erases students' relation to their home languages. The universality of the requirement suggests to me that this is, precisely, its point.

In any case, the requirement has nothing to do with what students need and everything to do with the academy's image of itself as a place where a special language is in use. The discourse of needs positions composition teachers as servants of a student need that is spoken, not by students themselves, but by people speaking for powerful institutions. Like the narrative of progress, the discourse of needs interpellates composition teachers as subjects who implement the regulatory desires of the academy and the culture at large.

REQUIRED COMPOSITION AND THE DISCOURSE OF NEEDS

In her analysis of the discourse of needs, feminist philosopher Nancy Fraser remarks that "needs claims have a relational structure; implicitly or explicitly, they have the form 'A needs x in order to y'" (163). The needs claims made within composition studies take this form: students need composition in order to write better, to write error-free prose, to survive in the academy, to prosper in a job or profession, to become acquainted with the best that has been thought and said, to become critics of the society in which they live. Fraser posits that such relational claims about needs are noncontroversial when they are very general, or "thin": thin needs include the human need for food and shelter, for example. But as soon as needs discourse descends to lower levels of generality, its claims become "thicker" and more controversial. For example: "Everyone needs an education in order to succeed." Most Americans might assent to this claim, and if so, this is a relatively thin claim about needs. But thicker needs claims can follow fast on the heels of this one: "Everyone needs the same education in order to succeed," or "Every American needs higher education in order to succeed." As needs claims become thicker, that is, as they descend from the plane of mythology to the plane of ideology, they invite contest.

However, even relatively thick needs claims cannot be contested if the relevant power relations silence those who might contest them. My readers will have noticed, perhaps, that in public discussions about the needs of welfare mothers and their dependent children, it is not mothers or children who define which needs are at stake. Nor do public discussions about teenage pregnancy typically construct teenage fathers as persons in need of state intervention into their sexual habits. Of course, current relations of power mitigate against welfare mothers' being delegated the cultural authority or the channels through which to speak and be heard, and the discourse of patriarchy consistently overlooks the responsibility of men in the getting of children. As the unfair, myopic, and interested terms of popular discussion about welfare indicate, even thick needs claims can seem thin (that is, uncontested and uncontestable), if they are manifested within a network of relations that disguises their constructed, and hence political, nature.

Fraser observes that analysts of needs discourse often overlook the power relations within which it circulates, and as a result they overlook some fairly important political effects:

> they take the interpretation of people's needs as simply given and unproblematic. . . . they assume that it doesn't matter who interprets the needs in question and from what perspective and in the light of what interest. . . . they take for granted that the socially authorized forms of public discourse available for interpreting people's needs are adequate and fair. . . . they thus neglect such important political questions as Where in society, in what institutions, are authoritative need interpretations developed? and What sorts of social relations are in force among the interlocutors or co-interpreters? (163)

The claim that students need required composition instruction is situated in a nexus of power relations that often go unexamined within composition theory and pedagogy. As a result, the political, interested aspects of such claims are obscured, as a point-by-point consideration of Fraser's analysis demonstrates. First: when power relations are not taken into account, *the interpretation of people's needs is given and unproblematic.* Now, the claim that students need composition is deeply embedded in a number of institutional and cultural discourses. The academic discourses that affect or have affected composition instruction include liberal education, humanism, general education, and progressivism, as well as the discursive practices of testing, grading, and ranking; the cultural discourses that affect composition include those of literacy, class, and race. That is to say, composition is administered and taught in a much thicker discursive network than are many other academic courses.

Despite its considerable ideological freight, however, within the current discursive climate of composition studies the claim that students need composition is treated as a thin claim. That is, it is very difficult to contest it without being written off as either an elitist or a troublemaker (White). This is particularly frustrating because support for the claim is virtually unarticulated: no empirical studies have ever been done to test it, and historical research reveals reiterated but unsubstantiated statements of it (e.g., McElroy, and see Templeman). I conclude that the claim that students need composition is "privatized," to use Fraser's lexicon once again; in other words, the claim is so widely accepted in the relevant communities that it is simply not available for argument.

Fraser argues that three kinds of needs discourses are presently in circulation: oppositional discourses, "which arise when needs are politicized 'from below'"; reprivatization discourses, which emerge in response to oppositional discourses and attempt to modify or halt their circulation; and expert needs discourses, "which link popular movements to the state" (171). All three discourses can be found in the history of composition studies, but they have emerged with unequal force.

Reprivatization discourses have appeared periodically in support of the universal requirement, even though there has never been much concerted opposition to it "from below." The single sustained example of opposition to compulsory composition instruction "from below"—the student protests of the late 1960s and early 1970s—resulted in the temporary abandonment of the requirement at a few universities. However, the lack of organized opposition by students has not prevented reprivatization discourses from occurring. Examples of such discourses are the media-manufactured literacy crisis of the late 1970s, which resulted in the reinstatement of the universal requirement at many universities; and postwar concern about the reentry of GIs into American culture, which stimulated the introduction of required "basic skills" programs in a large number of American universities during the 1940s. Interestingly enough, in the twentieth century, reprivatization discourses about composition have emerged with most vigor during postwar periods (1919, 1944, 1978), when America's ideological integrity was perceived to be threatened either internally or externally (Connors 1996; Spanos).

The role of expert needs discourse, according to Fraser, is to connect social or political discourse to a bureaucracy in order that a perceived need can be administered. The perceived need for composition was administered, virtually upon its appearance, by Adams Sherman Hill and his phalanx of instructors, exams, textbooks, bluebooks, and error cards. I suggest that the invention of required introductory composition at Harvard during the 1880s was an administered response to the perceived literacy crisis, as well as the unarticulated class anxiety, that permeated genteel American discourse of the period. By the 1920s, large composition programs, complete with administrators and elaborate testing apparatus and accelerated or remedial sections of the introductory course, had begun to take shape at many universities (Berlin 1987, 65–69). Today, writing programs constitute a huge administrative unit on almost every American campus that has no comparable peer anywhere else in the university.

According to Fraser, administered responses to perceived needs have the effect of repositioning the people whose needs are at issue: "They become individual 'cases' rather than members of social groups or participants in political movements. In addition, they are rendered passive, positioned as potential recipients of predefined services rather than as agents involved in interpreting their needs and shaping their life conditions" (174). Certainly the required introductory course positions students as consumers of a predefined pedagogy. In composition programs that require teachers to adhere to a predetermined grading scale, students' performances are always already ranked against a predefined scale of possibilities. And I would argue, along with Richard Ohmann, that the mass-taught course also positions students as people who have no culture, no history, that might distinguish them in any way from the thousands of their peers who are also writing about abortion or capital punishment or their most moving experience (1976, 145). Required composition, in other words, configures students as people who exist only in the institutional present, and who perform exercises that meet the institutional needs to rank and exclude.

To return to Fraser's analysis of the politics of needs interpretation: her second point is that when power relations are not interrogated, *it doesn't matter who interprets the needs in question and from what perspective and in the light of what interest.* It is worth repeating, I think, that it is not students but the academy that is served by the universal requirement, insofar as the requirement fulfills the gatekeeper function I described above, and insofar as the symbolic capital accrued by the requirement relieves academics from the responsibility of teaching literacy in their own classes and programs. In addition, composition teachers' willingness to speak for their students' needs entails a suspicious politics of representation.

Third: naive claims about needs interpretation assume that *fair and adequate socially authorized forms of public discourse are available for interpreting people's needs*. Aside from course evaluations, there is no authorized discourse within the academy that allows students to voice their concerns about curricula. Teachers use student evaluations of their courses to improve the course next time it is offered; administrators use them to evaluate teachers. But student evaluations are not considered to be valid input regarding the worth of a program or a requirement (unless, of course, students have good things to say, like "this course really taught me how to write"). Students do engage in many unauthorized discourses about curricula, of course: they circulate subrosa lists of good and bad courses and instructors; they complain to teachers or administrators about a bad experience in a course or program; they write letters to the campus newspaper; they call their parents, who sometimes call the board of regents. But none of these unauthorized channels give the mass of students regular and equal access to the groups who actually make curricular decisions: curriculum committees, faculty senates, and boards of regents or trustees.

Fourth: when the politics of needs discourse is not foregrounded, *political questions are neglected, such as, What sorts of social relations are in force among the interlocutors or co-interpreters?* The hierarchical social relations within the American university are quite clearcut, if hardly ever articulated in authorized public forums. There are hierarchies of disciplinarity (the natural sciences, the social sciences, the humanities, applied or pragmatic fields such as education or home economics). There are yet more hierarchies within each of these divisions (physics is purer than chemistry and both are purer than biology; philosophy is superior to literature and both are superior to rhetoric or composition). There are hierarchies of position (president and provost, dean, senior faculty, junior faculty, staff, graduate students, undergraduates). Composition teachers and their students occupy the very bottom rungs of all these hierarchical ladders. Thus, Murphy's suggestion that compositionists remain in thrall to the discourse of the institution might be fruitfully situated in a fuller analysis of their institutional position. Why indeed have composition teachers been so eager to adopt the institution's definition of their role? Could it be that they have seen accommodation as a means of survival, however marginally, within the institution? As Fraser notes, "members of subordinated groups commonly internalize need interpretations that work to their own disadvantage" (169). Or could it be that composition teachers are themselves somehow served by their adoption of an ethic of service and the discourse of student need?

I think it is time for people who profess composition studies to consider what would be lost, and what could be gained, if we dropped the discourse of student need as our legitimating claim. Throughout our history we have acquiesced to definitions of our profession and our disciplinary goals, given us by others. We work in academic and cultural climates in which misperceptions abound concerning our work. I wonder why we think that our professional interests are served by continuing to speak discourses that are imposed upon us, hierarchical and exclusive as they are.

WRITING BEYOND FRESHMAN ENGLISH

The universal requirement has obscured the potential of composition instruction at the college level, and it has delayed the development of composition studies as well. I conclude my indictment of the universal requirement by considering what might be possible in its absence.

Many universities and colleges already offer an array of upper-division courses in creative, technical, and professional writing. There are courses in editing and document design, as well. I would like to see this array of courses supplemented by a vertical elective curriculum in composing, a curriculum that examines composing both in general and as it takes place in specific rhetorical situations such as workplaces and community decision making. While I can envision challenging courses in invention or style or argumentation being offered in such a curriculum, I would hope that such a course of study would not confine students to practice in composing. Rather, it would help them to understand what composing is and to articulate the role it plays in shaping their intellectual lives. The topmost reaches of an undergraduate curriculum in composing would study histories of writing, debate the politics of literacy, and investigate the specialized composing tactics and rhetorics that have evolved in disciplines, professions, civic groups, women's organizations, social movements, and political parties—to name only a few sites where such investigations could fruitfully take place.

Elective vertical curricula in composing will require the development of new ways to think about composing subjects, and they will of necessity develop ethical technologies to inculcate those subjectivities in students who take the courses. I cannot anticipate what those subjectivities and technologies might be, but I can imagine one or two directions in which composition theory might develop. Composition has always been eclectic; composition teachers have almost always been *bricoleurs*—handypeople—who pick up bits of this theory and parts of that practice in order to get their work done. Composition teachers and theorists have begun to explore the relevance for our work of the exciting thinking that is being done in feminist theory, ethnocentric criticism, cultural studies, poststructural and postmodern thought, critical pedagogy, and neo-Marxism. The usefulness to writing teachers of other theoretical developments remains to be considered: Molefi Asante's notion of "the rhetorical condition" and his construction of an Afrocentric subjectivity, Pierre Bourdieu's notion of *habitus,* and Judith Butler's notion of performativity—to give just three examples—all seem to me to hold promise for composition theory and pedagogy (Bourdieu 1990).

The intellectual eclecticism of composition theory and pedagogy, where it has existed, has been a good thing, I suppose. I hope, however, that teacher-theorists of composition will in the future be wary of theoretical and pedagogical suggestions that turn them away from a commitment to understanding and teaching public discourse. We have, in ancient rhetorics, model theories of composing whose proponents were unabashedly interested in influencing the course of cultural and political events. Teachers of ancient rhetorics assumed that people compose only when they are moved by some civic exigency. Unlike the composing principles taught in current-traditional pedagogy (and in some versions of process pedagogy), which describe the shape of texts and are thought to apply universally, the composing principles taught in ancient rhetorical theories were fully situated in public occasions that required intervention or at any rate stimulated a composer's desire to intervene. Moreover, ancient teachers recognized the importance of location. Quintilian, for example, directs rhetors to begin the process of invention by asking questions about the situation that brought them to composition: "what there is to say; before whom; in whose defence, against whom, at what time and place, under what circumstances; what is the popular opinion on the subject; and what the prepossessions of the judge are likely to be; and finally of what we should express our deprecation or desire" (4.1.52–53). In this brief passage (taken from a very large treatise on pedagogy) we glimpse a subjectivity that is configured quite differently from those constructed in modern composition lore. Quintilian's rhetor is located in time and space; she inhabits a community where public opinion influences the course of events; where discourse itself is acknowledged to bring about change; where emotions influence behavior, and where people express their "deprecation or desire" when the course of events requires them to make and state moral judgments. Nor are ancient rhetorics as rule-governed as modern pedagogies. Where current-traditional pedagogy insists that essays always have introductions, for example, Cicero teaches that an introduction is necessary only if the audience is indifferent or hostile either to the rhetor or the issue she wishes to raise (*De Inventione* 1.15.21ff). Current-traditional rhetoric hardly admits that hostility toward a composer or her position might exist, while process pedagogy assumes that readers are always reasonable people—a liberal fiction that overlooks human interest and desire.

Ancient rhetoric offers other advantages to teachers as well. I like its emphasis on invention, its sense that making more arguments than can ever be used on a given occasion is a useful intellectual exercise. Aristotle's *Rhetoric* takes very seriously the potential of emotions, both as a source of argument and as persuasive strategy. This is a welcome relief from the assumption of modern rhetorical theory that reason is the only form of legitimate argumentative appeal. Ancient teachers of rhetoric had a consuming interest in language, as well, especially in the persuasive effects that can be achieved through its artful uses. This is a healthy corrective to the tendency of modern school rhetorics to discourage students from engaging in linguistic play. Ancient rhetorics also provide teachers with an extensive vocabulary about composing. Of particular use to me are its terms for public belief (now called ideology): the commonplace and *doxa,* or popular opinion. Ancient pedagogy has also provided us with a carefully sequenced set of composing exercises, called the *progymnasmata.*

But there are serious limits to the uses of ancient rhetorics. Classical rhetorical theory was devised a long time ago in cultures that were rigidly classbound and whose economies depended upon slavery. They were invented for the use of privileged men, speaking to relatively small audiences. Those audiences were not literate, and the only available technology of delivery was the human body. Greek rhetorics, in particular, rely on a logic of parts and wholes that was long ago supplemented by other means of reasoning. And so, while ancient rhetorical theory offers much that is absent from modern composing theory, it should be exploited with caution.

I see no reason why contemporary teachers cannot develop theories of composition that are fully as rich as those developed in ancient times. Much thinking remains to be done, and I do not doubt that enterprising teachers of composition will do it—because there is a place for composition in the university, and that place does not depend upon Freshman English.

NOTES

I. COMPOSITION IN THE UNIVERSITY

1. A conservative way to figure the magnitude of introductory composition is to consider that there are more than 3,600 colleges and universities in the country. If only one hundred freshmen enroll in introductory composition at each of these schools, more than 360,000 students take the course every semester. However, there are over 300 large public universities in the country that enroll more than 10,000 students. Universities of this size presumably enroll about 2,500 freshmen annually, and so they need to offer at least 100 sections of the freshman course if they limit enrollment to 25 students per section. They need to hire at least 50 teachers, if they limit teaching loads to two sections (as is commonly done in research universities, where graduate teaching assistants staff the composition program). A few very large public universities—Arizona State, Michigan State, Minnesota, Ohio State, Texas, Texas A&M—enroll 6,000 to 8,000 students in their freshman classes every fall semester. If universities of this size limit enrollments to 25 students per section, they need to offer at least 240 sections of the course and employ 120 people to teach it. These figures do not include courses taught at community colleges, where Freshman English is the largest program mounted by English departments.

2. In 1992 the Modern Language Association published a sizeable collection of essays entitled *Redrawing the Boundaries: The Transformation of English and American Literary Studies,* edited by Stephen Greenblatt and Giles Gunn. The stated purpose of this collection was to provide graduate students with an "adequate sense" of the reconstitution of English studies that has been brought about by contemporary literary theory as well as feminist and ethnic criticisms (3). The collection includes over twenty essays on fields such as medieval studies, Victorian studies, American literary studies prior to the Civil War, gender, feminist, African-American, and Marxist criticisms, deconstruction, postcolonialism, and the new historicism. Now, while composition studies has also been affected by recent developments in theory, the collection contains only one essay on composition. The editors of the collection did not find a prominent scholar in the field to write the essay on composition, as they did for other areas; rather, they commissioned a historian who happens to direct the composition program at Harvard. Although the essay cites a few pieces of composition scholarship published during the 1970s and early 1980s, its author basically concludes, as Tom Miller notes, that composition "does not exist as a

scholarly discipline" (1997, 313). If the layout of this collection represents the way in which English studies is configured in the imagination of literary scholars (and certainly this is the way the editors of the collection must have intended graduate students to understand the field), then composition is not very important, and nothing interesting has happened there for over twenty years.

3. These alterations were also motivated by the redesign of American colleges, increases in student populations, and the social upheaval that characterized the last three decades of the nineteenth century. For histories of the change from the traditional college to the university, see chapter 4 and the sources cited there. For the standard account of social upheaval during the late nineteenth century, see Wiebe; for the implications of American pragmatism with the social chaos of these years, see West (79ff).

4. Obviously, Arnoldian humanism has not been the only rationale put forward to authorize academic literary studies, and there have been occasional disagreements over how the humanist study of literature should be carried out. See Graff's first chapter. There are as many definitions of humanism as there are scholars who study it. Most definitions of humanism are circular or self-validating, as in this bit from R. S. Crane, who defines "a humanity" as "'education and training in the good arts' or disciplines; and the goodness of these arts is made to reside in the fact that those who earnestly desire and seek after them come to be most highly humanized, in the sense of being endowed with the virtues and knowledge that separate men most sharply from the lower animals" (7). For standard treatments of humanism, see Coates, White, and Shapiro; and Jaeger. For histories of humanist education, see Grafton and Jardine, and Kimball. For an attempt to distinguish humanism from a rhetorical educational tradition, see Atwill; for an attempt to meld rhetoric with humanism, see Mailloux.

5. I am indebted to my colleague Marie Secor for this succinct statement of the difference between humanism and composition.

6. For accounts of humanism's exclusions, see (for starters) Brodkey 1996 (88–105), hooks 1989, Kolodny, Spanos, Trinh, Villanueva, Woolf; for a theory of humanist exclusion, see Minnich.

3. THE BOURGEOIS SUBJECT AND
THE DEMISE OF RHETORICAL EDUCATION

1. Reading as a feminist, I cannot resist imagining the scene where Zeuxis looks over the virgins. I picture the sculptor gazing at the women from a distance, perhaps clucking his tongue over a perceived defect or gaping with admiration at some heretofore unperceived excellence, while their proud fathers looked on (mothers too? were their mothers allowed to attend?). But, post-Puritan that I am, mostly I am only able to picture Zeuxis licking his chops, and I wonder about those silent, silenced virgins: what did they think about this most unusual display of their bodies for a stranger? Were they charmed? frightened? Cicero does not tell us. Who were these women? Did they know one another? Were they friends, or perhaps cousins? While

Cicero claims that poets recorded the virgins' names, he does not report them.

2. Eagleton does make the point about education and the formation of subjectivity in "The Subject of Literature" (1985). For the theoretical basis of the notion of ethical subjectivity, see Michel Foucault, *Technologies of the Self* (1988).

3. In taking this position I dissent from mainstream thought in composition studies, wherein rhetoric and composition are yoked, as here, with a companionly "and." See Susan Miller (1989) for an elaboration of the argument that composition instruction and rhetorical education are very different things.

4. Bevilaqua is correct in the main when he opines that scientific rhetoric pays less attention to values than ancient rhetorics did. Certainly the pseudoscientific school rhetoric that developed during the nineteenth century, called "current-traditional rhetoric" by historians, throve in American universities for more than a hundred years partly because it was perceived to be value-neutral. On the other hand, Bevilaqua is wrong about the valence of "imaginative-poetic" concerns for rhetoric, at least with reference to the modern period. Modern rhetoricians' investment in the aesthetic notion of taste was every bit as deadly for rhetorical education as its supposed collusion with scientific discourse proved to be.

5. Gregory Clark traces the influence of this tradition of taste on American Calvinist rhetoric in "The Oratorical Poetic of Timothy Dwight" (1993).

6. The belles-lettres tradition can be opposed to the scientific-empirical tradition of American school rhetoric, a tradition carried forward by writers like Alexander Bain and Henry Noble Day, who were inspired by George Campbell's *Philosophy of Rhetoric* (1776) rather more than by Blair. It was this tradition that spawned current-traditional rhetoric. However, even those authors most tightly wedded to the scientific paradigm, like Bain, devoted a few pages of their texts to the cultivation of taste (1877, 120–21).

4. THE INVENTION OF FRESHMAN ENGLISH

1. This change has often been recounted by historians of higher education: see Earnest, Horowitz, Rudolph, Vesey.

2. For accounts of the tie between liberal arts education and manliness or gentlemanliness, see also Brauer and Kelso. See Shapin for an interesting study that ties gentlemanliness to truth telling.

3. Judicial criticism is enjoying a renewed vogue today, perhaps in response to a burst of antihumanist literary theory. See, for example, Harold Bloom's *The Western Canon* and E. D. Hirsch's *Cultural Literacy*.

4. Women constitute a partial exception to this generalization. While women did demand admission to higher education with increasing success after the war, many women educators insisted that women study precisely the traditional liberal arts curriculum that was being condemned by innovators, on the ground that women needed to prove that they could master the supposedly rigorous classical education heretofore deemed suitable only for gentlemen. See Jo Ann Campbell (1996, 1992a, 1992b); Hobbs; Horowitz. However, Robert J. Connors argues that the admission of

women to higher education played an important role in the demise of the classical curriculum (1995).

5. These developments have been recounted in detail by Gerald Graff in *Professing Literature*. See Payne for contemporary accounts of early English offerings. See Brereton 1995 and Graff and Warner for collections of relevant documents from the period. See Shumway for a theoretical treatment of the importance of disciplinarity to the development of English studies.

6. Here I part company with historians of composition who treat Freshman English as an extension of the universally required exercises in composition that took place within the classical college (Berlin 1984; Halloran 1982, 1990). A continuous history of required work in composition overlooks the momentous alterations to notions of grammar, rhetoric, and literature that occurred with the development of English studies. Some historians do take the position that Freshman English is very different from the more rhetorical exercises required by the classical colleges. See, for example, Kitzhaber (1990) who poses the difference as a theory-practice split, and Susan Miller (1989) who discusses it as a dichotomy between oral and written discourse. While I am not exactly indebted to her for what follows, I am aware that Miller's elegant theoretical analysis of the social and cultural roles played by Freshman English (1994) parallels my history of the invention of the course in many respects.

7. See Graff, chapter 4. Craik's *Shakespeare*—the text recommended on the Harvard entrance exam for 1869—is a fine example of nineteenth-century pedantry. When I was an undergraduate in the 1960s (in the heyday of new criticism), literature textbooks still featured lengthy annotation and meaty historical commentary, probably because collected works of canonical authors were then being edited by scholars who were in graduate school during the 1920s and 1930s, during the heyday of literary history. By the time I finished graduate school my secondhand copy of F. N. Robinson's *Chaucer* had so many notes in the margins that the poet's lines were unreadable.

8. According to Broome, Columbia and Cornell did not require English composition for entrance until 1882. Michigan followed in 1878, and Yale waited "with characteristic conservatism" until 1894 to require composition in English (223).

9. The story of Harvard's attempt to "raise standards" in English in the preparatory schools has often been recounted by historians. See, for example, Kitzhaber (1990) and Trachsel. For the reaction of faculty at other universities, see Donald Stewart on Fred Newton Scott.

10. Here I counter Cmeil, who takes the position that Hill and other nineteenth-century rhetoric teachers dropped the classical habit of associating style with character (240). Perhaps we disagree over a term; see Cmeil's distinction between *ethos* and *persona* (27). Or perhaps Cmeil misses the bourgeois interest in character development because he equates *ethos* with self-development, which is precisely its bourgeois sense. In classical rhetoric, on the other hand, *ethos* meant "reputation" or "public character."

5. LITERATURE AND COMPOSITION:
NOT SEPARATE BUT CERTAINLY UNEQUAL

1. Williams notes further that this shift occurred under the auspices of three "complicating tendencies": "a shift from 'learning' to 'taste' or 'sensibility' as a criterion defining literary quality"; "an increasing specialization of literature to 'creative' or 'imaginative' works"; and "a development of the concept of 'tradition' within national terms" (48). See Berlin's discussion of these three points (1996, 5–8). Literary scholars' disdain for composition may have impeded the growth of courses in "the production of literature"—that is, in creative writing (Payne 137). This would perhaps explain why most of the early courses in creative writing were offered by composition teachers, among them Wendell and Copeland at Harvard, Gertrude Buck at Vassar, Katharine Bates at Wellesley, George Rice Carpenter at MIT, and John Erskine at Columbia. See Myers for a history of creative writing in American higher education.

2. The humanist habit of denying or regretting the importance of rhetoric characterizes Lindeman's proposal as well, even though her position is not manifestly humanist. If the universally required course concentrates on the specialized issues and audiences developed within disciplines, it cannot focus on the public issues that concern citizens. That is, in the terms of Lindemann's proposal, composition can be reclaimed as rhetoric only in the limited sense that it maintains and circulates the specialized rhetorics developed within academic disciplines.

3. The term *character* is very rich, and I hope that my use of it in this book does not cause confusion. I sometimes use it as a substitute for *subjectivity*. Subjectivity and subject-formation are of interest in contemporary theory, I think, partly because notions such as Foucault's "political technologies of the subject" or "ethical technologies" reclaim the ancient understanding that subjectivities are constructed within culture and language rather than given by nature (1988). Subjectivities are, as a result, fully implicated in the differentiating and classifying movements of power, as Foucault demonstrates in almost all of his work. In most contexts, though, I prefer to use the term *character* because of its resonance within the history of rhetoric. It functions in the passage noted here just as the term *ethos* functioned in ancient rhetorics, to mean "reputation," that is, public estimates of a person's intellectual and moral status. The term works the same way within Arnoldian humanism, but the public nature of character assessment was and is suppressed in that formulation. Bourgeois humanists continually evaluate character; they simply don't admit that public constructions of a person's worth are constitutive of his or her character. This is so because liberal individualism has caused character to be associated with an individual's life experiences, so much so that we often assume a character to be unique to a given individual. Furthermore, we assume that since character is formed by experience, it is not subject to change by means of verbal persuasion.

4. General histories of Freshman English include Berlin (1984, 1987), Nan Johnson (1991), Kitzhaber (1990), and Susan Miller (1990). Robert J. Connors has also written numerous essays on the history of composition, and now see his

Composition-Rhetoric (1997). Brereton (1995) collects relevant documents. See Varnum for a history of introductory composition at Amherst; Jo Ann Campbell (1996, 1992a, 1992b) for Gertrude Buck's pedagogy at Vassar and for the teaching of composition at Radcliffe; Douglas, Simmons, and Newkirk for Wendell's teaching at Harvard.

5. I base this claim on my reading of professional literature, particularly upon my examination of surveys of Freshman English. Surveys of the course have been repeatedly undertaken ever since William Mead reported to MLA's pedagogical section in 1901 on "The Undergraduate Study of Composition" (see Brereton 1995 for a reprint of Mead's report). I studied over a dozen such surveys, many of which are cited in the text.

6. This is a misnomer, because current-traditionalism is not a rhetoric. For arguments in support of this claim and a history of current-traditionalism, see Crowley 1990.

7. This perception may have something to do with the fact that throughout Western history rhetoric had been one of the "trivial" or elementary subjects. In Europe it was taught in the lower schools until the nineteenth century, and hence it was ineluctably associated with the gymnasium or grammar school. But I suspect that humanists' disdain for composition had much more to do with their elevation of literary study than with their knowledge of the history of rhetorical education.

8. Of course there were local exceptions to this generalization, as at Amherst. See Varnum.

6. TERMS OF EMPLOYMENT: RHETORIC SLAVES AND LESSER MEN

1. See Bledstein, Shumway and Messer-Davidow, and Shumway for accounts of academic professionalization and the growth of disciplinarity in English. See chapter 8 of this book for the impact of specialization on undergraduate curricula.

2. A growing body of scholarship addresses the inequities in salary, benefits, and workloads of composition teachers. See, for example, Schell ("Costs," *Gypsy Academics*), Susan Miller 1990, 1991; Connors 1991. See, in addition, the extensive literature on the professional lives of part-time and graduate teachers of composition. Schell lists many of these in the bibliography of *Gypsy Academics*. For accounts of efforts to alleviate the working conditions of part-time and graduate student teachers, see the references to chapter 11 of this book.

7. "YOU CAN'T WRITE WRITING:" NORMAN FOERSTER AND THE BATTLE OVER BASIC SKILLS AT IOWA

1. I base this and other generalizations about internal discussions of the required courses at Iowa on documents and papers housed in special collections at the University of Iowa Libraries in Iowa City, Iowa. I also rely on interviews I conducted with people who were involved in the design and implementation of the Liberal Arts program during the early 1940s. For more complete histories of the

struggle over adoption of the new undergraduate program at Iowa see Crary, Flanagan, and Wilbers.

2. Foerster's innovation did not "throw out" the dissertation requirement, as Brereton avers (1988, 51). For evaluations of Foerster's contribution to creative writing, see Myers and Wilbers.

3. There can be no doubt that Foerster was aware of the complicity of romanticism and naturalism. He had, after all, only to read Babbitt's *Rousseau and Romanticism* to see the connection articulated and vilified. And see *Toward Standards* or any of Foerster's tirades against Rousseau, as, for example, in *The American State University*, 34ff.

8. FRESHMAN ENGLISH AND WAR

1. Robert J. Connors, Lisa Ede, and Andrea Lunsford assume that interest in rhetoric was "revived" among teachers of the introductory course during the middle of the twentieth century (1984, 10). For an objection to this reading of the history of composition, see Schilb (1986). I disagree with Connors, Ede, and Lunsford's use of the term *revival* because Freshman English was never informed by rhetoric prior to the advent of communication skills. Furthermore, I think that professional interest in rhetoric was stimulated by the war. Tressidder's is not the earliest reference I have found in the professional literature to support that assumption. In 1938, Warren Taylor published a quite remarkable essay in *College English* that called for the study of rhetoric to combat the flow of public misinformation, and for the invention of a new rhetorical theory (see Berlin 1987, 86–88).

2. I am not implying that literary study is not or cannot be practical. During the early decades of the twentieth century, however, advocates of a practically oriented composition course uniformly rejected literary study as a basis for a practical course in composition. Nor can it be denied that in modern humanism, literature was conceived as having no immediate practical use.

3. Dewey's legacy was also crucial to the development of process pedagogy (see chapter 11). For the relevance of Dewey's work to composition and composition studies, see Fishman, Fishman and McCarthy (1995, 1992), Holt, and Russell (1991, 1993).

4. Later in this passage, Dewey noted the class interests served by traditional humanism. He expressed reservations about the moral worth of Greek culture, because of its economic basis in slavery. A humanism based on this culture, given that it "omitted economic and industrial conditions from its purview," was "one-sided" since it "represented the intellectual and moral outlook of the class which was in direct social control" (1985 [1916], 298).

5. The phrase "skills of human communication" appears in the report forwarded to the steering committee in February 1943, although at that time the basic skills subcommittee was thinking not about a single course but three: they envisioned two 4-hour courses in speaking and writing and a 2-hour course in reading. However, a memo to Newburn from the subcommittee, dated July 1944, does use the term

communication skills, and the term now designates a single course into which work in speaking, writing, and reading was to be combined. I spent considerable time at the University of Iowa trying to find out who first suggested that instruction in writing, reading, and speaking be combined in one course and housed in a single administrative unit. The most satisfactory answer came from a former dean of the College of Liberal Arts, Dewey Stuitt. In the summer of 1944, Dean Stuitt served on the basic skills subcommittee. He told me in an interview that "we had these three clinics operating in three different departments—English, Speech, and Psychology—and it just made administrative sense to combine them." This instance may serve as a warning to historians who like to invest institutional innovations with all sorts of intellectual freight: the landmark yoking of individualized instruction in reading, writing, and speaking at Iowa began as an administrative convenience.

6. For descriptions of Denver's program, see Paul et al.; Davidson and Sorenson; Sorenson; Berlin 1987. Berlin treats the programs at Iowa and Denver, respectively, as conservative and radical incarnations of communication skills, and he discusses those programs in detail.

7. Although he does not mention it by name, Dunn's indebtedness to the philosophy of General Semantics is clear in the passage where he discusses coding, as well as in his insistence that the basic principles of communications pedagogy were generalization and abstraction (33ff). General Semantics exerted no little influence on communication skills pedagogy during the 1940s. It was also incorporated into basic composition and speech courses during the 1950s and was still in use in the required first-year composition course during the 1960s at a few schools. Berlin briefly treats General Semantics in *Rhetoric and Reality* (1987). The movement now seems to have exerted a degree of influence on pedagogy that was entirely out of proportion with its intellectual worth. No doubt, its essentially conservative attitude toward language and language use had something to do with its popularity. Because of this, it deserves fuller historical treatment than it has yet received. General Semantics was introduced to America by a seminar held in Chicago in 1938, taught by Count Alfred Korzybski. The seminar expounded the principles of language use that Korzybski had supposedly discovered through his study of recent research in biology and neurology and presented in his masterwork, *Science and Sanity* (originally published in 1933). Irving J. Lee and S. I. Hayakawa, American popularizers of Korzybski's work, both attended the Chicago seminar. Hayakawa's enormously popular textbook was called *Language in Action* (1939) and then *Language in Thought and Action* (1949). Lee's more scholarly introduction to General Semantics is called *Language Habits in Human Affairs* (1941). Lee also published a useful bibliographical essay on General Semantics in the *Quarterly Journal of Speech* 38, 1 (February 1952): 1–12.

8. The linguistic insight that students use the languages spoken in their communities had the potential to democratize instruction in the basic course, had its teachers been willing to follow up on its inferred premise: language use is multivalent, and hence nontraditional usages will naturally emerge and are acceptable in the communities that sponsor them. But the institutional pressure exerted by the

history of Freshman English was simply too overpowering; most teachers simply could not deny the urge to direct students toward "correct" use, despite the findings of structural linguistics that no such thing existed outside the minds of English teachers. See Crowley (1989).

9. While I agree with Spanos with specific reference to the subjectivizing function of the universal requirement in composition, I am not convinced that Freshman English continues to be required in the service of the state because it seems to me that "the state" is no longer the most serious threat to democratic education hovering on our horizon. I take that threat to be coming currently from the ideological Right.

9. AROUND 1971: THE EMERGENCE OF PROCESS PEDAGOGY

1. I'd like to thank Janice Lauer for encouraging me to write this chapter. She pointed out to me that the story of process should have been the final chapter of my history of current-traditional rhetoric (1990). My title riffs on Jane Gallop's *Around 1981* (1992). I began my university teaching career in 1971, and so, like Gallop, I choose this date from my personal history around which to organize a professional history.

2. I place the heyday of process pedagogy between 1970 and 1985. A keyword search (done on November 7, 1995) for *writing* and *process* in ERIC turned up 1,253 entries. The first entry, written by Arthur Draper and entitled "Teaching the Process of Writing," was dated 1969. The second was dated 1971. A veritable deluge of entries followed, tapering off in the late 1980s. A remarkable set of books about teaching writing appeared between 1965 and 1975, anticipating this spate of professional articles. They included E. P. J. Corbett's *Classical Rhetoric for the Modern Student* (1965), Donald Murray's *A Writer Teaches Writing* (1968), James Moffett's *Teaching the Universe of Discourse* (1968), Ken Macrorie's *Uptaught* (1970), Janet Emig's *The Composing Processes of Twelfth-Graders* (1971), James Kinneavy's *Theory of Discourse* (1971), Richard Young, Alton Becker, and Kenneth Pike's *Rhetoric: Discovery and Change* (1971), Peter Elbow's *Writing Without Teachers* (1973), James Britton, Tony Burgess, Nancy Martin, and Harold Rosen's *The Development of Writing Abilities* (1975), and Frank D'Angelo's *A Conceptual Theory of Rhetoric* (1976). This outpouring is remarkable given that current-traditional textbooks were virtually the only books published about the teaching of writing in universities prior to this time. Two innovative and eccentric textbooks appeared somewhat later: Anne Berthoff's *Forming, Thinking, Writing: The Composing Imagination* (1982), and Linda Flower's *Problem-Solving Strategies for Writing* (1981). Both of these books concentrate on invention. Berthoff's work was animated by her reading in philosophical pragmatics and the philosophy of mind and language; Flower's text was drawn from her reading and work in cognitive psychology. Both texts demonstrate the instructional possibilities that were opened by the use of heuristics and the legitimation of composition theory. Unfortunately, neither text enjoyed

anything like the longevity accorded to current-traditional textbooks like McCrimmon's *Writing With a Purpose*, which was flourishing around 1971 just as it had been ever since 1950.

3. Kuhn refined his notion of paradigm shifts in subsequent editions of *The Structure of Scientific Revolutions*. I cite the first edition here because that is the edition cited by Hairston.

4. Something else happened to composition when its teachers turned to process pedagogy, something that has not been widely remarked: the profession's politics altered from conservative to liberal (see chapter 10).

5. Berlin is correct when he argues that Bruner's influence on the invention of process pedagogy cannot be overestimated (1987, 122). However, other workers in developmental psychology—William Perry, Jean Piaget, and Lev Vygotsky—also influenced composition theory during the 1960s and 1970s. See Emig 1983; Gere; Zebroski.

6. This emphasis on inquiry indicates Bruner's indebtedness to some strain of Deweyan pragmatism. For Dewey's theory of inquiry, see his *Logic*.

7. For additional accounts of Emig's influence, see Faigley 1986, 532; Faigley et al.; Voss 279. For a critical reception, see France.

8. Free writing was authorized by Macrorie's *Writing to Be Read* (1968) and *Telling Writing* (1970), and by Elbow's *Writing Without Teachers* (1973). Kenneth Burke's dramatistic pentad was introduced into composition lore by William Irmscher in *The Holt Guide to English* (originally published in 1972). For Burke's formulation of the pentad and his rationale for it, see *A Grammar of Motives* (1945). Burke's terms—*agent, act, scene, agency,* and *purpose*—occasionally appear as a heuristic strategy in contemporary textbooks, shorn of their intellectual context as well as their theoretical dimension.

9. Advocates of process pedagogy sometimes assert that current-traditional rhetoric had no theory of invention (see Young 1976, for example). In *The Methodical Memory* (1990), I tried to establish that current-traditional rhetoric had a well-formed theory of invention consisting of at least three steps: select a subject, narrow it, and compose a thesis statement.

10. For this study, I reviewed currently best-selling rhetorics published during the years 1990–96 by major publishing houses that cater to the textbook trade in freshman composition: Harper-Collins, Macmillan (now Allyn and Bacon), McGraw-Hill, Prentice Hall, St. Martin's, and Simon and Schuster. I forestall the objection that textbooks may not be representative of teaching practice by pointing out that these books are bestsellers—purchased if not read in the hundreds of thousands annually. I remind skeptical readers that composition is taught for the most part by untrained teachers whose anxious supervisors attempt to teacher-proof their instruction by requiring them to use these massive books. Composition textbooks provide syllabi, lectures, discussion questions, and assignments—almost everything a novice teacher needs to survive a semester of Freshman English.

10. THE POLITICS OF COMPOSITION

1. The subject constructed in classical liberal theory is male, since eighteenth- and nineteenth-century liberals were unable to confer liberal notions of freedom and sovereignty upon women. See Brown 1995; Hirshmann 1992.

2. It has been difficult for Western women to find and inhabit a "private" arena of thought, since the discourses of medicine, reproductive technology, housekeeping, and child care, which address supposedly private areas of women's lives, are thoroughly inscribed within the discourses of patriarchy and capitalism. See Phelan.

3. For examples of this habit in liberal rhetorical theory, see the chapter on "party spirit" in George Campbell's *Philosophy of Rhetoric* (1776) or, two hundred years later, Wayne Booth's discussions of the limits of pluralism in *Critical Understanding* (1979). The educational pragmatisms that currently circulate in composition lore, such as Kenneth Bruffee's "social constructionism," are also liberal in their politics. Even though they emphasize collaboration and communal learning, their instrumentalism or functionalism thoroughly disassociates their notions of community from active engagement with social change. See France for an explanation of how this works out in pedagogical practice.

4. I have taught first-year composition at several universities during my long career, and so the stories I tell here should not be thought to have occurred at my present location (although they may have). Odd how the politics of location operates to silence references to one's location.

11. A PERSONAL ESSAY ON FRESHMAN ENGLISH

1. The locus classicus of "the tradition of complaint" about Freshman English is Greenbaum, but see Robertson (1989) and Connors (1996) for updates.

2. Other analyses of the cultural politics of the course can be found in Berlin and Vivion, Bullock and Trimbur, Douglas, France, Hurlbut and Blitz, and Slevin (1991). See Ohmann for a Marxist analysis of the cultural role played out by Freshman English (1976); see Zavarzadeh and Morton for a neo-Marxist analysis.

3. Interestingly enough, none of its conservative critics actually read the syllabus for the course (Brodkey 1994). This refusal to read the texts they condemn is characteristic of contemporary hard-right conservativism. See Berube.

4. For the texts of the Wyoming Resolution and the Statement of Professional Standards, see Slevin (1989). For histories of the resolution's genesis, see McCleary and two pieces by Robertson and her coauthors. For discussions of the resolution and accounts of attempts to implement it, see Ronald; Rose and Wyche-Smith; and Trimbur and Cambridge. In accordance with the first provision of the resolution, NCTE established a committee that developed a Statement on Professional Standards for postsecondary writing instruction. The final version of the statement appeared in the October 1989 issue of *College Composition and Communication*.

5. I have been accused of antifeminism when making abolitionist arguments. One accusation of antifeminism goes like this: most composition teachers are women;

if the requirement is abolished jobs will be lost; women will lose most of these jobs. A second one goes like this: composition specialists who claim to be feminists should hang onto the universal requirement since it is a power base from which to advance feminist projects. Both arguments advocate support of the (patriarchal) status quo, which seems to me to be a dangerous practice for adherents of any would-be revolutionary ideology to fall into. In addition, the second argument proposes that feminists take advantage of a situation that harms women in order to advance feminist agendas.

WORKS CITED

Adams, Charles F., Edwin L. Godkin, and George R. Nutter. 1895. "Report of the Committee on Composition and Rhetoric." In *Reports of Visiting Committees of the Board of Overseers*, 275–87. Cambridge: Harvard University.

———. 1897. "Report of the Committee on Composition and Rhetoric." In *Reports of Visiting Committees of the Board of Overseers*, 401–24. Cambridge: Harvard University.

Adams, Charles F., Edwin L. Godkin, and Josiah Quincy. 1892. "Report of the Committee on Composition and Rhetoric." In *Reports of Visiting Committees of the Board of Overseers*, 117–57. Cambridge: Harvard University.

Adams, John Quincy. 1810. *Lectures on Rhetoric and Oratory, Delivered to the Senior and Junior Sophisters in Harvard College*. Cambridge, Mass.: Hilliard and Metcalf.

Allen, Don Cameron. 1968. *The PhD in English and American Literature*. New York: Holt, Rinehart, and Winston.

Allen, Harold B. 1949. "The Minnesota Communication Program." In *Communication in General Education*, ed. Earl James McGrath, 58–73. Dubuque: William C. Brown.

———. 1952. "Preparing the Teacher of Composition and Communication—A Report." *College Composition and Communication* 3 (1952): 3–13.

Allen, James Sloan. 1983. *The Romance of Commerce and Culture: Capitalism, Modernism, and the Chicago-Aspen Crusade for Cultural Reform*. Chicago: University of Chicago Press.

Althusser, Louis. 1970. "Ideology and Ideological State Apparatuses." In *Lenin and Philosophy and Other Essays*. Trans. Ben Brewster. New York: New Left Books.

Anderson, Dorothy. "Edward T. Channing's Teaching of Rhetoric." *Speech Monographs* 16 (1949): 69–81.

Anderson, Melville. 1895. "The Leland Stanford, Junior, University." In *English in American Universities*, ed. William M. Payne, 49–59. Boston: Heath.

Arblaster, Anthony. 1984. *The Rise and Decline of Western Liberalism*. Oxford: Basil Blackwell.

Arnold, Aerol. 1960. "The Limits of Communication." *College Composition and Communication* 11 (1960): 12–16.

Arnold, Matthew. 1971. "The Function of Criticism at the Present Time." In *Critical Theory Since Plato*, ed. Hazard Adams, 583–95. New York: Harcourt, Brace, Jovanovich.

Aronowitz, Stanley, and Henry Giroux. 1985. *Education Under Siege: The Conservative, Liberal and Radical Debate Over School*. South Hadley, Mass.: Bergin & Garvey.

Asante, Molefi Kete. 1987. *The Afrocentric Idea*. Philadelphia: Temple University Press.

Atwill, Janet. 1997. *Arts of Virtue/Arts of Democracy: Aristotle, Rhetoric, and the Liberal Arts*. Ithaca: Cornell University Press.

"Await S.U.I. Liberal Arts Revision Plan." *Des Moines Sunday Register*. 27 February 1944, 6-L.

Aydelotte, Frank. 1914. "The Correlation of English Literature and Composition in the College Course." *English Journal* 3 (1914): 568–74.

Babbitt, Irving. 1908. *Literature and the American College: Essays in Defense of the Humanities*. Boston: Houghton Mifflin.

Bagwell, Paul. 1945. "A Composite Course in Writing and Speaking." *Quarterly Journal of Speech* 31 (1945): 79–87.

Bain, Alexander. 1877. *English Composition and Rhetoric: A Manual*. 4th ed. London: Longmans, Green.

Baker, Sheridan. 1976. *The Complete Stylist and Handbook*. 3d ed. New York: Crowell.

Balch, Stephen, and Rita Zuercher. "Less Costs More in Today's Colleges." Editorial. *Centre Daily Times*, 18 March 1996, A4.

Baldwin, Charles Sears. 1906. "Freshman English." *Educational Review* 32:385–94.

"The Basic Issues in the Teaching of English." Supplement to *College English* 21 (1959).

Bell, Marvin. 1964. "Poetry and Freshman Composition." *College Composition and Communication* 15: 1–5.

Berlin, James A. 1991. "Composition and Cultural Studies." In *Composition and Resistance*. Ed Mark Hurlbut and Michael Blitz, 47–57. Portsmouth, N.H.: Boynton Cook.

———. 1982. "Contemporary Composition: The Major Pedagogical Theories." *College English* 44:765–77.

———. 1988. "Rhetoric and Ideology in the Writing Class." *College English* 50:477–94.

———. 1987. *Rhetoric and Reality: Writing Instruction in American Colleges, 1900–1985*. Urbana: NCTE.

———. 1996. *Rhetorics, Poetics, and Cultures: Refiguring College English Studies*. Urbana: NCTE.

———. 1984. *Writing Instruction in Nineteenth-Century American Colleges*. Urbana: NCTE.

Berlin, James A., and Michael J. Vivion, eds. 1992. *Cultural Studies in the English Classroom*. Portsmouth, N.H.: Boynton Cook.

Bernard, Jessie Shirley. 1964. *Academic Women*. University Park, Penn.: Pennsylvania State University Press.

Berube, Michael. 1994. *Public Access: Literary Theory and American Cultural Politics*. London: Verso.

Bevilaqua, Vincent. 1985. "Campbell, Vico, and the Rhetorical Science of Human Nature." *Philosophy and Rhetoric* 18:23–30.

Bizzell, Patricia. 1992. *Academic Discourse and Critical Consciousness*. Pittsburgh: University of Pittsburgh Press.

———. 1991a. "Marxist Ideas in Composition Studies." In *Contending with Words: Composition and Rhetoric in a Postmodern Age*, ed. Patricia Harkin and John Schilb, 51–68. New York: MLA.

———. 1991b. "Professing Literacy: A Review Essay." *Journal of Advanced Composition* 11:315–22.

Blair, Hugh. 1965. *Lectures on Rhetoric and Belles-Lettres*. 2 vols. Ed. Harold Harding. Carbondale: Southern Illinois University Press.

Bledstein, Burton. 1978. *The Culture of Professionalism: The Middle Class and the Development of Higher Education in America*. New York: Norton.

Bleich, David. 1993. "Feminist Philosophy and Some Humanists' Attitudes Towards the Teaching of Writing." *Journal of Advanced Composition* 13:137–52.

Bloom, Harold. 1994. *The Western Canon: The Books and Schools of the Ages*. New York: Harcourt Brace.

Bonheim, Helmut W. 1956. "Teaching a Novel to Improve Writing Mechanics." *College English* 18:40–41.

Booth, Wayne C. 1979. *Critical Understanding: The Powers and Limits of Pluralism*. Chicago: University of Chicago Press.

———. 1956. "Imaginative Literature Is Indispensable." *College Composition and Communication* 7:35–38.

Bourdieu, Pierre. 1984. *Distinction: A Social Critique of the Judgement of Taste*. Trans. Richard Nice. Cambridge: Harvard University Press.

———. 1990. *The Logic of Practice*. Trans. Richard Nice. Palo Alto, Calif.: Stanford University Press.

Bowers, C. A. 1987. *Elements of a Post–Liberal Theory of Education*. New York: Teachers' College Press.

Boyd, James R. 1867. *Elements of English Composition, Grammar, Rhetoric, Logic, and Practice, Prepared for Academies and Schools.* 1st ed. 1860. New York: A. S. Barnes.

Brannon, Lil. 1995. "(Dis)Missing Compulsory First-Year Composition." In *Reconceiving Writing, Rethinking Writing Instruction*, ed. Joseph Petraglia, 239–48. Mahwah, N.J.: Erlbaum.

Brauer, George C. 1959. *The Education of a Gentleman: Theories of Gentlemanly Education in England, 1600–1775*. New York: Bookman.

Brereton, John C. 1988. "Composition and English Departments, 1900–1925." In *Audits of Meaning: A Festschrift in Honor of Ann E. Berthoff*. Ed. Louise Z. Smith, 41–54. Portsmouth, N.H.: Boynton-Cook Publishers.

———, ed. 1995. *The Origins of Composition Studies in the American College, 1875–1925: A Documentary History*. Pittsburgh: University of Pittsburgh Press.

Briggs, Harold E. 1948. "College Programs in Communication as Viewed by an English Teacher." *College English* 9:327–32.

Briggs, Le Baron Russell. 1896. "The Harvard Admission Examination in English." In *Twenty Years of School and College English*, ed. Adams Sherman Hill, Le Baron Russell Briggs, and Byron Satterlee Hurlbut. Cambridge: Harvard University Press.

Britton, James, Tony Burgess, Nancy Martin, Alex McLeod, and Harold Rosen. 1975. *The Development of Writing Abilities (11–18)*. Urbana: NCTE.

Brodkey, Linda. 1994. "Making a Federal Case Out of Difference: The Politics of Pedagogy, Publicity, Postponement." In *Writing Theory, Critical Theory*, ed. John Shilb and John Clifford, 236–61. New York: MLA.

———. 1996. *Writing Permitted in Designated Areas Only*. Minneapolis: University of Minnesota Press.

———. 1995. "Writing Permitted in Designated Areas Only." In *Higher Education Under Fire: Politics, Economics, and the Crisis of the Humanities*. Ed Michael Berube and Cary Nelson, 214–37. New York: Routledge.

Broome, Edwin C. 1903. *A History and Critical Discussion of College Admission Requirements*. New York: Macmillan.

Brown, Rollo Walter. 1926. *Dean Briggs*. New York: Harper and Brothers.

Brown, Wendy. 1995. *States of Injury: Power and Freedom in Late Modernity*. Princeton: Princeton University Press.

Bruner, Jerome S. 1962. *On Knowing: Essays for the Left Hand*. Cambridge: Belknap Press of Harvard University Press.

———. 1963. *The Process of Education*. Cambridge: Harvard University Press.

———. 1966. *Toward a Theory of Instruction*. Cambridge: Belknap Press of Harvard University Press.

Bryan, Adolphus. 1951. "The Problem of Freshman English in the University." *College Composition and Communication* 2, no. 2: 6–7.

Bullock, Richard, and John Trimbur, eds. 1991. *The Politics of Writing Instruction: Postsecondary*. Portsmouth, N.H.: Boynton Cook.

Burke, Kenneth. 1945. *A Grammar of Motives*. Berkeley and Los Angeles: University of California Press.

Butler, Judith. 1997. *Excitable Speech: A Politics of the Performative*. New York: Routledge.

———. 1990. *Gender Trouble: Feminism and the Subversion of Identity*. New York: Routledge.

Calderwood, Natalie. 1957. "Composition and Literature." *College Composition and Communication* 8:201–04.

Campbell, George. 1963. *The Philosophy of Rhetoric*, ed. Lloyd Bitzer. 1st ed. 1776. Carbondale: Southern Illinois University Press.

Campbell, James. 1995. *Understanding John Dewey: Nature and Cooperative Intelligence*. Chicago: Open Court.

Campbell, Jo Ann. 1992a. "Controlling Voices: The Legacy of English A at Radcliffe College 1883–1917." *College Composition and Communication* 43:472–85.

———, ed. 1996. *Toward a Feminist Rhetoric: The Writing of Gertrude Buck*. Pittsburgh: University of Pittsburgh Press.

————. 1992b. "Women's Work, Worthy Work: Composition Instruction at Vassar College, 1897–1922." In *Constructing Rhetorical Education*, ed. Marie Secor and Davida Charney, 26–42. Carbondale: Southern Illinois University Press.

Campbell, O. J. 1939. "The Failure of Freshman English." *College English* 28:177–85.

————. 1926. "The Value of the Ph.D." *English Journal* 15:191–97.

"Campuses with the Highest Enrollments, Fall 1994." *Chronicle of Higher Education* 43 (2 September 1996): 16.

Cardozier, V. R. 1993. *Colleges and Universities in World War II*. Westport, Conn.: Praeger.

Carruthers, Mary. 1990. *The Book of Memory: A Study of Memory and Medieval Culture*. Cambridge: Cambridge University Press.

Cicero, Marcus Tullius. 1949. *De Inventione*. Trans. H. M. Hubbell. Cambridge: Harvard University Press.

————. 1942. *De Oratore*. Trans. E. W. Sutton and H. Rackham. Cambridge: Harvard University Press.

Clark, Gregory. 1993. "The Oratorical Poetic of Timothy Dwight." In *Oratorical Culture in Nineteenth-Century America: Transformations in the Theory and Practice of Rhetoric*, ed. Gregory Clark and S. Michael Halloran, 57–77. Carbondale: Southern Illinois University Press.

Clifford, John. 1991. "The Subject in Discourse." In *Contending with Words: Composition and Rhetoric in a Postmodern Age*, ed. Patricia Harkin and John Schilb, 38–51. New York: MLA.

Cmeil, Kenneth. 1990. *Democratic Eloquence: The Fight Over Popular Speech in Nineteenth-Century America*. New York: William Morrow.

Coates, Willson, Hayden White, and J. Salwyn Shapiro. 1970. *The Emergence of Liberal Humanism: An Intellectual History of Western Europe*. 2 vols. New York: McGraw-Hill.

Cohen, Herman. 1994. *The History of Speech Communications: The Emergence of a Discipline, 1914–1945*. Annandale, Vir.: Speech Communication Association.

Collier, William Francis. 1991. *A History of Literature in a Series of Biographical Sketches*. New York: T. Nelson.

Connors, Robert J. 1983. "Handbooks: History of a Genre." *Rhetoric Society Quarterly* 13:87–98.

————. 1996. "The New Abolitionism: Toward a Historical Background." In *Composition in the Twenty-first Century: Crisis and Change*, ed. Lynn Z. Bloom, Donald A. Daiker, and Edward M. White, 47–63. Carbondale: Southern Illinois University Press. (Rpt. in *Reconceiving Writing, Rethinking Writing Instruction*, ed. Joseph Petraglia, 3–26. Mahwah, N.J.: Erlbaum, 1995.)

————. 1991. "Rhetoric in the Modern University: The Creation of an Underclass." In *The Politics of Writing Instruction: Postsecondary*, ed. Richard Bullock and John Trimbur, 55–84. Portsmouth, N.H.: Boynton Cook.

————. 1981. "Thirty Years of Writing with a Purpose." *Rhetoric Society Quarterly* 11:208–21.

———. 1995. "Women's Reclamation of Rhetoric in Nineteenth-Century America." In *Feminist Principles and Women's Experience in American Composition and Rhetoric*, ed. Louise Wetherbee Phelps and Janet Emig, 67–90. Pittsburgh: University of Pittsburgh Press.

———. 1997. *Composition-Rhetoric: Backgrounds, Theory, and Pedagogy*. Pittsburgh: University of Pittsburgh Press.

Connors, Robert J., Lisa S. Ede, and Andrea A. Lunsford. 1984. "The Revival of Rhetoric in America." In *Essays on Classical Rhetoric and Modern Discourse*, ed. Robert J. Connors, Lisa S. Ede, and Andrea A. Lunsford, 1–15. Carbondale: Southern Illinois University Press.

Connors, Robert J., and Andrea Lunsford. 1988. "Frequency of Formal Errors in Current College Writing, or Ma and Pa Kettle Do Research." *College Composition and Communication* 39:395–409.

Cooper, Lane. 1910. "On the Teaching of Written Composition." *Education* 30:421–30.

Cooper, Marilyn, and Michael Holzman. 1989. *Writing as Social Action*. Portsmouth, N.H.: Boynton Cook.

Copeland, Charles Townsend, and H. M. Rideout. 1901. *Freshman English and Theme-Correcting in Harvard College*. New York: Silver, Burdett.

Coppee, Henry. 1860. *The Elements of Rhetoric*. New rev. ed. Philadelphia: E. H. Butler.

Corbett, Edward P. J. 1970. "A Composition Course Based Upon Literature." In *Teaching High School Composition*, ed. Gary Tate and Edward P. J. Corbett, 195–204. New York: Oxford University Press.

Craik, George Lillie. 1869. *The English of Shakespeare Illustrated in a Philological Commentary on His Julius Caesar*, ed. William J. Rolfe. New York: Macmillan.

Crain, Jeannie C. 1993. "Four Comments on 'Two Views on the Use of Literature in Composition.'" *College English* 55:673–79.

Crane, Ronald Salmon. 1967. *The Idea of the Humanities and Other Essays*. 2 vols. Chicago: University of Chicago Press.

Crary, Ryland Wesley. 1946. "History of the State University of Iowa: The College of Liberal Arts in the Gilmore and Hancher Administrations." Ph.D. diss., University of Iowa.

Creek, Herbert L. 1955. "Forty Years of Composition Teaching." *College Composition and Communication* 6:4–10.

Cremin, Lawrence A. 1961. *The Transformation of the School: Progressivism in American Education 1876–1957*. New York: Knopf.

Crowley, Sharon. 1989. "Linguistics and Composition Instruction 1950–1980." *Written Communication* 6:480–505.

———. 1990. *The Methodical Memory: Invention in Current-Traditional Rhetoric*. Carbondale: Southern Illinois University Press.

———. 1988. "Three Heroines: Women in the Profession." *Pre/Text* 9:202–06.

Cunliffe, John W. 1912. "College English Composition." *English Journal* 1:591–99.

Davidson, Levette, and Frederick Sorenson. 1946. "The Basic Communications Course." *College English* 8:83–86.

Davis, W. R. 1925. "Ten Years of Cooperative Effort." *English Journal* 14:784–89.

Day, Jeremiah, and James L. Kingsley. 1961. "The Yale Report." In *American Higher Education: A Documentary History.* 2 vols. Ed. Richard Hofstadter and Wilson Smith, 275–91. Chicago: University of Chicago Press.

Denney, Joseph V. 1896. "Two Problems in Composition-Teaching." In *Contributions to Rhetorical Theory,* ed. Fred Newton Scott. Ann Arbor: Inland Press.

Dewey, John. 1985. *Democracy and Education.* In *The Middle Works.* Vol. 9, 1899–1924. Carbondale: Southern Illinois University Press. First published in 1916.

———. 1938a. *Experience and Education.* New York: Collier Books.

———. 1989. *Experience and Nature.* 1st ed. 1925. LaSalle: Open Court.

———. *Liberalism and Social Action.* In *The Later Works.* Vol. 11, 1935–37. 3–65.

———. 1938b. *Logic: The Theory of Inquiry.* New York: Holt.

———. 1963. *The School and Society.* Rev. ed; 1st ed., 1899. Chicago: University of Chicago Press.

DeBeers, Henry A. 1892. "Entrance Requirements in English at Yale." *Educational Review* 8:427–43.

DeBoer, John J. 1945. "English in a 'Communications' Program." *Quarterly Journal of Speech* 21:291–95.

DeVoto, Bernard. 1928. "English A." *American Mercury* 13:204–12.

Deemer, Charles. 1967. "English Composition as a Happening." *College English* 29:121–26.

Douglas, Wallace. 1976. "Rhetoric for the Meritocracy." In *English in America,* ed. Richard Ohmann, 97–132. New York: Oxford University Press.

Dow, Clyde W. 1948. "A Speech Teacher Views College Communication Courses." *College English* 9:332–36.

Dunn, Thomas. 1955. "The Principles and Practice of the Communication Course." *College Composition and Communication* 6:31–38.

Eagleton, Terry. 1990. *The Ideology of the Aesthetic.* Oxford: Basil Blackwell.

———. 1985–86. "The Subject of Literature." *Cultural Critique* 2:95–104.

Earnest, Ernest. 1953. *Academic Profession: An Informal History of the American College 1636–1953.* Indianapolis: Bobbs-Merrill.

Eble, Kenneth E. 1956. "The Freshman Composition Course Should Teach Writing." *College English* 17: 475–77.

Eliot, Charles Norton. 1890. "Address of Welcome." *PMLA* 5:1–4.

———. 1884. "What Is a Liberal Education?" *Century Magazine* (June): 203–12.

Emig, Janet. 1971. *The Composing Processes of Twelfth-Graders.* Urbana: NCTE.

———. 1967. "On Teaching Composition: Some Hypotheses as Definitions." *Research in the Teaching of English* 1:127–35.

———. 1980. "The Tacit Tradition: The Inevitability of a Multi-Disciplinary Approach to Writing Research." In *Reinventing the Rhetorical Tradition,* ed. Aviva Freedman and Ian Pringle, 9–17. Ottawa: CCTE.

————. 1964. "Uses of the Unconscious in Composing." *College Composition and Communication* 15: 6–11.

————. 1983. *The Web of Meaning: Essays on Writing, Teaching, and Thinking*, ed. Dixie Goswami and Maureen Butler. Upper Montclair, N.J.: Boynton Cook.

.   England, Kenneth. 1957. "The Use of Literature in the Freshman Research Paper." *College English* 18:367–68.

Eschbacher, Robert L. 1963. "*Lord Jim*, Classical Rhetoric, and the Freshman Dilemma." *College English* 25:22–25.

Faigley, Lester. 1986. "Competing Theories of Process: A Critique and a Proposal." *College English* 48:527–42.

————. 1992. *Fragments of Rationality: Postmodernity and the Subject of Composition*. Pittsburgh: University of Pittsburgh Press.

Faigley, Lester, Roger Cherry, David Jolliffe, and Anne Skinner. 1985. *Assessing Writers' Knowledge and Processes of Composition*. Norwood, N.J.: Ablex.

Fish, Stanley. 1989. *Doing What Comes Naturally: Change, Rhetoric, and the Practice of Theory in Literary and Legal Studies*. Durham: Duke University Press.

Fishman, Stephen M. 1993. "Explicating Our Tacit Tradition: John Dewey and Composition Studies." *College Composition and Communication* 44:315–30.

Fishman, Stephen M., and Lucille P. McCarthy. 1995. "Community in the Expressivist Classroom: Juggling Liberal and Communitarian Visions." *College English* 57:62–81.

————. 1992. "Is Expressivism Dead? Reconsidering Its Romantic Roots and Its Relation to Social Constructionism." *College English* 54:647–61.

Flanagan, Frances Mary. 1971. "The Educational Role of Norman Foerster." Ph.D. diss., University of Iowa, Iowa City.

Flower, Linda, and John R. Hayes. 1977. "Problem-Solving Strategies and the Writing Process." *College English* 39:449–61.

Foerster, Norman. 1937. *The American State University: Its Relation to Democracy*. Chapel Hill: University of North Carolina Press.

————. 1943. "For the Steering Committee May 1, N.F." Foerster Papers, University of Iowa Archives, Iowa City.

————. 1938. *The Future of the Liberal College*. New York: Appleton.

————. 1944. *The Humanities After the War*. Princeton: Princeton University Press.

————. 1946. *The Humanities and the Common Man: The Democratic Role of the State Universities*. Chapel Hill: University of North Carolina Press.

————. 1916. "The 'Idea Course' for Freshmen." *English Journal* 5:458–66.

————. 1944. "A Letter to the Editor." *Daily Iowan*, 23 March 1944.

————. Letter to Harry K. Newburn, 17 May 1943. Foerster Papers. University of Iowa Archives, Iowa City.

————. Letter to Harry K. Newburn, 14 January 1944. Foerster Papers, University of Iowa Archives, Iowa City.

————. Letter to Harry K. Newburn, 15 May 1943. Foerster Papers. University of Iowa Archives, Iowa City.

————. Letter to W. R. Boyd, 27 March 1944. Foerster Papers. University of Iowa Archives, Iowa City.

————. 1936. *Literature and the Art of Writing*. Iowa City: University of Iowa Press.

————. 1915. *Outlines and Summaries: A Handbook for the Analysis of Expository Essays*. New York: Henry Holt.

————. 1949. "Teaching the College Student to Write." In *Communication in General Education*, ed. Earl James McGrath, 199–214. Dubuque: William C. Brown.

————. 1928. *Toward Standards: A Study of the Present Critical Movement in American Letters*. New York: Farrar/Rinehart.

Foerster, Norman, and J. M. Steadman. 1919. *Sentences and Thinking: A Handbook of Composition and Revision*. Boston: Houghton Mifflin.

————. 1931. *Writing and Thinking*. Boston: Houghton Mifflin.

"Foerster Resigns in Protest Against Curriculum Change." 1944. *Cedar Rapids Gazette*, 7 July 1944.

Fontaine, Sheryl I., and Susan Hunter, eds. 1993. *Writing Ourselves into the Story: Unheard Voices from Composition Studies*. Carbondale: Southern Illinois University Press.

Foucault, Michel. 1979. *Discipline and Punish: The Birth of the Prison*. Trans. Alan Sheridan. New York: Vintage, 1979.

————. 1991. "Governmentality." In *The Foucault Effect, Studies in Governmentality: With Two Lectures by and an Interview with Michel Foucault*, ed. Graham Burchell, Colin Gorden, and Peter Mill. London: Harvester Wheatsheaf.

————. 1988. *Technologies of the Self: A Seminar with Michel Foucault*, ed. Luther H. Martin, Huck Gutman, and Patrick H. Hutton. Amherst: University of Massachusetts Press.

France, Alan. 1994. *Composition as a Cultural Practice*. Westport, Conn.: Bergin & Garvey.

Fraser, Nancy. 1989. *Unruly Practices: Power, Discourse and Gender in Contemporary Social Theory*. Minneapolis: University of Minnesota Press.

Frost, Clare. 1993. "Looking for a Gate in the Fence." In *Writing Ourselves into the Story: Unheard Voices from Composition Studies*, ed. Sheryl Fontaine and Susan Hunter, 59–69. Carbondale: Southern Illinois University Press.

Garnett, James M. 1886. "The Course in English and Its Value as a Discipline." *PMLA* 2:61–73.

Garvin, Harry R. 1959. "Novels and Freshman Composition." *College English* 21:175–77.

Gates, Theodore. 1941. "The First Instruction in Composition." *College English* 3:64–69.

General Education in a Free Society: Report of the Harvard Committee. (The "Redbook.") 1945. Cambridge: Harvard University Press.

Gerard, Alexander. 1970. *An Essay on Taste*. New York: Garland.

Gerber, John C. 1950. "The Conference on College Composition and Communication." *College Composition and Communication* 1:12.

————. 1967. "Literature—Our Untamable Discipline." *College English* 28:351–58.

———. 1993. Personal interview. September.

———. 1947. "A Training Program for a Communication Skills Staff." *College English* 8:31–37.

———. 1952. "Three-Year History of the CCCC." *College Composition and Communication* 3:17–18.

Gere, Anne Ruggles. 1987. *Writing Groups: History, Theory, and Implications.* Carbondale: Southern Illinois University Press.

Gladden, Washington. 1909. *Recollections.* Boston: Houghton Mifflin.

Glockler, George. 1944. Letter to Harry K. Newburn, 11 March 1944. Newburn Papers. University of Iowa Archives, Iowa City.

Goodwin, W. W. 1893. "The Root of the Evil." *Harvard Graduates' Magazine* 1:189–93.

Gorrell, Robert. 1972. "The Traditional Course: When Is Old Hat New." *College Composition and Communication* 23:264–70.

Gorrell, Robert, and Charlton Laird. 1972. *The Modern English Handbook.* 5th ed. Englewood Cliffs, N.J.: Prentice Hall.

Gradin, Sherrie L. 1995. *Romancing Rhetorics: Social Expressivist Perspectives on the Teaching of Writing.* Portsmouth, N.H.: Boynton Cook.

Graff, Gerald. 1987. *Professing Literature: An Institutional History.* Chicago: University of Chicago Press.

Graff, Gerald, and Michael Warner, eds. 1989. *The Origins of Literary Studies in America: A Documentary Anthology.* New York: Routledge.

Grafton, Anthony, and Lisa Jardine. 1986. *From Humanism to the Humanities: Education and the Liberal Arts in Fifteenth- and Sixteenth-Century Europe.* Cambridge: Harvard University Press.

Greenbaum, Leonard. 1969. "The Tradition of Complaint." *College English* 31:174–87.

Greenblatt, Stephen, and Giles Gunn, eds. 1992. *Redrawing the Boundaries: The Transformation of English and American Literary Studies.* New York: MLA.

Greenhut, Morris. 1962. "Great Books and English Composition." *College English* 24:136–40.

Gray, Giles Wilkeson. 1964. "The Founding of the Speech Association of America: Happy Birthday." *Quarterly Journal of Speech* 50:342–45.

Grey, Lennox. 1944. "Toward Better Communication in 1944, and After." *Quarterly Journal of Speech* 30 (April): 131–36.

Gruber, Carol. 1975. *Mars and Minerva: World War I and the Uses of Higher Learning in America.* Baton Rouge: Louisiana State University Press.

Hackett, Herbert. 1955. "A Discipline of the Communication Skills." *College Composition and Communication* 6:10–15.

Hairston, Maxine. 1992. "Diversity, Ideology, and Teaching Writing." *College Composition and Communication* 43:179–93.

———. 1982. "The Winds of Change: Thomas Kuhn and the Revolution in the Teaching of Writing." *College Composition and Communication* 33:76–88.

Halloran, S. Michael. 1990. "From Rhetoric to Composition: The Teaching of Writing in America to 1900." In *A Short History of Writing Instruction: From*

Ancient Greece to Twentieth-Century America, ed. James J. Murphy, 151–82. Davis, Calif.: Hermagoras Press.

————. 1982. "Rhetoric in the American College Curriculum: The Decline of Public Discourse." *Pre/Text* 3:245–69.

[Hancher, Virgil.] 1945. *The New Progam in Liberal Arts*. Iowa City: University of Iowa Publications, New Series No. 1350. 1 January 1945.

Haraway, Donna. 1991. *Simians, Cyborgs, and Women: The Reinvention of Nature*. New York: Routledge.

Harrington, David V. 1968. "Teaching Students the Art of Discovery." *College Composition and Communication* 19:7–14.

Hart, James Morgan. 1874. *German Universities: A Narrative of Personal Experience*. New York: Putnams.

————. 1884–85. "The College Course in English Literature, How It May Be Improved." *PMLA* 1:84–95.

Hart, John A., Robert C. Slack, and Neal Woodruff. 1958. "Literature in the Composition Course." *College Composition and Communication* 9:236–41.

Hart, Sophie Chantal. 1902. "English in the College." *School Review* 10:364–73.

Hayford, Harrison. 1956. "Literature in English A at Northwestern." *College Composition and Communication* 6:42–45.

Heyda, John. 1979. "Captive Audiences: Composition Pedagogy, the Liberal Arts Curriculum, and the Rise of Mass Higher Education." Ph.D. diss., University of Pittsburgh.

Hill, Adams Sherman. 1887. "English in Our Colleges." *Scribners' Magazine* 1:507–12.

————. 1890. *Our English*. New York: Harper and Brothers.

————. 1878. *The Principles of Rhetoric and Their Application*. New York: American Book.

Hill, Adams Sherman, Le Baron Russell Briggs, and Byron Satterlee Hurlbut. 1896. *Twenty Years of School and College English*. Cambridge: Harvard University Press.

Hirsch, E. D. 1987. *Cultural Literacy: What Every American Needs to Know*. New York: Vintage.

Hirschmann, Nancy J. 1992. *Rethinking Obligation: A Feminist Method for Political Theory*. Ithaca: Cornell University Press.

Hobbs, Catharine, ed. 1995. *Nineteenth-Century Women Learn to Write*. Charlottesville: University of Virginia Press.

Hoblitzelle, Harrison. 1967. "A Study of Freshman English: An Informal Survey." *College English* 28:596–600.

Hoeveler, J. David. 1977. *The New Humanism: A Critique of Modern America, 1900–1940*. Charlottesville: University of Virginia Press.

Hofstadter, Richard, and Walter P. Metzger. 1955. *The Development of Academic Freedom in the United States*. New York: Columbia University Press.

Hofstadter, Richard, and Wilson Smith. 1961. *American Higher Education: A Documentary History*. 2 vols. Chicago: University of Chicago Press.

Holt, Mara. 1994. "Dewey and the 'Cult of Efficiency': Competing Ideologies in Collaborative Pedagogies of the 1920s." *Journal of Advanced Composition* 14:73–92.

———. 1993. "Knowledge, Social Relations, and Authority in Collaborative Practices of the 1930s and the 1950s." *College Composition and Communication* 44:538–55.

hooks, bell. 1989. *Talking Back: Thinking Feminist, Thinking Black.* Boston: South End.

———. 1994. *Teaching to Transgress: Education as the Practice of Freedom.* New York: Routledge.

Hoover, Regina. 1974. "Taps for Freshman English?" *College Composition and Communication* 25:149–54.

Hopkins, Edwin M. 1912. "Can Good Composition Teaching Be Done Under Present Conditions?" *English Journal* 1:1–7.

———. 1923. "The Labor and Cost of the Teaching of English in Colleges and Secondary Schools." 16th ed. Urbana: NCTE.

Horowitz, Helen Lefkowitz. 1993. *Alma Mater: Design and Experience in the Women's Colleges from Their Nineteenth-Century Beginnings to the 1930s.* 2d ed. Amherst: University of Massachusetts Press.

Hughes, Merritt Y. 1938. "Some Prophecies of Our Doom." *English Journal* 28:323–37.

Hultzen, Lee S. 1949. "The Course in Verbal Communication at the University of Illinois." In *Communication in General Education,* ed. Earl James McGrath, 113–26. Dubuque: William C. Brown.

Hurlbut, Byron Satterlee. 1896. "College Requirements in English." In *Twenty Years of School and College English,* ed. Adams Sherman Hill, Le Baron Russell Briggs, and Byron Satterlee Hurlbut, 46–53. Cambridge: Harvard University Press.

Hurlbut, C. Mark, and Michael Blitz, eds. 1991. *Composition and Resistance.* Portsmouth, N.H.: Boynton Cook.

"Humanities." *Encyclopedia Britannica.* 1963.

Hunt, Theodore W. 1896. "The Study of English in American Colleges." *Educational Review* 12:140–50.

———. 1884–85. "The Place of English in the College Curriculum." *PMLA* 1:118–32.

Huyssen, Andreas. 1988. *After the Great Divide: Modernism, Mass Culture, Postmodernism.* Basingstoke, Hampshire: Macmillan.

"Imaginative Writing in the Freshman Course." 1951. *College Composition and Communication* 2, 4:33.

"Iowa's School of Letters Admits Imaginative, Critical Writing for Ph.D. Thesis." *Daily Iowan.* 26 March 1931, 3.

Irlen, Harvey Stuart. 1970. "Toward Confronting Freshmen." *College Composition and Communication* 21:35–40.

Jaeger, Werner. 1943. *Paideia: The Ideals of Greek Culture.* Oxford: Oxford University Press.

Jamieson, Alexander. 1844. *A Grammar of Rhetoric*. New Haven: A. H. Maltby.

Jay, Gregory. 1993. "Four Comments on 'Two Views on the Use of Literature in Composition.'" *College English* 55 (October): 672–79.

Johnson, Nan. 1991. *Nineteenth-Century Rhetoric in North America*. Carbondale: Southern Illinois University Press.

Johnson, Wendell. 1943. "A Core Curriculum: Explanatory Note." 17 September. Newburn Papers. University of Iowa Archives, Iowa City.

Johnson, Wendell. 1944. Letter to Harry K. Newburn, 11 March. Newburn Papers. University of Iowa Archives, Iowa City.

———. 1943. "You Can't Write Writing." *ETC: A Review of General Semantics* 1:25–32.

Kellogg, Brainerd. 1893. "On Teaching English." *School Review* 1:96–105, 152–62.

Kelly, Dennis. 1996. "Taking Education to Task: E. D. Hirsch Jr. Argues that Knowledge Is Lost in 'Progressive' Approach." *USA Today*, 3 October 1996, 10D.

Kelso, Ruth. 1929. *The Doctrine of the English Gentleman in the Sixteenth-Century. University of Illinois Studies in Language and Literature* 14, 1–288. Urbana: University of Illinois Press.

Kennedy, X. J., Dorothy Kennedy, and Sylvia Holladay. 1993. *The Bedford Guide for College Writers*. 3d ed. Boston: Bedford Books of St. Martin's.

Kimball, Bruce. 1986. *Orators and Philosophers: A History of the Idea of a Liberal Education*. New York: Teachers' College Press.

Kitzhaber, Albert. 1960. "Death—or Transfiguration?" *College English* 21 (April): 367–73.

———. 1990. *Rhetoric in American Colleges*. (Ph.D. diss., Washington University, 1953.) Dallas: Southern Methodist University Press.

———. 1963. *Themes, Theories, and Therapy: The Teaching of Writing in College*. New York: McGraw-Hill.

Knight, Leon. 1993. "Four Comments on 'Two Views on the Use of Literature in Composition.'" *College English* 55 (October): 672–79.

Koller, Kathrine. 1955. "Broadening the Horizon: Cultural Values in Freshman English." *College Composition and Communication* 6:82–85.

Kolodny, Annette. 1986. "Dancing Through the Minefield: Some Observations on the Theory, Practice, and Politics of a Feminist Literary Criticism." In *Critical Theory Since 1965*, ed. Hazard Adams and Leroy Searle, 499–512. Tallahassee: Florida State University Press.

Kuhn, Thomas. 1961. *The Structure of Scientific Revolutions*. Chicago: University of Chicago Press.

Kuklick, Bruce. 1992. "The Emergence of the Humanities." In *The Politics of Liberal Education*, ed. Darryl J. Gless and Barbara Herrnstein Smith, 201–12. Durham: Duke University Press.

Kytle, Ray. 1970. "Pre-writing by Analysis." *College Composition and Communication* 21:380–85.

———. 1971. "Slaves, Serfs, or Colleagues—Who Shall Teach College Composition?" *College Composition and Communication* 12:339–41.

Laird, Charlton. 1956. "Freshman English During the Flood." *College English* 28:131–38.

Lanham, Richard. 1983. *Literacy and the Survival of Humanism.* New Haven: Yale University Press.

Larson, Richard. 1988. "The Ford Foundation Study of the Writing Curriculum: Implications." NCTE Convention, St. Louis, November 1988.

———. 1992. "Freshman Composition: Is it a Waste of Time?" *The Council Chronicle* 1 (April): 9.

Lathrop, H. B. 1893. "Entrance Examinations in English at Stanford." *Educational Review* 9:289–95.

Latosi-Sawin, Elizabeth. 1993. "Four Comments on 'Two Views on the Use of Literature in Composition.'" *College English* 55 (October): 672–79.

Lauter, Paul. 1995. "Political Correctness and the Attack on American Colleges." In *After Political Correctness: The Humanities and Society in the 1990s,* ed. Christopher Newfield and Ronald Strickland, 212–15. Boulder: Westview.

———. 1991. "A Scandalous Misuse of Faculty—Adjuncts." In *Canons and Contexts,* ed. Lauter, 198–209. New York: Oxford University Press.

Lindemann, Erica. 1993. "Freshman Composition: No Place for Literature." *College English* 55 (March): 311–16.

———. 1995. "Three Views of English 101." *College English* 57 (March): 287–302.

"Literature." *Oxford English Dictionary.* 2d ed. CD-Rom.

Lounsbury, Thomas. 1911. "Compulsory Composition in Colleges." *Harper's Monthly Magazine* 123:866–80.

Lutz, William. 1971. "Making Freshman English a Happening." *College Composition and Communication* 22:35–38.

Mailloux, Stephen. 1989. *Rhetorical Power.* Ithaca: Cornell University Press, 1989.

Malinowitz, Harriet. 1990. "The Rhetoric of Empowerment in Writing Programs." In *The Right to Literacy,* ed. Andrea A. Lunsford, Helene Moglen, and James Slevin, 152–62. New York: MLA.

Malmstrom, Jean. 1956. "The Communication Course." *College Composition and Communication* 7:21–24.

Martin, Harold C., and Richard Ohmann. 1963. *The Logic and Rhetoric of Exposition.* New York: Rinehart.

McCleary, Bill. 1988. "Two Committees to Implement Wyoming Resolution Begin Their Work." *Composition Chronicle* 1:1–3.

McCloskey, John. 1935. "The Breakdown of Tradition." *English Journal* 24:116–25.

McCrimmon, James. 1969. "Will the New Rhetorics Produce New Emphases in the Composition Class?" *College Composition and Communication* 20 (May): 124–30.

———. 1967. *Writing With a Purpose: A First Course in College Composition.* 4th ed. Boston: Houghton Mifflin. (1st ed., 1950; 6th ed., 1976).

———. 1970. "Writing as a Way of Knowing." In *The Promise of English: 1970 Distinguished Lectures.* 115–30. Urbana: NCTE.

McDonald, Robert L. 1992. "Interview with Gary Tate." *Composition Studies* 20:36–50.

McDowell, Tremaine. 1946. "General Education and College English." *College English* 7:351–57.

McElroy, John G. R. 1884–85. "The Requirements in English for Admission to College." *PMLA* 1:195–203.

Mead, William E. 1902. "The Undergraduate Study of Composition." *School Review*: 317–31.

Middlebrook, Samuel. 1947. "English I in Cellophane." *College English* 9:140–43.

Miller, Gary E. 1988. *The Meaning of General Education: The Emergence of a Curriculum Paradigm*. New York: Teachers' College Press.

Miller, Susan. 1994. "Composition as a Cultural Artifact: Rethinking History as Theory." In *Writing Theory and Critical Theory*, ed. John Clifford and John Schilb, 19–32. New York: MLA.

———. 1991. "The Feminization of Composition." In *The Politics of Writing Instruction: Postsecondary*, ed. Richard Bullock and John Trimbur, 39–53. Portsmouth, N.H.: Boynton Cook/Heinemann.

———. 1989. *Rescuing the Subject: A Critical Introduction to Rhetoric and the Writer*. Carbondale: Southern Illinois University Press.

———. 1990. *Textual Carnivals: the Politics of Composition*. Carbondale: Southern Illinois University Press.

Miller, Tom. 1997. *The Formation of College English: Rhetoric and Belles Lettres in the British Cultural Provinces*. Pittsburgh: University of Pittsburgh Press.

———. 1990. "Where Did College English Studies Come From?" *Rhetoric Review* 9:50–69.

Mills, Barriss. 1953. "Writing as Process." *College English* 15:19–26.

Mills, Glen E. 1947. "Speech in a Communication Course." *Quarterly Journal of Speech* 32:40–45.

Minnich, Elizabeth Kamarck. 1990. *Transforming Knowledge*. Philadelphia: Temple University Press.

Minot, Walter S. 1974. "Friendship: A Parody." *College Composition and Communication* 25:154.

Minutes of the Steering Committee. 30 January 1943. Foerster Papers. University of Iowa Archives, Iowa City.

———. 27 December 1943. Foerster Papers. University of Iowa Archives, Iowa City.

———. 30 December 1943. Foerster Papers. University of Iowa Archives, Iowa City.

Minutes of the Sub-committee on Literature. 25 May 1942. Foerster Papers. University of Iowa Archives, Iowa City.

———. 17 May 1943. Foerster Papers. University of Iowa Archives, Iowa City.

Moffett, James. 1994. "Coming Out Right." In *Taking Stock: The Writing Process Movement in the '90s*, ed. Lad Tobin and Thomas Newkirk, 17–30. Portsmouth, N.H.: Boynton Cook/Heinemann.

Moore, Marianne. 1967. "Poetry." In *Complete Poems of Marianne Moore*. New York: Macmillan.

Morison, Samuel Eliot. 1930. *The Development of Harvard University Since the Inauguration of President Eliot 1869–1929.* Cambridge: Harvard University Press.

————. 1965. *Three Centuries of Harvard.* Cambridge: Harvard University Press.

Moulton, Richard. 1989. From "Shakespeare as a Dramatic Artist: A Study of Inductive Literary Criticism (1888)." In *The Origins of Literary Studies in America: A Documentary Anthology,* ed. Gerald Graff and Michael Warner, 61–74. New York: Routledge.

Murray, Donald M. 1972. "Teach Writing as a Process Not Product." *The Leaflet* (November): 11–14. Rpt. in *Rhetoric and Composition: A Sourcebook for Writing Teachers,* new ed., ed. Richard Graves, 89–92. Upper Montclair, N.J.: Boynton Cook, 1984.

Murray, Robin. 1990. "Fordism and Post-Fordism." In *New Times: The Changing Face of Politics in the 1990s,* ed. Stuart Hall and Martin Jacques, 38–53. London: Verso.

Murphy, Michael. 1993. "After Progressivism: Modern Composition, Institutional Service, and Cultural Studies." *Journal of Advanced Composition* 13 (fall): 345–64.

Myers, D. G. 1996. *The Elephants Teach: Creative Writing Since 1880.* Englewood Cliffs, N.J.: Prentice Hall.

Newburn, Harry K. 1943. "The Challenge to Liberal Education When Peace Comes." Baconian Lectures, Series on Aims and Progress of Research 74, News Series 1324, Study Series 405. Iowa City: University of Iowa.

Newkirk, Thomas. 1991. "Barrett Wendell's Theory of Discourse." *Rhetoric Review* 19:20–30.

Newman, Samuel. 1851. *A Practical System of Rhetoric.* New York: Mark H. Newman. First published in 1827.

Nightingale, Augustus Frederick. 1879. *Handbook of Requirements for Admission to Colleges in the United States.* New York: Appleton.

North, Stephen. 1987. *The Making of Knowledge in Composition: Portrait of an Emerging Field.* Upper Montclair, N.J.: Boynton Cook.

Nystrand, Martin, Stuart Greene, and Jeffrey Wiemelt. 1993. "Where Did Composition Studies Come From?" *Written Communication* 10 (July): 267–333.

Ohmann, Richard. 1976. *English in America.* New York: Oxford University Press.

————. 1991. Foreword, *The Politics of Writing Instruction: Postsecondary,* ed. Richard Bullock and John Trimbur, ix–xvi. Portsmouth, N.H.: Boynton Cook.

Oliver, Kenneth. 1950. "The One-Legged, Wingless Bird of Freshman English." *College Composition and Communication* 1:3–6.

Olson, Keith. 1974. *The G.I. Bill, The Veterans, and the Colleges.* Lexington: University of Kentucky Press.

Osgood, Charles G. 1915. "No Set Requirement of English Composition in the Freshman Year." *English Journal* 4:231–35.

————. 1922. "Humanism and the Teaching of English." *English Journal* 11:159–66.

O'Sullivan, Noel. 1993. "Conservatism." In *Contemporary Political Ideologies,* ed. Roger Eatwell and Anthony Wright, 50–77. Boulder: Westview.

Palmer, Glenn. 1912. "Culture and Efficiency Through Composition." *English Journal* 1:488–92.

Parker, Richard Green. 1846. *Aids to English Composition, Preparation for Students of All Grades*. New York: Harper and Brothers.

Paul, Wilson B., Frederick Sorensen, and Elwood Murray. 1946. "A Functional Core for the Basic Communications Course." *Quarterly Journal of Speech* 32:232–44.

Payne, William Morton. 1895. *English in American Universities: By Professors in the English Departments of Twenty Representative Universities*. Boston: Heath.

Perrin, Porter G. 1936. "The Teaching of Rhetoric in American Colleges Before 1750." Ph.D. diss., University of Chicago.

Petraglia, Joseph, ed. 1995. *Reconceiving Writing, Rethinking Writing Instruction*. Mahwah, N.J.: Erlbaum.

Phelan, Shane. 1989. *Identity Politics: Lesbian Feminism and the Limits of Community*. Philadelphia: Temple University Press.

Phelps, William Lyon. 1912. *Teaching in School and College*. New York: Macmillan.

———. 1896. "Two Ways of Teaching English." *Century Magazine* 51:793–94.

[Pitcher, Seymour]. 1944. Memorandum of a Conversation with Dean Newburn. 29 January 1944. Foerster Papers. University of Iowa Archives, Iowa City.

Plato. 1961. *Gorgias*. Trans. W. D. Woodhead. In *The Collected Dialogues of Plato*, ed. Edith Hamilton and Huntington Cairns, 229–307. Princeton: Princeton University Press.

Porter, Noah. 1870. *The American Colleges and the American Public*. New Haven: Charles Chatfield.

Pratt, Mary Louise. 1992. "Humanities for the Future: Reflections on the Western Culture Debate at Stanford." In *The Politics of Liberal Education*, ed. Darryl J. Gless and Barbara Herrnstein Smith, 13–31. Durham: Duke University Press.

Pumphrey, Jean. 1973. "Teaching English Composition as a Creative Art." *College English* 34:666–73.

Quackenbos, George Payn. 1864. *Advanced Course of Composition and Rhetoric*. New York: D. Appleton.

Quintilian, Marcus Fabius. 1920. *The Institutes of Oratory*. 4 vols. Trans. H. E. Butler. Cambridge: Harvard University Press.

"Report: Subcommittee on Basic Skills." n.d. Foerster Papers. University of Iowa Archives, Iowa City.

Report of the Subcommittee on Basic Skills. 6 July 1944. Foerster Papers. University of Iowa Archives, Iowa City.

Report of the Subcommittee on Literature. n.d. Foerster Papers. University of Iowa Archives, Iowa City.

Roberts, Edgar V. 1973. *Writing Themes About Literature*. 3d ed. Englewood Cliffs, N.J.: Prentice Hall.

Robertson, Linda. 1989. "Alliances Between Rhetoric and English: The Politics." *Composition Chronicle* 2:5–7.

Robertson, Linda, Sharon Crowley, and Frank Lentricchia. 1987. "The Wyoming Conference Resolution Opposing Unfair Salaries and Working Conditions for Post-Secondary Teachers of Writing." *College English* 49:274–80.

Robertson, Linda, and James Slevin. 1987. "The Status of Composition Faculty: Resolving Reforms." *Rhetoric Review* 5:190–94.

Rohman, D. Gordon. 1965. "Pre-writing: The Stage of Discovery in the Writing Process." *College Composition and Communication* 16 (May): 106–12.

Rohman, D. Gordon, and Albert O. Wlecke. 1962. "The Construction and Application of Models for Concept Formation in Writing." U.S. Office of Education Cooperative Research Project Number 2174.

Ronald, Ann. 1990. "Separate but (Sort of) Equal: Permanent Non-Tenure-Track Faculty Members in the Composition Program." *ADE Bulletin* 95:33–37.

Rorabacher, Louise E. 1952. "The Professional Status of the Composition Teacher." *College Composition and Communication* 2:10.

Rose, Shirley K., and Susan Wyche-Smith. 1990. "One Hundred Ways to Make the Wyoming Resolution a Reality." *College Composition and Communication* 41:318–24.

Rubinstein, S. Leonard. 1946. "Composition: A Collision with Literature." *College English* 27:273–77.

Rubin, Joan Shelly. 1992. *The Making of Middlebrow Culture*. Chapel Hill: University of North Carolina Press.

Rudolph, Frederick. 1977. *Curriculum: A History of the American Undergraduate Curriculum Since 1636*. San Francisco: Jossey-Bass.

Russell, David R. 1995. "Activity Theory and Its Implications for Writing Instruction." In *Reconceiving Writing, Rethinking Writing Instruction*, ed. Joseph Petraglia, 51–77. Mahwah, N.J.: Erlbaum.

———. 1988. "Romantics on Writing: Liberal Culture and the Abolition of Composition Courses. *Rhetoric Review* 6:132–48.

———. 1993. "Vygotsky, Dewey, and Externalism: Beyond the Student/Discipline Dichotomy." *Journal of Advanced Composition* 13:173–97.

———. 1991. *Writing in the Academic Disciplines, 1870–1990: A Curricular History*. Carbondale: Southern Illinois University Press.

Rutland, J. R. 1923. "Tendencies in the Administration of Freshman English." *English Journal* 12:1–9.

Ryland, Frederick. 1914. *Chronological Outlines of English Literature*. New York: Macmillan.

Sampson, Martin Wright. 1895. "The University of Indiana." In *English in American Universities*, ed. William Morton Payne, 92–98. Boston: Heath.

Schell, Eileen E. n.d. "The Costs of Caring: Feminin-ism and Contingent Women Workers in Composition Studies." In *In Other Words: Feminism and Composition Studies*, ed. Susan Jarratt and Lyn Worsham. Unpublished ms.

———. 1997. *Gypsy Academics and Motherteachers: Gender, Contingent Labor, and Writing Instruction*. Portsmouth, N.H.: Boynton Cook/Heinemann.

Schilb, John. 1996. *Between the Lines: Relating Composition Theory and Literary Theory*. Portsmouth, N.H.: Boynton Cook.

———. 1986. "The History of Rhetoric and the Rhetoric of History." *Pre/Text* 7:11–34.

Schiller, Andrew. 1954. "The Use of Creative Writing in the Teaching of Literature." *College Composition and Communication* 4:110–17.

Scott, Frank W. 1918. "The Relation of Composition to the Rest of the Curriculum." *English Journal* 7:512–20.

Scott, Franklin W., J. M. Thomas, and Frederick A. Manchester. 1918. "Preliminary Report of the Special Committee on Freshman English." *English Journal* 7:592–99.

Shapin, Steven. 1994. *A Social History of Truth, Civility and Science in Seventeenth-Century England*. Chicago: University of Chicago Press.

Shaw, Patrick W. 1974. "Freshman English: To Compose or Decompose, That Is the Question." *College Composition and Communication* 25:155–59.

Shaw, Thomas Budd. 1867. *Outlines of English Literature, A New American Edition*. New York: Sheldon. First published in 1852.

Shelley, Percy Bysshe. 1971. "A Defense of Poetry. In *Critical Theory Since Plato*, ed. Hazard Adams, 499–516. New York: Harcourt Brace Jovanovich.

Shipherd, H. Robinson. 1929. "Required Composition for College Freshmen." *Education* 49:18–25.

Shumway, David R. 1994. *Creating American Civilization: A Genealogy of American Literature as an Academic Discipline*. Minneapolis: University of Minnesota Press.

Shumway, David R., and Ellen Messer-Davidow. 1991. "Disciplinarity: An Introduction." *Poetics Today* 12 (summer): 201–25.

Simmons, Sue Carter. 1995. "Radcliffe Responses to Harvard Rhetoric: 'An Absurdly Stiff Way of Thinking.'" In *Nineteenth-Century Women Learn to Write*, ed. Catharine Hobbs, 264–92. Charlottesville: University of Virginia Press.

———. 1995. "Constructing Writers: Barrett Wendell's Pedagogy at Harvard." *College Composition and Communication* 46:327–52.

Slevin, James. 1991. "Depoliticizing and Politicizing Composition Studies." In *The Politics of Writing Instruction: Postsecondary*, ed. Richard Bullock and John Trimbur, 1–21. Portsmouth, N.H.: Boynton Cook.

———. 1989. "Statement of Principles and Standards for Postsecondary Teaching of Writing." *College Composition and Communication* 40:329–36.

Smallwood, Mary L. 1935. *An Historical Study of Examinations and Grading Systems in Early American Universities: A Critical Study of the Original Records of Harvard, William and Mary, Yale, Mount Holyoke, and Michigan from Their Founding to 1900*. Cambridge: Harvard University Press.

Smith, Ron. 1974. "The Composition Requirement Today: A Report on a Nationwide Survey of Four-Year Colleges and Universities." *College Composition and Communication* 25:138–48.

Snyder, Franklin B. 1935. "Twenty-five Years of Trying to 'Teach' English." *English Journal* 24:196–208.

Sorenson, Frederick. 1949. "The Basic Communications Course Reconsidered." *College English* 10:324–28.

Spanos, William V. 1993. *The End of Education: Toward Posthumanism*. Minneapolis: University of Minnesota Press.

"Statement of Principles and Standards for the Postsecondary Teaching of Writing."
    1989. *College Composition and Communication* 49:329–36.

Steeves, Harrison Ross. 1912. "Ideas in the College Writing Course." *Educational
    Review* 44:45–54.

Steeves, Harrison Ross, and Frank H. Ristine, eds. 1913. *Representative Essays in
    Modern Thought: A Basis for Composition*. New York: American Book.

Stegner, Wallace. 1950. "Writing as Graduate Study." *College English* 11:429–32.

Steinberg, Edwin. 1995. "Imaginative Literature in Composition Classrooms?"
    College English 57 (March): 266–80.

Stewart, Donald. 1982. "Two Model Teachers and the Harvardization of English
    Departments." In *The Rhetorical Tradition and Modern Writing*, ed. James J.
    Murphy, 118–29. New York: MLA.

Stewart, Randall. 1955. "The Freshman Course Needs a Current of Ideas." *College
    English* 17:16–19.

Stone, Edward. 1955. "The Freshman Composition Course: A Study in Shame and
    Glory." *College Composition and Communication* 7:91–94.

Stuckey, J. Elspeth. 1991. *The Violence of Literacy*. Portsmouth, N.H.: Boynton
    Cook/Heinemann.

Stuitt, Dewey. 1994. Telephone interview, May.

Sullivan, Patricia, and Donna J. Qualley, eds. 1994. *Pedagogy in the Age of Politics:
    Writing and Reading (in) the Academy*. Urbana: NCTE.

Tate, Gary. 1995. "Notes on the Dying of a Conversation." *College English* 57
    (March): 303–09.

———. 1993. "A Place for Literature in Freshman Composition." *College English* 55
    (March): 317–21.

Taylor, Warner. 1929. *A National Survey of Conditions in Freshman English*.
    University of Wisconsin Bureau of Education and Research Bulletin no. 11.
    May.

Taylor, Warren. 1938. "Rhetoric in a Democracy." *English Journal* 27:851–58.

Templeman, William. 1962. "Thirty-Seven Departments on Freshman English."
    College Composition and Communication 13:35–40.

Thoma, Henry F. 1957. "Freshman Texts, 1931–1945." *College Composition and
    Communication* 8 (February): 35–39.

Thomas, J. M. 1916. "Training for Teaching Composition in Colleges." *English
    Journal* 5:447–57.

Thompson, Stith. 1930. "A National Survey of Freshman English." *College English*
    19:553–57.

Thorson, Gerald H. 1953. "Literature in Freshman English." *College Composition and
    Communication* 4 (May): 38–40.

———. 1956. "Literature: The Freshman's Key." *College Composition and
    Communication* 7: 38–40.

Tibbetts, A. M. 1965. "A Short History of Dogma and Nonsense in the Composition
    Course." *College Composition and Communication* 16:90–96.

Tobin, Lad. 1994. "How the Writing Process Was Born—And Other Conversion
    Narratives." In *Taking Stock: The Writing Process Movement in the '90s*, ed. Lad

Tobin and Thomas Newkirk, 1–14. Portsmouth, N.H.: Boynton Cook/ Heinemann.

Tobin, Lad, and Thomas Newkirk, eds. 1994. *Taking Stock: The Writing Process Movement in the '90s*. Portsmouth, N.H.: Boynton Cook/Heinemann.

Trachsel, Mary. 1992. *Institutionalizing Literacy*. Carbondale: Southern Illinois University Press.

Tressider, Argus J. 1944. "Speech in the Military Program." *Quarterly Journal of Speech* 30:387–94.

Trimbur, John, and Barbara Cambridge. 1988. "The Wyoming Conference Resolution: A Beginning." *WPA: Writing Program Administration* 12:13–17.

Trinh, T. Minh-Ha. 1989. *Woman, Native, Other: Writing Postcoloniality and Feminism*. Bloomington: University of Indiana University Press.

Tyler, Moses Coit. 1879. *A Manual of English Literature by Henry Morley, Thoroughly Revised with an Entire Rearrangement of Matter and With Numerous Retrenchments and Additions*. New York: Sheldon.

Varnum, Robin. 1996. *Fencing With Words: A History of Writing Instruction at Amherst College During the Era of Theodore Baird, 1938–1966*. Urbana: NCTE.

Vesey, Laurence. 1965. *The Emergence of the American University*. Chicago: University of Chicago Press.

Villanueva, Victor. 1993. *Bootstraps: From an American of Color*. Urbana: NCTE.

Voss, Richard. 1983. "Janet Emig's Composition Processes of Twelfth-Graders: A Reassessment." *College Composition and Communication* 34:278–83.

Walker, Barbara. 1985. *The Crone: Woman of Age, Wisdom, and Power*. San Francisco: Harper and Row.

Warner, Michael. 1985. "Professionalization and the Rewards of Literature: 1875–1900." *Criticism* 27:1–28.

Weaver, Richard. 1970. "Language is Sermonic." *In Language Is Sermonic: Richard M. Weaver on the Nature of Rhetoric*, ed. Richard L. Johannesen, Rennard Strickland, and Ralph T. Eubanks, 201–25. Baton Rouge: Louisiana State University Press.

Wendell, Barrett. 1891. *English Composition*. New York: Scribners'.

———. 1888. "Lecture Notes for English 12." Ms. Curriculum Materials. Harvard University Archives, Cambridge.

West, Cornel. 1989. *The American Evasion of Philosophy: A Genealogy of Pragmatism*. Madison: University of Wisconsin Press.

White, Edward M. 1995. "The Importance of Placement and Basic Studies: Helping Students Succeed Under the New Elitism." *Journal of Basic Writing* 14:75–84.

Wiebe, Robert H. 1967. *The Search for Order 1877–1920*. New York: Hill and Wang.

Wikelund, Philip R. 1959. "'Masters' and 'Slaves': A Director of Composition Looks at the Graduate Assistant." *College Composition and Communication* 10:226–30.

Wiksell, Wesley. 1947. "The Communications Program at Stephens College." *College English* 9:143–48.

Wilbers, Stephen. 1980. *The Iowa Writers' Workshop: Origins, Emergence, and Growth*. Iowa City: University of Iowa Press.

Wilcox, Thomas. 1973. *The Anatomy of College English*. San Francisco: Jossey-Bass.

———. 1972. "The Varieties of Freshman English." *College English* 33: 686–701.

———. 1967. "Non Serviam: The Reintegration of English." *College Composition and Communication* 18:146–51.

———. 1965. "Composition Where None is Apparent: Contemporary Literature and the Course in Writing." *College Composition and Communication* 16:70–75.

Williams, Raymond. 1977. *Marxism and Literature*. New York: Oxford University Press.

Wilson, Gordon. 1967. "CCCC in Retrospect." *College Composition and Communication* 18:127–34.

Wise, J. Hooper. 1949. "The Comprehensive Freshman English Course at the University of Florida." In *Communication in General Education*, ed. Earl J. McGrath, 157–72. Dubuque, Iowa: William C. Brown.

Wise, J. Hooper. 1953. "The Comprehensive Freshman English Course—Reading, Speaking, and Writing—at the University of Florida." *College Composition and Communication* 4:131–37.

Woolf, Virginia. 1957. *A Room of One's Own*. New York: Harcourt, Brace, and World.

Wozniak, John Michael. 1978. *English Composition in Eastern Colleges, 1850–1940*. Washington, D.C.: University Press of America.

Wykoff, George S. 1945. "Army English Experiences Applicable to Civilian, Postwar English." *College English* 6:338–42.

———. 1949. "Toward Achieving the Objectives of Freshman Composition." *College English* 10:319–23.

———. 1940. "Teaching Composition as a Career." *College English* 1:426–37.

Young, Richard. 1976. "Invention: A Topographical Survey." In *Teaching Composition: A Bibliographical Survey*, ed. Gary Tate, 1–43. Fort Worth: Texas Christian University Press.

Young, Richard, Alton Becker, and Kenneth Pike. 1970. *Rhetoric: Discovery and Change*. New York: Harcourt, Brace, and World.

Zavarsadah, Mas'ud, and Donald Morton. 1986–1987. "Theory Pedagogy Politics: The Crisis of the 'Subject' in the Humanities." *Boundary 2* 15:1–21.

Zebroski, James. 1994. *Thinking Through Theory: Vygotskian Perspectives on the Teaching of Writing*. Portsmouth, N.H.: Boynton Cook.

Zilversmit, Arthur. 1993. *Changing Schools: Progressive Educational Theory and Practice, 1930–60*. Chicago: University of Chicago Press.

INDEX